PRINCETON VERSUS THE NEW DIVINITY

PRINCETON VERSUS THE NEW DIVINITY

Articles from the
Princeton Review

THE MEANING OF
SIN – GRACE – SALVATION –
REVIVAL

THE BANNER OF TRUTH TRUST

THE BANNER OF TRUTH TRUST
3 Murrayfield Road, Edinburgh EH12 6EL, UK
PO Box 621, Carlisle, Pennsylvania 17013, USA

*

Articles first published in the *Biblical Repertory and
Theological Review* (from 1837, *Biblical Repertory and
Princeton Review*) between 1830 and 1842

First Banner of Truth edition 2001

ISBN 0 85151 801 X

*

Typeset in 11/12 pt OldStyle 7 at the
Banner of Truth Trust, Edinburgh
Printed in Great Britain at
The University Press,
Cambridge

Contents

PUBLISHER'S INTRODUCTION

The 'New Divinity' was a movement in theological thought which had pervasive influence in parts of the United States in the 1830s. While diverse elements went into its composition, its leading ideas were a revision of teaching on the fallen condition of man, the nature of the atonement and the extent to which man is dependent upon the Holy Spirit for regeneration. Widespread controversy attended the promotion of the new teaching and its results included the division of the Presbyterian Church in 1838.

The professors and teachers at Princeton Theological Seminary and University were the main opponents of the New Divinity. As a subject it dominated the Seminary's *Biblical Repertory and Theological Review* (renamed *Biblical Repertory and Princeton Review* in 1837) for over a decade and in this book some of the most significant of the articles from that source are now reprinted.

Why these articles should be reprinted at a date so far removed from the controversy which occasioned them warrants introductory comment. Some controversies represent no more than a passing disturbance in the church. It was not to be so with the New Divinity. Both contending parties in the controversy saw this clearly. Those who introduced the new ideas were insistent that they would have revolutionary and long-term benefits for the advance of the gospel. Especially would this be so, they claimed, with respect to effective evangelism

and the promotion of revival. The Princeton men, and those
who supported them, were equally convinced that, should the
new teaching succeed, it would mean a change of direction
exceedingly adverse to the spiritual interests of later generations. Where the 'New School' were certain of the practical
benefits resulting from the changes for which they were working, the 'Old' saw disaster.

For a time the proponents of the New Divinity appeared to
win the debate. The evangelists who adopted the new thinking
– most notably Charles Grandison Finney (1792–1875)[1] –
appealed effectively to the numbers of professed converts
under their preaching. They claimed a recovery of 'the gospel',
and results seemed to show it. Churches grew impatient about
questions of doctrine when there were fields ripe for harvest.
Time, however, changed the perspective and during the twen-
tieth century there was an increasing questioning of the alleged
benefits which the New Divinity was supposed to have introduced. One of the first influential questioners on the North
American side of the Atlantic was William G. McLoughlin,
Jr.[2], while in Britain, Martyn Lloyd-Jones (Minister of Westminster Chapel, London, 1938-68[3]) was a leader and evangelist
who challenged the correctness of what had been so long
assumed.[4]

The time is now ripe for a re-examination of the thinking
which led to the changes in evangelism[5], and for that purpose
there is no better starting point than the articles concerning the
New Divinity which the Princeton teachers published in the
Biblical Repertory and Theological Review. Those brought
together in the present volume are considered among the most
important for such a re-examination.

[1] See Garth M. Rosell and R. A. G. Dupuis (eds.), *The Memoirs of Charles G.
Finney: The Complete Text* (Grand Rapids: Zondervan, 1989).
[2] *Modern Revivalism: Charles Grandison Finney to Billy Graham* (New
York: Ronald Press Co., 1959
[3] Initially (1938–43) as the colleague of Dr G. Campbell Morgan.
[4] *Knowing the Times: Addresses Delivered on Various Occasions 1941–1977*
(Edinburgh: Banner of Truth, 1989), Chapter 1, *The Presentation of the
Gospel*, and Chapter 6, *Conversions: Psychological and Spiritual*.
[5] On these changes see Iain H. Murray, *Revival and Revivalism: The
Making and Marring of American Evangelicalism 1750–1858* (Edinburgh:
Banner of Truth, 1994).

Two of the authors are well known. Archibald Alexander (1772–1851), the founding professor of Princeton Seminary, and Charles Hodge (1797–1878), perhaps the leading American Reformed theologian of the nineteenth century, require little introduction. Much information about both men can be found in David B. Calhoun's *Princeton Seminary: Faith and Learning, 1812–1868* (Edinburgh: Banner of Truth, 1994). Alexander and Hodge were responsible for the first five articles in this volume. Albert Baldwin Dod (1805–45), the author of the sixth article, was a native of New Jersey and a graduate of both Princeton College and Princeton Seminary. He was 'a winsome and effective professor of mathematics and of almost everything else'.[1] His article represented Princeton's answer to Finney's view of revivals of religion. John Woodbridge, born in Massachusetts in 1784, was a pastor in several Congregational and Presbyterian churches and an active opponent of the New Divinity. Dr Thomas Cleland (1778–1858) was born in Virginia and present at the Cane Ridge revival in Kentucky in June 1801.[2] He sided with the New School when the division of the Presbyterian Church took place in 1838.

The Princeton men countered the New Divinity both by direct discussion and refutation (as in Articles 1 and 5–7) and by historical reviews, such as Articles 2–4 in this collection, showing that aspects of the new views had already been debated in earlier centuries. The final article is an account drawn largely from eyewitness sources of some of the phenomena which occurred during revivals in Kentucky in the early years of the nineteenth century, the period from which many of the features of the later revivalism sprang. The author's concluding reflections are of permanent value.

David Calhoun's history provides valuable information on the background to the controversy and on Finney, who became president of Oberlin College, Ohio, in 1835.[3] Other New-Divinity spokesmen mentioned in the articles include

[1] Calhoun, *Princeton Seminary: Faith and Learning,* p. 168.
[2] See Iain H. Murray, *Revival and Revivalism,* pp. 152–4.
[3] *Ibid.,* pp. 221–30. See also Keith J. Hardman, *Charles Grandison Finney* (Grand Rapids: Baker Book House, 1987); and Iain H. Murray, *Pentecost – Today?* (Edinburgh: Banner of Truth, 1998), pp. 33–53.

Asa Mahan (1799–1889), a colleague of Finney's at Oberlin, whose views on sanctification are discussed in Article 7, and Samuel H. Cox (1793–1881), whose sermon on regeneration is critically reviewed by Charles Hodge in the first article in this volume. Cox was a prominent Presbyterian minister in New York. The circumstances in which the articles were written are indicated by Calhoun.[1]

All but one of the articles are taken from *Theological Essays: Reprinted from the Princeton Review: First Series*, published in New York by Wiley and Putnam in 1846. The exception is No. 6 in the present collection, *On Revivals of Religion* by Albert B. Dod, which is taken from *Essays Theological and Miscellaneous, Reprinted from the Princeton Review: Second Series,* published in the following year.

---

[1] *Princeton Seminary*, pp. 226–9.

1

REGENERATION[1]

Voltaire, in one of his historical works, sneeringly inquires, 'How were the priests employed while the Saracens were desolating the fairest portion of their church?'

'Disputing', he answers, 'whether Christ has one will or two!'

It will be well if the theologians of the nineteenth century do not furnish occasion to some future infidel historian for a similar taunting remark. There is scarcely any subject in the history of the church which is more humiliating than that of theological discussions of this nature. The evil appears to have arisen early, for Paul, in his epistles to Timothy, repeatedly and earnestly exhorts him 'not to strive about words to no profit', but to avoid 'foolish questions which gender strifes'. Yet not a century has passed from that day to this which has not been disturbed and disgraced by disputes fairly within the apostle's description. That there are serious evils attending controversies of this character no one will deny. They bring discredit on religion; they alienate brethren who should live together in love; they call off the attention from the practical duties of benevolence and piety; and they are from their nature destructive of the spirit of true religion.

[1]By Charles Hodge. Published in 1830 in review of *Regeneration and the Manner of Its Occurrence*. A Sermon from John 5:24. Preached at the Opening of the Synod of New York, in the Rutgers Street Church, on 20 October 1829, by Samuel H. Cox, D.D., Pastor of the Laight Street Presbyterian Church.

These disputes, in nine cases out of ten, turn not on the correct exposition of the Bible, but on the decision of some point in mental or moral science. Philosophy, instead of being the handmaid of religion, has become the mistress of theology. This is a fact deeply to be lamented. The subjects, we admit, are so nearly allied that they cannot be kept entirely distinct; still, theology might have, and ought to have, much less of a philosophical and more of an exegetical character than it has commonly assumed. The predominance of the former over the latter element in theology has been unquestionably one of the most prolific sources of evil to the church. What is Pelagianism, Arminianism, or almost any other *ism,* but a particular system of religious philosophy? And what are the questions which now alienate and divide Christians in this country, but questions in mental or moral science? If a man tells you his theory of virtue, you need ask no questions about his theology.

Hence it is that these diversities of opinion are in a great measure confined to professed theologians, clergymen, or laymen. The views which ordinary Christians, under the guidance of *common sense* and sanctified feeling, take of divine truth are in all ages and countries very nearly the same. Nor does it seem to us correct to say that common sense is nothing more than the popularized results of philosophical speculations, because we find it the same in countries where entirely different systems of philosophy have for ages prevailed.

Look at Germany and England for an illustration. The philosophical theologians of these countries differ *toto coelo*[1] in their views. They have hardly a single principle in common. But how is it with common Christians? They are as much united in opinion as they are in feeling. And why? Because their opinions are formed from the Bible, under the guidance of the Spirit, and the influence of those essential and consequently universal principles of our nature which it has been the grand result of philosophy to sophisticate and pervert.

Is all philosophy then to be proscribed? By no means. The very statements we have made demonstrate its importance. If a man's speculative opinions do thus influence his views of religious truth and duty, it is a matter of unspeakable moment

[1] literally 'by the whole heavens', diametrically.

that these opinions should be correct. And in a multitude of cases, the only means of preventing the evils which flow from erroneous principles is to show the fallacy of the principles themselves. Besides, all truth is harmonious, whether taught in the word of God or learned from the constitution of our own nature, and in itself there can be no subject more worthy of accurate knowledge than that mysterious and immortal principle which was created in the image of God. All this we cheerfully admit.

At the same time the undeniable fact, that systems of philosophy have been as changeable as the wind; that each in its turn has been presented, urged and adopted with the utmost confidence, and each in its measure perverted the simple truths of the Bible, should teach us to be modest: it should teach us to separate the human from the divine element in our theology, and to be careful not to clothe the figments of our own minds with the awful authority of God, and denounce our brethren for not believing him when they do not agree with us. It should teach us, too, not to ascribe to men opinions which, according to our notions, may be inferred from the principles which they avow.

This is an impropriety of very frequent occurrence, and of which we think we have great reason to complain in the sermon before us. To state what appears to us to be fair deductions from principles assumed, as arguments against them, is one thing; but to charge those who hold these principles with holding our deductions, is a very different affair.

With regard to the author of this sermon, we can truly say that we entertain for him the highest respect. We love his honesty. We admire the frankness and decision with which he always avows his opinions. We rejoice to see that there is little of that evil spirit in the discourse which so often converts investigations of truth into angry disputations. But while we give Dr Cox full credit for sincerity and acquit him of entertaining any bad feelings towards his brethren, we still think that he is chargeable with grossly misrepresenting their opinions and holding them up to a contempt and reprobation due only to his acknowledged caricature. We refer specially to page 6 of the Introduction, where, after stating that there are certain dogmas, 'some of them not proved, or even suspected by those who employ them', which have a tendency 'to solace the sinner in his distance from Christ' and 'excuse his disobedience to the gospel, and which ought to be rejected as false and ruinous', he gives the following specifications: –

'A man has no ability to do his duty.

'Where the means of grace are purely and abundantly vouchsafed by the sovereign goodness of Providence, a man can do nothing for, but can only counteract, his own salvation; having no ability, even if he had the inclination, to believe the gospel and be saved.

'The wickedness of men consists in physical defect or disorganization of the faculties of the soul, so that total depravity and physical depravity are nearly synonymous, and both equally true.

Regeneration is the implantation of *a certain kind of* 'principle of holiness', which is incapable of definition or demonstration, and has no connection with human consciousness; which precedes all active mental holiness, and is antecedent also to all 'the fruit of the Spirit' as specified in the New Testament, in the susception and sustentation of which, the Creator is sole as well as sovereign agent; man no agent at all, but only a passive receiver, an unconscious subject of the mysterious gratuity; and which is the happy contrary of a *principle of sin,* which is concreated with us, and is the permanent fund of all our depravity, in which also we are passive – though quite active in exercising all the wickedness which flows (full copiously) from such an inserted fountain, and which has its residence and location somewhere in the texture of the soul, which is itself a very wicked thing somehow physiologically, in the very nature of it, antecedent to any agency at all of ours.

'Regeneration consists in some secret physical motion on the soul which restores its dislocated powers and cures the connatural diseases of its texture; since the work of the Creator, as such, is not 'good', but lays the foundation in the very entity of the soul for all its overt wickedness, and for the necessity of regeneration.

'The soul is passive, entirely passive, and God the sole agent of regeneration.

'The means of grace and the gospel itself are in no sense moral causes of regeneration; since their important use is merely to illustrate the strength of an invincible depravity, to make the sinner worse and worse, till he is physically regenerated, and then to signalize the prodigious efforts and labours of Omnipotence, in this department of constant miracle-working – as if there were no considerable difference between dividing the Red Sea symbolically by the rod of Moses, and conciliating the human mind by the revealed glories of the *everlasting* gospel!

'It is wrong to require a sinner in the name of God to repent immediately and believe the gospel, and to urge him to this as the only way of salvation.

'The offer of salvation is not made to every hearer; or if it be, to accept it is impracticable, and to require this of the sinner, wanton and absurd.

'If there is a universal offer in the gospel, it is founded – not on the atonement of Jesus Christ at all, but only on the ministerial commission, or on human ignorance of who the elect are; or it has no moral foundation, or it is only man's offer, and not God's; or it is a matter of mere sovereignty, and so insoluble; or it is an offer in form, and in fact no offer or overture at all: and this, although there is no salvation known to the gospel but that of our Lord Jesus Christ as an *atoning Saviour – Prov.* 1:20–33; *Luke* 14:24; *Acts* 4:12; *Acts* 13:26, 46.'

The doctor then says, 'If I have caricatured these dogmas, I have done so intentionally; but only by representing them as they are, and making the reality govern the appearance.'

It is not probable that Dr Cox in writing these paragraphs had any one class of theologians exclusively in his eye; because some of 'these dogmas' are inconsistent with each other. We have no doubt, however, that most of what is here stated was intended as an exhibition of the doctrines of the old Calvinists (*sit venia verbo*[1]). Our reason for thinking so is that we are accustomed to see such, and even still more gross misrepresentations of these doctrines, though, we acknowledge, not often from such men as Dr Cox. It is, however, notorious that this class of theologians are constantly represented as maintaining that 'man has no ability, even if he had the inclination, to believe the gospel and be saved' – that man's depravity 'is a physical defect' – that regeneration is 'a physical change', etc. Representations have been made of these doctrines which we had supposed no man who felt the obligation 'of interpreting language in conformity with the known and declared nature of the thing described' could ever allow himself to make.

[1] If the expression may be allowed; so to speak.

Belonging as we do to the class, which for the sake of convenience and distinction we have called old Calvinists, we feel ourselves aggrieved by such representations and called upon to show that no such doctrines can be fairly imputed to the elder Calvinists. It will not be expected that in a single article we should go over the formidable list presented by Dr Cox. We shall for the present at least, confine ourselves to the doctrine of this sermon and show that the old standard Calvinistic authors expressly disclaim the opinions here imputed to them, and that they are not fairly deducible from any of the principles which they avow. Should we entirely fail as to the second point, it would still be very unjust to charge men with holding doctrines which they constantly disclaim because we consider them as flowing from their principles.

The two main points of Dr Cox's sermon are, first, that regeneration is a moral, in distinction from a physical change; and secondly, that it occurs in a manner perfectly accordant with the active powers of the soul. We use the word 'physical', not as synonymous with 'natural', but in the sense in which it is used in this sermon, implying something referring to the substance or essence. By physical regeneration in this sense is intended a change in the essence or essential properties of the soul, or in the language of Dr Cox, an influence by which 'the connatural diseases in the texture of the soul are healed'.

Our object is to show that Dr Cox has misrepresented the views of his brethren on this subject; that they hold to no change in the substance of the soul nor in any of its essential properties, but uniformly teach that the change is a moral one and takes place in a manner perfectly congruous to the nature of a rational and active being. We appeal to the language and doctrines of all the old Calvinistic divines in support of this assertion.

Charnock, in his discourse on regeneration contained in Vol. II of the folio edition of his works, proposes in the first place to state in reference to the nature of this change, what it is not. On page 72 he says:

It is not a removal or taking away of the old substance or faculties of the soul. Some thought that the substance of Adam's soul was corrupted when he sinned, therefore suppose the substance of his soul to be altered when he is renewed. Sin took not away the essence but the rectitude; the new creation, therefore, gives not a new faculty but a new quality.[1]

Who the 'some' were, to whom Charnock refers as holding that the substance of Adam's soul was corrupted by the fall, we know not; all we know is that such is not the doctrine of any respectable body of Calvinists, nor of any standard writer on the subject. The only man of whom we have heard who taught this doctrine was Flaccius Illyricus, Professor at Jena, and a pupil of Luther; but we know, too, that his opinions on this subject were condemned almost without a dissenting voice by the reformed theologians of Germany and England.

On the 73rd page[2] Charnock says expressly, 'the essence and faculties remain the same.' 'The passions and affections are the same as to the substance and nature of the acts; but the difference lies in the objects.' 'When a man loves God, or fears God, or loves man, or fears man, it is the same act of love and the same act of fear; there are the same motions of the soul, the same substantial acts simply considered,' etc. 'This new creation is not a destruction of the substance of the soul, but there is the same physical being, and the same faculties in all, and nothing is changed in its substance as it respects the nature of man.' – p. 85. We have here a most explicit disavowal of the doctrine of physical regeneration in the sense in which Dr Cox represents the old Calvinists as holding it.

As to the manner in which this work is effected, he remarks in the first place, that 'it is a secret work, and therefore difficult to explain'.

Yet secondly, this is evident, that it is rational, that is, congruous to the essential nature of man. God does not deal with us as beasts or as creatures destitute of sense, but as creatures of an intelligent order. Who is there that believes in Christ, as heavy things fall to the earth, or as beasts run at the beck of their sensual appetites without rule or reason? – p. 217.[3]

---

[1] In the Banner of Truth edition of Stephen Charnock's *Works* this passage will be found in *Volume 3: The New Birth* (Edinburgh: Banner of Truth, 1986), p. 91.
[2] *ibid.*, p. 91–2.
[3] *ibid.*, p. 278–9.

God that requires of us a reasonable service would work upon us by a reasonable operation. God therefore works by the way of a spiritual illumination of the understanding, in propounding the creature's happiness by arguments and reasons; and in the way of a spiritual impression on the will, moving it sweetly to embrace that happiness and the means to it which he doth propose; and indeed without this work preceding, the motion of the will could never be regular.' – p. 218.[1]

In speaking more particularly of the direct operation of the Holy Spirit on the will, his first proposition is that there is such an influence; second that

this work, though immediate, is not compulsive . . . It is a contradiction for the will to be moved unwillingly; any force upon it destroys its nature . . . It is not forced, because it is according to reason, and the natural motion of the creature; the understanding proposing, and the will moved to an embracing; the understanding going before with light, the will following after with love . . . The will, being a rational faculty, cannot be wrought upon but rationally. – p. 221.[2]

The instrumentality of the truth in regeneration is strongly asserted by all old Calvinists. Charnock says that

to make an alteration in us according to our nature of understanding, will, and affection, it is necessary there should be some declaration of things under those considerations of true, good, delightful, etc., in the highest manner, to make a choice change in every faculty of the soul; and without this a man cannot be changed as a rational creature, etc. – p. 233.[3]

The word operates, first, objectively, as it is a declaration of the will of God, presenting the objects of all holy acts; and secondly, it has an active force. 'It is operative in the hand of God for sanctification.' 'The Spirit doth so edge the word that it cuts to the quick, discerns the very thoughts, insinuates into the depths of the heart', etc. – p. 235.[4]

[1] *ibid.*, p. 279.
[2] *ibid.*, p. 286–7.
[3] *ibid.*, p. 313.
[4] *ibid.*, p. 319.

To conclude . . . the promise in the word breeds principles in the heart suitable to itself; it shows God a Father and raises up principles of love and reverence; it shows Christ a Mediator and raises up principles of faith and desire. Christ in the word conceives Christ in the heart; Christ in the word, the beginning of grace, conceives Christ in the soul, the hope of glory. – p. 236.[1]

The use of the word in regeneration is surely according to this view something more than 'the rod of Moses stretched out over the Red Sea'. We presume, however, that the paragraph in which Dr Cox denounces the opinion that the means of grace have no tendency to produce holiness, was designed for a different quarter. Old Calvinists have generally been charged with laying too much stress on the use of means.

Charnock was by no means singular in the views here expressed. Living as he did in the days of the Puritan ascendancy in England, the companion of Owen, Goodwin, Burgess, Bates, and many others of the same class, he was united with them in opinion as well as in labours.

Owen, in his work on the Spirit, when speaking of regeneration, lays down the following proposition (page 270 of the folio edition): 'In or towards whomsoever the Holy Spirit puts forth his power, or acts his grace for their regeneration, he removes all obstacles, overcomes all oppositions, and infallibly produces the effect intended.'[2] But how is this done? Is it by changing the substance of the soul or violating any of the laws of its being? The words which immediately follow and which are intended to explain this general proposition contain the answer.

The power which the Holy Spirit puts forth in our regeneration is such, in its actings or exercise, as our minds, will, and affections are suited to be wrought upon, and to be affected by, according to their natures and natural operations . . . He doth not act in them any otherwise than they themselves are meet to be moved and move, to be acted and act, according to their own nature, power and ability.

---

[1] *ibid.*, p. 319.
[2] In the Banner of Truth edition of Owen's *Works* this and the following statements will be found in Vol. 3 (London: Banner of Truth, 1965), p. 318–20.

He draws us with 'the cords of a man.' And the work itself is expressed by *persuading*; 'God shall persuade Japheth'; and *alluring*, – I will allure her into the wilderness and speak comfortably unto her': for, as it is certainly effectual, so it carries no more repugnancy unto our faculties than a prevalent persuasion doth.

One can hardly imagine how men who use such language can be charged with holding a 'physical regeneration' by which 'the connatural diseases of the texture of the soul' are cured. Owen proceeds to say secondly that the Holy Spirit

doth not, in our regeneration, possess the mind with any enthusiastical impressions . . . but he works on the minds of men in and by their own natural actings, through an immediate influence and impression of his power. 'Create in me a clean heart, O God.' He 'worketh both to will and to do.' Thirdly, he therefore offers no violence or compulsion unto the will. This that faculty is not naturally capable to give admission unto. If it be compelled it is destroyed.

And again on the next page,

The Holy Spirit, who in his power and operation is more intimate, as it were, unto the principles of our souls than they are to themselves, doth, with the preservation and in the exercise of the liberty of our wills, effectually work our regeneration and conversion unto God. This is the substance of what we have to plead for in this cause, and which declares the nature of this work of regeneration, as it is an inward spiritual work.

Bates' view of the manner in which this change is effected is the same with that of Owen. In the fourth volume of his works (octavo edition) page 140, he says,

The effectual operation of grace does not violate the native freedom of the will, but is congruous to it. God's drawing is by teaching: 'every one who hath heard and learned of the Father cometh unto me.' When the Author of the gospel is a teacher of it, the most stupid and obstinate sinners shall be convinced and obedient.

Again:

God draws sinners to himself 'with the cords of a man', in a rational way, without violence to their faculties, and fastens them by the bonds of love.

In another place, Vol. II, page 298, he says,

The Holy Spirit does not work grace in us, as the sun forms gold in the earth, without any sense in ourselves of his operations: but we feel them in all our faculties congruously to their nature, enlightening the mind, exciting the conscience, turning the will, and purifying the affections.

The opinions of the reformed, or Calvinistic divines of Germany and Holland, were the same on these points as those of the Calvinists of England. Turrettin, *Theol. Elenct.* loc. 15, quaest. 4, para. 15, says,

The action of efficacious grace is not simply physical, because it acts on the moral faculty, which must be moved according to its own nature; nor is it simply moral, as if God only acted by suggestion and gentle persuasion, as the Pelagians insist: but it is supernatural and divine, transcending all these categories . . . It is powerful, and cannot be frustrated; it is gentle, and cannot be resisted. Its strength is supreme and unconquerable so that it might defeat the corruption of nature and the ruling inability to do well and necessity of doing evil: but it is nevertheless kind and agreeable, as is fitting for an intelligent and rational nature.

The Synod of Dort, in order to prevent any misapprehension of their views of efficacious grace, as though it were inconsistent in its operation with the rational and moral powers of our nature, say in reference to the fourth article in dispute between them and the Remonstrants,

But as man did not cease by the fall to be a creature endowed with understanding and will, neither did the sin which pervaded the entire human race deprive him of his human nature, but brought on him depravity and spiritual death; so also this divine grace of regeneration does not treat men as wooden pillars or stones, nor take away their will and its properties, nor do violence to it, but spiritually heals and corrects and at the same time sweetly and powerfully bends it; so that where, before, the rebellion and resistance of the flesh prevailed, now a prompt and sincere obedience of spirit begins to reign; in which the true and spiritual liberty of our will consists.

Spanheim, in his *Elench. Controv. Cum August. Confess. Theol. Oper.* tom. iii., col. 909, after stating how nearly the

views of the Lutheran divines coincided with those of Calvinists on this subject, says that the difference which did exist
seemed to result from a misapprehension of the Calvinistic
doctrine. 'They suppose us,' he says, '1) by irresistible grace to
mean a violent act of compulsion, as with wood and stones;
and 2) to deny that there is resistance to grace on the part of
corrupt nature, and the flesh which is enmity against God,
which certainly does resist as much as it can.'

Stapfer, in his *Institut. Theol. Polem.*, cap. iii., § 136, maintains in unison with the common mode of speaking among
Calvinists of his day that there was in regeneration a divine
illumination of the understanding and a divine influence on the
will. What he intended by these expressions he carefully
explains: 'By illumination we understand a supernatural conviction of the truths revealed, bound up with a distinct
awareness of these things.'

And this, he says, though certainly producing conviction,
offers no more violence to the mind that the demonstration of
a proposition in geometry:

Nor can this remove human liberty, or at all detract from it, any more
than when, by sunlight after darkness, the things around us are seen
clearly again, or when, by means of a demonstration, one is
convinced of a truth of geometry.

With regard to the influence which operates on the will, he
says,

I say that he acts thus so that man might remain free in his conclusions and not be seized by the throat and dragged unwillingly; he
does this so that man might act willingly. He brings the truth to our
minds so clearly that they cannot fail to assent, and suggests such
powerful motives to the will that it cannot refuse, but is won over:
Thou hast persuaded me, O Lord, and I was persuaded, for thou art
stronger than I and hast prevailed – *Jer.* 20:7.

This he asserts, over and over, is the true Calvinistic
doctrine. This he does not only in his chapters on Pelagianism
and Arminianism, where he is answering precisely the same
objection which (and it is one of the wonders of the age)
Calvinists are now urging against Calvinism, viz., that efficacious grace, as explained by them, is inconsistent with the

nature of man as a rational and responsible creature; but also in his chapter *De Consensu et Dissensu Protestantium* and in his preliminary statement of the general truths of theology.

We fear that we have already exhausted the patience of our readers in proving a point concerning which every one acquainted with Calvinistic writers must have been satisfied before we began. We hope, however, that our labour will not be regarded as altogether unnecessary, because when an imputation comes from a source in every way so respectable, and in fact so highly respected, the inference will be that in sober truth old Calvinists do hold that the texture of the soul is diseased; that its substance is changed in regeneration; that some unknown violence to its faculties is suffered under the Spirit's influence.

It is proper, therefore, that it should be shown that the direct reverse of all this is distinctly declared by them to be their opinion; that they profess to believe regeneration to be a moral and not a physical change; and that it takes place without any violence being done to the soul or any of its laws. Our readers, too, will be led, we trust, to think with us, that there should be something more than mere inferential reasoning to justify ascribing to men a set of opinions which they constantly and earnestly disclaim.

We are perfectly willing to admit that old Calvinists, when treating on the subject of regeneration, often speak of a direct and physical influence of the Spirit on the soul. But in what sense? In the sense in which Dr Cox represents them as holding physical regeneration? Far from it. He says that physical regeneration and depravity stand together. He thus uses the word as qualifying the effect produced. They use it to qualify the influence exerted in producing the effect.

But what do they mean when they speak of a physical influence being exerted on the soul in regeneration? They mean precisely what we suppose Dr Cox means when he speaks of 'the agency of the Spirit apart from the power of the truth which is his instrument'. – p. 27. They mean to assert that regeneration is not effected by mere moral suasion; that there is something more than the simple presentation of truth and urging of motives. The idea of Calvinists uniformly was that the truth, however clearly presented or forcibly urged, would never produce its full effect without a special influence of the Holy Spirit. This influence they maintained was supernatural, that is, above the mere moral power of the truth, and such as infallibly to secure the results, and yet, to use their own illustration, did the soul no more violence than demonstration does the intellect or persuasion the heart.

This opinion is not confined to any one class of Calvinists: as far as we know it is common to them all. We understand Dr Cox as teaching the same doctrine. In fact we know no Calvinist who denies it. The author of the review in the last number of the *Christian Spectator*, of the strictures of Dr Tyler on some previous articles in that work, says, 'We have never called in question the doctrine of an immediate or direct agency of the Spirit on the soul in regeneration.' This is all the old Calvinists intended by physical influence. That this assertion is correct is evident from the fact that they taught, as we have seen above, that this influence is perfectly 'congruous' to the nature of the soul, doing it no more violence than, in the language of Owen, 'an effectual persuasion doth'; and that it produces no physical change in the substance of the soul or any of its faculties.

Unless, therefore, we mean to interpret their language not according to their clear and often repeated statements of their meaning, but according to the sense which a particular expression has attained among ourselves, we must admit that no part of the proof of the charge which we are considering can be made to rest on the occurrence of the phrase 'physical influence' in their writings.

But there is still further evidence that our assertion on this subject is correct, which is derived from the fact that it is in controversy with those who taught that there was no influence beyond 'moral suasion' and 'common grace' exerted in regeneration that the older writers maintained what they sometimes called a physical influence of the Spirit.[1]

Turrettin, in the passage quoted above, describing the nature of the influence exerted in regeneration, says that it is not merely a moral influence such as the Pelagians contended for, but supernatural and divine; and immediately adds, '*aliquid*

---

[1] This expression, however, is by no means so common as that of 'direct and immediate influence', and is so carefully guarded as to prevent any justifiable mistake as to its meaning.

de ethico et physico participat' (it partakes of the moral and the physical), where it is plain that it is in opposition to the Pelagian doctrine that he uses this expression; precisely as Dr Cox would do the words, direct and immediate.

When the Remonstrants arose, they objected strongly to the modes of expression which had become common among the Reformed theologians on the subject of efficacious grace. This led to a more precise statement of what their real doctrines were on this subject, and they uniformly repelled the imputations of their opponents that they taught that this influence was inconsistent with the rational nature of the soul. They very unwillingly used even the word irresistible, which they said was no word of their selection, but was put upon them by the Jesuits and Remonstrants. It afterwards indeed became very common; but they tell us they intended by it nothing more than certainly efficacious.

Stapfer, cap. 17, p. 540, says in answer to such objections that when the Reformed speak of irresistible grace, 'they mean that divine grace operates efficaciously, so that it infallibly overcomes the resistance of man, and that, *by its own persuasion,* its efficacy is so great that man cannot but follow with complete spontaneity.' The necessity or certainty as to the result for which they contended was none other than that for which President Edwards and all other Calvinists contend, and which is inconsistent with no other theory of liberty than that of indifference. If any man would candidly compare one passage with another in the writings of old Calvinists and interpret their language agreeably to the fair rules of construction, there could be no doubt as to their meaning, by 'physical influence', what Dr Cox, we presume, means by 'an influence apart from the truth'.

Charnock, in speaking on this subjects says in the general that the work is secret, yet 'congruous to the essential nature of the soul'. He then states more particularly first, that there is 'an immediate and supernatural work on the will': as synonymous with this expression he on the next page uses the words 'physical operation'. His second proposition is that 'this work, though immediate, is not compulsive and by force'. 'The will being a rational faculty cannot be wrought upon but rationally' is one of his assertions in explanation of his idea of this immediate influence. 'God, who knows how to make a will with a principle of freedom, knows how to work upon the will without intrenching upon or altering the essential privilege he bestowed upon it' is another. His third position is that this immediate work 'is free and gentle'. 'A constraint not by force *but love.*' 'It is sweet and alluring: the Spirit of grace is called *the oil of gladness;* it is a ready and delightful motion which it causes in the will; it is a sweet efficacy and an efficacious sweetness.'

Is this 'to paralyse the soul, or to strike it through with a moral panic'? Surely Dr Cox will regret having made such a representation of the views of men whose opinions as to *the nature* of divine influence do not differ one tittle from his own. 'At what time,' Charnock goes on to say, 'God doth savingly work upon the will, to draw the soul from sin and the world to himself, it doth with the greatest willingness, freedom, and delight, follow after God, turn to him, close with him, and cleave to him, with all the heart and with purpose never to depart from him. – Song of Songs 1:4. *Draw me, and we will run after thee:* drawing signifies the efficacious power of grace; running signifies the delightful motion of grace: the will is drawn, as if it would not come; it comes, as if it were not drawn. His grace is so sweet and so strong that he neither wrongs the liberty of his creature nor doth prejudice his absolute power. As God moves necessary causes necessarily; contingent causes contingently; so he moves free agents freely, without offering violence to their natures. The Spirit glides into the heart by sweet illapses of grace and victoriously allures the soul. – Hosea 2:14. *I will allure her and speak to her heart;* not by crossing, but changing the inclination by the all-conquering and alluring charms of love', etc.[1]

The fourth proposition is that this influence is 'insuperably victorious' or, in other words, irresistible. In what sense is it irresistible? Let the following explanation from Charnock in this immediate connection answer, and prevent those brethren reproaching us for a word, who agree with us as to the thing intended.

[1] Charnock, *The New Birth*, p. 287–8.

As the demonstration of the Spirit is clear and undeniable, so the power of the Spirit is sweet and irresistible; both are joined, 1 Cor. 2:4. An inexpressible sweetness allures the soul, and an unconquerable power draws the soul; there are clear demonstrations, charming persuasions, and invincible efficacy combined in the work. He leaves not the will in indifference. [This is what they were arguing against.] If God were the author of faith only by putting the will into an indifference, though it be determined by its own proper liberty, why may not he also be said to be the author of unbelief, if by the same liberty of this indifference it be determined to reject the gospel? . . . *This irresistibleness takes not away the liberty of the will.* Our Saviour's obedience was free and voluntary, yet necessary and irresistible . . . Is not God freely and voluntarily good, yet necessarily so? He cannot be otherwise than good; he will not be otherwise than good. So the will is irresistibly drawn, and yet doth freely come to its own happiness.[1]

It is perfectly evident, therefore, that nothing more was intended by this expression than what President Edwards and all other Calvinists contend for, viz., moral or philosophical necessity.

Now, when it is remembered that all the expressions which we have quoted, and much more of the same import, are used in explanation of the nature of that divine influence by which regeneration is effected, we think that our readers will feel that the strongest possible evidence should be required to sustain the charge against those who use them of holding doctrines utterly inconsistent with their most clearly expressed opinions. We think that any candid man will acknowledge, who should take the trouble to read the writings of the older Calvinists, that they held no other doctrines on the subject of divine influence than such as are common among all classes of opposers of Arminianism. Their 'supernatural' or 'physical' influence meant nothing more than what is now intended by 'a direct and immediate influence'.

Owen, whose language on this subject is as strong as that of any writer with whom we are acquainted, states clearly, as we have already seen, his belief that the influence for which he contended is perfectly 'congruous' to the nature of the soul. He

[1] *ibid*, p. 288.

tells us also, page 257, that it is against the Pelagian theory that he is arguing when he maintains that moral suasion alone does not effect our regeneration, but that there is a direct agency of the Spirit in the work, which is such 'as our minds, wills, and affections are suited to be wrought upon and affected by, according to their natures and natural operations.'

But if old Calvinists held such opinions (and they hold them still) on 'the nature of regeneration and the mode of its occurrence', where is the difference between them and Dr Cox? None in the world, as far as these general statements go. His general propositions, that regeneration is a moral and not a physical change, and that it takes place in a manner accordant to the nature of the soul, are as orthodox as Owen or Charnock could wish them. We take it for granted, however, that Dr Cox would think we had treated him rather unhandsomely thus to convict him of *old* orthodoxy.

We proceed, therefore, to state where the difference really lies. It is simply this. All the old Calvinists, and the great majority, we hope and believe of the new school also, hold that the *result* of the Holy Spirit's operation on the soul is a holy principle or disposition; Dr Cox says, if we understand him, that the result is a holy act. This is the whole ground of debate, and to lookers on it may appear rather too narrow to be worth disputing about. Dr Cox, however, seems to think that this is a subject of vital importance affecting deeply our views of the whole system of divine truth and our manner of preaching; involving the high questions of the grounds of man's accountability, the nature of sin and holiness, and of human liberty.

And here we are sorry to say we agree with him. We are afraid that this is a turning point. We do not see how it is possible to hold together the tattered shreds of Calvinism if this ground be assumed. Is Calvinism, then, a mere metaphysical system? We think not. But there are some metaphysical opinions utterly inconsistent with it; that indifference is necessary to the freedom of the will is one, and that morality consists in acts only, we fear, is another.

All the ground that we have for supposing that Dr Cox holds this latter opinion is found in the pamphlet under review. And even here it is not distinctly asserted; but it seems to be constantly implied and to be the foundation of all that is peculiar in the sermon or introduction. The principle assumed is that there is nothing in the soul but its substance, with its essential attributes and its acts. Therefore, if regeneration be not a change in its acts, it must be a change in the substance. If sin be not an act, then it is substance, 'an entity', 'a disease of the texture of the soul'.

This we take it, is the ground of the imputation that Calvinists believe in physical depravity and physical regeneration; for if this principle be not assumed, there is not even the slender and insufficient ground of these doctrines being deducible, in the author's opinion, from Calvinistic principles, to justify the charge. Besides, every one knows that this is the ground on which this charge has been made before, in a manner far more offensive and unfair than Dr Cox is capable of making it. It is on this ground also, we presume, that Dr Cox maintains that the soul is as active in regeneration as in repentance or the exercise of faith.

And it is on this ground, we suppose, that he ridicules the idea of regeneration being the production of a holy principle in the soul, 'the happy contrary', as he calls it, 'of a principle of sin, which is concreated with us.' This view of the doctrine of regeneration (that it is the production of a holy principle), he says, can 'command the confidence of no well disciplined mind' (rather a bold assertion by the way), and then adds, 'By holy principle I mean love to God, and not anything antecedent to it; and by love to God, I mean loving him; and in that the subject is active.'

Dr Cox, we believe, pins his faith to no man's sleeve and is the follower of no party. His opinions are his own; but what they are we pretend not to know further than they are developed in this discourse. He has here brought forward the charge against many of his brethren whom he loves, and who love him, of believing in physical depravity and physical regeneration. On what grounds he rests the charge we have no means of ascertaining but from the opinions advanced in this discourse. We are anxious to show that, as far as old Calvinists are concerned, the imputation is unfounded. And we think that we have shown to the satisfaction of every candid reader that these doctrines are constantly and explicitly disclaimed by this class of theologians.

When it is asserted, therefore, in the face of such positive declarations to the contrary, that they do entertain these opinions, it can only be on the ground that they are fair inferences from the principles which they avow. This, though a very improper ground for a direct imputation, is all, we are persuaded, that can exist. How Dr Cox would endeavour to make it appear that these are fair inferences we do not know, and therefore do not wish to be considered in our further remarks on this subject, as having reference to Dr Cox's theological opinions any further than they are distinctly avowed in this sermon. Our object is simply this: to endeavour to show that the Calvinistic doctrine that regeneration consists in the production of a holy habit or principle in the soul, fitting and disposing it to holy acts, is not liable to the charge here advanced.

It will not be necessary to take up much time or space in proving that the doctrine of regeneration as just stated is that which is held by old Calvinists. Charnock, page 85, vol. ii, says, 'This new creation consists in gracious qualities and habits which beautify and dispose the soul to act righteously and holily.' Owen says the new creation is 'an habitual holy principle wrought in us by God and bearing his image', or, as in the next sentence, 'a divine supernatural principle of spiritual actions and operations'.

We prefer, however, referring to the statements of a few of the theologians of our own country, some of whom do not belong to the class which for the sake of convenience we have called old Calvinists. *President Edwards* not only admits that moral principles or habits may and must exist in the soul prior (in the order of nature) to moral action, but his whole system of practical theology, as it seems to us, rests on this foundation. The great fundamental principle of his work on the affections is this: All gracious or spiritual affections presuppose and arise from spiritual views of divine truth. These views the natural man neither has, nor can have, while he remains such. Hence arises the necessity of such a change being wrought in the state of the soul that it can perceive the real beauty and excellence of divine things. This change consists in imparting to the soul what he calls 'a new sense', or a new taste, or relish, or principle, adapted to the perception and love of spiritual excellence.

Were we to attempt to exhibit all the evidence which might be adduced in proof of the fact that his views were such as we have represented, we should be obliged to quote a great part of the work just mentioned. We refer the reader especially to what he says on the first and fourth signs of gracious affections. With regard to the nature of regeneration, we quote only a single passage. After having stated that the exercises of the true Christian are specifically different from those of unsanctified men, he infers that if the exercises are different, the principle whence they proceed must be different, or there must be, 'as it were, a new spiritual sense, or a principle of new kind of perception or spiritual sensation.' And he hence explains why it is that 'the work of the Spirit of God in regeneration is often in Scripture compared to giving a new sense, giving eyes to see and ears to hear, unstopping the ears of the deaf and opening the eyes of them that were born blind, and turning them from darkness unto light'. The nature of this 'new sense' he thus explains:

This new sense and the new dispositions that attend it are no new *faculties,* but are new *principles* of nature. I use the word *principles* for want of a word of a more determinate signification. By a *principle of nature,* in this place, I mean that foundation which is laid in nature, either old or new, for any particular manner or kind of exercise of the faculties of the soul; or a natural habit or foundation for action, giving a person ability and disposition to exert the faculties in exercises of such a certain kind; so that to exert the faculties in that kind of exercises may be said to be his nature. So this new spiritual sense is not a new faculty of understanding, but it is a new foundation laid in the nature of the soul for a new kind of exercises of the same faculty of understanding. So that new holy disposition of the heart that attends this new sense, is not a new faculty of the will, but a foundation laid in the nature of the soul for a new kind of exercises of the same faculty of will. The Spirit of God, in all his operations on the minds of natural men, only moves, impresses, assists, improves, or some way acts upon natural principles, but gives no new spiritual principle.[1]

[1] Jonathan Edwards, *The Religious Affections* (London: Banner of Truth, 1961), p. 134.

We have never met with a stronger or more formal statement of the doctrine which we are endeavouring to support than is found in this passage. And it should be considered that this is not a passing remark on the part of President Edwards, or the statement of an isolated opinion, but it is a fundamental principle of his whole theology as we understand it. Take this away, and his whole theory of original righteousness, original sin, of the nature of holiness and the nature of sin, and of the liberty of the will, go with it. Whether his views on these subjects are correct, although the main question, is one thing, but that he really entertained the opinion here so clearly expressed we wonder that any man should ever have doubted. We trust that respect for the memory of President Edwards and the obligation 'to interpret language according to the known and declared nature of the thing described' will prevent any one saying that he believed that 'this new sense' is an entity, or 'this foundation' for moral exercises is 'something inserted in the soul', 'an agent within an agent,' etc., etc.

Dr Bellamy seems to teach the same doctrines as President Edwards with regard to spiritual blindness, the necessity of divine illumination prior to the exercise of any holy affections, and the nature of regeneration. In the second volume of his works, page 502, he says, 'In regeneration there is a new, divine, and holy taste begotten in the heart by the immediate influences of the Holy Spirit.' And on the opposite page, 'The idea of a natural beauty supposes an internal sense implanted by our Creator by which the mind is capacitated to discern such kind of beauty.' 'And that the idea of spiritual beauty supposes an internal spiritual sense communicated to the soul by the Spirit of God in the work of the new creation, is clearly illustrated and proved by a late divine whose praise is in all the churches.' He here refers his readers to Edwards on *Religious Affections*.

Dr Dwight taught the same doctrine, and that clearly and definitely. In his discourse on the nature of regeneration, he says, 'This change of heart consists in a relish for spiritual objects communicated to it by the power of the Holy Ghost.' That 'this relish' was antecedent, according to his view, to all holy acts, there can be no doubt, because he expressly asserts it, and because his arguments go to prove it. What he calls 'a relish for spiritual objects' he elsewhere calls a holy disposition and refers to the case of Adam for an illustration of its nature. 'When God created Adam,' he remarks,

there was a period of his existence after he began to be, antecedent to that in which he exercised the first volition. Every man who believes the mind to be something besides ideas and exercises and does not admit the doctrine of casualty, will acknowledge that in this period the mind of Adam was in such a state that he was propense to the exercise of virtuous volitions rather than that of sinful ones. This state of mind has been commonly styled disposition, temper, inclination, heart, etc. In the Scriptures it usually bears the last of these names: I shall take the liberty to call it disposition. This disposition in Adam was the cause whence his virtuous volitions proceeded; the reason why they were virtuous and not sinful. Of the metaphysical nature of this cause I am ignorant; but its existence is, in my view, certainly proved by its effects.

Again, on the same page,

In regeneration, the very same thing is done by the Spirit of God for the soul which was done for Adam by the same Divine Agent at his creation. The soul of Adam was created with a relish for spiritual objects. The soul of every man who becomes a Christian is renewed by the communication of the same relish. In Adam this disposition produced virtuous volitions. In every child of Adam who becomes the subject of virtue, it produces the same effects.

The same idea is expressed if possible even more formally in the same volume, page 451, where, among other things equally explicit, he says that by this disposition he intends 'the cause which in the mind of man produces virtuous affections and volitions'. The same doctrine is repeatedly taught in other passages of his works, as in the sermons on the *Probation of Man,* vol. i., 394, on the *Fall,* 410, 413, on *Depravity as derived from Adam,* etc.

From various passages which occur in the pamphlet of Dr Tyler already mentioned, we infer that he holds the same doctrine. The same principle (that moral disposition may exist antecedently to all moral acts) is also frequently and clearly asserted by Dr Woods of Andover, in his controversy with Dr Ware. We refer to the opinions of these distinguished men, to show how united Calvinists, old and new, are in their views on this point, and that if the charge of believing in physical depravity and physical regeneration be sustained, it lies on almost the whole Calvinistic world. Still the main question recurs – is the charge well founded?

The main principle, as before stated, which is assumed by those who make this charge is that we can only regard the soul as to its substance on the one hand and its actions on the other. If therefore there be any change wrought in the soul other than of its acts, it must be a physical change. And if any tendency, either to sin or holiness, exist prior to choice, it is a positive existence, a real entity. Thus the charge of physical depravity and physical regeneration is fairly made out. We are constrained to confess that if the premises are correct, the conclusions, revolting as they are and affecting as they do the fair names of so large a portion of the Christian church, are valid.

The principle itself, however, we believe to be a gratuitous assumption. It is inconsistent with the common and, as we believe, correct idea of habits, both connatural and acquired. The word habit (*habitus*) was used by the old writers precisely in the same sense as 'principle' by President Edwards, as explained above, or disposition, as used and explained by President Dwight. That there are such habits or dispositions which can be resolved neither into 'essential attributes' nor 'acts', we maintain to be the common judgment of mankind.

Let us take for illustration an instance of an acquired habit of the lowest kind, the skill of an artist. He has a soul with the same essential attributes as other men; his body is composed of the same materials; and the same law regulates the obedience of his muscular actions to his mind. By constant practice he has acquired what is usually denominated skill; an ability to go through the processes of his art with greater facility, exactness, and success than ordinary men. Take this man while asleep or engaged in any indifferent occupation, you have a soul and body not differing in any of their essential attributes from those of other men. Still there is a difference. What is it? Must it be either 'a real existence, an entity', an act, or nothing? It cannot be 'an entity', for it is acquired, and it will hardly be maintained that a man can acquire a new essential attribute.

Neither is it an act, for the man has his skill when it is not exercised. Yet there is certainly 'something' which is the ground of certainty, that when called to go through the peculiar business of his art, he will do it with an ease and rapidity impossible for common men.

It is as impossible not to admit that this ground or reason exists in order to account for the effect, as it is not to admit the existence of the soul to account for its exercises. By constant practice, a state of mind and body has been produced adapted to secure these results and which accounts for their character. But this is the definition of principle or habit as given above.

A single circumstance is here wanting which is found in other 'habits' and that is, there is not the tendency or proneness to those particular acts to which this state of mind is adapted. This difference, however, arises not from any difference in the 'habits' themselves, but from the nature of the faculties in which, so to speak, they inhere. A principle in the will (in its largest sense, including all the active powers), is not only a state of mind adapted to certain acts, but prone to produce them. This is not the case, at least to the same degree, with intellectual habits. Both classes, however, come within the definition given by President Edwards and Dr Dwight: 'a state of mind' or 'foundation for any particular kind of exercise of the faculties of the soul'.

The same remarks may be made with regard to habits of a more purely intellectual character. A man, by devoting himself to any particular pursuit, gradually acquires a facility in putting forth the mental exercises which it requires. This implies no change of essence in the soul; and it is not merely an act which is the result of this practice. The result, whatever it is, is an attribute of the man under all circumstances, and not merely when engaged in the exercises whence the habit was acquired.

But to come nearer to the case in hand. We say a man has a malignant disposition, or an amiable disposition. What is to be understood by these expressions? Is it merely that he often indulges malignant or amiable feelings? or is it not rather that there is an habitual proneness or tendency to their indulgence? Surely the latter. But, if so, the principle stated above, that we can regard the soul only as to its substance or its actions, cannot be correct. For the result of a repetition of acts of the same kind is an abiding tendency which is itself neither an act (eminent or imminent) nor an 'entity'.

Here, then, is the soul with its essential attributes – and habitual tendency to certain exercises, and the exercises themselves. The tendency is not an act, nor an active state of the feelings in question; for it would be a contradiction to say that a man whose heart was glowing with parental affection, or filled for the time with any other amiable feeling, had at the same moment the malignant feeling in an active state, although there might exist the greatest proneness to their exercise.

We have seen no analysis of such dispositions which satisfies us that they can be reduced to acts. For it is essential to the nature of an act that it should be a matter of consciousness. This is true of those which are imminent acts of the will or ultimate choices (by which a fixed state of the affections is meant to be expressed), as well as of all others. But a disposition or principle, as explained above, is not a matter of consciousness. A man may be aware that he has a certain disposition, as he is aware of the existence of his soul, from the consciousness of its acts, but the disposition itself is not a subject of direct consciousness. It exists when the man is asleep or in a swoon and unconscious of any thing.

Neither can these habits be with any propriety called a choice or permanent affection. For in many cases they are a mere proneness to acts which have their foundation in a constitutional principle of the mind. Our object at present is merely to show that we must admit that there are mental habits which cannot be resolved either into essential attributes of the soul, fixed preferences, or subordinate acts; and consequently, that those who believe in dispositions prior to all acts do not necessarily maintain that such dispositions are of the essence of the soul itself. If it be within the compass of the divine power to produce in us that which by constant exercise we can produce in ourselves, then a holy principle or habit may be the result of the Spirit's influence in regeneration without any physical change having been wrought.

But it is not only objected that regeneration is a physical change, if anything beyond a change in the exercises of the soul

is effected; but it is said that the thing contended for is utterly
unintelligible, incapable of definition or explanation. We are
ready to acknowledge that it admits of no other explanation
than that which is derived from stating its effects and referring
to cases of analogous kinds. There is in all men a social
principle, as it is called, which is something else than a desire
to live in society, because it is connatural, as may be inferred
from its universality; there is a tendency in all men to love their
children, which is something besides loving them; there is a
tendency in man also to sympathize in the sufferings of others,
etc. It may be said these are all constitutional tendencies
implanted in our nature.

This is very true; but does saying this enable us to understand their nature? May it not be objected to those who employ
this language, You are using words without meaning; what do
you know of a social principle distinct from the actual desire to
live in society, or prior to its exercise? What idea can you form
of a principle of self-love, excepting actually loving one's self?
Are we then to deny that there are any such original propensities or tendencies as these implanted in our nature, because
we cannot directly conceive of them?

Yet Dr Cox says, in reference to this subject, 'By holy
principle, *I* mean love to God, and by love to God I mean
actually loving him.' On the same principle, he might deny the
existence of any of the original dispositions or tendencies of the
soul. For they are as incapable of being defined as the holy
principle which is produced in regeneration. The soul itself is
in the same predicament. We know nothing of it but from our
consciousness of its acts.

And if the objection which we are now considering be valid
against the existence of principles prior to acts, then it is valid
against the existence of the soul. We are conscious only of its
exercises, and therefore some philosophers and theologians tell
us we are not authorized to go any further. The existence of a
substance apart from the exercises is not necessary to account
for their existence, and therefore is a gratuitous assumption.
An assumption, too, of the being of something which we are
incapable of defining, explaining, or even conceiving.

The reply which Dr Cox would make to this reasoning is
probably the same that we should be disposed to make to his

objection against the existence of holy principles prior to holy acts. For the mind as instinctively seeks a reason for the choice which the soul makes in loving God, as it does for the various ideas and exercises of which it is constantly conscious. And we should probably be as little satisfied with the reasons which Dr Cox could assign to account for this choice, as he would be with those of the defenders of the exercise scheme to account for these exercises without resorting to a thinking substance.

If he were to say that the effect is produced by the Holy Spirit, we should answer that this can only be done in one of three ways that we can conceive of. First, either by his direct agency producing the choice, in which case it would be no act of ours; or secondly, by addressing such motives to our constitutional and natural principle of self-love as should induce us to make the choice, in which case there would be no morality in the act; or, thirdly, by producing such a relish for the divine character that the soul as spontaneously and immediately embraces God as its portion, as it rejoices in the perception of beauty.

The thing contended for is not more unintelligible than a hundred things of like nature. Taste is the ready perception and quick feeling of natural beauty. That is, these are its effects. But no one can directly conceive of it, as it is an attribute of the mind, either original or acquired. It is absolutely certain, however, that the man who does thus readily perceive and feel the beauty of natural objects has a quality of mind which a clown does not possess. And we should be astonished to hear any one maintain that there was no such thing as taste, but the exercise. 'By taste I mean the love of beauty, and by love of beauty I mean actually loving it, and that is an act and not a principle.'

But why does one man see and feel a beauty in certain objects when others do not? Is there no difference between the clown and the most refined votary in the arts, but in their acts? Is any man satisfied by being told that one loves them, and the other does not; that it is in vain to ask why; the fact is enough, and the fact is all; there is no difference in the state of their minds antecedent to their acts; there can be no such thing as a principle of taste or sense of beauty, distinct from the actual love of beauty?

We are disposed to think that no man can believe this: that the constitution of our nature forces us to admit that if one man, under all circumstances and at all times, manifests this quick sensibility to natural beauty, and another does not, there is some difference between the two besides their acts; that there is some reason why, when standing before the same picture, one is filled with pleasure and the other is utterly insensible. We cannot help believing that one has taste (a quality, principle, 'or inward sense') which the other does not possess. It matters not what it may be called. It is the ground or reason of the diversity of their exercises which lies back of the exercises themselves, and must be assumed to account for the difference of their nature.

Now, there is moral as well as natural beauty, and it is no more unintelligible that there should be a 'sense', or taste, for the one than for the other. The perfect character of God, when exhibited to different men, produces delight and desire in some, repugnance in others. We instinctively ask, Why? Why do some perceive and delight in his moral beauty, while others do not? The answer, some love, and others do not, is no answer at all. It is merely saying the same thing in other words. There must be some reason why one perceives this kind of beauty, to which others are blind; why one is filled with love the moment it is presented, and the other with repugnance. And this reason must lie back of the mere exercise of this affection, must be something besides the act itself and such as shall account for its nature.

It may be said, however, that the cases are not analogous: that the emotion excited by beauty is involuntary, while moral objects address themselves to the voluntary affections; and that it is admitted that there is not only 'something' back of each exercise of love, but we are told distinctly what it is, namely, the soul with its essential attributes, its ultimate or supreme choice, or dominant affection, and the object in view of the mind. Accordingly, it is easily accounted for that when the character of God is presented, one man is filled with love, another with repugnance. The reason of the difference in *these* acts does indeed lie back of the acts themselves; for it is found in the ultimate or supreme choice of the different individuals.

But how is this to be accounted for? If there is no necessity for accounting for the particular character of the first or ultimate choice (if so it must needs be called), there is no need of accounting for the others. The difficulty is not at all met by this statement. It is only pushed back from the secondary and subordinate to the primary and dominant preference. There it returns. The question still is, why does the soul of one man make this supreme choice of God, or in other words, love him, while another sets his affections on the world? There is precisely the same necessity for assuming some ground or reason for the nature of the first choice, as for any acts subordinate and subsequent to it.

Let us suppose two individuals called into existence, in the full maturity of their faculties; each has a soul with the same constitutional powers, or essential attributes; the one is filled with delight the moment the character of God is presented, and the other is not; or the one loves his Maker as soon as the idea of his excellence is presented, the other does not. According to this theory, there is no reason for this difference. There is nothing back of the first act of choice that is not common to both.

If, instead of two individuals, we suppose two millions, one portion having their affections spontaneously called forth on their first view of their Maker, the other unaffected; we have only a greater number of effects without a cause, but the case is the same. It will not do to answer that the choice is made under the influence of the desire of happiness, for this being common to all, is no reason for the difference of the result, which is the very thing to be accounted for. To say that the choice is made under the influence of the desire of happiness is only to say that when the character of God is presented it gives pleasure. But the same character is presented in both cases, the same desire exists in both, yet in one it gives pleasure, is an object of desire; in the other not.

This is the fact which is left entirely unaccounted for on the theory in question, and for which the mind as instinctively seeks a cause, as it does for any other effect. To account for the difference from the nature of agency is to assume the liberty of indifference. For if the choice be made prior to the rising of desire towards the object, then it is made in indifference and is of no moral character. If the desire rise, it is love; which is the very thing to be accounted for. We are at a loss to see how this theory is to be reconciled with the Calvinists' doctrine on the will, which is not peculiar to Edwards, but constituted the great dividing line between Calvinists and Arminians from the beginning.

We feel, therefore, a necessity for assuming that there is 'something' back of the first moral act besides the soul and its essential attributes, which will account for the nature of that act, which constitutes the reason why, in the case supposed, the soul of the one individual rose immediately to God, and the other did not; and the 'something' assumed in this case is no more indefinite and undefineable than the constitutional propensity to live in society, to love our children, or the mental quality called taste, all which are assumed from a necessity not more imperious than that which requires a holy principle to account for the delight experienced in view of the character of God. And if our Maker can endow us not only with the general susceptibility of love, but also with a specific disposition to love our children; if he can give us a discernment and susceptibility of natural beauty, he may give us a taste for spiritual loveliness. And if that taste, by reason of sin, is vitiated and perverted, he may restore it by the influences of his Spirit in regeneration. Neither, therefore, the objection, that what is not an act must be an essential attribute; nor the unintelligible nature of a 'principle of nature' is, in our view, any valid objection to the common doctrine on regeneration.

There is a third objection, however, to this doctrine, and that is that it renders the sinner excusable, because it makes regeneration to consist in something else than the sinner's own act. This objection, as it seems to us, can only be valid on one or the other of two grounds; the first is that the common doctrine supposes sin to be a physical defect, and regeneration a physical change; and the second is that a man is responsible solely for his acts, or that there can be no moral principle anterior to moral action. With regard to the first, it is enough to say that no physical change, according to the constant declaration of Calvinistic writers, is held to take place in regeneration, and that no such change is implied in the production of a holy principle, as we have already endeavoured to show.

The second ground is inconsistent with the common notions of men on the nature of virtue, and if true would render the commencement of holiness or regeneration impossible. It is according to the universal feeling and judgment of men that the moral character of an act depends upon the motive with which it is done. This is so obviously true that Reid and Stewart, and almost all other advocates of the liberty of indifference, readily admit it. And so do the advocates of the theory on which this objection is founded, with regard to all moral acts excepting the first. All acts of choice, to be holy, must proceed from a holy motive, excepting the first holy choice which constitutes regeneration; that may be made from the mere desire of happiness or self-love.

We confess that this strikes us as very much like a relinquishment of the whole system. For how is it conceivable that anything should be essential to the very nature of one act as holy, that is not necessary to another? Is not this saying that that on which the very nature of a thing depends may be absent, and yet the thing remain the same? Is it not saying that that which makes an act what it is and gives it its character, may be wanting or altered, and yet the character of the act be unaffected?

It is the motive which gives the moral character to the act. If the motive is good, the act is good; if the motive is bad, the act is bad; if the motive is indifferent, so is the act. The act has no character apart from the motive. This, it seems, is admitted with regard to all moral acts excepting the first. But the first act of a holy kind is an act of obedience, as well as all subsequent acts of the same kind. How then is it conceivable that the first act of obedience performed from the mere desire of happiness or self-love can be holy, when no other act of the same kind and performed from the same motive, either is or can be? How does its being first alter its very nature? It is still nothing more than an act done for self-gratification, and cannot be a holy act.

It is said we must admit this, from the necessity of the case, or acknowledge that there can be holiness before moral action. We prefer admitting the latter and believing that 'God created man upright', and not that he made himself so. That there was a disposition, or relish, or taste for holiness, before there was any holy act, which to us is far more reasonable than that an act is holy because the first of a series, which, if performed from the same motive at a different point of the line, would have a different character.

The grand objection, we know, that is made to all this is that holy beings have fallen, which it is maintained would be impossible if the ground here assumed is correct. If the character of an act depends on its motive, a sinful act cannot be performed by a being in whom sin does not already exist; and, consequently, neither the fallen angels, nor Adam, could ever have apostatized.

We think, however, that there is a broad difference between the commencement of holiness and the commencement of sin, and that more is necessary for the former than for the latter. An act of obedience, if it is performed under the mere impulse of self-love, is virtually no act of obedience. It is not performed with any intention to obey, for that is holy, and cannot, according to the theory, precede the act. But an act of disobedience performed from the desire of happiness is rebellion. The cases are surely widely different. If to please myself I do what God commands, it is not holiness; but if to please myself I do what he forbids, it is sin.

Besides, no creature is immutable. Though created holy, the taste for holy enjoyments may be overcome by a temptation sufficiently insidious and powerful, and a selfish motive or feeling excited in the mind. Neither is a sinful character immutable. By the power of the Holy Spirit the truth may be so clearly presented and so effectually applied as to produce that change which is called regeneration; that is, as to call into existence a taste for holiness, so that it is chosen for its own sake, and not merely as a means of happiness.

It is evident, therefore, that the theory which denies the possibility of moral distinctions being carried back of acts of choice forces its advocates to adopt the opinion that the first holy act is specifically different from all others. That Adam was not created holy, but by choosing God made himself holy, and that this choice, though made with no holy motive or intention but merely from a desire of happiness, has a moral character. This we think not only contradictory to the express declaration of Scripture, which says that man was created in the image of his Maker (which includes his moral as well as his natural image, as we are taught in the New Testament), but is inconsistent with the very first principles of morals, as it teaches that an act performed without any good intention or motive is yet holy.

It seems to us liable also to this further objection, that it represents man's obligation to love God to rest upon the fact that it will promote his happiness. This is involved in the principle that the choice made from this motive is a good choice; for it can only be good as it is in obedience to a moral obligation. If the obligation fulfilled is to God, then to fulfil it must be the motive. If the motive which prompts the choice have reference to himself, then the only obligation which he fulfils is to himself. It is a wise decision, but it is no holy act. If it be said that the excellence of the choice lies in the nature of the object chosen, it is giving up the question. For if the excellence of the object be the ground of the choice, it can act as a motive only by exciting a desire for it as excellent, which must needs be a holy desire, and if this determines the choice, then the man is holy before he chooses God as his portion, and the choice is the result, and not the cause of his holiness.

Or, if we call the desire itself the choice (which is an incorrect use of terms), still the case is the same. For the best definition that can be given of a holy being is that holy objects excite in him desire as soon as they are presented. If Adam, therefore was filled with desire and pleasure as soon as his mind rested on the character of God, then he was created holy. As we remarked above, this theory, that the first moral act is not performed from a holy motive but from the constitutional desire of happiness, is not only inconsistent with the nature of a holy act, but affords no relief in the case. For the difficulty still remains, why the character of God should appear desirable to one being and not to another, if both are called into existence *in puris naturalibus* (with purely natural qualities).

That Adam was created holy, that is, with a holy disposition which existed prior to his first holy act, though necessarily destructive of the very first principle of the theory referred to, has been considered as a fixed point among Calvinists. We have already seen that Dr Dwight did not think it necessary to prove it. Because he says, 'every man who believes the mind to be something more than ideas and exercises, and *does not admit the doctrine of casualty*, will acknowledge' it. President Edwards, in his work on original sin, has a whole chapter in which he endeavours to prove that our first parents were created in righteousness, or as he expresses it, 'with holy principles and dispositions'. The grand objection against this doctrine, he says, is this:

that it is utterly inconsistent with the nature of virtue that it should be concreated with any person; because, if so, it must be by an act of God's absolute power without our knowledge or concurrence; and that moral virtue in its very nature implieth the choice and consent of the moral agent, without which it cannot he virtue and holiness: that a necessary holiness is no holiness;

and he quotes from Dr Taylor of Norwich, the words, 'Adam must exist, he must be created, yea, he must exercise thought and reflection before he was righteous.'

To this he replies,

In the first place, I think it a contradiction to the nature of things as judged of by the common sense of mankind. It is agreeable to the sense of the minds of men in all ages, not only that the fruit or effect of a good choice is virtuous, but the good choice itself from which that effect proceeds; yea, and not only so, but also the antecedent good disposition, temper, or affection of the mind from whence proceeds that good choice, is virtuous. This is the general notion, not that principles derive their goodness from actions, but that actions derive their goodness from the principles whence they proceed; and so that the act of choosing that which is good is no further virtuous than it proceeds from a good principle or virtuous disposition of mind; which supposes that a virtuous disposition of mind may be before a virtuous act of choice; and that therefore *it is not necessary that there should first be thought, reflection, and choice before there can be any virtuous disposition.* If the choice be first, before the existence of a good disposition of heart, what signifies that choice? There can, according to our natural notions, be no virtue in a choice which proceeds from no virtuous principle but from mere self-love, ambition, or some animal appetite.' – p. 140.[1]

---

[1] Jonathan Edwards, *Works*, vol. 1 (Edinburgh: Banner of Truth, 1974), p. 177.

If there was a holy disposition before there was 'thought, reflection, or choice', Edwards most assuredly carried moral distinctions back of moral acts. That by so doing he carried them into the 'essential attributes of the soul' is an assertion founded on the assumption that what is not an act must be an essential attribute, which we believe few are prepared to admit.

God has created man with various susceptibilities, dispositions, or tendencies of mind towards objects without himself; these tendencies are not necessarily 'real existences, entities', or essential attributes, for tendencies or habits may, as before remarked, be acquired as the skill of an artist or a proneness to any particular mental exercise. They may result from the relative state of all the essential attributes and yet be 'no part of the soul' themselves. Their nature, however, is confessedly as inconceivable as the nature of the soul, and no more so; and they are as necessarily assumed to account for the results which meet our view, as the soul or any of its attributes. If a million of intelligent beings, the first moment they think of the character of God, are filled with desire and delight, it is as evident that they were created with a proneness or disposition to take pleasure in holiness, as it is that the hearts of mothers have an innate tendency to love their children, because they glow with delight the first moment they are given to them.

Nothing, we think, but the most determined adherence to a speculative opinion, can prevent any man acknowledging that it is as possible for the mind to be created with this 'instinctive' love of holiness, as with a disposition for any other specific class of objects. And we think, too, that the vast body of men will agree with President Edwards in thinking that 'such a disposition being natural or from a kind of instinct implanted in the mind in its creation', is no objection to its being of a virtuous or moral character. Does the maternal instinct cease to be amiable because it is natural? Does a disposition to kindness and gentleness lose its character by being innate? Are not the instinctive love of justice, abhorrence of cruelty, admiration of what is noble, which God has implanted in our nature, objects of approbation?

If our feelings and the general sense of mankind answer these questions in the affirmative, they as certainly will decide that an innate disposition to love God, existing in the mind of Adam at the moment of his creation, does not lose its moral character by being innate. The common feelings and judgment of men, therefore, do carry moral distinctions back of acts of choice, and must do so unless we deny that virtue ever can commence, for 'there can, according to our natural notions, be no virtue in a choice which proceeds from no virtuous principle but from mere self-love.'

If this be so, the very foundation of the objection that the common doctrine of regeneration destroys the responsibility of the sinner is taken away. This responsibility rests upon the fact that he stands in the relation of a rational and moral creature to God. He has all the attributes of a moral agent – understanding, conscience, and will. He has unimpaired the liberty of acting according to his own inclinations. His mind is not subject to any law of causation which determines his acts independently of himself. Motives, as external to the mind, have no influence, but as the mind itself, according to the laws of all rational creation, is affected by them and *voluntarily* admits their influence, and yields to it.

The responsibility of man, therefore, resting on the immutable obligations which bind him to love and obey God, and on the possession of all the attributes of moral agency, is not destroyed by his moral depravity of which the want of a disposition to holiness is an integral part. He does not love God, not because there is any physical defect in his constitution, but because his moral taste is perverted by reason of sin. He is so corrupt that even infinite loveliness appears hateful to him. There can in the nature of things be no reason why an intelligent and moral being should be blind to moral excellence, excepting moral corruption. And if this be an excuse, then the more depraved, the less he is to blame.

How he became thus depraved is another question – but it has nothing to do with the point before us, which is the nature of the inability which it involves to love God. He may have been born so, or he may have made himself so. It makes no difference as to this point. So long as this depravity is his own, his own moral character, it can furnish no excuse or palliation for not complying with the great command of the law and gospel. An object worthy of all affection is presented to his view, viz., the divine character; he is capable of intellectually apprehending this object. If blind to its loveliness it is, in his own judgment and that of all men, his sin; it is the very height of corruption to view as unlovely what is the perfection of moral beauty.

That men do labour under this moral blindness is one of the most frequently asserted doctrines of the Scriptures. 'The natural man receiveth not the things of the Spirit of God, for they are foolishness unto him; neither can he know them, because they are spiritually discerned.' 'These things,' says our Saviour, 'will they do unto you because they have not known the Father nor me.' 'To know God is eternal life.' We are said to be saved through knowledge. The gospel is 'hid to them that are lost'. Their eyes are binded

Light has shined into the hearts of those that believe. The saints of old prayed to have their minds illuminated; and Paul intercedes for his fellow Christians earnestly and frequently for this blessing as the only possible means of their sanctification. This is so plain that President Edwards, in speaking on this subject, says, 'There is such a thing, *if the Scriptures are of any use to teach us anything,* as a spiritual, supernatural understanding of divine things that is peculiar to the saints, and which those who are not saints know nothing of' – page 298, *On the Affections.* [1]

The cause of this blindness is sin, and therefore it is inexcusable. But if it exists, there is an evident necessity for such a change in the soul that it shall be brought to see this beauty of holiness, and from the constitution of our nature, this change must precede the exercise of love. For how can we love that which we do not see? The affections must have an object, and that object must be apprehended in its true nature in order to be truly loved. It is obvious therefore that regeneration, to be of a moral character at all, must consist in such a change as brings the soul into a state to see and love the beauty of holiness. It matters not what the change be called – a 'spiritual sense' or 'a taste' or 'disposition'; it is as necessary as that an object should be seen in order to be loved.

Now it is evident that all this must be denied by those who make regeneration to consist in the 'act of loving God', who

[1] Edwards, *The Religious Affections*, p. 195.

deny that there is any change prior in the order of nature to the exercise of love. For if the sinner is blind to God's loveliness, it is absolutely impossible that he should love it until he is brought to see it. It may be said that this is to render the sinner's case absolutely hopeless. So it is. And they do but delude and mock him, who represent it otherwise. It is thus the Bible represents it. It tells him that the natural man cannot know the things of the Spirit of God. And it is moreover necessary that the sinner should be brought to feel that his case, as far as he himself is concerned, is absolutely hopeless; that he may be brought to fall, with his blind and wicked heart, at the feet of sovereign mercy, and cry, Lord save me! or I perish.

But does this make the sinner excusable? Not unless his sin is his excuse. It is this, and this alone, which prevents his perception of the loveliness of God, and therefore, the more complete his blindness, the greater his loathsomeness and guilt. The two sentiments of complete helplessness and of entire blame-worthiness are perfectly consistent, and are ever united in Christian experience. The believer feels them every day. He knows that it is his duty, at once, to love God as purely and fervently and constantly as do the saints made perfect. Yet he feels that no mere efforts of his own, no use of means, no presentation of motives, no summoning of his powers, will ever enable him to raise his carnal heart to heaven. Does this free him from a sense of guilt? No. He covers his face with both his hands and bows down in the dust, and cries, Behold, I am vile. Have mercy on me, O Lord, and create within me a clean heart.

That the denial of the sinner's blindness to the holiness of God is involved in the theory of regeneration under consideration is perfectly evident, and is not, we presume, denied. If the mere choice of God as the supreme portion of the soul is regeneration, and the performance of this act constitutes the change, then of course no previous change is admitted to be necessary to enable him to make the choice; no opening of his eyes to see the moral excellence of the object he is to choose, no production of any sense of its loveliness; the choice itself is all that is demanded; and for this, everything is present that the act requires – the object, the capacity of viewing it in its true moral excellence, and the motive whence the choice is to proceed. For he need not choose God from any holy motive or intention (which would be to make holiness precede moral action), the simple desire of happiness is all that is required. The character of this first act does not depend on its motive. It is holy, though performed merely from the desire of self-gratification. This is a conclusion from which our minds instinctively revolt, and which Edwards says is contrary to the natural notions of men. It is, however a conclusion which is legitimate and acknowledged, and being, in our view, a complete *reductio ad absurdum,* the system is fairly, in our humble apprehension, *felo de se.*[1]

Dr Cox asks whether it is not 'intrinsically absurd' that a man should be regenerated before he does his duty? We think the absurdity is all the other way, that he should do his duty without being regenerated. That he should love God without having any proper perception of his character; or that an unholy soul should have this perception of the beauty of holiness. It appears to us a contradiction in terms to say that a holy object can be viewed as excellent and desirable by a carnal mind; for a holy mind is best defined by saying that it perceives and relishes the beauty of holiness. It is inconceivable to us, therefore, that any sinner should love God without this previous change, except on one or the other of these two grounds: that all his acts are created in him and he is really no agent at all, or that an act proceeding from mere self-love is holy. Both which contradict what to us are primary principles or intuitive truths.

But how is it that regeneration precedes the exercise of love? As the opening of the eyes precedes sight; as a sense of the beautiful precedes the emotion of beauty; as the maternal instinct precedes maternal love. As it is impossible for a man to have his eyes open in the day-time without seeing, so it is impossible for a man to be regenerated without delighting in God. Yet opening the eyes is not seeing, nor is regeneration delighting in God.

What the metaphysical nature of this change is, no one can tell. All the soul can say is, Whereas I was blind, now I see. What once appeared repulsive and 'foolishness' now appears

[1] Literally 'a felon of itself', a suicide.

supremely desirable and excellent. What once excited enmity, now calls forth love. What once was irksome and difficult is now easy and delightful. To say that these exercises themselves constitute the change, and the whole change, is to say that a wicked man is suddenly transformed in all his views, feelings, and conduct, without any reason for it. And to refer all to the immediate operations of the Spirit is to make man a machine, or mere instrument on which a mysterious hand plays what tune it pleases, to the delight or torment of the conscious but passive subject.

There is still another point. Dr Cox speaks of this 'certain kind of principle' as 'a mysterious gratuity' with which the receiver has nothing to do. A something inserted in the soul in some magic manner to influence his exercises, but which forms no part of his character. We are persuaded that a fundamental difference as to the nature of agency and human liberty lies at the foundation of all such objections. We are as yet only fighting in the dark. The real turning point is yet in the background. We do not mean that it is intentionally kept there, but that these objections have not even the semblance of force, if (what is yet considered common ground) the Calvinistic theory of the will is retained.

Was it a mere 'mysterious gratuity' without moral character for him, that Adam was created in the image of God 'with holy principles and dispositions'? Were these not voluntary principles? Was he not free in all his exercises of love determined by them? A disposition is not the less voluntary because it is innate. The affections are all voluntary, although concreated with us. Is a man less free in loving himself because self-love is a constitutional propensity? Does a mother love her child against her will because she acts agreeably to her nature? Does not the disposition so to do enter into her character? If this be true with regard even to constitutional propensities, it is still more obviously true with respect to moral disposition, whether originally implanted or restored in regeneration.

There is a continual play upon the double sense of the word 'voluntary'. When the faculties of the soul are reduced to understanding and will, it is evident that the latter includes all the affections. In this sense, all liking or disliking, desiring or being averse to, etc., are voluntary, or acts of the will. But when we speak of the understanding, will, and affections, the word 'will' includes much less. It is the power of the soul to come to a determination to fix its choice on some object of desire. These two meanings are distinct, though they may relate only to different states of the same faculty. In the latter sense, will and desire are not always coincident. A man may desire money and not will to take it or make it an object of pursuit; he may not fix his choice upon it. The will is here determined by some other desire of greater force; desire of doing right, for example.

When we speak of a volition of a choice, of a decision or determination of the will, the word 'will' is used in the restricted sense. A man may have many objects of desire before his mind; the decision which the will makes among them, or its selection, is its choice. There are a thousand things capable of ministering to our happiness; riches, honour, sensual pleasure, the service of God; the selection which the soul makes is made by the will in the narrower sense. This is a voluntary act in one sense of the term. But in another, the desire itself which the soul has for these objects, and not merely its decision or choice, is a voluntary act. For, according to Edwards, 'all choosing, refusing, approving, disapproving *liking, disliking,* directing, commanding, *inclining,* or being averse, a *being pleased* or *displeased with'*, are acts of the will. In this sense, all the affections and all desires are voluntary exercises, whether constitutional or not, and not merely the decisions to which they lead. Hence self-love, the love of children, the love of society, the desire of esteem, are all voluntary, although all springing from native tendencies of the mind.

This distinction between these different senses of the word will, although frequently made and formally stated, is yet, time after time, lost sight of in discussions of this nature, which gives rise to endless confusion. The word is often used in one sense in the premises of an argument and in the other in the conclusion. How often is it said that a man can love God if he will? What does this mean? If 'will' be here used in its narrower sense, this is not true. The affections no more obey a determination of the mind than the emotions do. A man can no more will to love, to hate, to be pleased or displeased, than he can will to be joyful or sorrowful, gay or sad, or even hot or cold at any given moment. But if the word be taken in its larger sense, as including the affections, then the proposition is identical; it is saying a man can love God if he does love God. And when Dr Cox says there are some men who teach that a man has no ability to believe even if he has the inclination; the very statement is absurd. For if the mind is inclined to embrace the truth in its real character, it does believe.

Although the advocates of the theory that morality attaches only to acts of choice lay down as the foundation of their doctrine Edwards' definition of the will as given above, yet it is plain that in a multitude of cases they confine acts of choice to acts of the will in the restricted sense. Thus the desire of money becomes avarice, they say, only when the will comes in and decides on money as the main object of pursuit. Self-esteem is not pride until the will decides on preferring our own claims unduly. In all such cases, it is the will as the faculty of decision between different objects of desire, that is intended. It is to acts of the will in this restricted sense, and to the states of mind thence resulting, and not to voluntary acts in the broad sense of President Edwards, that morality is made to attach.

Hence, in the case of Adam, the desire excited by a view of the divine perfections has no moral character. That belongs only to the act of the will which fixes on God as the chief good. And the first holy act of a newborn soul is not the desire which rises in view of the Divine Being, but the act of the will by which he is chosen as a portion. Hence, in the distinction between constitutional and voluntary propensities, the social affections, the love of children, desire of esteem, etc., are referred to the former class, and are not considered as voluntary. Yet in the broad sense of the word 'will', assumed as the foundation of the theory according to which all 'inclining or being averse', all 'being pleased or displeased with', are acts of the will, they are as truly voluntary as the others.

Now, when it is asserted that no disposition is of a moral character except so far as it depends on choice or preference, and that all morality lies in the will, the whole meaning turns on the sense in which the word 'will' is taken. If taken in its broader sense, this would be admitted; if in the restricted sense, we should deny it altogether. Those who make the assertion doubtless take it in the latter; for they say that all that precedes the decision of the soul, its fixing on some object of desire as its chief portion, is neither sinful nor holy; that holiness consists in the selection of God, and sin in the choice of the world, and that there is nothing sinful nor holy but these primary or ultimate choices and the subordinate acts resulting from them.

But it is clear that the term voluntary applies not only to such acts of choice, but to all exercises of the affection or desires preliminary thereto. No one would say that the disposition to love ourselves or our children depends on choice; and yet these dispositions are properly and truly voluntary. We cannot love otherwise than voluntarily.

When, therefore, these gentlemen use the word voluntary, it is in reference to acts of the will in the restricted sense, excluding the spontaneous exercises of the native propensities of our nature. They of course deny that Adam was created holy. The spontaneous rising of desire in his mind to God was neither holy nor unholy. His moral character commenced with the first act of choice, that is, with his selection of God from among the various sources of happiness as his chief good.

Here lies one great point of difference between them and common Calvinists. President Edwards maintains clearly that Adam was holy before this act of choice, yea, before he exercised 'thought or reflection'. And he says that it is according to our natural notions of things that there could be no virtue in this choice unless it was determined by a virtuous disposition.

The common judgment of men is that moral character belongs to the desire of moral objects. The morality lies in its nature independently of its origin. Its being from 'a kind of instinct' does not destroy its moral character. The desire of holiness is holy, no matter how it rises in the mind.

If this be so, a similar tendency of mind and a similar desire, if produced in our mind by the power of the spirit in regeneration, is not 'something inserted in the soul' without influence on our character. It constitutes us holy, as truly as Adam was holy at his first creation, though much of sin may yet remain. It is indeed 'a mysterious gratuity'; the Scriptures call it GRACE; but it is still ours, from its nature, voluntary and active. It is an inclination of the heart; and as Dr Bellamy remarks, an 'involuntary inclination of the heart is a contradiction in terms'. He uses the word voluntary in its larger sense, as Edwards does, and not merely in that which applies to a decision or selection from among different objects of desire. With him all spontaneous exercises of the mind are voluntary; self-love, the love of children, and all other similar affections. A disposition therefore to these or any other exercises existing prior to the exercises, in his view, does not destroy their character as voluntary nor their morality, if they have reference to moral objects; this depends upon their nature, not their origin.

We have already remarked that the opposite system destroys the moral character of the first act (in reference to moral objects) in Adam and in regeneration. We are ready to admit that as the desire of a holy object is from its nature holy, so the choice of such an object as holy is from its nature good. But it is inconceivable that holiness, as such, can be chosen without a previous apprehension of its real excellence, and desire for it as such; for the choice is but the determination of the desire. If, therefore, moral character be denied to the antecedent desire, the choice loses its moral character also. It cannot be confined to the act of choice, for there can in fact be no choice of a holy object as such, but from a desire for it in its true character, and this is a holy desire and precedes the choice.

If self-love be only so far the motive to this choice, that it 'prompts to the choice, but not determines it', what, we ask, does determine it? There are but two answers to this question. The one is that the will determines itself, *i.e.,* the choice is made in indifference and has clearly no moral character; or it is determined by a desire of the object as such (not mere desire of happiness, for that only prompts the choice, *not determines it),* and then the whole theory is relinquished, for here is the desire of a holy object not merely as a means of happiness, but for the object as holy, which must needs be a holy desire, and being antecedent to the choice, would be, according to the theory, anterior to the commencement of holiness.

The truth is, that this whole system is a forced and unnatural union between Arminian philosophy and Calvinistic facts: a union which can neither be peaceful nor lasting. Nor is this the first time that it has been attempted. The favourite principle of the opposers of the doctrines which are now called Calvinistic, in all ages, has been that moral character can only belong to acts of choice; and of course, that no such thing as original righteousness or original sin is possible or conceivable; that any other influence in regeneration than that of moral suasion, by which one man is led to make a good choice, which another man, under the same influence, might refuse to make, is inconsistent with moral agency; that doctrines of election and perseverance of the saints, presupposing that of efficacious grace, must necessarily be untrue.

The first departures from these doctrines have commenced by adopting the main principle and endeavouring to reconcile it, as far as possible, with the facts involved in the doctrines themselves; viz., that all men do sin, with absolute certainty, the moment they become moral agents; that the influence of the Spirit is infallibly efficacious: and that all whom God has chosen certainly believe and attain eternal life. But less than a generation has commonly been sufficient to break the connection and leave the philosophical principle undisputed master of the field.

That this principle is inconsistent with the doctrine of original righteousness is formally admitted. That it involves the denial of original sin, as this doctrine has been commonly held among Calvinists, is equally clear. According to the prevalent doctrine on this subject, original sin consists, first, in the imputation of Adam's sin. This, it seems, has been long exploded. Secondly, in the want of original righteousness. This is gone too, for there never was any such thing. And thirdly, in the corruption of nature, that is, a tendency to do what God has prohibited existing prior to all acts of choice and independently of them; and now this is gone. There is no such tendency to sin as can be considered a moral disposition.

Although this article has already swollen far beyond our expectations, we cannot pass this subject without a single remark on the charge of physical depravity. The futility and unfairness of the same charge as it regards the subject of regeneration we have endeavoured to expose above. As this rests on precisely the same grounds, it must stand or fall with the other. If there may be moral principles prior to moral acts (as we think must be assumed in the case of Adam, or we make the commencement of holiness impossible), then there is not a shadow of ground for this charge.

Nor is it the Calvinistic doctrine that there is a specific propensity to sin (analogous to the holy disposition implanted in the heart of Adam) connatural with the soul of man. None such need be assumed, and none such is believed to exist. The mere absence of a native tendency to God leaves the soul in moral confusion and ruin. There is no positive infusion of wickedness. The essential attributes and constitutional propensities are there, and nothing more. But they are there without a principle of moral order and subordination. There is no presiding spirit to turn them to the service of God. The result of this absence is all manner of evil, and a tendency to all this evil lies in this very state of the soul and exists prior to any of its moral acts.

Does the withholding this predisposition to holiness from a being to whom all the essential attributes of his nature are left unimpaired, make God the author of sin? Then must he be accused of being the author of all sin that results from the abandonment of the reprobate, and of all that by the utmost exertion of his power he could prevent. Nor is it more difficult to reconcile this fact (that God should withhold from the fallen race of man those communications which resulted in the innate tendency to holiness which fill the soul of Adam) with the divine justice and goodness, than it is the admitted fact that he has brought, and is still bringing, the countless millions of the human family into existence under circumstances so unfavourable that all, without exception, incur the penalty of eternal death at the first moment of moral agency. And that moment arriving, too, at the first dawn of intellect and when the first faint flushes of moral feeling rise in the soul. If this be no penalty, we know not what is. 'To be placed under a law,' says Coleridge (*Aids to Reflection,* p. 168),

the difficulty of obeying, and the consequences of not obeying, which are both infinite, and to have momently to struggle with this difficulty, and to live in momently hazard of these consequences – if this be no punishment! – words have no correspondence with thoughts, and thoughts are but shadows of each other, shadows that own no substance for their anti-type. Of such an outrage on common sense, Taylor (Bishop Jeremy) was incapable. He himself calls it a penalty; he admits that in effect it is a punishment.'

It is a penalty, too, according to this theory, without transgression; a punishment without a crime. We cannot see,
therefore, that anything is gained by the new theory over the
old doctrine, which represents our race as having enjoyed a full
and fair and favourable probation in their first parent, and as
being regarded and treated as an apostate race on account of
his rebellion; so that the withholding those divine communications which resulted in the first man, in the moral image of his
Maker, is a penal evil from which, it is true, utter ruin results;
but it is the ruin not of innocent, but of fallen human beings.
This doctrine involves no mysterious confusion of the identity
of the race with that of Adam, and no transfer of moral character from him to us. His act was personally his own, and only
his; it is ours only on the representative principle, which is
recognised not only by Dr Hopkins and his followers distinctly,
but by Arminians and Pelagians,[1] and is so clearly taught by
the fact that the race fell when Adam fell, that it is admitted in
reality even by those who formally deny it.

But to return to our subject. This theory not only overthrows
the doctrines which we have just mentioned, but it throws the
Spirit's influences almost entirely out of view. We are not
speaking of the opinions of its advocates, but of the tendency
of the theory. According to their views, regeneration consists in
the choice of God as the supreme portion of the soul. This
requires that the soul should view him as supremely desirable.
This the sinner is not only naturally, but morally able to do; for
his corruption does not blind him to the excellence of holiness
or its adaptedness to promote his happiness. To secure this
happiness is the only impulse or motive necessary to make this
choice, and he is urged to make it, assured that if he will
summon all his powers to the effort, the result, by the grace of
God, may follow.

We think the grace of God acts a part scarcely more
conspicuous in all this scheme than it does in the enumeration
of the titles of a European monarch. There is no blindness to
the excellence of the object of choice to be removed, no holy
motive is necessary for the grand decision; all that is required
is a practical conviction that it will be for the sinner's interests.

[1] See Daniel Whitby (1638–1726), author of a *Paraphrase and Commentary
on the New Testament* (1703), on Romans 5:12.

Firmly as these brethren may believe in the necessity of the Spirit's interference, it is evident that necessity is left out of view almost entirely in their theory. Accordingly, when they come to describe the process of this great change, the sinner is the only agent brought to view; he is to consider, ponder, and decide, for all which he absolutely needs no assistance, though it may be graciously afforded. This mode of representation stands in strong contrast with the language of Scripture in those passages in which we are said 'to be born of the Spirit', 'to be created anew in Christ Jesus', to experience the workings 'of the exceeding greatness of the power of God', and many others of a similar character.

As to the point which Dr Cox thinks so 'intrinsically absurd' and about which he says so much, whether man is passive in regeneration, it will be seen that, for its own sake, it does not merit a moment's discussion. It depends entirely on the previous question. If regeneration be that act of the soul by which it chooses God for its portion, there is an end of all debate on the subject. For no one will maintain that the soul is passive in acting. But if there be any change in the moral state of the soul prior to its turning unto God, then it is proper to say that the soul is passive as to that particular point. That is, that the Holy Spirit is the author, and the soul the subject of the change. For all that is meant by the soul's being passive is that it is not the agent of the change in question. Its immediate and delightful turning unto God is its own act, the state of mind which leads to this act is produced directly by the Spirit of God.

The whole question is whether any such anterior change is necessary; whether a soul polluted and degraded by sin, or in Scripture language, carnal, needs any change in its moral taste before it can behold the loveliness of the divine character. For that this view must precede the exercise of affection, we presume will not be denied.

If this point be decided, the propriety of using the word 'passive' to denote that the soul is the subject and not the agent of the change in question, need not give us much trouble. Sure it is that this change is in Scripture always referred to the Holy Spirit. It is the soul that repents, believes, hopes and fears, but it is the Holy Spirit that regenerates. He is the author of our faith and repentance by inducing us to act, but no man regenerates himself. The soul, though essentially active, is still capable of being acted upon. It receives impressions from sensible objects, from other spirits, and from the Holy Ghost. In every sensation, there is an impression made by some external object and the immediate knowledge which the mind takes of the impression. As to the first point, it is passive or the subject; as to the second, it is active, or the agent. These two are indeed inseparably connected, and so are regeneration and conversion.

It is even allowable to say that the mind is passive considered as the recipient of any impression, no matter how communicated. Coleridge says, 'In ATTENTION, we keep the mind *passive;* in THOUGHT, we rouse it into activity. In the former, we submit to an impression, we keep the mind steady in order to receive the stamp.' – p. 252. Whether this is technically 'wretched, philosophically wrong, and theologically false' or not, we do not pretend to say. All that we say is that it is perfectly intelligible and perfectly according to established usage to speak of the mind as passive when considered as the subject of an impression. And if the Holy Spirit does make such an impression on the mind or exert such an influence as induces it immediately to turn to God, then it is correct to say that it is passive in regeneration, though active in conversion.

However, this is a very subordinate point; the main question is whether there is not a holy 'relish', taste' or principle produced in the soul prior, in the order of nature, to any holy act of the soul itself. If Dr Cox can show this to be 'intrinsically absurd', we shall give up the question of 'passivity' without a moment's demur.

To relinquish the other point, however, will cost us a painful struggle. It will be the giving up the main point in debate between the friends and opposers of the doctrines of grace from Augustine to the present day. It will be the renunciation not only of a favourite principle of old Calvinists, but of one of the fundamental principles of the theology of Edwards, Bellamy, Dwight and, as we believe, of the great body of the New England clergy. It will be the renunciation of what Calvinists old and new have believed to be the scriptural doctrine of original righteousness, original sin and efficacious grace. It will be the rejection of that whole system of mingled sovereignty and love which has been the foundation for ages of so many hopes and of so much blessedness to the people of God.

And all for what? Because it has been discovered that what is not an act is an entity; that to suppose the existence of moral disposition prior to moral action is making morality a substance. As we are incapable of seeing the truth of these axioms and believe their assumption to be encumbered with all the difficulties above referred to, we are not disposed to renounce, on their behalf, doctrines which have for ages been held dear by the best portion of the Christian church.

Dr Cox demands, What has been the moral history of these doctrines? It would require more time and space than we can now command fully to answer this question. Not to enter on questionable ground, however, we would refer him for an answer to the history of the Reformation. These doctrines were held sacred by all those men who were God's great instruments in that blessed work, and are incorporated in the confessions of all the Reformed churches. We would point him to the history of the English Puritans and Nonconformists; to the Puritans of New England, from the time of their landing down to a late period in their history, and to the present opinions of the great body of their descendants.

We would refer him to any age or any church peculiarly distinguished for genuine piety. For there is scarcely one of the doctrines which he has empaled in his introduction (with the exception of the mere extent of the atonement, a point of very subordinate importance to that of its nature), which does not enter into the faith of the great body of evangelical Christians. We have no doubt that Dr Cox believes these doctrines. What we lament is that he should have caricatured the manner in which the vast majority of those who hold them have been accustomed to represent them, and that he should even seem to advocate a principle which we fear is subversive of them all.

2

THE EARLY HISTORY
OF PELAGIANISM[1]

With propriety the term 'militant' has been applied to the church upon earth. No sooner was the light of truth sent down from heaven, than it fell into interminable conflict with the darkness of error. And not only was it necessary to contend with the powers of darkness without the kingdom of Christ, but hideous forms of error were generated within the bosom of the church, according to the prophetic warning of our Saviour: 'Beware of false prophets which come to you in sheep's clothing'; and that of the apostle Paul, in his solemn valedictory to the elders of Ephesus: 'For I know this, that after my departing shall grievous wolves enter in among you, not sparing the flock. Also of your own selves shall men arise, speaking perverse things, to draw away disciples after them.'

Even while Paul lived, the churches were exceedingly disturbed and distracted by false teachers who brought in 'another gospel' and endeavoured to overthrow from the foundation the doctrine of gratuitous justification by faith without works, and to substitute a legal system according to which justification before God could be expected only from obedience to the ceremonial law of Moses. A large portion of the inspired writings of this apostle have direct reference to the opinions of these Judaizing heretics. Others arose in the church who

[1]By Archibald Alexander. Published in 1830.

denied the resurrection of the body and maintained that all the resurrection to be expected was already past. They seem to have explained all that our Lord had said respecting the resurrection spiritually or as relating to the purification or revivification of the soul. As the former errorists manifestly came out from the sect of the Pharisees, the latter might have derived their origin from the Sadducees or from some of the schools of heathen philosophy.

From these facts in the history of the apostolic church, we learn that when converts were made to the society of Christians, many of them retained something of the leaven of their old errors and endeavoured to modify and corrupt the pure doctrines of the gospel by accommodating them to their preconceived opinions. And as all the first Christians had been brought up in another religion, it is not wonderful that errors abounded among those professing Christianity, even in the times of the apostles. This is, indeed, contrary to the vulgar opinion, which considers the primitive church as being in all respects near perfection. This opinion, however, is not founded on any information given to us in the apostolic writings; for, in addition to what has already been observed, we may refer to the epistles of our Lord to the seven churches of Asia for further proof of the existence and prevalence of error in the days of the apostles. And towards the close of that age, the impudence and licentiousness of the propagators of error may be learned from the catholic epistles of John, the second of Peter, and the epistle of Jude; all of which are filled with descriptions of false teachers and warnings against their pestiferous influence.

Of the age immediately succeeding that of the apostles, our information is very imperfect, either because there were few who had leisure or inclination for writing, or because their works have perished, which we know to have been the fact in regard to some important records. But from all the authentic history which has reached our times, we learn that swarms of heretics infested the church even while she was struggling under the direful strokes of sanguinary persecution. No age has produced more monstrous errors than the second century, of which Irenaeus has given us a detailed account: and all this congeries of extravagant opinions originated in the false philosophy of those who professed to embrace Christianity. The loathsome spawn of Gnosticism was cast upon the church from the corrupt but fertile source of the Oriental philosophy. The original fountain of this extraordinary inundation of absurd heresy was a fanciful doctrine of the nature of God. It would be interesting to pursue this subject, but we are admonished by the narrowness of our limits to forbear.

It does not appear, however, that amidst the multifarious errors which were broached in the first four centuries, any controversy arose respecting the doctrines of *sin* and *grace*. In regard to the person of the Mediator, error had assumed almost every possible shape, both as it related to his humanity and divinity, and the nature and effects of the union between them. Council after council had been convened to discuss and decide on points connected with this important subject; and theologians of the first learning and highest reputation employed their pens in defence of the catholic doctrine.

But early in the fifth century a new doctrine began to be published by Pelagius, a British monk, on the subject of man's natural condition, and the connection which subsisted between Adam and his posterity. That the doctrine of Pelagius was new and different from the opinions which had commonly been received in the church, needs no other proof than the impression which it made on the minds of the great majority of learned theologians who lived at that time. And that the doctrine of original sin then received by the church was the same which had been always held from the times of the apostles, is exceedingly probable, from the fact that the subject never underwent any public discussion; while it is rarely the case that a doctrine entirely new can be introduced and propagated everywhere without giving rise to much controversy and exciting much public attention.

Pelagius did, indeed, in his controversy with Augustine, allege that this father had invented the doctrine of original sin, which was unknown to preceding ages; but in answer to this charge, Augustine appealed to many writers of the first ages to show that they entertained the same views as those which he now advocated. These testimonies are not so explicit as could be collected from the writings of those who lived after the discussion of this subject took place. But this is always the case. When any point of doctrine is undisputed and received by all, while it is everywhere tacitly admitted or incidentally referred to, it is never made the subject of accurate definition; nor is it expounded with that fulness and caution which become necessary after it has been called in question or opposed. When Augustine was urged to bring forward proof from the fathers who preceded him, he answered the demand in the following sensible manner: 'What occasion is there that we should search the works of those, who, living before this heresy arose, had no necessity of handling this difficult question, which doubtless they would have done, if they had been obliged to answer such men as we have to deal with?'

Jerome, in several places in his works, ascribes the new opinions propagated by Pelagius to Rufin, who he alleges borrowed them from Origen. But as Jerome is known to have cherished an implacable hostility to Rufin, and also to the memory of Origen, his testimony on this subject ought to be received with caution. And we cannot find that he brings forward any passages from the writings of Rufin which are sufficient to gain credit to the allegation against him.

Pelagius is admitted by his keenest opposers to have been a man of learning and of estimable character. And on other points, especially on the warmly-contested doctrine of the Trinity, he not only was orthodox, but wrote three books in defence of the catholic opinion, in which he gave deserved praise to Athanasius for his great constancy and soundness in the faith, and did not hesitate to pronounce the opinions of Arius impious.

He moreover published fourteen books, containing an exposition of the epistles of Paul, which in the opinion of several learned men are still extant in the commentaries subjoined to those of Jerome on Paul's epistles. One thing is certain in relation to these commentaries: They do not contain the opinions of Jerome on the subject of original sin, but precisely those of Pelagius. Besides the books already mentioned, he wrote many letters to distinguished individuals, most of which are lost; and also a book, DE NATURA, in which he extols the powers and virtues of human nature; and a small book addressed to Pope Innocent containing a confession of the catholic faith as he had received it.

But it was a complaint against him by some of his contemporaries, that he left it to his disciples principally to write, so that he might have the opportunity when he judged it expedient, of denying that the opinions published by them were his own. Yet on the whole it cannot be denied that the reputation of Pelagius stood high in the church before he began to propagate his heretical opinions. Jerome, who was never inclined to spare his adversaries, seems to have respected him, for in his first piece against his opinions, he refrains from mentioning his name, but speaks of himself under the fictitious name of Atticus, and of his adversary by the name of Clitobolus. Another writer of that age who seemed solicitous to speak evil of Pelagius, found nothing to hold up to censure or ridicule but his bodily defects. Augustine acknowledges that he was a man of chaste and unblemished character; and Chrysostom laments that a man of so great probity should have fallen into heresy.

But, although Pelagius was the author of the system which has been denominated from him, yet some of his disciples were much more distinguished in the defence and propagation of these opinions. Among these, the most celebrated was Cœlestius. Augustine admits that he was a man of most penetrating genius. Before he became a follower of Pelagius, he published three small treatises addressed to his parents, in the form of epistles, which contained nothing erroneous, but were full of incitements to a virtuous life. What he wrote afterwards we know only from the citations and references of Augustine and others of his opponents. When he was condemned by the council of Carthage, he travelled into Asia, where, it is said, he was ordained a presbyter and afterwards took up his residence in Sicily, where he continued by his discourses and writings to propagate the doctrines of Pelagius.

Julian, an Italian bishop, the son of Memorius, Bishop of Capua, was, however, the most zealous and able writer in favour of the opinions of Pelagius. When quite a young man he was known to Augustine and greatly beloved by him, as appears from a letter which he addressed to the father of Julian. This young man was so rich in mental endowments and possessed of an eloquence so commanding and persuasive that he received the appellation of the Roman Demosthenes. And from what remains of his controversial works, it is manifest that he had a mind of uncommon vigour and penetration. The character given of him by Gennadius of Marseilles is, 'that he was a man of a penetrating genius, learned in the Scriptures, and an accurate scholar both in the Greek and Latin languages.'

Before he embraced the impious doctrine of Pelagius, he was distinguished among the doctors of the church. Afterwards he undertook the defence of the Pelagian errors against Augustine, first in a work consisting of four books, and then in another work of eight books. He is said also to have written a work in the form of a dialogue, in which the parties in this controversy are introduced as defending their respective opinions.

But Gennadius, and others who followed him, are entirely mistaken in ascribing this dialogue, or *disputation,* to Julian. It is the production of Augustine, who selects from the eight books of Julian the arguments which are there used in favour of Pelagianism, and then answers them in his own name. The title of this disputation is *Altercatio Amborum.* The occasion of writing this book Augustine himself has informed us of in his own preface, where he says that an illustrious man sent him certain extracts which some person had made from the books of Julian, the Pelagian heretic, and requested that he would give an answer. 'To these,' says he, 'I now return an answer, first setting down the very words of Julian, and then subjoining my answers to each particular in order.'

Julian also indited two letters which were published, the one addressed to Zosimus, Bishop of Rome, the other in the name of eighteen bishops who united with him, to Rufus, Bishop of Thessalonica. The venerable Bede, in his commentary on the *Song of Solomon,* mentions and refutes a work of Julian on the same subject. Julian prefixed to his exposition of the *Canticles* a work entitled *De Amore,* in which he labours to prove that there is implanted in all men a natural principle of love which continues from infancy to old age, and is preserved without loss of vigour by mere human exertion.

He wrote, moreover, a book concerning the virtue of constancy, and an epistle to Demetrius, in both of which, according to Bede, he defended the Pelagian doctrine of free-will.

Pelagius came to Rome about AD 410, when Innocent, the bishop, was absent, in consequence of the capture of the city by Alaric; and there began to scatter the seeds of his doctrine under the specious veil of certain interrogatories which he proposed for consideration and discussion. Cœlestius, in Sicily, pursued the same policy and about the same time. Not long after this, both Pelagius and Cœlestius passed over to Africa, but Pelagius did not long continue there, but travelled on to Asia Minor.

By this time the rumour of his heresy was spread abroad; Jerome in the east, and Augustine in the west, had taken up their polls against what they considered a pestiferous doctrine. A council was therefore called at Diospolis, or Lydda, in Palestine, and fourteen bishops met to investigate the doctrines of Pelagius. Everything here was as favourable to him as he could have wished; for neither of the two bishops who were his accusers were present; and as the writings of Pelagius were in the Latin language, his judges were totally incompetent to form an accurate judgment of his doctrines, for want of a correct knowledge of the Latin tongue. Moreover, John, Bishop of Jerusalem, warmly espoused the cause of Pelagius, and he was without difficulty acquitted of the charge of heresy, and received by the assembled bishops as an orthodox brother.

The presbyter Orosius, coming to Carthage from Palestine, brought with him the accusation preferred against Pelagius by Herus and Lazarus, and communicated this document to a council then sitting at Carthage, on the affairs of the church. The bishops there assembled, before they heard of the decision of the council of Diospolis were much alarmed, and wrote to Innocent of Rome their view of the opinions of Pelagius; adding, that if he and his partisans did not unequivocally reject these errors they ought to be immediately excommunicated. These resolutions were signed by sixty-eight bishops. Another synod met shortly afterwards at Milevum, Numidia, and addressed letters on the same subject to the Bishop of Rome.

The result of the Eastern council being now known in Africa, Augustine, Alypius, and Aurelius, with two other bishops, wrote a more full and particular account of the whole controversy to Innocent, and explained how the council of Diospolis had most probably been imposed on by the subtilty of

Pelagius. Innocent entered fully into the views of the African bishops, and in his answer expressed the same conditional condemnation of the authors of the heresy. But as Pelagius had diffused his doctrine extensively and put on it a fair face, it was necessary that he should be met with arguments as well as decisions of councils: and no man in the church was so well qualified for this work as Augustine, who did not shrink from the arduous task, but entered into this field of controversy in which he was occupied for twenty years.

Pelagius gloried greatly in his acquittal; on which occasion he wrote to a friend that fourteen bishops had agreed with him that man might live without sin and easily keep the commandments of God if he would. He also wrote to Augustine an account of his acquittal; and immediately proceeded to publish his opinions more boldly, in four books which he wrote on the subject of free-will, and in which he entirely denied the doctrine of original sin.

The first thing which Augustine wrote expressly against the opinions of Pelagius was three books addressed to Marcellinus, *Concerning the Demerit and Remission of Sins, and the Baptism of Children.* In these Pelagius is treated very respectfully, because Augustine still believed him to be a pious man, and because his reputation in the church was very high. In these books Augustine said that it was possible for a man, by the aids of divine grace, to live without sin, but that no one had ever yet attained to that perfection, or ever would in time to come. At this opinion, Marcellinus expressed some surprise; which gave occasion to Augustine to write another book, *Concerning the Letter and Spirit,* in which he keenly contends with the opposers of the doctrine of grace.

As Pelagius had now, by means of his letter to Demetrius, made known his opinions and spread them abroad, Augustine did not any longer consider it necessary to forbear mentioning his name; he therefore provided an antidote to the aforesaid letter, in an epistle addressed to Juliana, the mother of Demetrius, which is numbered 143 in the *Collection* of his epistles.

In the year 414 he seems to have written his famous work *De Natura et Gratia,* which he dedicated to two young gentlemen, Timasius and Jacobus, who had recently been converted, from being disciples of Pelagius, to the catholic faith. These two young men had been induced by the persuasions of Pelagius to devote themselves to a monastic life, and at the same time drank in his self-righteous spirit; but by the exertions of Augustine they were brought back to the acknowledgment of the truth.

In the following year, 415, Augustine wrote a particular account of the proceedings in relation to Pelagius which had taken place in the council of Palestine, and addressed it to Aurelius, Bishop of Carthage.

In the year 416 the council of Carthage met and addressed a letter to Innocent; and Augustine, in addition, wrote one in his own name and that of several of his friends, Aurelius, Alypius, Euodeus and Possidius. As Augustine had already commenced writing against Pelagius, a request was made by this council that he should go on with the controversy; in consequence of which he published this year two books; the one *Concerning the Grace of Christ,* the other *Concerning Original Sin.*

About this time also it is supposed that his letter to Dardanus was written, which is numbered fifty-seven in the *Collection* of his epistles, and moreover, his book against Cœlestius, addressed to the Bishops Eutropius and Paulus, *Concerning the Perfection of Righteousness.*

In the year 417, Augustine, having heard that there were some persons at Nola who had imbibed the doctrine of Pelagius, wrote to Paulinus, bishop of that place, *Concerning the Pelagian Heresy,* which letter is the one-hundred-and-sixth in the *Collection.*

In 418 he wrote two epistles to the Roman presbyter, Sixtus, one of which was intended as an express refutation of the Pelagian heresy.

Thus it appears how indefatigable this father was in opposing the heresy of Pelagius. Almost every one of the above works is particularly mentioned in *The Retractations of Augustine.*

Innocent, Bishop of Rome, dying about this time, was succeeded by Zosimus, to whom both Pelagius and Cœlestius addressed epistles in which they gave such a complexion to their system and spoke in language so plausible and ambiguous, that Zosimus was completely deceived by their fair speeches. He accordingly wrote to the bishops of Africa that he considered Pelagius an orthodox man. But they showed in their answer that it was not enough for these men to acknowledge the truth in general terms; but that they should explicitly confess that we need the grace of Jesus Christ in every act. Zosimus did not remain obstinate, but upon receiving accurate information from Augustine of the true nature of the opinions of these men, issued a sentence of condemnation against them.

Upon this, the Emperor Honorius also passed a sentence of banishment from Rome against the Pelagians. This was in the year 418. Cœlestius, on being condemned, went to Constantinople, where he met with determined opposition from Atticus, the bishop of that city; so that his designs of propagating his opinions there were disappointed.

Pelagius still continued in Palestine and complained grievously of the hard treatment which he received by the decisions and acts respecting him at Rome, and by the books written against him; and again succeeded in imposing on some respectable persons who held a conference with him, by leading them to think that his doctrine did not materially differ from the common belief. Those persons on whom he made this impression were so much interested in his favour, that they wrote to Augustine stating their favourable views of the doctrine of Pelagius. This communication seems to have been the occasion of Augustine's writing his books *Concerning Grace and Original Sin.*

Julian, of whom we have already spoken, having published severe animadversions on the conduct of Zosimus and his clergy, Boniface, the successor of Zosimus, sent them to Augustine for the purpose of having them refuted; which he did in four books, inscribed to Boniface. And Count Valerius, having received another of Julian's writing, in which he charges the Catholics with condemning marriage, deriving this as an inference from their doctrine of original sin, caused this work to be sent to Augustine, who soon published an answer in his work *De Nuptiis et Concupiscentia.*

To this work Julian replied in four books. To these Augustine opposed six books, in the first three of which he answers what is contained in Julian's first book; but the fourth, fifth, and sixth are employed in refuting the second, third, and fourth of

Julian, the one answering to the other in order. Julian was not a man to be easily silenced, for he now came out with eight books against the six of Augustine. These the venerable polemic was preparing to answer when he was called away from all his earthly labours. Only two books of this last work were completed; these have come down to us with his other works.

The death of Augustine occurred, according to the testimony of Prosper, in his *Chronicon,* AD 430; the latter was the friend and correspondent of Augustine, from whom this father received particular information of the progress of Pelagianism, or rather semi-Pelagianism, at Marseilles, where these opinions took deep root and continued long to flourish.

It may be satisfactory now to give a more particular account of the decisions of the several councils which met for the consideration of this subject in their chronological order.

The first was the council of Carthage, convened, AD 407, on account of the dissemination by Cœlestius of the opinions of Pelagius, which also he pertinaciously defended. Of the proceedings of this council no fragment remains but one preserved in Augustine's work on original sin. Mention is made of this council, however, in the letter of the fathers of the second council of Carthage, addressed to Innocent. From the fragment preserved by Augustine, we learn that the accusation against Cœlestius was that he had taught 'that the sin of Adam hurt himself alone'. Cœlestius acknowledged that he had doubted concerning the communication of sin by descent from Adam, but professed his willingness to be better instructed by those to whom God had given greater wisdom; yet observed that he had heard from presbyters of the church a doctrine different from that which was held by the council. And being called upon to name one from whom he had heard such an opinion, he mentioned Rufin, a holy presbyter of Rome. On being asked whether he had not asserted that infants are born in the same state in which Adam was before transgression, he would make no other reply but 'that infants needed baptism, and ought to be baptized'.

The council of Diospolis, in Palestine, consisted, as has been mentioned before, of only fourteen bishops. The accusers of Pelagius were not able to attend, one of them being prevented by sickness, and the other by some other cause. Augustine mentions this council in several of his works, and ascribes the acquittal of Pelagius to his artful use of equivocal terms by which his judges were deceived and were induced to pronounce him innocent. Jerome, in his seventy-ninth epistle, calls this 'a miserable synod'; and says that although they did not err in doctrine, they were deceived in the man, who deceitfully seemed to condemn his own opinions. Photius, in his *Bibliotheca,* gives a more particular account of this council; but his information seems to have been derived from the works of Augustine, already referred to.

AD 416. Another council met at Carthage, which has already been noticed; not convened, indeed, to attend to this controversy, but Prosius having brought intelligence respecting the proceedings instituted against Pelagius in Palestine, the fathers of this council took up the business and wrote a letter to Innocent, in which they expressed their opinion freely and fully, relative to the heresy of the opinions of which Pelagius was accused, and of the course which ought to be pursued in regard to him if he did not explicitly abjure them. Sixty-seven pastors were present at this synod.

About the same time or a little later, a synod met at Milevum, in Numidia, consisting of sixty bishops, or pastors, who took up the subject of the errors of Pelagius and Cœlestius, and in imitation of the council of Carthage, addressed a letter to Innocent, Bishop of Rome.

It appears from several notices in the writings of Augustine that another full synod met in Africa and addressed letters on this subject to Zosimus the successor of Innocent; but all traces of the acts and proceedings of this council, except the short notices referred to above, have disappeared. This synod is said to have consisted of two hundred and twenty-four bishops, and is supposed to have been held, AD 417 or 418. But great obscurity rests upon the whole matter.

AD 428. When Cœlestinus was Bishop of Rome, a council was held in Gaul, occasioned by a deputation from Britain, who represented that the poison of Pelagianism had been imported into that country by one Agricola the son of Jenerianas, a bishop; and that they greatly needed aid to prevent its diffusion among the people. On this occasion a large council convened, and two eminent men, Germanus and Lupus, were sent on a mission to Britain to check the progress of Pelagianism. By their exertions the catholic doctrine appeared to be everywhere restored; but no sooner had they taken their departure than heresy began again to germinate; so that the request to the Gallican church for help was repeated, and Germanus was again sent and was accompanied by Severus, a disciple of Lupus, his former colleague. The witnesses for these facts are Constantius, in his *Life of Germanus,* and Bede, in his *History of the British Churches.*

The next council in which the subject of Pelagianism was brought up for consideration was that of Ephesus, AD 431. This is called an Ecumenical council. It was convened, not on account of the heresy of Pelagius, but to condemn Nestorianism; but as the followers of Pelagius would not join in the censure of Nestorius, the council expressed their disapprobation of that heresy also, which they denominate *the wicked doctrine of Cœlestius.* And in their synodical epistle to Cœlestinus, Bishop of Rome, they approve of the sentence of condemnation which had been passed on Pelagius, Cœlestius, Julian, and their abettors, whom they call impious men.

The Pelagian doctrine was next condemned in a council which met at Arles, in France; the exact year is not settled. This synod denounced an anathema against the impious doctrines of Pelagius and especially against the opinion, *'that man was born without sin; and that he could be saved by his own exertions'.* They considered it a presumption worthy to be condemned for any man to believe that he could be saved without grace.

The council of Lyons met soon after that of Arles, and approved its decrees; but some other doctrines were also brought under consideration and subjected to censure.

AD 494. Gelasius, Bishop of Rome, convened a council of seventy bishops in that city, by whom the writings of Augustine and Prosper were approved and recommended; while those of the semi-Pelagians, Cassian and Faustus, were censured.

Other councils were held in after ages which condemned the Pelagian heresy; but our object now is to give a view of this controversy in its first rise in the fifth century.

Before we proceed to give a view of the opinions entertained and propagated by Pelagius and his followers, it will be satisfactory to ascertain what were the opinions of the church on this subject.

The doctrine of the church, then, on the subject of original sin, may be thus stated: It has ever been the judgment of the catholic church that the first sin of Adam was imputed to all his posterity by the righteous appointment of God, and that its effects are transmitted to all his children; which effects, the church always believed, were that they were born destitute of original righteousness, subject to the sentence of death and obnoxious to eternal separation from God.

Man being created in the image of God and being fully endued with all powers necessary for obedience; and, moreover, being blessed with everything requisite for his comfort, did transgress the law of his Maker by disobeying that commandment which was given as a test of his whole obedience.

This first act of transgression, it is true, was the criminal act of Adam as an individual; but as he was the root and principle of our whole nature, it may be considered the sin of the human race: so that his voluntary act, in opposition to the will of his Creator, may be reckoned that of his descendants; not indeed strictly and properly (for those not yet born could not perform an act), but interpretatively or by imputation; for this act was not only imputed to Adam to condemnation, but to all his posterity.

That the above is a correct statement of the commonly received doctrine of the church at the period of which we treat will appear from many explicit declarations, not only of Augustine and other individuals, but from the decrees and letters of councils, consisting of numerous bishops, living in every region of the earth to which the universal church extended.

Augustine, in book xvi of his work *De Civitate Dei,* has these words: '*Nascuntur, non proprie, sed originaliter, peccatores.*' 'Men are born, not properly, but originally, sinners.' And in book i., c. 15 of his *Retractations,* he says, '*Peccatum eos ex Adam dicimus originaliter trahere; id est, reatu eos implicatos, et ob hoc poenae obnoxios detineri.*' 'We affirm that they derive sin originally from Adam; that is, they are involved in guilt, and on this account are held liable to punishment.'

In his work concerning the demerit and remission of sin, he says that to *impute* and to *remit* are opposites; therefore, he asserts, to *impute* is to subject one to guilt; to *remit* is, *not to impute* to condemnation. Here it may be proper to remark that by *imputation* Augustine meant not a transfer of moral acts or moral characters, but the opposite of remission; to *impute a sin,* therefore, according to him, is to hold the person bound to suffer his punishment. And by the word *reatus,* or *guilt,* he understood an obligation to suffer the punishment of sins or a subjection to the penalty of the law.

It is necessary to understand accurately the meaning of these terms as used by theologians, or we shall be involved in perpetual perplexity in relation to their opinions. Most of the objections now made to the doctrine of imputation and to the transfer of guilt proceed from a misapprehension of the true import of these terms. We therefore hear a great deal of declamation respecting the impossibility of making a transfer of moral character, and respecting the impossibility of ever removing the guilt of a sinner; but if the exact meaning of these terms was apprehended, the supposed difficulty or absurdity would vanish. For, although personal acts cannot be transferred, the consequences or legal penalties of those acts may be transferred; and although the ill-desert of one man cannot be transferred to another, the punishment due to one can be inflicted on another.

But to return, Augustine says again, book xiv., c. 11, *De Civitate Dei:* 'From the first pair so great a sin has been transmitted, that by it, human nature is changed for the worst; also the bond of iniquity and the necessity of death are transmitted to their posterity.'

And this manner of speaking of original sin was not peculiar to Augustine; for we find the same sort of language in Bernard. When speaking of the first sin, he has the following words: 'That this first sin, of which he is here treating was *another's,* inasmuch as in Adam we sinned; being unconscious of it, *our own,* inasmuch as, although by another, yet we ourselves have sinned, and in the just judgment of God it is imputed to us.'

Nicolas Lyra, who lived about four hundred years ago, speaks the same language when explaining the fifth of

Romans: 'The sin of Adam is imputed to all descending from him by natural generations because they are his members, on which account it is called original sin.'

And the later writers, until the council of Trent, do not deviate from this language of the ancient church. Cajetan, commenting on the same (Romans 5) says, 'The punishment of death is inflicted on him with his whole posterity; by which it is proved that the sin of which death is the punishment is imputed to him and to his whole posterity.'

And even Bellarmine uses as strong language on the subject of imputation as any who went before him. 'Adam,' says he, 'alone committed that (sin) by actual volition; but it is communicated to us by generation in that mode in which it was possible for that which is past to be communicated, viz., by imputation.'

It is scarcely necessary to adduce testimonies from early Protestant writers; for it is known to all in the least acquainted with the opinions of the reformers, that with one consent they held that the sin of Adam was imputed to his posterity; and that in consequence of this imputation a corrupt nature was communicated to all his natural descendants. We could fill volumes with citations in proof of this fact, but it is unnecessary. Indeed, until Socinus arose, no one connected with the reformation ever intimated a doubt concerning the imputation of Adam's first sin to his posterity. This ingenious but heretical man utterly denied, as all his followers do, the whole doctrine of original sin. His words are: 'Although all the posterity of Adam are liable to eternal death, this is not because the sin of Adam is imputed to them, but because they are his natural descendants: so that their doom to death does not arise from imputation, but from the propagation of the human race.'

It is now, by many who would be esteemed orthodox, and Calvinistic too, considered so absurd to hold the doctrine of the imputation of Adam's sin to his posterity, that they will not even condescend to argue the point and demonstrate its falsehood. If these be correct in their views of the subject, it must create some surprise that all theologians, from the days of Augustine, who were not acknowledged heretics, believed firmly in this doctrine and considered it as fundamental in the Christian system. Is it certainly the fact that these modern

impugners of the ancient doctrine of the church understand the
Scriptures better than all who have gone before them? Or is it
undoubted that they are endowed with a perspicacity so much
superior to that of Augustine, Calvin, Owen, and Edwards,
that what these thought after profound consideration might be
defended as reasonable, is so absurd as not to merit a
refutation?

Now, we confess ourselves to be of the number of those who
believe, whatever reproach it may bring upon us from a certain
quarter, that if the doctrine of imputation be given up, the
whole doctrine of original sin must be abandoned. And if
this doctrine be relinquished, then the whole doctrine of
redemption must fall, and what may then be left of Christianity, they may contend for that will; but for ourselves, we shall
be of opinion that what remains will not be worth a serious
struggle.

But we must return to our proper subject. It will next be
satisfactory to know by what sort of arguments the ancient
theologians defended the doctrine of original sin. And although
we will not vouch for the soundness of every interpretation of
Scripture which the ancient expositors gave, yet it cannot but
be satisfactory to the advocates of this doctrine now, that as far
back as we can trace the history of opinions, the same views
were entertained of the meaning of the principal texts which
bear on this point as are now maintained.

The fathers, then, supported the doctrine of original sin by
such texts as Genesis 6:5, 8:21: 'And God saw that the wickedness of man was great on the earth, and that every imagination
of the thoughts of his heart was only evil continually . . . For
the imagination of man's heart is evil from his youth.'
Ambrose, in his remarks on this text, does not confine it to the
antediluvians, but considers it a description of human nature
in every age, and extends it to persons in every period of
human life: For he says, 'Even the child of a day old is not
without sin, for infancy cannot be exempt from sin on account
of the infirmity of the body.'

Another text which they adduced in proof of original sin was
Genesis 17:14: 'And the uncircumcised man child, whose flesh
of his foreskin is not circumcised, that soul shall be cut off from
his people; he hath broken my covenant.' On this text

Augustine remarks that 'the soul which is not regenerated shall perish, since he, with all others, sinned in Adam'. It seems that they interpreted the breach of the covenant to have reference to the covenant made with Adam, and not the covenant of circumcision. For thus we find Bede commenting on this text, 'Not the covenant of circumcision which an infant that could neither will good nor evil could not break, though his parents might; but that covenant is signified which God entered into with the first man, and which every one who has only lived a day upon earth has violated, and so stands in need of a saving remedy.'

Job 14:4: 'Who can bring a clean thing out of an unclean? not one', is another text on which the ancient theologians relied for the proof of original sin. As they followed the Seventy, however, they found more to their purpose in this text than is contained in the Hebrew. For in the Greek version the text reads, literally translated: 'For who is clean from filth? Not one, if even his life has been but of one day on the earth.' Hence, we find Augustine, in reference to this text, saying:

The stain of the vitiated root is diffused through the branches, being transmitted by natural generation; so that there is not an infant of one day old free from the guilt of sin, unless saved by unmerited grace. For he who has no sin properly of his own has derived to him the sin of another, concerning which the apostle speaks, where he says, by one man sin entered into the world, etc.

The next argument the fathers derived from Psalm 51:5: 'Behold I was shapen in iniquity, and in sin did my mother conceive me.' It was left for modern critics to discover that David was here bewailing the sinfulness of his mother; such an idea never seems to have entered the mind of any of the ancient commentators. They argue thus from the text: If David, that most holy king, and born of pious parents, contracted pollution in his conception, then certainly the same must be true of all other men. Thus reasoned Origen, Basil the Great, Theodoret, Rufin, Cassiodorus, Euthymius and Remigius, in their notes on this text. Likewise Hilary, Ambrose, Chrysostom, Faustus, Isychius, Gregory the Great, Alcuin, Bede, and every other orthodox commentator for seventeen centuries after Christ. They who still believe that the Psalmist is here speaking of the sin of his birth, notwithstanding the learned criticisms which have recently appeared on this text, have the comfort of knowing that they are supported by the opinions of all the ancients and all the moderns whose opinions carry weight in matters of this kind.

Another text adduced by the ancient advocates of this doctrine is Isaiah 48:8: 'And wast called a transgressor from the womb.' On which Cyril, on *Hosea*, makes several remarks, tending to show the original depravity of man.

But let us now come to the New Testament; and here the first text which the fathers urge in proof of original sin is John 3:3, 6. 'Verily, verily I say unto you . . . that which is born of the flesh is flesh, and that which is born of the spirit is spirit.' From which it was argued that whatever was carnally propagated could only savour of carnal things, which, in order to become spiritual, must be born of the Spirit; without spiritual regeneration it was impossible to enter into the kingdom of heaven. Augustine often makes use of this text in his controversy with the Pelagians; and it is used in the same manner by Prosper and by Gregory the Great.

But the passage of Scripture on which they depended above all for the support of the doctrine of original sin was the fifth of Romans, from the twelfth verse to the end of the chapter: 'As by one man sin entered into the world, and death by sin, so death passed on all men, because that [or in whom] all have sinned.'

Verse 14: 'Nevertheless, death reigned from Adam to Moses, even over them that had not sinned after the similitude of Adam's transgression.'

Verse 18: 'Therefore as by the offence of one, judgment came upon all men to condemnation.'

Verse 19: 'For as by the disobedience of one many were made sinners.'

From these passages they reasoned in the following manner: That sin which the apostle so describes as that which has brought death on all men; – that by it all men have sinned, and by it have been constituted sinners, even those who have not sinned after the similitude of Adam's transgression (that is, have not committed actual sin); – and in consequence of this sin all are become subject to death and condemnation;

therefore this sin, although committed by Adam alone, as it was a personal act, yet may be considered as the sin of human nature, since he stood as the representative of us all, who were then included in his loins; and are all therefore laid under an obligation to suffer the punishment of his sin.

The fathers also were particular in noticing that Adam was here called the type of Christ, whence they inferred that as we are justified by the imputation and not the imitation of Christ's obedience, so the disobedience of Adam becomes ours, not by imitation but by imputation. They moreover remarked that the particles *eph ho* ('in whom') teach us that the posterity of Adam sinned in him: or if you prefer rendering these words *'because that'*, or *'inasmuch as'*, all have sinned, they must contain a sufficient reason for the death of all, infants as well as others; and therefore the word *all* must be considered as including infants; when it is said, therefore, all have sinned, it will follow that infants also have sinned. This method of reasoning is pursued by Augustine in many different parts of his works; and the same method of reasoning from this passage is followed by Theodoret, by Prosper, by Faustus, by Gennadius, and also by the Carthaginian and Arausicanian councils.

Another passage of Scripture which the ancient theologians considered conclusive on the subject of original sin was Romans 7, where Paul speaks of a law in his members warring against the law of his mind. 'For I know that in me, that is, in my flesh, there dwelleth no good thing. For to will is present with me, but to perform that which is good I find not.' The necessity of the aids of divine grace is argued from this passage by Irenaeus, Tertullian, and Augustine, in more places than one. This father, indeed, gives us two distinct expositions of the apostle's meaning in the afore-cited words. According to the first of these, the conflict here described is between conscience and sinful desires drawing the soul to evil; but according to the latter, the struggle is between the sinful nature which remains in the regenerate, and the new man or principle of grace implanted by the Holy Spirit. In either sense it furnishes strong proof of the natural proclivity of man to evil: but especially in the latter sense, in which a remaining leaven of iniquity is found in the regenerate continually hindering his holy

exercises, it furnishes an undoubted proof of the depravity of
our nature.

They also appealed to 1 Corinthians 15:22: 'For as in Adam
all die, so in Christ shall all be made alive.' On this text the
writer of certain ancient commentaries which have been
ascribed to Ambrose, says, 'Paul says this because as Adam by
sinning found death, so he subjected all his posterity to the
same punishment; so also Christ by not sinning overcame
death and acquired life for all those who are of his body; that
is, the resurrection.' And again, 'As all die in Adam, whether
they be just or unjust, so also all, whether believers or
unbelievers, shall be raised from the dead by Christ; but they
who believe not, to punishment.'

Augustine expresses his views of the import of this passage
thus:

The opinion of the apostle is here clearly exhibited, that none are
subject to death but through Adam, and that none enter into eternal
life unless by Christ. For by the word *all* repeated in this verse, we
are to understand in the first instance, all who are naturally
descended from Adam, and in the second all who are united to Christ
by a spiritual regeneration: so then it is declared that none die except
by their connection with Adam, and none are made alive but those
who are quickened in Christ.

The argument is simply this: As all are vivified in Christ, in
like manner all die in Adam; but Christ vivifies those for
whom he has merited the forgiveness of sin, and on whom he
bestows a new life by regeneration: Therefore Adam, in like
manner by his sin has merited death for all his posterity and
transmitted to them a corrupt nature by ordinary generation.

The last text of Scripture which we will mention as furnishing satisfactory proof to the fathers of the doctrine of original
sin, is Ephesians 2:3: 'And were by nature the children of
wrath, even as others.' On this many ancient writers comment,
and all agree in the opinion that it means that when born we
are under condemnation, from which Christ came to deliver
us.

Four of the texts above cited as teaching the doctrine of
original sin, Jerome applies to the same purpose in a single
paragraph of his commentary on Ezekiel. Of his remarks, how-

ever, we shall only cite that which relates to the famous text in the fifty-first Psalm:

David says, I was conceived in iniquity and in sin did my mother bring me forth: not in the iniquity of his mother's or his own personal sin, but in the sin of human nature. Whence, the apostle says, death reigned from Adam to Moses, even over those who had not sinned after the similitude of Adam's transgression.

From this remark we learn not only what Jerome thought was the meaning of being conceived in sin, but also that he understood the apostle to mean infants, where he speaks of those who had not sinned after the similitude of Adam's transgression. And we believe that in regard to both these texts he speaks the language of all antiquity.

Among the reasons by which the doctrine of original sin as held by the ancients was supported, the sufferings and death of infants were believed to hold the first place, because it was considered that it would be altogether unjust that they should be thus punished, unless they were charged with the guilt of some sin. Hence, Augustine, in his fourth book against the two letters of Pelagius, says:

But how is it that the Pelagians hold that death only is derived to us from Adam? According to them, we die because he died; but he died because he had sinned. They hold, therefore, that punishment passes upon us without any fault: Innocent infants, then, are punished by an unjust sentence; suffering death without having merited this punishment.

And again, in his sixth book against Julian, he says:

The sins of parents in one respect are not ours, but in another respect they are ours. They are not ours as it relates to the personal act, but they are ours by the contagion of our descent; which, if it were not true, a grievous yoke would be upon the children of Adam from the day of their birth, which could by no means be reconciled with justice.

And in his last answer to Julian he says, 'This judgment [viz. death] on infants would be altogether unjust if there were no original sin.' And again, 'Why are little children so grievously afflicted if they have no sin at all? Could not an omnipotent and just God prevent these unjust punishments from falling on infants?'

The writer of the book entitled *Hypognosticon* argues in a similar manner:

If the sin of our first parents hurt no one but themselves, how does it happen that the punishment of their fault falls upon us? unless you maintain that God is unjust, who suffers those who are free from all sin to be held bound under the chain of punishment.

Prosper reasons in the same manner. In his book against Collator he says:

Unless you choose to affirm what is evidently false, that punishment, not sin, has been transmitted to the posterity of Adam; for it is too impious to think this of the justice of God, that it is his will to condemn those who are free from sin to the same punishment as the guilty. But wherever punishment is manifest, there is complete evidence of the existence of sin; for sin and punishment are indissolubly united; therefore human misery is not from the constitution of the Creator, but from the retribution of the Judge.

It must be confessed, however, that some among the orthodox of that age held that God, as a sovereign, might punish his creatures, and even doom them to eternal death, although they had never sinned. Of this opinion was Macarius the Egyptian. The opinion of Augustine and Prosper, however, has commonly been entertained by sound theologians in all ages. Some indeed think that the two opinions may be reconciled by supposing that the one party speak of the punishment of loss merely, while the others speak of the punishment of sense. But this is not very satisfactory; and the opinion of Macarius, which has been received by some since the reformation, is dishonourable to God.

And so it was esteemed by the council of Arausicanum; for in their second canon they declare that 'to say that God inflicts death, which is the punishment of sin, where no sin exists, is to charge him with injustice'. The same opinion is given by Anselm, who says, 'It is repugnant both to wisdom and justice that they whom God hath fitted for eternal happiness should, without being chargeable with sin, be forced to suffer punishment.'

The fathers also relied on this argument, that 'if infants were not involved in the guilt of sin, Christ cannot be their Saviour.' On this subject Augustine says in his first book against the two letters of Pelagius, 'They contend that infants are in a safe state already, so that they dare deny that they owe their salvation to the Saviour.' And again, in book second, 'The Pelagians assert that God is not the Purifier, Saviour, and Deliverer of men of all ages.' And in his answer to Julian, ch. xxxi., 'The multitude whom you despise, that acknowledge the catholic faith, confess that infants are redeemed by the Saviour; and therefore they detest the error of the Pelagians who deny this.' The same sentiments are found in many other passages of the writings of this father.

But scarcely any argument was more frequently resorted to by the advocates of the doctrine of original sin, than that derived from the baptism of infants. This argument is handled by Augustine in the following manner:

The church borrows for them [infants] the feet of others that they may come, the heart of others that they may believe, the tongue of others that they may confess. For being sick, they are oppressed with the sin of another; so, when made whole, they are saved through the confession of another for them. This practice the church always had; always held. Let no one, therefore, whisper in your ears a contrary doctrine. The church received it from the faith of our ancestors, and perseveringly holds it fast, even to the end. For where there are none sick, there is no need of a physician. What need, therefore can infants have of Christ, if they are not sick? If they are well, why seek a physician to take care of them? If they are infected with no sin when they are brought to Christ, why is it not said to those who bring them into the church, 'Carry these innocents hence; they that be whole need not a physician, but the sick'? 'Christ came not to call the righteous, but sinners.'

So also the council of Milevum, or rather of Carthage, denounced such as denied that infants should be baptized for the remission of original sin. Canon 17:

For in no other sense can that be understood which was spoken by the apostle – that by one man sin entered into the world; and death by sin; and so death hath passed upon all men, in whom all have sinned – than in that adopted by the universal church everywhere diffused. For by reason of this rule of faith, even infants who were never capable of committing any sin themselves are nevertheless baptized according to truth for the remission of sins: so that the pollution contracted by them in their birth might be cleansed by their regeneration.

But that which was thought to give peculiar force to this argument was that Cœlestius himself, in a book which he edited at Rome, was constrained to confess, that 'Infants are baptized for the remission of sins, according to the rule of the universal church, and according to the doctrine of the gospel.' It seems, then, that from this argument the Pelagians were never able to extricate themselves; but of this more hereafter.

The view which has been given of the opinions of the universal church on the subject of original sin relate only to the age of the Pelagian controversy. It may still be a matter of proper and important inquiry, what opinions were commonly entertained on this point before the commencement of the fifth century?

From the almost universal concurrence of theologians in Africa, Asia, and Europe, in the belief of this doctrine, we may infer that it did not originate in this age. We may be sure, from this consideration, that the doctrine of original sin was not invented by Augustine, as some have pretended. Jerome was more learned, and at this time much more known than Augustine, and he held the same doctrine and commenced writing against the heresy of Pelagius before Augustine took up his pen; and these distinguished fathers lived in parts of the church widely separated from each other, the one in Africa, the other in Palestine.

But in every council except the little one of Diospolis, the doctrine of Pelagius was condemned and the doctrine of original sin affirmed; and commonly without a dissenting voice. At some of these councils there were present several hundreds of theologians. Even in the council of Diospolis, which acquitted Pelagius, there was nothing determined inconsistent with the catholic doctrines; but the case was that Pelagius, by artfully concealing his true opinions under plausible but ambiguous terms, deceived the fathers who sat in that council, as Augustine has shown.

If it be a fact, then, that at the commencement of the fifth century all the theologians in the world, except a few who were soon rejected as heretics, agreed in maintaining the doctrine of original sin, how shall we account for the universal prevalence of such a doctrine, but by supposing that it was handed down from the first planting of the Christian church? For if it had been an error introduced by some particular doctor, or by some section of the church, it would not have been universal in its diffusion, nor would it have united the suffrages of all the faithful ministers of the gospel, as we see it did.

And again, supposing that by extraordinary efforts this doctrine, so repugnant to the natural feelings of men, could have been everywhere propagated by the commencement of the fifth century, would there be no trace of such an universal change of opinion, and no record of the extraordinary efforts necessary to bring it about?

Among all the writers who have touched on this subject, is it not strange that not one is found who gives the least hint of any such thing? Surely a change in relation to a doctrine so radical must have occasioned controversy. All would not have adopted a new and distasteful doctrine upon its first proposal. These are things which can never be cleared up on the hypothesis that the doctrine of original sin was not the doctrine of the apostolic churches.

Here we might gather up from the writings of almost all the fathers who preceded Augustine, testimonies incidentally given, which would serve to show that they all believed in the same doctrine of original sin, which was so strenuously defended by the whole Christian church in the beginning of the fifth century; and it would be easy to pursue this course, because Augustine has travelled over the same ground before us and has adduced testimonies on this subject from Ignatius, from the work under the name of Dionysius the Areopagite, from Justin Martyr, Irenaeus, Origen, Basil, Gregory Nazianzen, Chrysostom, and others who, although they do not enter into any discussion on this subject (for it was not a matter of dispute), yet drop such expressions incidentally when treating other subjects, as are sufficient to prove that there was from the beginning one uniform faith on this fundamental point. The reader who is desirous of further information on this subject is referred to the various treatises of Augustine on original sin.

But our limits and our plan require that we should now exhibit a brief but impartial view of the real opinions of Pelagius and his followers, which shall as far as possible be given in their own words; which testimonies, however, are taken from the writings of Augustine and others, their own works having for the most part perished.

Pelagius, in his book *De Natura,* as quoted by Augustine, says: 'When it is declared that all have sinned in Adam, it should not be understood of any original sin contracted by their birth, but of imitation.' Again: 'How can a man be considered guilty by God of that sin which he knows not to be his own? for if it is necessary, it is not his own; but if it is his own, it is voluntary; and if voluntary, it can be avoided.' In his exposition of the epistle to the Romans he says:

The opposers of the propagation of sin thus endeavour to impugn the doctrine: The sin of Adam has not injured those not sinning, just as the righteousness of Christ does not profit those not believing: for it is said that in like manner, yea much more, is salvation by one, than perdition by one. And if baptism cleanses that ancient sin, then they who are born of two baptized persons must be free from that sin; for they could not transmit that to posterity which they no longer possessed themselves. Moreover, they say that if the soul is not by traduction, but the flesh only, then the flesh only is concerned in the propagation of sin, and it alone deserves to be punished; for they allege that it would be altogether unjust that a soul just born should be obliged to bear that ancient sin of Adam, from whom it has not derived its origin. For they allege that it can by no means be conceded that God, who pardons our own sins, should impute to us the sin of another person.

Pelagius does not speak here in his own name, but as personating others, whose opinions and arguments he exhibits; for at this time he durst not openly declare his real sentiments. In like manner Cœlestius disseminated the same doctrine, as will be shown below, and also pursued the same insidious policy in propagating his opinions.

Julian also, in his last work against Augustine, charges this father with holding that 'infants were oppressed with the guilt of no sin of their own, but only with that of another person'. Again he says, 'Whoever is accused of a crime, the charge is made against his conduct, and not against his birth.' And in the conclusion, where he recapitulates what he had written, he says, 'Therefore we conclude that the triune God should be adored as most just; and it has been made to appear most irrefragably that the sin of another never can be imputed by him to little children.'

And a little afterwards, 'Hence that is evident, which we defend as most reasonable, that no one is born in sin, and that God never judges men to be guilty on account of their birth.' Again, 'Children, inasmuch as they are children, never can be guilty until they have done something by their own proper will.'

And as the ground on which the doctrine of communicated guilt was held was a certain natural conjunction of the parties, by reason of which Paul declares that we sinned in Adam, therefore they used their utmost exertion to elude the force of this argument.

Julian reasons thus: 'If there was no such thing as one man imitating another, and the apostle had declared that all had sinned in Adam, yet this mode of speaking might be defended by Scripture use: for Christ called the devil a father, although he is incapable of generation; so the apostle, in describing how the first man was imitated by those who came after him, might without impropriety use such language as that before cited.' And again, 'The apostle Paul gave no occasion to error and said nothing improper when he declared that the first man was a sinner, and that his example was imitated by those who followed him.' 'By one man sin entered into the world; but one man was sufficient to furnish an example which all might imitate.' 'He speaks of one, that he might teach that the communication of sin was by imitation, not by generation.' 'Which sin, although it did not become a part of our nature, was, however, the pattern of all sin; and hence, although it is not chargeable on men in consequence of their birth, it is by reason of their imitation of it.'

Prosper, in his epistle to Demetrius, expresses the opinion thus: 'The sin of Adam hurts his posterity by its example, but not by natural communication.' These opinions were rejected and firmly opposed by the orthodox. Jerome, at the close of his third book against the Pelagians, writes thus:

If it be objected that it is said there are some who have not sinned, it is to be understood that they did not actually commit the sin of which Adam was guilty by transgressing the commandment of God in Paradise, but all men are held to be guilty, either in consequence of the sin of Adam, their ancient progenitor, or by their own personal act. The infant, by the engagement of his parent in baptism, is released: and he who has arrived at years of understanding is delivered, both by another's engagement and his own, namely, by the blood of Christ. And let it not be supposed that I understand this in a heretical sense, for the blessed martyr Cyprian, in the letter which he wrote to Tidus the bishop concerning the baptism of infants, says, 'How much more ought infants not to be debarred from baptism, who, being recently born, have committed no sin, unless that by their carnal birth from Adam they have contracted the contagion of that ancient death in their first nativity. They ought, therefore, more readily to be admitted to receive the remission of sins, that which is forgiven them is not their own sin, but that of another.'

Augustine also strenuously opposed this opinion of the Pelagians in all his writings, 'For,' says he, 'we were all in that one man, when he, being one, corrupted us all.' *De Civ. Dei*, lib. xiii., c.14. And in lib. i, c.10, of his *Retractations*, he says:

The opinion which I delivered, that sin injures no nature but that in which it is committed, the Pelagians apply to the support of their own doctrines that little children cannot be hurt by the sin of another, but only by their own; not considering that, as they belong to human nature, which has contracted original sin, for human nature sinned in our first parents, it is true, therefore, that no sins hurt human nature but its own.

Orosius, in his *Apology for Free Will*, says:

All have sinned and come short of the glory of God, either in Adam or in their own proper persons: the universal mass, therefore, is obnoxious to punishment. And if the punishment of condemnation due to all should be indicted, certainly it is not unjustly indicted.

In like manner, the writer of the book entitled *Hypognosticon* says:

Truly then the sin of Adam hurt him alone while he was alone, and Eve his wife: but in them we were all included, because they were the nature of the whole human race, which is one in all of us, for we partake of their nature.

What has been brought forward relates to the imputation of the first sin; let us next inquire what was the Pelagian doctrine respecting the communication of its stain or pollution. Pelagius, in his book *De Natura*, says:

First it is disputed concerning this, whether our nature is debilitated and deteriorated by sin. And here, in my opinion, the first inquiry ought to be, what is sin? Is it a substance, or is it a mere name, devoid of substance; not a thing, not an existence, not a body, nor anything else (which has a separate existence), but an act: and if this is its nature, as I believe it is, how could that which is devoid of substance debilitate or change human nature?

And in his book *Concerning Free Will*:

Everything, good or evil, praiseworthy or censurable, which we possess, did not originate with us, but is done by us; for we are born capable both of good and evil, but not in possession of these qualities; for in our birth we are equally destitute of virtue and vice; and previously to moral agency, there is nothing in man but that which God created in him.

Cœlestius held precisely the same doctrine. Augustine testifies that he held and taught that 'the sin of Adam hurt himself alone, and that infants are born in that state in which Adam was before he sinned'. Julian maintained the same doctrine, which he repeatedly expresses and pertinaciously defends: 'Human nature,' says he, 'in the time of our being born, is rich in the gift of innocence.' Again:

Even if the devil should create men, they would be free from all evil in their origin; and so now they cannot be born in sin because no one can help being born, nor can it be just to demand from anyone what is to him altogether impossible.

The same says, 'There is no sin in the condition of our nature'; and, 'Nobody is born with sin; but our free will is so entirely unimpaired that before the exercise of our own proper will, nature in everyone is free from every taint.' Hence

Prosper, in his *Chronicon* for the year 414, has this remark:

About this time Pelagius the Briton published his doctrine that the sin of Adam injured himself alone and did not affect his posterity; and that all infants are born as free from sin as Adam was before his transgression.

It cannot be a matter of surprise that the Pelagians held that Adam's posterity inherited from him no corrupt nature, when they did not believe that his own nature was deteriorated by sinning. Julian, therefore, says:

A man's natural state is not changed by sinning, but he becomes guilty and the subject of demerit; for it is of the very essence of free will that the man should have it in his power as much to cease from sinning as to deviate from the path of rectitude.

In opposition to these opinions, the doctors of the catholic church held that all the posterity of Adam were now destitute of the original righteousness with which he was endowed, and hence proceeds an inordinate exercise of all the powers of the mind, which is called the fuel of sin, the law in the members, concupiscence, etc.

Augustine is full and explicit on this subject. Lib. xxi., c.3, *De Civitate Dei,* he says, 'On account of the greatness of the crime, the nature of man was changed in its punishment; so that what was inflicted as a punishment on our sinning first parents comes naturally on others born of them.' Again, lib. xiv. c.12:

Human nature was changed by the sin of the first pair; so that a silent corruption pervades it, such as we see and feel, and by reason of which we are subjected to death and to so many and great evils, and are disturbed and agitated with so many contrary and conflicting passions such as had no existence in Paradise before man sinned, although he was there invested with an animal body.

Also: 'How else shall we account for that horrible depth of ignorance from which all error originates, by which all the sons of Adam are involved in a certain dark gulf from which they cannot be delivered without labour, sorrows, and fear?' Speaking again of the many kinds of vices to which men are subject, he adds, 'All these sins of wicked men proceed from the same root of error and perverse love with which every child of Adam is born.'

Prosper also expresses himself strongly on this subject. 'By the wound of original sin the nature of all men is corrupted and mortified in Adam, whence the disease of all manner of concupiscence hath sprung up.' The same writer says in another place:

Whence is it that, if what Adam lost his posterity did not lose, he himself is not alone the sufferer by his sin, and not his posterity? But the truth is, all have sinned in one, and every branch from this corrupt root is justly condemned. What Adam lost, then, by the fall, all have likewise lost.

The writer concerning the *Vocation of the Gentiles,* lib. i., c. 6, has these words:

Human nature was vitiated by the transgression of the first man; so that even in the reception of blessings and in the midst of helps and divine precepts, there is a continual proclivity of the will to evil; in which, as often as we confide we are deceived.

Again: 'All men were created in the first man without fault, and we all have lost the integrity of our nature by his transgression.' 'Adam was by nature free from sin, but by the disobedience of his will he contracted many evils and transmitted them to be multiplied more and more by his posterity.'

Vincentius Lyra asks, 'Who, before Cœlestius, that monstrous disciple of Pelagius, ever denied that the whole human race was held guilty of Adam's sin?'

Peter, the deacon, in his book concerning the Incarnation, says:

Therefore, seduced by the cunning of the serpent, of his own accord he became a transgressor of the divine law; and so, agreeably to the threatening, he was in the just judgment of God condemned to the punishment of death; that is, both body and mind were changed for the worse, and having lost liberty, he was enslaved under the servitude of sin; hence it is that no man is born who is not bound by the bond of this sin, with the exception of Him who was born by a new mode of generation, that he might lose the bond of sin; even the Mediator between God and man, the man Christ Jesus.

It was also a doctrine of the Pelagians that temporal death was by the necessity of nature, and did not fall on the human race in consequence of the sin of our first parents. They alleged that Adam would have died, although he had never sinned. Very far, then, were they from acknowledging that we had incurred eternal death by the sin of Adam. Augustine relates that it was one of the charges against Pelagius in Palestine that he held the doctrine of Cœlestius, that 'Neither by the death nor transgression of Adam do the whole human race die, nor do the whole human race rise from the dead in virtue of Christ's resurrection'. 'Death,' said he, 'passed to the posterity of Adam by imitation of his sin, not by generation.'

Augustine, in his last answer to Julian, addresses him thus:

You will not agree that by reason of original sin death passes on the human race, for then you would be forced to acknowledge that sin had been propagated through all our race. For you cannot but perceive how unjust it would be to inflict punishment where there is no guilt.

Orosius, against Pelagius, has these words: 'Your followers, who have sucked the poison abundantly from your breast, assert that man was made mortal and that he incurred no loss from the transgression of the precept.' And the writer of the *Hypognosticon* says, speaking of the Pelagians, 'They tell us that whether Adam had sinned or not, he would have died.'

On the other hand, the orthodox maintained that 'death, temporal and eternal, together with all pains and diseases connected with the death of the body, flow from the first sin; and that unless Adam had sinned, he never would have died.'

Augustine fully expresses the opinion of the church catholic in his book *De Peccat. Mer. et Remiss:*

Although as to his body, he was of the earth and partook of an animal nature, yet if he had not sinned, his body would have changed into a spiritual body and into that incorruptibility which is promised to the saints at the resurrection.

Again:

If Adam had not sinned, he never would have been divested of his body, but would have been clothed with immortality and incorruption; so that mortality would have been swallowed up of life;

that is, there would have been a transition from animal to spiritual life . . . According to my judgment, he had a resource in the fruits of the trees of the garden against the decays of nature, and in the tree of life against old age . . . So great a sin was committed by the first two of our race, that human nature underwent a change for the worse: also the obligation of their sin and the necessity of dying have been transmitted to posterity. And the reign of death over men will prevail until due punishment shall precipitate into the second death which has no end, all except those whom the unmerited grace of God shall bring into a state of salvation.

From this last question arose another. Why are infants baptized? And if they should depart without baptism, in what state do they deserve to be placed? Pelagius, lest he should be obliged to confess that they were under the bond of original sin and by their birth exposed to eternal death, denied that they received baptism for the remission of the guilt of the first sin or that they might be translated from the power of darkness into the kingdom of God. Thus Augustine declares that 'the Pelagians will not believe that original sin is removed by baptism, for they contend that no such thing exists in those just born.' Hence many inferred that they did not believe that infants were redeemed by Christ: and some affirmed that they denied the propriety of the baptism of infants altogether.

But Pelagius, in the book which he addressed to Innocent, Bishop of Rome, clears himself from imputations of this kind. 'Who was ever so impious,' says he, 'as to wish to interdict infants from a share in the common redemption of the human race?' And the council of Carthage acknowledges that Cœlestius admitted the redemption of infants. Augustine also, in his 89th epistle, addressed to Hilary, among other things says:

He was forced to confess, on account of the baptism of infants, that redemption was necessary for them also. Where, although he was unwilling to speak explicitly concerning original sin, yet by the very naming of redemption he involved himself into difficulty; for from what should they be redeemed but from the power of the devil, under which they could not be, unless they were under the guilt of original sin. Or with what price are they redeemed, unless with the blood of Christ, concerning which it is most manifestly declared, that it was shed for the remission of sin?

But Pelagius put another meaning on the word redemption, concerning which Augustine speaks in another place. Hilary expresses their opinion thus, that 'An infant dying unbaptized cannot justly perish, since it is born without sin.' And Augustine describes it in these words: 'Nor do little children need the grace of the Saviour, by which through baptism they may be delivered from perdition, because they have contracted no guilt from their connection with Adam.'

The Pelagians, however inconsistent it may appear, not only retained the baptism of infants, but also the very form which had been long in use, according to which it was said to be for the remission of sins. On which subject Augustine remarks, 'Of what advantage is it that you make use of the same words in the baptism of infants as adults, when you take away the thing signified in this sacrament?' And the author of the *Hypognosticon* addresses them with severity respecting the same thing:

> Who is not shocked at the mere naming of your practice, in which you make the faithful word of God in part true and in part a lie; that is, true as it relates to adults, for you admit that they are indeed baptized for the remission of sins: but false as it relates to infants, who are not, according to you, baptized for the remission of sins, although you use in their baptism, this very form of words.

To these things the Pelagians had nothing to reply, except that although infants were free from sin, they were the subjects of the same sacrament which, when applied to adults, was for the remission of sins. But when urged to state why they were at all baptized, they offered two reasons: The one was that by baptism they were adopted into the number of sons; the other, that by it they received the promise of the kingdom of heaven.

This made it necessary for Pelagius to feign some intermediate place between heaven and hell to which unbaptized infants might be sent after death. But he was cautious about what he said on this point. We learn from Augustine that he was wont to say, 'Whither infants do not go I know, but whither they do go, I know not.' This same father, therefore, in writing against Julian, adverts to this opinion in the following words: 'You make two places of everlasting happiness; the one within and the other without the kingdom of God.' From what

has been said, it is evident what were the opinions of the
Pelagians respecting the future state of infants, and the reasons
of their baptism.

The opinions of the orthodox on these points were far different, for although they disputed among themselves what kind
of punishment was due to infants on account of original sin,
whether of loss or of sense, yet there was an almost universal
consent among them that in consequence of original sin, we are
children of wrath and obnoxious to eternal punishment; and,
moreover that baptism was for the remission of sins; and that
by baptism infants were regenerated and thus made partakers
of life and eternal felicity.

Augustine often brings up this subject and may be considered as speaking the sentiments of the whole church in his
time. He says:

I do not affirm that infants dying without baptism will be in a worse
condition than if they had never been born, for our Lord uses this
expression respecting sinners of the most abandoned character: for
from what he says about Sodom, and does not restrict to the wicked
inhabitants of that city, that it will be more tolerable for them than
some others in the day of judgment, the inference is clear that there
will be a difference in the future punishment of men; who then can
doubt but that unbaptized infants, who are chargeable with the guilt
of original sin only, which has not been aggravated by any actual
transgressions of their own, will fall under the lightest punishment of
all? But what will be the nature or the degree of their punishment,
although we cannot define, yet I should not dare say that it would
have been better for them never to have been born, than to exist in
the state which will be allotted to them.

Again:

It may be truly said that unbaptized infants, leaving the body without baptism, will suffer the very mildest punishment; yet he who says
that they will fall under no degree of condemnation both deceives
others and is deceived himself; for the apostle has said that the
condemnation is of one sin; and that by one offence condemnation
hath come upon all men . . . We say that little children should be
baptized; and of this no one doubts, for even they who differ from us
in other points all concur in this; we maintain, however, that this is

that they may be saved and may inherit eternal life, which they cannot possess unless they are baptized in Christ; but they say, it is not for salvation, not for eternal life, but for the kingdom of God.

Jerome also, in book iii. against the Pelagians, says:

This one thing I say, and will then conclude: Either you should have another creed, which after the words Father, Son, and Holy Spirit, should contain a clause that ye shall baptize infants for the kingdom of heaven; or if you use the same baptism for infants and adults, you should confess that the former as well as the latter are baptized for the remission of sins.

Paullinus, in his book addressed to Zosimus, after the condemnation of Pelagius and Cœlestius, says:

They strive against the apostolical doctrine of original sin, which hath passed on all men, for our race will possess that inheritance received from Adam, even unto the end of the world, and which is only by the sacrament of baptism removed from infants, who cannot inherit eternal life nor obtain the kingdom of God by any other means.

A multitude of testimonies might be adduced of the same import, but it is unnecessary. The reader will perceive from those above cited, what is exceedingly evident to every one in the least conversant with ecclesiastical history, that the fathers of this period seem universally to have fallen into the mistake of confounding baptism with regeneration. From an erroneous interpretation of John 3:5, they concluded that there was no salvation without external baptism; and the next step was that the internal grace of regeneration uniformly accompanied the external rite; and this notion had taken such full possession of their minds that they commonly gave the name *regeneration* to baptism. We have not kept back the evidence of this fact, whatever may be its operation; for we now have to act the part of faithful historians; and to exhibit fairly to the view of our readers the opinions of the ancient church on an important point of doctrine which may be considered as lying at the foundation of the Christian system.

The cardinal point of the Pelagian system was the denial of original sin; this was their *proton pseudos*, their radical error, from which all the rest naturally germinated. The controversy did, however, include many other distinct points of no small interest, concerning which our limits do not permit us to say anything at present. Probably in some future number we shall resume the subject and exhibit a view of other controversies which have arisen in the church respecting original sin.

It is attended with many advantages to bring into view ancient heresies; for often what modern innovators consider a new discovery and wish to pass off as a scheme suited to remove all difficulties, is found upon examination to be nothing else than some ancient heresy clothed in a new dress.

That the doctrine of original sin is involved in many difficulties which no mortal has the wisdom to explain, we are ready to admit: but the question with us is: Is it taught in the Bible? And if anyone choose to move a previous question, it will be: Can that book be divinely inspired which contains such a doctrine? And here, if we could get clear of the thing by rejecting the Scriptures, something would be gained; but the evidence of original sin is deeply recorded in the acknowledged depravity of our race and in the dispensations of God towards us.

To account for the facts which experience teaches beyond all possibility of contradiction, we need the testimony which the Bible contains, which if we reject we may escape one set of difficulties, but shall assuredly plunge into others more formidable and unmanageable, although they may be more out of sight.

It is our opinion, therefore, after looking on all sides, and contemplating the bearing and consequences of all theories on this subject, that none is on the whole so consistent with facts, with the Scriptures and with itself, as the old doctrine of the ancient church which traces all the sins and evils in the world to the IMPUTATION of the first sin of Adam; and that no other theory of original sin is capable of standing the test of an impartial scrutiny.

3

ORIGINAL SIN[1]

Although, as has been shown in the former Essay, the Pelagian doctrines respecting original sin were condemned by councils and by popes, the heresy was not soon extinguished; but was in whole or in part adopted by many learned and ingenious men. To many the opinions of Augustine appeared harsh and hardly reconcilable with moral agency and human accountableness. They therefore endeavoured to strike out a middle course between the rigid doctrines of Augustine and the unscriptural opinions of Pelagius. This led to the adoption of an intermediate system, which obtained the denomination of Semi-Pelagianism; and as these views seem to have been generally received about Marseilles, in the south of France, the abettors of this theory were very commonly called Massilienses. Augustine entered also into this controversy and carried on a correspondence on the subject with Prosper and Hilary, two learned men of that region; the former of whom ardently opposed the Semi-Pelagians, while the latter was inclined to favour them. By degrees, however, the public attention was called off from this subject. The darkness and confusion produced by the incursion of the northern barbarians took away all opportunity and disposition to discuss those abstruse matters. Ages of ignorance succeeded,

[1]By Archibald Alexander. Published in 1830.

which have emphatically been called 'the dark ages'. Super-stition advanced, indeed, with rapid strides, but doctrinal investigation was neglected; or degenerated into mere logomachies, or useless thorny disputations.

We shall therefore pass over this long dark period with this slight notice and will proceed to take a survey of the period antecedent to the Reformation; and endeavour to ascertain the opinions of some of those acute and metaphysical men, denominated schoolmen. It has become customary for almost all classes of modern writers to treat the scholastic theology with sovereign contempt; and this often without any adequate knowledge of the system which they contemn. It is true, these ingenious men often exhausted their energies and lost their labour by a vain attempt to fathom an abyss: but it would surprise some modern metaphysicians and theologians to learn how exactly they themselves are running in the track and pursuing the very footsteps of these despised schoolmen.

Our first object, therefore, will be to lay before the reader a brief abstract of the discussions of the angelical doctor, St Thomas Aquinas, on the subject of original sin. The subject is treated in the eighty-second question of his second book.

On this subject, he starts four queries. 1. Whether original sin is a habit? 2. Whether original sin is one, in man? 3. Whether it consists in concupiscence? 4. Whether it exists in an equal degree in all?

This author, in his vast work entitled SUMMA THEOLOGIAE, invariably commences his discussion by briefly stating some arguments on each side of the question.

On the first question proposed above, he brings forward the following objections to the affirmative. 1. 'Original sin consists in the privation of original righteousness, as is declared by Anselm; but a privation is not a habit, therefore original sin is not a habit.' 2. 'Actual sin is more deserving of blame than original sin, because it possesses more of a voluntary nature; but a mere habit of actual sin is not chargeable with guilt; for if it were, then a man would be guilty of sin all the time he was asleep. Original sin, therefore, is not a habit.' 3. 'Besides, in evil, the act always precedes the habit; for no evil habit is ever infused, but always acquired: but no act precedes original sin; therefore original sin is not a habit.'

'But on the other hand, Augustine declares that infants are the subjects of concupiscence; but they are not so in regard to the act; therefore original sin in them must be a habit.'

The conclusion which he draws from a view of both sides of the question is the following:

Original sin is a habit, but not in the same way as knowledge is a habit; but it is a certain inordinate condition of nature, and a debility consequent on the privation of original righteousness.

This proposition he proceeds to explain as follows :

The word habit is taken in a two-fold sense; in the first, it signifies a power by which one is inclined to act; in this sense knowledge and virtue are called habits: but in the other sense, habit is a disposition or state of nature composed of many particulars, according to which nature is in a condition favourable or unfavourable for any given exercise. Now, according to the first sense of the word, original sin is not a habit, but according to the second it is; just as we speak of health as a good habit or state of the body; and sickness as the contrary. Original sin may therefore be described to be a certain inordinate condition or disposition proceeding from the loss of harmony in the exercise of the moral powers, in which harmony original righteousness consisted: just as sickness is a certain disordered state of the body and its functions, arising from the loss of that equal temperament in which health consists. On account of this analogy, original sin is often called 'a disease of the mind'. And as in bodily sickness, there is not a mere privation of that regular state and action in which health consists, but also an inordinate disposition, so also, original sin includes both a privation of original righteousness and a disorder of the faculties of the mind: it is not, therefore, merely a privation, but is also a corrupt habit . . . Again, as actual sin consists in the irregularity of our moral exercises, and original sin in the inordinate disposition of our nature, original sin may have the true nature and ill-desert of sin; but such an inordinate condition of the soul has not the nature of an act, but of a habit: therefore, original and actual sin are distinct, although both are connected with ill-desert.

But in regard to the third objection, stated above, in which it was alleged that in evil, acts must precede the habits, as there can be no infusion of evil habits, he says:

I would observe that it has already been stated, that original sin does not consist in that kind of a habit in which there is a power inclining us to act; for although from original sin there does follow an inclination to inordinate action, yet not directly, but indirectly: namely, by the removal of original righteousness, by which these inordinate motions were restrained and everything preserved its regular condition: just as in the case of bodily sickness there follows indirectly an inclination to irregular bodily motions. Original sin, therefore, ought not to be considered 'an infused habit', nor a habit acquired by repeated acts, but an innate disposition derived from the voluntary transgression of the first man.

The above will serve as a specimen of the manner in which this subject was discussed in the thirteenth century. It is not to our purpose to take any notice of the author's answers to the other questions stated above.

It is now time to bring distinctly into view the opinions of the Reformers on the subject of original sin. And here it may be observed in the general that while these distinguished and holy men appealed to the Bible for the proof of their doctrines and would agree to submit to no other judge in matters of faith, yet they were all much in the habit of studying the writings of Augustine, whose views of doctrine appeared to them to be remarkably accordant with the sacred Scriptures. From a knowledge of this fact, it might readily be inferred that the reformers agreed with the father before mentioned in his views of original sin.

There is no occasion, however, to have recourse to reasoning on this point: the confessions, catechisms, and treatises of these men are as explicit as we could wish them to be, and although they fell into deplorable divisions about other matters, yet in regard to doctrine, it is remarkable, they were all of one mind. This unanimity is not a conclusion merely inferred from their writings; but at the famous conference between Luther and Zwingle and their respective friends and adherents at Marpurg, where they were unable to come to any agreement respecting the eucharist, it was ascertained by a particular comparison of ideas on all the important doctrines of religion that no difference of opinion existed among them on these points. And that this conference, from which the friends of peace had expected so much, might not be altogether without fruit, a paper, or confession, consisting of fourteen articles, was prepared and signed by all the theologians present. The fourth of these articles related to original sin and was in the following words:

Fourthly – We believe that original sin is innate to us and propagated from Adam to us. And that this sin is such that it renders all men liable to damnation. Indeed, unless the death and life of Jesus Christ had come to our aid, all men would have been damned on account of original sin, nor could they have attained to the kingdom of God and eternal happiness.

These doctrinal articles were subscribed by Luther, Melancthon, Jonas, Osiander, Brentius, Agricola, Oecolampadius, Zwingle, Bucer, and Hedio.

It is true, however, that Zwingle fell, for a while, under some suspicion of error in regard to the doctrine of original sin; because he maintained that infants, the offspring of believing parents, would not finally perish for want of baptism: and it has been alleged that in some of his writings he spake of original sin rather as our disease and curse than as our sin. On this account, Rhegius addressed an admonitory letter to him, to which Zwingle replied explicitly and fully, so as to give full satisfaction to Rhegius and to others; and now, AD 1529, at Marpurg, he and his followers were as ready to subscribe this doctrine as Luther himself.

After the breach was found to be irreconcileable on the subject of the sacrament of the Lord's Supper, the Lutherans indulged great bitterness of spirit towards this noble reformer, and often spoke of him and his adherents as *Pelagianising*; although, in fact, they were as orthodox on this point as the Lutherans themselves.

As it appears that no diversity of opinion existed among the reformed on this subject, it will be sufficient, in addition to what has been said already, merely to exhibit the words of the famous confession of Augsburg, sometimes called the Augustan confession: 'Original sin consists in the want of original righteousness, and in an inordinate disposition of the faculties of the soul: so that it is not merely a privation, but a certain corrupt habit.'

The perfect agreement of all the reformers on the subject of the imputation of the first sin of Adam to all his posterity must be well known to all who are conversant with their writings. Their opinions on this subject have, however, been collected by the very learned Andrew Rivet in his work on *Original Sin,* which is contained in the third volume of the folio edition of his works. It will be unnecessary, therefore, at present to exhibit their testimony on this point.

The far-famed council of Trent formed several canons on the subject of original sin, but they were expressed in the most ambiguous terms. Their object was, in general terms, to recognize the ancient doctrine of the church on this point but not to censure any of their own doctors who differed exceedingly from one another in their views of the subject. That this was indeed the motive which actuated them is explicitly declared by one of their most learned members, Andradius, who became also the principal defender of the canons and proceedings of that body. He informs us that the decrees of the council on this subject were not intended to condemn even the opinions which had been published by Albert Pighius, who confined original sin entirely to the imputation of the sin of Adam, and asserted that there was no such thing as inherent, hereditary depravity; for, he says, it was their purpose to leave all men at liberty to form what opinions they pleased respecting the nature of original sin.

Andradius himself, in treating this subject, makes a free use of this liberty, and discourses in the following manner:

Man, in his original creation, received a constitution in which were implanted a number of appetites, desires, and affections, between which, considered in themselves, there was not a perfect concord, for the flesh naturally lusted against the mind and *vice versa*: but over these purely natural affections there was superinduced a moral character called 'original righteousness', by which all the irregular tendencies of the nature of man were restrained within proper bounds, and the exercise of the whole rendered harmonious . . . The propension of these natural inclinations is not in itself sinful, but when original righteousness is removed, then it becomes sinful by its disorder and extravagance. The very essence of original sin, therefore, consists in the absence of original righteousness, from which defect all sinful concupiscence proceeds. These natural inclinations, therefore, called 'concupiscence', are not evil *per se,* but only by irregularity and excess; therefore, when the mind is renewed by the Holy Spirit, and they are again restrained within their proper limits, they cease to be sinful.

But as all sin supposes the transgression of a law, Andradius asks 'whether the loss of original righteousness is repugnant to any law'; and answers that 'there is, indeed, no express law to which it is opposed', but says, 'it is contrary to the general law of our nature, which requires everything essential to our moral perfection.' But here our ingenious author falls into a difficulty, for he lays it down as a principle that 'all sin is the act of an intelligent and voluntary agent in violation of the law of God; but the loss of original righteousness was owing to the personal fault of Adam, who was the only voluntary agent concerned in the transaction.'

His answer is subtle, though unsatisfactory; but it is borrowed from Augustine. 'As all men were then included in Adam, so our wills were included in his will, and thus original sin may be said to be voluntary in us.' But whereas there was but an obscure exercise of our will in the commission of the first sin, he maintains, and it is accordant with the common opinion of Popish theologians, that 'of all sins, original sin is the least'; but as this is directly contrary to the declaration of the fathers, they say that the reason why it had been called *'great'* by them was on account of its wide diffusion and universal propagation.

It is very evident, therefore, from the explicit declarations of this great defender of the council of Trent, how much they obscured and misrepresented this fundamental doctrine of Scripture: and, accordingly, he finds great fault with a writer of his own church who had taught that from the soul infected with original sin no good thing could naturally proceed; asserting that human nature was not so entirely depraved, but that from it, by proper discipline, some good thing might proceed without the aid of grace; and this good he does not confine to external acts, but extends to spiritual exercises; therefore, according to him, the seeds of genuine piety must exist in our corrupt nature previous to regeneration.

Chemnicius [*Martin Chemnitz* (1522–86)], from whose EXAMEN the preceding account is taken, gives his own views and those of his brethren on this subject; an abstract of which we will here insert, and which may be considered as expressive of the opinions of all the reformers, as this defence of their opinions met with universal approbation.

He utterly denies the truth of the principle asserted by Andradius, that in the original constitution of man there existed a tendency to disorder, which was only restrained by the superadded gift of righteousness; and maintains that man in his state of original integrity possessed perfectly the image of God, which consisted in a conformity to his law; so that with his whole heart and mind, with all the faculties of the soul, and all the appetites and members of the body, there was perfect strength, and no tendency to excess or evil. The law of God which required him to love his Creator with all his soul, and mind, and strength, was fully written in his heart, to which there was a perfect conformity in every thought and desire. There existed, therefore, in man thus pure and holy, nothing of that struggling of carnal appetites and desires against spiritual exercises which is now experienced by the regenerate and which is called concupiscence.

Now the law of God requires a complete conformity to its precepts in our acts and in the whole frame and state of our minds, and where this is not found, condemns us as sinners. Experience, as well as the word of God, teaches that man's mind in its unrenewed condition, instead of being illumined with the rays of truth, is replete with horrible darkness; that his will is turned in aversion from God and indulges enmity towards him; that the affections are perverse; and that in all the powers there is a horrible *ataxia* (disorder) and depravation so far as relates to spiritual things.

Then this able polemic goes on to adduce the texts of Scripture which bear on this point, which we shall at present omit, and only remark that no modern author has insisted more strenuously on the depth of original sin and the total depravity of the human heart in all ages and in all persons. As to the seat of depravity, he says that the Scriptures refer it to the mind, the will, and the heart; it has infested all our faculties, and commences with our very being.

He continues:

Nor need we fear, as does Andradius, lest we should exaggerate the evil and extent of our innate corruption; for if we attend to the language of Scripture, we shall be convinced that the depth of the disease exceeds all conception; as says David, 'Who can understand his errors?' And Jeremiah, 'The heart is deceitful above all things, and desperately wicked, who can know it?'

The papists acknowledge that original sin exists, but pretend that it is not safe to define what it is; and allege that the ancient church never defined it. But let the impartial reader only compare the awful descriptions of this evil in the word of God with the frigid, mitigating discourses of the papists and their absurd philosophising respecting *puris naturalibus,* and he will be convinced that their doctrine is not that of the Bible.

And as to the pretence of Andradius that the council of Trent did not think proper to give any definition of original sin, we oppose to it the explicit testimony of the Holy Spirit repeatedly given in the Scriptures, in which the nature of this fountain of all iniquity is clearly exhibited. And in regard to the fathers, they certainly call it *the vice of our nature, pollution, inbred corruption, etc*.

And he concludes his proofs of the doctrine of original sin with the following weighty sentence: 'And when the mouth of the Lord calls on all flesh to be silent and heaven and earth to give ear, Andradius, with the Council of Trent, would rather give an opinion than believe with Scripture.'

The doctrine of total depravity, derived as an inheritance from our first father, is not inculcated more strongly by any writer than by Luther, in his work entitled *De Servo Arbitrio,* written against the celebrated Erasmus. It was our first purpose to have given an abridgment of this treatise of the great reformer; but Luther's style and manner are so peculiar that his writings do not bear to be abridged without much loss; and having met with a treatise on the subject of original sin by a celebrated professor of the Lutheran church, D.G. Sohnnius, who lived and wrote in the sixteenth century, we have concluded to lay before our readers an abstract of this discourse, from which may be learned what views were entertained on this subject in the age immediately after that of Luther and Calvin.

This theologian received the first part of his education at Marpurg, but when he was only fifteen years of age, his residence was transferred to Wittenberg, AD 1589, where his progress in learning was astonishing. At first his extraordinary talents were most assiduously devoted to the study of the civil law: but, in the twenty-first year of his age, he seems to have been led by a remarkable divine influence on his mind, to relinquish the profession which he had chosen and devote himself to theology, which he pursued with unremitting ardour at Marpurg for two years, when his proficiency was so remarkable that although no more than twenty-three years of age, he was made theological professor and continued in this office to give instructions to candidates for the ministry with extraordinary diligence and conspicuous success for ten years.

But differing in opinion with some of his older brethren respecting the doctrine of the ubiquity of Christ's body, which he strenuously opposed, and also in some other points of theology; for the sake of a good conscience he resigned his office at Marpurg; but after a very short interval, such was his celebrity, he received two invitations, the one from Prince Casimir to become professor of theology at Heidelberg, and the other to a similar station at Herborn. He accepted the first and was inaugurated July 18, 1584. In this situation he conducted himself with consummate wisdom and incessant diligence in promoting the cause of truth, and by giving his aid and influence to every enterprise for the benefit of learning and religion; and AD 1588, he was chosen as one of the ecclesiastical counsellors and senators, but without any interference with his office as professor.

But this extraordinary young man soon finished his work upon earth. While in the midst of his useful labours, and when the influence of his peaceful and pious example had become extensive, he was unexpectedly taken out of the world by a pleurisy in the thirty-seventh year of his age. His theological writings, in Latin, were published soon after his decease, including something like a system of theology; and are remarkable for profound research and accurate discrimination, as we think will be acknowledged by all who impartially peruse the following translation, or rather abstract, of his treatise on original sin.

Our object in bringing forward this work is not so much for the sake of its explanations and arguments, in all of which we do not concur, as to furnish the inquisitive reader with a full view of the opinions of Protestants on this point in the period immediately succeeding the reformation. And no one acquainted with ecclesiastical history will suppose that the doctrines here inculcated were peculiar to this author: the very same are found in the works of every Protestant writer of credit in that age.

The first part of the treatise of Sohnnius, in which he discusses the nature of sin and its various distinctions, we omit, as not being now to our purpose. We shall therefore commence with his answer to the objections urged in his day against the doctrine of original sin, from which it will clearly be understood what opinions were then commonly entertained on this subject.

'Having given some account of the nature and divisions of sin, our next object will be to refute some of those errors which relate to original sin. The first question then is whether there is any such thing; and this inquiry is the more necessary because many of the papists so extenuate original sin, that they will scarcely admit that it partakes of the nature of sin. And the Anabaptists have gone to the impudent length of asserting that original sin is a mere figment of Augustine.

In opposition to this error of the Anabaptists and of some of the Romanists, we assert that their doctrine is not countenanced by Scripture, and therefore cannot be true. They appeal, indeed, to Ezekiel 18:20, where it is said, 'The son shall not bear the iniquity of the father; but the soul that sinneth it shall die.' From which they infer that the posterity of Adam cannot be guilty in consequence of his fall.

To which it may be replied that Ezekiel is not speaking of the sin of our first father and federal head, which was the sin of the whole species, but of the sins of individuals of the Jewish nation. In this sense, it is true that the son shall not bear the punishment of his father's sin unless by imitation he is led to do the same; but the sin of Adam was not the sin of an individual, but of the whole race, for he represented the whole species.

The first man stood in a situation in regard to his posterity which no other man ever did, and his first sin was theirs in a sense in which no other of his sins could be; for his after sins were personal, and he alone was answerable for them; but his first sin was public, and that which brought death upon all his posterity. The gifts with which Adam was endowed, if they had been retained, would have been for the benefit of all his posterity, but being lost, they were not only forfeited for himself but for them. For as Levi paid tithes while in the loins of his progenitor Abraham, so the whole human race were included in Adam, to stand or fall with him.

Hence Paul, in Romans 5, says that Adam was a type of Christ, so that 'As by the disobedience of the first Adam many were constituted sinners, by the obedience of the second Adam many were constituted righteous.' In this passage it is clearly signified that the integrity which was given to our first father would have been available for our benefit if he had stood firmly in innocence: but that it was also committed to him to forfeit and lose all blessings for his posterity as well as for himself if he should prove disobedient. This was the event, and accordingly the precious deposit with which he was intrusted for the whole human race, was lost.

Now, this being the state of the case, it is manifest that no son bears the sins of any other father as he does those of Adam, but the soul that sinneth in the common administration of God's government, dies: but surely this general principle in relation to sin and punishment does not in the least affect our condition as fallen in the fall of our federal head and representative. The son does not bear, commonly, the sins of his other progenitors with which he has nothing to do, but he does and must bear the first sin of Adam, which was his own; for though not guilty of the act in his own person, he did commit it by his representative.

2. Another argument brought against the doctrine of original sin is that what is not voluntary cannot be sinful, because nothing can have the nature of sin which does not proceed from the exercise of understanding and choice; but what is called original sin, especially in infants, is not voluntary, therefore it cannot possess the nature of sin.

The maxim on which this argument rests is acknowledged in courts of justice among men; but it ought not to be transferred to the church, so as to affect the doctrine of original sin, which she always held and believed. Moreover, this maxim has relation altogether to actual sins, but not to original sin: and it is repugnant to the declaration of Paul, Romans 7: 'What I will that I do not, but what I hate that I do.' And Galatians 5: 'The spirit lusteth against the flesh, so that ye cannot do the things that ye would.' Augustine, in his *Retractations,* lib. i. c. 13, declares that 'this political maxim ought to have no place in relation to this point'. And in his book against Julian he says, 'In vain do you pretend that there can be no sin in infants because they are not and cannot be the subjects of voluntary exercise.' The maxim is true enough in regard to our own proper acts, but can by no means be admitted in relation to the contagion of original sin; which, however, had its origin in the voluntary act of the first man.

3. A third argument against original sin is that all sin consists in acts, but infants are capable of no acts, therefore they cannot be the subjects of sin; for 'to sin' is an active verb and signifies to do something actively; original sin, therefore, cannot exist.

To which it may be answered that in the Hebrew language, the words which signify 'to sin' express not only acts, but habits; not only positive actions, but defects and inherent pravity which is born with us.

4. It is again argued that that which is the property of an individual cannot be propagated through a whole race, but the sin of our first parents was the property of those individuals, and cannot be communicated to their posterity.

It is true that the qualities or properties of individuals are not universally propagated through the whole species, except such as are of the nature of *adunamiai*, or imperfections; for these are constantly propagated through the whole race. For example, that corruption of human nature which is the cause of death, whatever it may be, is universally propagated, for all the descendants of Adam are mortal; so also original sin is *adunamia*, or a natural impotency, or a defect, or a depraved inclination, or *ataxia* – a disorder of the affections of the mind.

Besides, the proposition on which the argument is founded is only true of separable qualities, but does not apply at all to such as are inseparable and which perpetually inhere in the subject, so that they cannot even in thought be severed from it. We do in fact witness many evils which are propagated from both parents. Moreover, the proposition stated above is only true of those qualities which are only found in some individuals, but not to those which are common to the whole species; but original sin is not a quality of a few individuals, but of the whole race; for Adam was the representative of the whole race, and forfeited that *depositum* with which he was intrusted as the head of the whole family.

5. It is again alleged that punishments are not sins, but those defects and irregular inclinations which belong to human nature are the punishment of the sin of the first man, and cannot be of the nature of sin.

Here again, there is an application of a political maxim to a subject to which it does not belong; for it is a fact clearly established in the divine government that the privation of the divine image and favour is both a sin and a punishment, but in different respects. In respect to God inflicting it, it is a punishment, for he in just judgment may deprive his creatures of his grace; but in respect to man, this privation is a sin, which by his own fault he has brought upon himself and admitted into his own soul.

6. It is again objected, that nature being from God must be good: therefore there can be no such thing as original sin or a vitiated nature.

To which it may be replied that nature was good before the fall and before sin entered to corrupt it; and nature still, so far as it is the work of God, is good; that is, the substance of the soul, the faculties and the natural principle of rational action are good; but nature, as it is depraved, is not the work of God, but something added to his work, namely, *ataxia*, or disorder and corruption in the faculties which God created in a state of order and integrity. God is the creator and preserver of the faculties, but not of the sin.

7. The Anabaptists argue that Adam having been received
into favour, was in a state of grace when his children were
procreated; and therefore, upon the principle that everything
begets its like, he could not propagate offspring infected with
original sin.

Answer: There is more in the conclusion than in the
premises; for the procreation of offspring is not according to
grace, but according to nature; so that whatever the nature of
man is since the fall, that only can be propagated. Adam
obtained freedom from guilt, not from nature, but from grace;
but grace cannot be propagated. Man, therefore, cannot
propagate anything but that corrupt nature derived from the
fall.

Moreover, the regenerate are not perfectly delivered from the
evil nature of sin, which still dwells in them and renders imperfect all that they do. So far as the regenerate act from nature,
they act sinfully: all the good which is in them is from the Spirit
of God, to whom they are indebted for every good thought: it
is evident, therefore, that grace, for every motion of which we
are dependent on another agent, cannot be propagated: but
sin, consisting in a defect or disorder of our nature, and having
its origin and proper seat in our own nature, may be
propagated. 'In me, that is, in my flesh,' says Paul, 'there
dwelleth no good thing.' 'That which is born of the flesh is
flesh.' And we never hear of a man being regenerated by a
natural birth from pious parents, but the regenerate are 'born
of the Spirit – born of God'.

They further allege, indeed, that men cannot propagate what
they do not possess; and therefore the regenerate cannot
communicate original sin to their offspring, for the guilt of all
their sins is removed by a full pardon. To which we reply as
before, that though it is true that a man cannot propagate what
he has not, yet as far as nature prevails, all men are sinful, and
it is that which properly belongs to our nature which is
capable of being propagated; therefore, when a sinful nature is
communicated to posterity it is the communication of what a
man does possess; for neither remission of sins nor the infusion
of grace do in the least affect the laws by which the propagation of the human species is regulated, for reasons already
stated.

8. But the opposers of the doctrine of original sin even appeal to Scripture for support to their opinion. They allege Romans 11:16 and 1 Corinthians 7:14 as texts which declare in favour of the children of the saints being born free from original sin. In the former, Paul asserts that 'if the root be holy so are the branches'. But they are deceived by the mere sound of a word, for 'holiness' in this place does not refer to internal moral qualities, but to external consecration: whatever is devoted solemnly to the service of God, or has a relation to his worship is called 'holy'. Thus the tabernacle, the altar, the ark, the sacrifices, the priests, and even Jerusalem itself were holy. The whole nation of Israel, as being in covenant with God, are continually spoken of as 'a holy people'; and as the promises of God's covenant with Abraham have respect to his posterity even to the end of the world; so in a certain sense these branches which are now broken off are holy, as they stand in a peculiar relation to God, which other people do not. And in the latter passage, the children of believers are called 'holy' on account of their relation to the Christian church, as being connected with the visible church by baptism, or as being capable of such connection in consequence of their relation to parents who are members of the church. For God makes the same promise to each believer which he formerly made to Abraham, *I will be a God to thee and to thy seed after thee*. But this text by no means signifies that the children of believers are born in a state free from all pollution.

9. It is again objected that the phrase 'original sin' never occurs in Scripture and never should have been introduced into the church.

Answer: Many words are conveniently used in theology which are not found in Scripture; and this must be the case where the truth is denied and error introduced: and appropriate words and phrases expressing a clear and definite meaning save us the necessity of much circumlocution. Now the truth is that the Scriptures use various words to express what is usually denominated 'sin', without entering into the distinction between original and actual sin; but the idea conveyed by the phrase 'original sin' can be logically inferred from numerous passages of Scripture, as we shall show presently. When the Pelagians denied the doctrine of original sin, which the church had before held without dispute, the orthodox fathers invented this name for the sake of avoiding all ambiguity and that the matter in dispute might be clearly and distinctly exhibited; for the Pelagians strenuously maintained that all sins were actual, or consisted in acts; but the orthodox maintained that besides the acts of sin, there existed a corruption of nature – an inherent moral disorder in the faculties, which for conveniences they denominated 'original sin'.

Having shown that the doctrine of those who oppose original sin is not contained in Scripture, nor can be proved from it, we now proceed to demonstrate that it is absolutely repugnant to the testimony of God in his Word, and therefore is a false doctrine which should be exterminated from the church.

The first testimony which we adduce is from Genesis 6:5: 'And God saw that the wickedness of man was great in the earth, and that every imagination of the thoughts of his heart was only evil continually'; and Genesis 8:1: 'For the imagination of man's heart is evil from his youth.' The objection to this testimony is that 'this is only spoken of adults, and only shows that there is in man a proneness to go astray; but nothing is here said respecting a hereditary corruption of the human heart'. But is it not evident that if all the thoughts and imaginations of the heart are constantly evil from youth upwards, the nature of man must be corrupt? What stronger evidence could there be of a corruption of nature than the fact that all men sin and do nothing else but sin, from the moment that they are capable of actual transgression? An effect so universal can never be accounted for by imitation, for children begin to sin before they have much opportunity of imitating the sins of others, and even when the examples before them are pious and good. If from the fruits of holiness we may infer that the tree is good, then certainly on the same principle, from a production of bad fruit it is fairly concluded that the nature is evil. 'A good man out of the good treasure of his heart bringeth forth that which is good; but an evil man, out of the evil treasure of his heart, that which is evil.' 'Out of the abundance of the heart the mouth speaketh.'

Our next testimony we take from Romans 3:10: 'There is none righteous, no not one.' Now if man's nature be not corrupt, how can it be accounted for on any rational principles, that all men, without the exception of one, should be unrighteous? To this proof indeed, Albert Pighius excepts that it relates to the Jewish nation, and not to the whole race of man. But this is contrary to the express design of the apostle in this passage, which was to prove that both Jews and Gentiles were all under sin and wrath, and all stood in absolute need of salvation by faith in Christ. And in the preceding verse, he explicitly declares that he had 'proved both Jews and Gentiles, that they are all under sin'. And his general conclusion is 'that all the world may become guilty before God'. Indeed, if the nation of the Jews only was referred to in this passage, yet it might be fairly inferred that all other nations were in the same corrupt condition; for why should it be supposed that universal depravity should be confined to this one people? And history confirms the sentence of the apostle, for it represents other nations as wicked as the Jews. The apostle must, therefore, be considered as describing the moral condition, not of one nation or one age, but of human nature in all countries and at all times, so far as it is not restored by Christ.

A third testimony for original sin is found in Romans 7, where Paul, in strong language, describes the power and depth of indwelling sin as experienced by himself, now in his renewed state. He calls it 'a law of sin and death', as working in him 'all manner of concupiscence'; as 'deceiving him'. And he speaks of it as an abiding principle – 'sin that dwelleth in me'. As an evil ever present with him in all his exertions to do good; 'as a law in his members warring against the law of his mind', so that he exclaimed, 'O wretched man that I am, who shall deliver me from the body of this death?' The Pelagians, it is true, will not agree that Paul is here speaking in his own person, but pretend that he personates a Jew under conviction of the duty which the law requires, but sensible of his inability to comply with the demands of the law. But that the apostle is here giving us his own experience is evident from all the circumstances of the case; which opinion is not only held by Augustine in his controversy with Julian, but was maintained by the fathers who preceded him, particularly Cyprian and Hilary.

Other testimonies not less direct and conclusive are:

Job 15:14: 'What is man that he should be clean? and he which is born of a woman, that he should be righteous?

Psalm 51:5: 'Behold I was shapen in iniquity; and in sin did my mother conceive me.'

John 3:6: 'That which is born of the flesh is flesh.'

Romans 5:12: 'As by one man sin entered into the world . . . and so death passed upon all men, because that all have sinned.' On this text it is worthy of remark that it is not only asserted that the punishment of death hath passed upon all men, but the reason is added, namely, 'because all have sinned'; so that the fault and punishment, the guilt and pollution, are by the apostle joined together.

Romans 5:19: 'For as by one man's disobedience many were made sinners.'

Romans 8:7: 'Because the carnal mind is enmity against God, for it is not subject to the law of God, neither indeed can be.'

Ephesians 2:3: 'And were by nature the children of wrath, even as others.'

And as infants die, as universal experience teaches, it is evident that they must be chargeable with sin; for Paul clearly represents sin as the cause of death – of the death of all men. 'And the wages of sin is death.'

It would be tedious to enumerate all the objections which Pelagians and others make to the interpretation of these texts. The specimen given above may be taken as an evidence that they never can succeed in proving that their doctrine is consonant with the testimony of God in the Holy Scriptures.

Hitherto we have disputed with those of the Papists and Anabaptists who deny the existence of original sin altogether; but now we come to consider the opinion of those who acknowledge original sin, but insist that it is not anything inherent in man at his birth, but only the guilt of another's sin imputed. This opinion is maintained by some of the papists, who think that original sin is nothing else than the debt of punishment contracted from the sin of Adam, but that nothing

of the pollution of sin is propagated by natural generation.
AD 1542, Pighius, after the conference which was held at
Worms, expressed his opinion in writing as follows: 'Original
sin does not consist in any defect, nor in any vice, nor depravation of nature; not in any corrupt quality nor inherent vicious
habit in us, but solely in our subjection to the punishment of
the first sin; that is, in *contracted guilt,* without anything of
depravity in our nature.'

It is a sufficient refutation of this doctrine that it is nowhere
found in Scripture, and nothing should be received as an
article of faith which cannot be proved from this source. Its
abettors do indeed endeavour to establish it by an appeal to the
Bible, but they are obliged to beg the very point in dispute, as
will soon be made to appear.

Pighius, the chief advocate for this opinion, brings forward
Romans 5:12: 'By one man sin entered into the world, and
death by sin'; verse 15: 'By the offence of one, many are dead';
verse 16: 'For the judgment was by one to condemnation';
verse 1: 'For by one man's offence death reigned by one'; verse
18: 'Therefore, as by the offence of one judgment came upon
all men to condemnation.' In all these texts, says Pighius, the
apostle attributes condemnation to the sin of Adam, and
nothing else. To which it may be replied that when the apostle
declares that 'sin had entered into the world', he does not
mean merely that Adam had become a sinner, but that it had
come upon all his descendants; that is, upon all men in the
world; for he does not say in this place that *guilt* had entered,
but that *sin* had entered into the world. And this is not left to
be inferred, but is expressly asserted in the same verse, '*in
whom* all have sinned', or '*for that* all have sinned'.

Moreover, when he declares that all are subject to death and
condemnation by the sin of one, it is a just inference that they
are all partakers of his sin and are born in a state of moral
pollution. In the 19th verse it is said, 'By the disobedience of
one many are constituted sinners'; now to be constituted
sinners includes the idea not only of being made subject to the
penalty, but partaking of the nature of sin; for they who are
entirely free from the stain of sin cannot with propriety be
called 'sinners'. Again, the apostle in this chapter teaches that
'while we were yet sinners Christ died for us, to deliver us from

death and reconcile us to God'; certainly he died for none but sinners: but if infants are not sinners then Christ did not die for them, nor do they belong to him as their Saviour; which is most absurd.

'But', says Pighius, 'infants, being neither endued with the knowledge of the law nor with freedom of will, are not moral agents, and are therefore incapable of obedience or disobedience; they cannot therefore be the subjects of sin and cannot be bound to endure the penalty of the law on any other account than for the sin of another.'

Answer: Although infants have not the exercise of free will and are not moral agents, yet they possess a nature not conformable to the law of God: they are not such as the law demands that human beings should be, but are depraved; 'children of wrath', and guilty on account of their own personal depravity: for the authorized definition of sin is *anomia*, that is, whatever is repugnant to the law of God.

But they insist further that 'God being the author of nature, if that be depraved, he must be the author of sin.'

To which we reply in the words of Augustine:

Both are propagated together, nature and the depravity of nature; one of which is good, the other evil: the first is derived from the bounty of our Creator, the latter must be attributed to our original condemnation. The first has for its cause the good pleasure of God, the latter the perverse will of the first man: *that* exhibits God as the former of the creatures, *this* as the punisher of disobedience. Finally, the same Christ, for the creation of our nature, is the maker of man; but for the healing of the disease of this nature became man.

Again, this doctrine may be refuted by express testimonies from Scripture; and ought therefore to be rejected as unsound. Genesis 5:3: 'Adam begat Seth in his own image'; Job 14:4: 'Who can bring a clean thing out of an unclean? Not one'; Psalm 51:5: 'For I was shapen in iniquity and in sin did my mother conceive me'; Romands 5:19: 'By the disobedience of one man, many were made sinners'; Ephesians 2: 3: 'and were by nature the children of wrath, even as others'; that is, we were born subject to condemnation because born in a corrupt state. From all which passages it appears that original sin does not consist merely in guilt or liableness to punishment, but in a moral depravation of the whole nature; and that it is not contracted by imitation, but by generation. Paul often speaks of that which we call 'original sin' under the general name of 'sin'. In Romans 6:8 he speaks of the 'old man' being crucified'; of the 'body of sin' being destroyed; and in chapter 7 he speaks of being 'sold under sin', of no good thing dwelling in his flesh; of evil being present with him when he would do good; and of being led captive by 'the law of sin' in his members.

Another cogent proof of the heterodoxy of this doctrine may be derived from the baptism of infants, which certainly supposes that they are conceived and born in sin.

It is also worthy of observation that spiritual regeneration is, in Scripture, continually put in contrast with 'the flesh', and with our fleshly birth. But where is the propriety of this, if the flesh is naturally free from stain?

And finally, the catholic church has ever held an opinion contrary to the one which is now opposed. Augustine, in his second book against Pelagius and Cœlestius, expresses most explicitly what we maintain. Says he:

Whosoever contends that human nature, in any age, does not need the second Adam as a physician, on the ground that it has not been vitiated in the first Adam, does not fall into an error which may be held without injury to the rule of faith; but by that very rule by which we are constituted Christians, is convicted of being an enemy to the grace of God.

It is again disputed whether concupiscence, or that disease of our nature which renders us prone to sin, is itself of the nature of sin. This the papists deny; we affirm.

They allege that whatever exists in us necessarily, and is not from ourselves but from another, cannot be of the nature of sin; but this is the fact in regard to concupiscence, *ergo*, etc.

Answer: In a merely political judgment this may be correct, but not in that which is divine. And if the principle here asserted was sound, it would prove too much: it would prove that even the *acts* of concupiscence are not sinful: for there is a sort of necessity for these, supposing the principle of concupiscence to exist in the soul.

It is next objected that that which is wholly the work of God, as is the whole nature of man, cannot be corrupt, and therefore whatever belongs to this nature as it comes from the hand of God, cannot be otherwise than free from sin.

If there were any force in this argument, it would prove that there could be no such thing as sin in the universe, for all creatures are not only dependent on God for existence at first, but for continuance in being every moment; and if the power of God could not, consistently with its purity, be exerted to bring into existence the children of a corrupt parent in a state of moral corruption, neither could it be to continue their being, which equally requires the exertion of omnipotence. But the truth is, so far as human nature or human actions are the effect of divine power, the work is good; the essential faculties of the mind and members of the body are good, and the entity of every human act is good; but the evil of our nature is received by natural generation and is the consequence of the fall of our first parent, and the sinfulness of our acts must not be ascribed to God, 'in whom we live and move', but to the perversity of our own wills.

But they allege that God inflicts this depravity on the race of men, and therefore it cannot partake of the nature of sin without making God its author.

To which it may be replied that God inflicts it, as it is a punishment, but not as it is sin; that is, he withdraws all divine influence, and all the gifts of innocence with which the creature was originally endued, in just judgment. Does not God in just displeasure for obstinate continuance in sin, often send blindness of mind as a judgment: in the same manner he can inflict that pravity of nature which we bring into the world with us as a punishment for the sin of our first parents: that is, he withholds all those gifts and all that influence which are necessary to a state of moral purity. The texts of Scripture which might be adduced to establish the doctrine which has been advanced, have already been cited and need not now be repeated.

But Albert Pighius asserts that the divine law only prohibits vicious acts, not the latent qualities of the mind: the command says 'Thou shalt not covet', but it does not say thou shalt not have a disease which may induce you to covet. It is true, the act only is mentioned in this prohibition, but the disposition is doubtless included, as in the sixth commandment it is only said, 'Thou shall not kill'; and in the seventh, 'Thou shalt not commit adultery'; but we know from high authority that in the one case the law is violated by sinful anger, and in the other by a wanton desire; so in the eighth commandment, the act of theft only is forbidden expressly, but we know that to covet our neighbour's goods is sin; and in like manner, although the tenth commandment only prohibits expressly the act of concupiscence, yet undoubtedly the disease, or corrupt disposition from which the act proceeds, is included by implication in the prohibition.

And this will appear very clearly by considering the preceptive part of the law; this requires that we should love God with all our heart, and mind, and strength; and of course whatever in us that is opposed to a compliance with this command is forbidden, but such an obstacle is this disease of concupiscence, therefore, this being forbidden by the holy law of God, is sinful. Infants, therefore, are children of wrath because they have in them a disease of irregular propensity, although it has not yet been exerted.

Pighius still urges the objection already refuted in another form, that no law can prohibit equitably what it is impossible for the creature to avoid; but the infant can no more avoid being born with a proneness to irregular indulgences than it could avoid coming into the world with the sense of touch or taste; he concludes, therefore, that concupiscence is not prohibited in the tenth commandment.

Now we answer, as before, that if it is true that nothing is forbidden which cannot be avoided, then sinful acts are not forbidden, for with a nature labouring under the disease of concupiscence, sinful acts cannot be avoided; and so the argument is not sound, since it proves too much; nay, the renewed themselves cannot avoid sin in this life, as Paul abundantly teaches in the seventh of Romans; therefore God does prohibit what we cannot avoid, and does command what we cannot perform.'

The author then proceeds to refute the opinion of the Flaccians, that original sin corrupted the substance of the soul; an opinion industriously propagated by Flaccius Illyricus, one of the most learned of the reformers; and which was embraced and pertinaciously maintained in several places in Germany. But as this error is not now maintained by any with whom we are acquainted, we do not think it necessary to exhibit the elaborate and conclusive arguments by which Sohnnius refutes it.

As we stated before, our object in giving an abstract of this treatise is not so much to defend the doctrine of hereditary depravity, as to give a correct view of the state of opinion on this subject at the time of the Reformation and afterwards. And it cannot fail to occur to the intelligent reader that none of the objections now made to the doctrine are new, or supported by any new arguments. The whole ground of controversy now occupied by the various discordant opinions has been gone over before. And the result will probably be as before, that while those who adhere strictly to evangelical doctrine will continue to maintain the old doctrine, its opposers will deviate further and further from orthodoxy.

There has never yet been an instance in the history of the church of the rejection of any doctrines of the gospel, where the opposers of the truth have been contented to stop at the first step of departure from sound doctrine. If they who first adopt and propagate an error are sometimes restrained by habit, and by a lurking respect for the opinions of the wise and good, as also by a fear of incurring the censure of heresy, from going the full length which their principles require; yet those who follow them in their error will not be kept back by such considerations.

Indeed, the principles of self defence require that men who undertake to defend their opinions by argument should endeavour to be consistent with themselves: and thus it commonly happens that what was originally a single error soon draws after it the whole system of which it is a part. On this account it is incumbent on the friends of truth to oppose error in its commencement, and to endeavour to point out the consequences likely to result from its adoption; and to us it appears that nothing is better calculated to show what will be the effect of a particular error than to trace its former progress by the lights of ecclesiastical history.

4

THE INABILITY
OF SINNERS[1]

There has occurred within our recollection a considerable
difference in the manner of treating this subject,
especially in addresses to the impenitent from the pulpit. It was
customary formerly for Calvinistic preachers to insist much on
the helpless inability of the sinner. He was represented according to the language of the Scriptures to be 'dead in trespasses
and sins' and utterly unable to put forth one act of spiritual
life; and too often this true representation was so given as to
leave the impression that the person labouring under this total
inability was not culpable for the omission of acts which he
had no power to perform. The fact of man's being a free
accountable agent was not brought into view with sufficient
prominence; and the consequence was that in many cases the
impenitent sinner felt as if he were excusable, and the conclusion was too commonly adopted that there was no
encouragement to make any effort until it should please a
sovereign God to work. And if at any time the zealous preacher
urged upon his hearers in private the duty of repentance, he

[1]By Archibald Alexander. Published in 1831 in review of the work 'An
inquiry into that inability under which the sinner labours, and whether it
furnishes any excuse for his neglect of duty.'

was sure to hear the echo of his own doctrines: 'We are incapable of doing anything until God shall be pleased to work in us "to will and to do of his good pleasure"; it is useless for us to attempt anything.' We do not say that the inability of man was so represented by all as to produce these impressions, for we know that by some, not only man's dependence, but also his duty, was distinctly and forcibly inculcated.

Some excellent men, who saw the danger of so insisting on the inability of man as to furnish an apology for the careless sinner, borrowed a little aid from the Arminian scheme, and taught that if the sinner would do what was in his power, and continue faithfully to use the outward means of grace, the Spirit of God would assist his endeavours: and thus a connection was formed between the strivings of the unregenerate and the grace of God. But this was not consistent with the other opinions of these men, and involved them in many practical difficulties, and contradicted many clear passages of Scripture which teach that 'without faith it is impossible to please God'.

And it seemed to be obviously absurd that the promise of grace should be made to acts and exercises which, it could not be denied, were in their nature sinful. Some, indeed, spoke of a kind of sincerity which they supposed an unregenerate sinner might possess; but it was found difficult to tell what it was; and another difficulty was to quiet the minds of those convinced sinners who had been long using the means of grace. Such persons would allege that they had prayed, and read, and heard the Word for a long time, and yet received no communications of grace. To such, nothing could on this plan be said, but to exhort them to wait God's time, and to entertain the confident hope that no soul ever perished that continued to the last seeking for mercy.

The inconvenience and evil of these representations being perceived, many adopted with readiness a distinction of human ability into *natural* and *moral*. By the first they understood merely the possession of physical powers and opportunities; by the latter, a mind rightly disposed. In accordance with this distinction it was taught that every man possessed a natural ability to do all that God required of him; but that every sinner laboured under a moral inability to obey God, which, however, could not be pleaded in excuse for his disobedience, as it consisted in corrupt dispositions of the heart, for which every man was responsible. Now this view of the subject is substantially correct, and the distinction has always been made by every person, in his judgments of his own conduct and that of others. It is recognized in all courts of justice and in all family government, and is by no means a modern discovery.

And yet it is remarkable that it is a distinction so seldom referred to or brought distinctly into view by old Calvinistic authors. The first writer among English theologians that we have observed using this distinction explicitly is the celebrated Dr Twisse, the prolocutor of the Westminster Assembly of Divines, and the able opposer of Arminianism, and advocate of the Supralapsarian doctrine of divine decrees. It was also resorted to by the celebrated Mr Howe, and long afterwards used freely by Dr Isaac Watts, the popularity of whose evangelical writings probably had much influence in giving it currency. It is also found in the theological writings of Dr Witherspoon, and many others whose orthodoxy was never disputed.

But in this country no man has had so great an influence in fixing the language of theology as Jonathan Edwards, President of New Jersey College. In his work, *The Freedom of the Will,* this distinction holds a prominent place and is very important to the argument which this profound writer has so ably discussed in that treatise. The general use of the distinction between natural and moral ability may therefore be ascribed to the writings of President Edwards, both in Europe and America. No distinguished writer on theology has made more use of it than Dr Andrew Fuller; and it is well known that he imbibed nearly all his views of theology from an acquaintance with the writings of President Edwards. And it may be said truly that Jonathan Edwards has done more to give complexion to the theological system of Calvinists in America than all other persons together. This is more especially true of New England; but it is also true to a great extent in regard to a large number of the present ministers of the Presbyterian Church.

Those, indeed, who were accustomed either to the Scotch or Dutch writers did not adopt this distinction, but were jealous of it as an innovation and as tending to diminish, in their view, the miserable and sinful state of man, and as derogatory to the grace of God. But we have remarked that in almost all cases where the distinction has been opposed as false, or as tending to the introduction of false doctrine, it has been misrepresented. The true ground of the distinction has not been clearly apprehended; and those who deny it have been found making it themselves in other words; for that an inability depending on physical defect should be distinguished from that which arises from a wicked disposition or perverseness of will, is a thing which no one can deny who attends to the clear dictates of his own mind; for it is a self-evident truth which even children recognize in all their apologies for their conduct.

We do not assert, however, that the dispute between the advocates and opposers of this distinction has been a mere logomachy. There is one important point of difference. They who reject the distinction maintain that if we have lost any physical ability to perform our duty by our own fault, the obligation to obedience remains, although ability to execute it is utterly lost; while the advocates of the distinction between natural and moral ability hold that obligation and ability must be of equal extent; and although they admit that we are accountable for the loss of any faculty which takes place through our fault, yet the guilt must be referred entirely to the original act, and no new sin can be committed for not exercising a faculty which does not exist, or which is physically incapable of the actions in question.

To illustrate this point, let us suppose the case of a servant cutting off his hands to avoid the work required of him. The question then is, Is this servant guilty of a crime for not employing those members which he does not possess? It is admitted that he is chargeable with the consequences of his wicked act, but this only goes to show the greater guilt of that deed. It is also true that if the same perverse disposition which led to this act is still cherished, he is virtually guilty of the neglect of that obedience which was due. Sin consists essentially in the motives, dispositions, and volitions of the heart, and the external act only possesses a moral nature by its connection with these internal affections. But it cannot be truly said that a man can be guilty of a crime in not using hands which he does not possess. Let us suppose this servant to have become truly penitent and to have nothing in his mind but a strong desire to do his duty; can any impartial man believe that he commits a sin in not doing the work which he has no hands to execute? We think not.

The case will appear more evident if the faculty lost should be one which is essential to moral agency; as if a man should by his own fault deprive himself of reason. It is manifest that a man totally destitute of reason is incapable of any moral acts; and this is equally true, however this defect may have been contracted. If a man performs an act by which he knows reason will be extinguished or perverted, he is guilty in that act of a crime which takes its measure, in part, from the consequences likely to ensue. Thus in the case of the drunkard; he who destroys his reason by inebriation may be considered as guilty of an act, the guilt of which has respect to all the probable consequences. In human courts we are aware that intoxication cannot be pleaded as a justification of crime; but on this subject it may be observed that drunkards are not commonly so destitute of a knowledge of right and wrong as to be deprived of their moral agency. And again, it would be of dangerous consequence to admit the principle that a man might plead one crime in justification of another; and it would be exceedingly liable to abuse, as a man might become intoxicated for the very purpose of committing a great crime, or he might affect a greater degree of intoxication than was real; so that it is a sound political maxim that a man shall be held responsible for all acts committed in a state of inebriation.

But *at the bar of conscience* we cannot but view the matter in a different light. If by an intoxicating liquor reason is completely subverted, and the man is no longer himself, we cannot judge that he is as accountable for what he does, as when in his sober senses. You may accumulate as much guilt as you will on the act of extinguishing or perverting his reason; but you cannot think that what he madly perpetrates under the influence of strong drink is equally criminal as if committed while reason was in exercise. This we take to be the deliberate judgment of all impartial men.

The most difficult question relative to this matter is whether ignorance and error do wholly, or in any degree, exculpate from the guilt of actions committed under their influence. On this subject, it has been customary to distinguish ignorance (and all error is only a species of ignorance), into voluntary and involuntary. The former, however great, does not excuse; the latter, if invincible, does; or mitigates criminality in proportion as it approximates to insuperable ignorance. But when we speak of voluntary ignorance, we do not mean that there is a deliberate volition to remain in ignorance, or that it could be removed by an act of the will; but we mean that ignorance or misconception which is a part of our depravity or a consequence of it.

A mind depraved by sin is incapable of perceiving the beauty and sweetness of spiritual objects, and is therefore totally incapable of loving such objects. This ignorance constitutes an essential part of human depravity and can never be an apology for it, nor in the least exculpate from the guilt of sins committed under its influence. It is, in fact, that very blindness of mind and unbelief of heart which lies at the foundation of all departures from God. To which we may add that the actual exercise of corrupt affections obscures the intellect and perverts the judgment, as has been remarked by all moralists, and the same is observable in all the common transactions of life. Ignorance or error induced by criminal self-love or by malignant passions forms no excuse for the evil which flows from this source; but this very ignorance and error form a part of that sinful character which belongs to the moral agent.

We are aware that there has been current with many in our day a theory which separates entirely between the intellect and will, and maintains that the former in its operations is incapable of virtue or vice; and to corroborate this opinion, a distinction has been made of the powers of the soul itself, into natural and moral. By this division, the understanding or intellect belongs to the former class, the will and affections to the latter. According to this hypothesis, all sin consists in voluntary acts or in the exercise of the will, and the understanding is incapable of moral obliquity, because it is not a moral faculty. They who have adopted this theory (and they are many) entertain the opinion that depravity consists very much in the opposition of the heart to the dictates of the understanding.

In regeneration, according to them, there is no illumination of the understanding by the Holy Spirit. This, according to the theory under consideration, is altogether unnecessary. This work, therefore, consists in nothing else than giving a new heart, or a new set of feelings. If the person has received correct doctrinal instruction, no other illumination is needed; and the whole difference in the conceptions of truth between the regenerate and unregenerate, is owing to nothing else than a change in the feelings; for as far as mere intellect is concerned, the views of the understanding are the same before regeneration as afterwards; except that, a renewed heart disposing the person to the impartial love of truth, he will be more careful to collect and weigh its evidences, and will thus be preserved from errors into which the unregenerate, through the corrupt bias produced by the affections, are prone to fall.

Now against this whole method of philosophizing we enter our dissent. This total dissociation of the understanding and heart, and this entire repugnance between them, are contrary to all experience. There can be no exercise of heart which does not necessarily involve the conception of the intellect; for that which is chosen must be apprehended, and that which is loved and admired must be perceived. And although it is true that the knowledge of the unregenerate man is inefficacious, so that while he knows the truth he loves it not; yet we venture to maintain that the reason why his knowledge produces no effect is simply because it is inadequate. It does not present truth in its true colours to the heart. It is called speculative knowledge and may be correct as far as it goes; but it does not penetrate the excellence and the beauty of any one spiritual object; and it may be averred that the affections of the heart do always correspond with the real views of the understanding. The contrary supposition, instead of proving that man is morally depraved, would show that his rationality was destroyed.

If it be alleged that this apprehension of the beauty, sweetness, and glory of spiritual things, which is peculiar to the regenerate, arises merely from the altered state of the heart, I have no objection to the statement, if by *heart* be meant the moral nature of the renewed mind; but it is reversing the order of nature and rational exercise to suppose that we first have an affection of love to an object, and then see it to be lovely. We may ask what excited this affection of love. If anything is known of the order of exercises in the rational mind, the perception of the qualities on which an affection terminates is, in the order of nature, prior to the affection. The soul in an unregenerate state is equally incapable of seeing and feeling aright in relation to spiritual objects. And indeed, we hardly know how to distinguish between the clear perception of the beauty of an object, and the love of that object; the one might serve as a just description of the other.

Not but that the intellect and heart may be distinguished; but when beauty, sweetness, excellence, and glory, or good in any of its forms, is the object of the understanding, this distinction in experience vanishes. And accordingly the schoolmen distinguished between the understanding and will, not by referring nothing to the latter but blind feeling, but by dividing all objects which could be presented to the mind into such as were received as *true* merely, and such as were not merely apprehended as true, but as *good*. These last they considered as having relation to the will, under which all appetitive affections were included.

The Scriptures have been repeatedly appealed to as placing all moral acts in the will; but they furnish no aid to those who make this wide distinction between understanding and will. They do often use the word *heart* for moral exercise, but not to the exclusion of the intellect. Indeed, this word in the Old Testament, where it most frequently occurs, is used for the whole soul; or for any strong exercise of the intellect as well as the feelings. We are required to love with the understanding; and 'a wise and understanding heart' is a mode of expression which shows how little the inspired penmen were influenced by a belief of this modern theory. And in the New Testament, to 'believe with the heart' includes the intellect as much as what is called the will. It means to believe really and sincerely; so to believe, as to be affected by what we believe, according to its nature.

But is not all moral exercise voluntary, or an exercise of the will? Yes, undoubtedly; and so is all moral exercise rational, or such as involves the exercise of intellect. If the will were a moral power, as many suppose, then every volition would be of a moral nature – the instinctive preference of life to death would be moral; the choice of happiness in preference to misery, which no sentient being can avoid, would be moral. At this rate, it would follow that mere animals are moral beings, because it is certain they possess will. But the simple truth is that the understanding and will stand in the same relation to the morality of actions; and the latter no more deserves to be called the moral part of our constitution than the former. The only faculty belonging to our constitution which can properly be denominated moral, is conscience; not because its exercise furnishes the only instance of moral acts, for it may be doubted whether the monitions of this faculty partake of a moral nature; but because by this we are enabled to perceive the moral qualities of actions.

Our object in this discussion is to establish the point that ignorance is a part of the depravity which sin has introduced into our minds; and we maintain, in strict accordance with the Scriptures, that no unregenerate man has any adequate or true knowledge of God; nor, indeed, is he capable of such knowledge. It is a comprehensive description of the wicked that 'they know not God'; 'know not the way of peace'. To know the true God and Jesus Christ is eternal life. 'The natural man receiveth not the things of the spirit of God, they are foolishness unto him, neither can he know them, because they are spiritually discerned.' The regenerate have the eyes of their understanding enlightened and have been translated from darkness to the marvellous light of the gospel.

As to invincible ignorance, it is manifest that it must stand on the same footing with the want of the requisite physical powers. It is equally impossible for a man to see, whether he be deficient in the organs of vision or in light. If God has revealed his will on certain points and in consequence has demanded our faith and obedience, the obligation to perform these duties will be co-extensive with the communication of this revelation, and no further. The heathen, therefore, will not be condemned for not believing in the Messiah, 'for how could they believe in him of whom they have not heard?' This, however, will not be any excuse for not seeking after more light by every means in their power. If persons who are surrounded by the means of instruction obstinately neglect to avail themselves of the opportunity of knowing the will of God, they do render themselves exceedingly guilty by such perverseness and make themselves responsible for all the omission of duty which arises from this state of obstinate ignorance.

Let us now return to the inquiry respecting natural and moral inability. We asserted that all men, and even children, were in the constant habit of making a distinction between an impediment to the doing of a thing, which arose from want of physical power, and that which depended solely on the disposition or will. But it may be useful to inquire whether any advantage has been derived from the use of these terms, or whether they have not rather served to perplex and mislead the people for whose benefit they were devised. That this latter is probably a correct statement of the truth may with some probability be presumed from the fact that these terms are evidently falling into disuse with many who were once tenacious of them.

But to render this more evident, we would remark that there is an obvious inaccuracy in speaking of two kinds of ability, both of which are requisite to accomplish the same object. If both are necessary to the end, then evidently either by itself is not an ability. If the strength of a man, together with a machine of a certain power, be necessary to lift a weight, it is evidently incorrect to say that the hand of the man is able to elevate this heavy body; his strength is only an ability when combined with the machine which is needed to give it force; so, if the mere possession of natural powers to do the commandments of God is not of itself sufficient to reach the end, it is not properly called an *ability*; it is only such when combined with what is called moral ability.

Again, the word *natural* is here used in an uncommon and technical sense; and the term being already in common use in relation to the same subject in a sense entirely different, it is calculated to perplex and mislead. When we say man possesses a natural ability, we mean by the word *natural* that which is contra-distinguished from moral, that which is destitute of any moral quality; but we are accustomed to say, and the usage is derived from Scripture, that man is naturally depraved, naturally blind, naturally impotent: but in this case we mean that which is innate, that which is constitutional. And when applied to this subject, the meaning is entirely diverse from the one stated above; for while *there*, all idea of moral character is excluded, *here* it relates to moral qualities. 'Man is naturally able to obey the commandments of God' and 'Man is naturally a depraved and impotent being' are contradictions, if the word *natural* be used in the same sense in both cases; but as intended, there is no contradiction; for the word in the first instance has an entirely different meaning from what it has in the second.

But surely such confusion in the use of terms should be avoided. And if you will inquire of the common people what they understand by natural ability, you will be convinced that it is a phrase which perplexes and obscures, rather than elucidates the subject. We have known instances in which clergymen of some learning and even doctors of divinity have understood that they who held the doctrine of man's natural ability denied that of total depravity; whereas the fact is that there are no sterner advocates of universal and total depravity than those who make this distinction.

But an objection of a different but not less weighty kind lies against the use of the phrases 'moral ability' and 'moral inability'. By the former is meant that state of the heart or affections which leads a person to choose to perform any act of external obedience; by the latter, the contrary, or an indisposition or unwillingness to do our duty. Now, we know that the law of God extends to the heart and requires rectitude in every secret thought and affection; yea, the essence of obedience consists in this conformity of the heart to the law of God. But according to the import of this distinction, these internal affections are no more than a moral ability to obey. The phrase seems to contemplate external acts only as acts of obedience and the affections of the heart as the ability to perform them; but this is evidently incorrect. What is the sum of the obedience which the law of God requires of man? Is it not supreme and perfect love? What is moral ability? It is this very thing in which the essence of obedience consists. This moral ability should relate to something prior to love; but what ability is that which is prior to all holy affection? If you say the nature or disposition, the law requires that this be pure also as well as the acts and exercises. There is, then, no such thing as a moral ability to obey, as distinct from obedience itself. And, again, what is moral inability but sin itself? It is the want of a right temper and a holy will – the defect of that love which the law requires; and what is this but sin?

It certainly can have no other effect but to mislead, to call the essence of disobedience by the name of 'moral inability'. It can be no question whether sin can furnish any excuse for disobedience. Now, what is called 'moral inability', when it comes to be analysed, is nothing but the essence of sin as it exists in the heart. Man labours under a moral inability to obey God because he does not love him; but love is the sum and essence of all obedience; it is the same, therefore, as to say, that man in his natural state has no love to God. Man is in a state of sin which, while it continues, must be an effectual hindrance to the service of God.

We have already remarked that the distinction of inability into *natural* and *moral* is much less used of late than it was some fifteen or twenty years ago. It has not answered the purpose for which it was invented. If there be a real inability which man cannot remove, it must have the effect of discouraging human exertions. Let it be conceded that it does not render man excusable; yet it does render his unassisted efforts ineffectual; therefore, they who consider it all important, not merely to fix upon the conscience the conviction of ill-desert, but to rouse the powers of the soul to action, have adopted a new method of treating this subject which not a little alarms those who are tenacious of old notions and the ancient forms of speech.

These new preachers, in their addresses to the impenitent sinner, say nothing about natural and moral inability. They preach that man is in possession of every ability which is requisite for the discharge of his duty. That it is as easy for him to repent, to exercise faith, and to love God, as to speak, or eat, or walk, or perform any other act. And men are earnestly and passionately exhorted to come up at once to the performance of their duty. Nothing is more in the power of a man, they allege, than his own will; and the consent of the will to the terms of the gospel is all that is required to constitute any man a Christian. When sinners are awakened, and become anxious about their salvation, it is deemed by these teachers improper to manifest any sympathy with their feelings of pungent conviction; for the only reason of their remaining in distress is their obstinate continuance in impenitence. All conversation with such, therefore, should assume the character of stern rebuke, and continued earnest exhortations to *submit* to God, to give up their rebellion, and to make choice of the service of God. And if any convinced sinner ventures to express the opinion that he labours under any sort of inability to do what is required of him, he is severely reproved, as wishing to cast the blame of his impenitence on his Maker. And it is believed that upon the new plan of treating awakened sinners, they are brought to the enjoyment of peace much sooner than upon the old plan of treating them rather as unfortunate than as guilty. Men, upon being assured that salvation is in their power, are induced to make an exertion to submit to God, and do often persuade themselves that now they have complied with their duty and have passed from death unto life.

There is much reason to fear, however, that many souls who have very slight convictions of sin are deluded into the opinion that they have submitted and are reconciled to God, though they have never been led to any deep views of the dreadful sinfulness of their own hearts. And others who have deeper convictions find all their own efforts unavailing; and while they confess that the fault is in the total depravity of their nature, continue to profess their inability to repent; and whatever power others may have to change the heart, are more and more convinced that no such power belongs to them. The obstinate cases cannot but be perplexing and troublesome to the zealous preachers of full ability; but they contrive to reconcile them with their doctrine by various methods which it is not to our purpose to specify.

Now, as a large portion of our younger theologians appear to be adopting this new theory of ability and consider it a great improvement upon both the old Calvinistic doctrine and also upon the Edwardean theory of natural and moral ability; and especially, as it claims a near alliance with the many revivals of religion which are now in progress in the church, it becomes a duty of high obligation to bring these opinions, which are now so widely and confidently inculcated, to the test of reason and Scripture; and we trust that our readers will indulge us while we enter with some degree of minuteness into the discussion.

And to give our views clearly and fully on the subject of man's ability and inability, we shall endeavour to go back to first principles and cautiously examine those maxims which, by most who speak on this subject, are taken for granted.

On the subject of man's moral agency and accountableness, there is no controversy.

It is also agreed by most that an obligation to perform an act of obedience supposes the existence of the faculties or physical powers requisite for its performance. An irrational being cannot be under a moral obligation to perform a rational act. Man cannot be under obligation to do what requires powers which do not belong to his nature and constitution. For example, man could not justly be required to transport himself from earth to heaven as the angels do, because this exceeds the power which belongs to his nature. And it is admitted that where there is a willingness to perform a duty, anything which renders the execution of our desire impracticable, removes the obligation. For no man can be bound to perform impossibilities.

The maxim that *obligation to obey any command supposes the existence of an ability to do the action required,* relates entirely to actions consequent upon volitions. If we appeal to the common sense or universal judgment of mankind on this point, we must be careful to understand precisely the common principle respecting which all men are agreed; and must be careful not to extend the maxim to other things entirely distinct from its usual application. An infant cannot justly be required to build a house or a ship. A person of weak intellect and little invention cannot be obliged to write an elegant poem. No man can be under obligation to remember every word which he ever spoke and every thought which ever passed through his mind. A man who has lost his hands or his feet cannot afterwards be under a moral obligation to exercise these members. This case is so plain, and the judgment of men so uniform on the subject, that we need not dwell longer on the point.

The next thing to be inquired is whether this maxim applies to the ability of *willing* as well as *doing.*

And here it may be remarked that the possession of the faculty of willing, or of choosing and refusing, is essential to a moral agent; and, therefore, a being who has no such faculty can never be subject to a moral law. On this point there can be no difference of opinion. Neither is it supposed by any that we have the power of avoiding an exercise of will when an object is proposed, or when a particular action is in the contemplation of the mind; for if we do not choose a proposed object, we of course refuse it; and if we do not determine on an action which may be suggested, we of necessity let it alone. There is here no other alternative. Hence, it is evident that the liberty of man does not consist in the power to will or not to will. In regard to this, man may be said to lie under necessity; but it is obviously no hardship, since he is at liberty to will as he pleases. But the most important question is, Has the moral agent the power of willing differently from what he does in any particular case? This is a very intricate subject, and will require close attention and an impartial judgment in order to see clearly where the truth lies.

The word *will* is taken in a greater or less latitude. It signifies, according to some, every desire and inclination, every preference and choice. According to others, *volitions,* or the acts of the will, are properly such acts of the mind as result in some change of the body or mind. The whole active power of man consists in an ability, when he chooses to exercise it, to alter the train of thought by turning the mind from one subject of contemplation to another; and in the ability to move the members of the body within certain limits. Let any man seriously inquire whether he possesses any other power or ability than this.

We know that there are many things which he has no ability to perform. He cannot alter the nature of the perceptions of sense; he cannot excite in himself affections to any objects at will. If a man wish to enkindle love in his breast to any person, he cannot possibly do more than contemplate all the traits of character which are amiable in that person, or all those circumstances which have a tendency to create an interest in the person: but it is a vain effort to endeavour to love another by the mere effort of will. If we take the word *will* in the larger sense, all clear distinction between desire and will is removed. If we call every preference an act of volition, then obviously will and affection are confounded; for what is preference but a superior affection? and choice, if it result in no determination to act, is nothing else but preference, or the cherishing a stronger affection for one thing than another.

It seems to us, therefore, to be altogether expedient to confine the words *will* and *volition* to those distinctly marked actions which lead to some change in body or mind. Those determinations which lead directly to action, whether of body or mind, are properly called volitions, as when I resolve to raise my hand; to direct my eyes to this quarter or that; to turn my thoughts from one subject to another. These are acts which are clearly defined and which are easily distinguishable from mere desires or emotions. A late philosophical writer has indeed attempted to sweep away all controversies respecting the determination of the will by confounding will and desire together: but still he is obliged to acknowledge that some of our desires are followed by actions or by a change in the body or mind; and these being thus clearly distinguished by their effects, and being also the most important of all our acts, it is expedient to have them put into a class by themselves with an appropriate denomination.

But let us return to the inquiry already instituted, which is, when we will any particular thing, whether we have it in our power to will the contrary. Here it will be acknowledged at once that a man cannot will at the same time opposite things; for if he determines on an act, he cannot determine to let it alone. When it is asked whether the person who wills an action had it in his power to omit it, the answer is that if he had been so inclined, he could have willed the opposite.

The very nature of volition is the resolving on that which is agreeable to our inclinations. To suppose any constraint or compulsion in willing is absurd; for then it would not be a volition. No greater liberty can be conceived than freely to choose what we please. But if the import of the question is whether with an inclination one way, we are able to will the very contrary, the thing is absurd. If we were capable of such a volition, it would be a most unreasonable act. Such a self-determining power as would lead to such acts would render man incapable of being governed by a moral law, and would subject him, so far as such a power was exercised, to the most capricious control. He could no longer be said to be the master of himself; for while his whole soul was inclined to one thing he might be led in an opposite direction without having any reason or motive for his conduct. Such a power as this, no one, I think, will plead for who understands its nature. Man has the power to determine his own will, but in accordance with his own inclinations – the only kind of power over the will which any reasonable being can wish. If I can will as I please, surely I need not complain that I cannot will as I do not please. If I govern my volitions by my prevailing inclination, this is surely a greater privilege, and more truly liberty, than a power to determine the will without any motives and contrary to all my wishes. My actions are as truly my own and self-determined when they accord with inclination, as if they could spring up without any desire.

Many philosophical men, from a fear of being involved in the doctrine of necessity, have talked and reasoned most absurdly in relation to this point. And it is to be regretted that many writers who have substantially maintained the true doctrine of the will have employed language which has had the effect of confirming their prejudices. To talk of a necessity of willing as we do, although we may qualify the word by 'moral' or 'philosophical', is inexpedient. There can be no necessity in volition. It is the very opposite of necessity. It is liberty itself. Because volition has a determinate cause which makes it what it is, this does not alter the case. If the cause be a free agent, and the kind of volition be determined by the unconstrained inclinations of the heart, the freedom of our actions is in no way affected by this certain connection between volitions and their cause. The contrary doctrine involves the monstrous absurdity that volitions have no cause and no reason for being what they are. If, then, we can will as we please, we have all conceivable liberty and power, so far as the will is concerned. But the maxim that no man is under obligation to do that which he has no power to perform does not apply to the act of volition, as was before observed, but to the ability to act according to our will.

We come now to the inquiry whether a man has a power to change the affections of his heart, or to turn the current of his inclinations in a contrary direction to that in which they run. On this subject our first remark is that the very supposition of a person being sincerely desirous to make such a change is absurd, for if there existed a prevailing desire that our affections should not be attached to certain objects, then already the change has taken place; but while our souls are carried forth in strong affections to an object, it is a contradiction to say that that soul desires the affections to be removed from that object: for what is affection but the outgoing of the soul with desire and delight towards an object? But to suppose a desire not to love the object which has attracted our affections, is to suppose two opposite affections prevailing in the same soul at the same time and in relation to the same object.

It is true that there may exist conflicting desires in regard to the objects which are pursued; for while with a prevailing desire we are led on to seek them, there may, and often do, exist inferior desires which draw us, according to their force, in another direction. Thus, a drunkard may be prevailingly inclined to seek the gratification which he expects from strong drink; but while he is resolved to indulge his appetite, a regard to health, reputation, and the comfort of his family, may produce a contrary desire. In the case supposed, it is overcome by the stronger inclination which a vicious appetite has generated.

It is also true, as has been remarked by President Edwards, that in contemplating some future time, a man may desire that the appetite or affection which governs him may be subdued. And again, a man may be brought into such circumstances that his desire of happiness or dread of eternal misery may be so strong as to induce him to wish that his predominant affections might be changed, and under the powerful influence of these constitutional principles he may be led to will a change in the temper of his mind and the inclinations of his heart.

The question is whether a volition to change the desires or dispositions is ever effectual. If our philosophy of the mind be correct, this is a thing entirely out of the power of the will. Every person, however, can put the matter to the test of experience at any moment. The best way to prove to ourselves that we have a power over our affections, is to exercise it. Who was ever conscious of loving any person or thing merely from willing to do so? What power, then, has the sinner to change his own heart? He does not love God, but is at enmity with him

– how shall he change his enmity into love? You tell him that he has the power to repent and to love God, and urge him instantly to comply with his duty.

Now we should be exceedingly obliged to anyone who would explain the process by which a sinner changes the current of his affection. We have often tried the experiment and have found ourselves utterly impotent to accomplish this work. Perhaps the zealous preacher of the doctrine of human ability will say it is as easy to love God, or easier, as it is to hate him. He can only mean that when the heart is in that state in which the exhibition of the character of God calls forth love, the exercise of love in such a soul is as easy as the exercise of enmity in one of a different moral temperament. The ability to repent and love God, then, amounts to no more than this, that the human faculties when rightly exercised are as capable of holy as of sinful acts, which no one, we presume, ever denied; but it is a truth which has no bearing on the point in hand. The impenitent sinner cannot sincerely will to change his heart, and if under the influence of such motives as he is capable of feeling he does will a change of affection, the effect does not follow the volition.

Those persons, therefore, who are continually preaching that men have every ability necessary to repent are inculcating a doctrine at war with every man's experience and directly opposed to the word of God, which continually represents the sinner as 'dead' and impotent, and incapable of thinking even a good thought. But we shall be told that it is a maxim of common sense that whatever we are commanded to do we must have power or ability to perform – that it is absurd to suppose that any man is under obligation to do what he is unable to perform.

Now, we are of opinion that this is precisely the point where these advocates of human ability mistake, and their error consists in the misapplication of the maxim already mentioned – which is true and self-evident when properly applied – to a case to which it does not belong. We have admitted over and over that this doctrine is universally true in relation to the performance of actions consequent on volition; but we now deny that this is true when applied to our dispositions, habits, and affections. We utterly deny that, in order to a man's being accountable and culpable for enmity to God, he should have the power of instantly changing his enmity into love. If a man has certain affections and dispositions of heart which are evil, he is accountable for them; and the more inveterate and immovable these traits of moral character are, the more he is to be blamed, and the more he deserves to be punished.

But as it is alleged that the common judgment of man's moral faculty is that he cannot be culpable unless he possesses the power to divest himself of his evil temper by an act of volition, we will state one or two cases, and leave it to every reader to judge for himself after an impartial consideration of the facts.

In the first place, we take the case of a son who, being of a self-willed disposition and having a great fondness for sensual pleasure and a strong desire to be free from restraint, has been led to cherish enmity to his father. The father we will suppose to be a man of conscientious integrity, who, from natural affection and from a regard to higher principles, wishes to perform his duty by reproving, restraining, and correcting his child. But all this discipline, instead of working a reformation, has the effect of irritating the son, who every day becomes more stubborn and incorrigible, until he comes at length to look upon his father as a tyrannical master – an object of utter aversion. Hatred readily takes root in the bosom of such a one, and by the wicked counsels of ill advisers this feeling is cherished, until by degrees it becomes so inveterate that he cannot think of his father without being conscious of malignant feelings. The effect of such feelings will be to pervert every action of the hated person, however kind or just. Malice also causes everything to be seen through a false medium.

Now suppose this process to have been going on for years, the first question is, can this ungrateful son change in a moment these feelings of enmity and ill-will for filial affection? The impossibility is too manifest to require any discussion; he cannot. But is he, on account of his inability to change his affections, innocent? Surely the guilt of such a state of mind does not require that the person be at once, or at all, able to change the state of his heart. And we maintain that according to the impartial judgment of mankind, such a man would be the object of blame without regard to any ability to change his heart. And this is the case with regard to impenitent sinners. Their enmity to God and aversion to his law is deep and inveterate; and though they have neither ability nor will to change the temper of their minds, they are not the less culpable on that account; for the nature of moral evil does not consist in that only which can be changed at will, but the deeper the malignity of the evil, the greater the sinfulness, and the more justly is the person exposed to punishment. We are of opinion, therefore, that the new doctrine of human ability which is so much in vogue is false and dangerous. And to corroborate this opinion, we remark that men who are forsaken of God and given over to believe a lie, and to work all uncleanness with greediness; or, who have committed the unpardonable sin so that they cannot be 'renewed again to repentance', are surely unable to change their hearts, and yet they are exceedingly guilty.

The same thing may be strongly illustrated by a reference to the devils. They are moral agents and act freely, for they continue to sin; but who would choose to assert that they can change their nature from sin to holiness, from enmity to love? But they possess, as fully as man, what has been called 'natural ability'. They have all the physical powers requisite to constitute them moral agents and to perform the whole will of God, and are continually adding to their guilt by their willing commission of sin. But it is impossible for the devils to become holy angels; and this one fact is sufficient to demonstrate that a power to change the heart is not necessary to render a man guilty for continuing in sin.

The very reverse comes nearer the truth. The more unable a sinner is to cease from his enmity, the deeper is his guilt: yet on the very same principles on which it is argued that it is as easy for man to love God as to hate him, it might be proved that it was perfectly easy for the fallen angels to love God, or for the spirits shut up in the prison of despair to begin to love God, and thus disarm the law of that penalty which dooms them to everlasting death. If holiness is anything real, if it has any foundation or principle in the mind in which it exists, and if this principle was lost by the fall of men and angels, then it is certain that man cannot restore to his own soul the lost image of God.

Again: they who insist upon it, that the sinner has all ability to repent and turn to God and who so peremptorily and sternly rebuke the impenitent for not doing instantly what they have it in their power to do so easily, ought to set the example which these sinners should follow. Surely the renewed man has the same kind of ability, and as much ability, to be instantly perfect in holiness as the unregenerate man has to renew his own soul or to change his own heart. Let the preacher give an immediate example of this ability by becoming perfectly holy, and we will consent that he preach this doctrine.

But the strongest argument against this notion of human ability is derived from the scriptural doctrine of the necessity of regeneration by the operations of the Holy Spirit. It is a maxim in philosophy that no more causes should be admitted than are both true and sufficient to account for the effects. And it is equally clear, that if supernatural influence is necessary to repentance and other holy exercises, then man has not the ability to repent without such aid. It is manifestly a contradiction to assert that man is able to commence the work of holiness by his own exertions; and yet that he cannot do this without divine aid.

Every text, therefore, which ascribes regeneration to God, is a proof of man's inability to regenerate himself. Indeed, the very idea of a man regenerating his own heart is absurd; it is tantamount to a man's creating himself or begetting himself.

Besides, the Scriptures positively declare man's inability to turn to God without divine aid. 'No man,' says the Lord Jesus, 'can come to me except the Father which hath sent me draw him.' 'Without me ye can do nothing.' 'Christ is exalted a Prince and a Saviour, to give repentance and the remission of sins.' 'Which were born not of blood, nor of the will of the flesh, nor of the will of man, but of God.' 'So then, it is not of him that willeth, nor of him that runneth, but of God that showeth mercy.' 'Not that we are sufficient of ourselves to think anything as of ourselves'; but see 2 Corinthians 3:5: Our sufficiency is of the Lord. Everything is ascribed to the grace of God, and man, in Scripture, is continually represented as 'dead in trespasses and sins', as 'blind', 'not subject to the law of God, neither indeed can be'.

It will be objected with much confidence that if man has no ability to repent he cannot be blamed for not repenting. But this is only true if he desires to repent and is unable to do it. This, however, is not the case of the impenitent sinner. He does not wish to repent – if he did, there is no hindrance in his way. But his soul is at enmity with God, and this opposition is so deep and total that he has neither the will nor the power to convert himself to the love of God.

But will his wickedness, therefore, excuse him because it is so great that it has left no desire nor ability to change his mind? Certainly the judgment of mankind is sufficiently ascertained on this point and is entirely different from this. The wretch who is so abandoned to vice that he never feels a wish for reformation is not on this account free from blame; so far from it, that THE GREATER THE INABILITY, THE GREATER THE GUILT. The more entirely a murderer has been under the influence of malice, the more detestable his crime. The object of all judicial investigation is to ascertain first, the fact, and then the motive; and the more deliberate, unmixed, and invincible the malevolence appears to have been, the more unhesitating is the determination of every juror or judge to find him guilty. It is the common sense of all men that the more incorrigible and irreclaimable a transgressor, the more deserving is he of severe punishment.

It cannot, therefore, be a fact that men generally think that where there is any kind of inability there is no blame. The very reverse is true. And it will be found to be the universal conviction of men in all ages and countries that a totally depraved character creates an inability to do good, and that the greater this inability, the more criminal is the person who is the subject of it.

Another objection is that if impenitent men are informed that they can do nothing, they will sit still and make no manner of exertions but will wait until God's time, as it is certain all their efforts will be in vain until God works in them to will and to do. To which we reply that unregenerate men are ever disposed to pervert the truth of God so as to apologise for their own negligence; but this must not hinder us from embracing it and preaching it, though this should teach us to exercise peculiar caution when there is danger of mistake or perversion. Again, it answers no good end to set such persons to strive in their own strength and sometimes fatally misleads them; for either they become discouraged, not finding their strength to answer to the doctrine of the preacher, or they are led to think that the exertions which they make are acts of faith and repentance, and thus without feeling their dependence on God are induced to rely on their own strength.

Now, the true system is to exhort sinners to be found in the use of God's appointed means; that is, to be diligent in attendance on the word and at the throne of grace. They should also be exhorted to repent and to perform all other commanded duties, but at the same time distinctly informed that they need the grace of God to enable them rightly to perform these acts; and their efforts should be made in humble dependence on divine assistance. While they are reading or hearing, or meditating or praying, God may by his Holy Spirit work within their hearts, and while they are using the means of repentance, the grace of repentance may be bestowed upon them. We should not exhort men to perform any duty otherwise than as God has commanded it to be done; but we may exhort an unregenerate sinner to read and pray, for in attending on these means he is making the effort to believe and to repent; and while engaged in the use of these external means, God may give a believing and penitent heart.

Besides, we do not know when men cease to be unregenerate. They are often renewed before they are aware that they have experienced a saving change; and if we omit to exhort them to pray, etc., under the apprehension that they cannot perform the duty aright, we may be hindering the access of some of God's dear children to his presence. And in regard to those who pray with an unregenerate heart, we are persuaded that they do not, by making the attempt to pray, sin so egregiously as by omitting the duty altogether. If the principle on which some act in their treatment of the awakened were carried out to its legitimate consequences, they should be told neither to plough nor sow; no, nor perform the common duties of justice and morality, because they sin in all these as certainly as in their prayers.

It is thought that inculcating the doctrine of the inability of sinners has a tendency to lead them to procrastinate attention to their salvation upon the plea that it is useless for them to strive until God's grace shall be granted; and it has been admitted that this abuse may be made of the doctrine; but is there no danger of abuse on the other side? When men in love with sin are taught that they possess all necessary ability to turn to God and that they can repent at any moment by a proper use of their own powers, will they not be led to postpone attention to the concerns of the soul, under the persuasion that it is a work which they can perform at any time, even on a death-bed? Will they not run the risk of being suddenly cut off, when they are informed that in a moment or in a very short time they can give their hearts to Christ?

In fact, this is precisely the practical system of every careless sinner. He knows that he is going astray at present; but then he flatters himself that after enjoying his sinful pleasure awhile longer he will give them all up and become truly pious; and this common delusion is carried so far that the secret thought of many is that if on a death-bed they should only be favoured with the exercise of reason for a short time, they can easily make their peace with God and prepare for another world. Therefore, faithful ministers have felt it to be their duty to endeavour to dissipate this delusion and to convince men that their hopes of future repentance are fallacious; and they have found nothing more effectual to remove this dangerous self-confidence than to insist on the utter helplessness and total inability of the sinner to convert his own soul.

But now the strain of preaching which is heard from many coincides most perfectly with the erroneous persuasion which ignorance of their depravity leads natural men to cherish. We are persuaded, therefore, that much evil will result from this new method of preaching respecting man's ability. The evil will be twofold: first, multitudes will be confirmed in their false persuasion of their ability to become truly religious whenever they please; and will in this persuasion go on presumptuously in their indulgence of sin with the purpose to repent at some future day; the second evil will be that multitudes under superficial conviction, being told that they have the power to turn to God, will, upon entirely insufficient grounds, take up the opinion that they have complied with the terms of salvation because they are conscious they have exerted such power as they possess, and thus false hopes will be cherished which may never be removed. We are of opinion, therefore, that what is cried up as 'new light' in regard to the proper method of dealing with sinners is really a dangerous practical error; or, if what is inculcated can by any explanation be reconciled with truth, yet this method of exhibiting it is calculated to mislead and has all the pernicious effects of error.

The truth is that no unregenerate man can change his own heart, and yet he is accountable for all its evil and culpable for all the inability under which he labours. Man is a moral agent and free in his sinful actions; that is, they are voluntary. He does what he pleases, and he wills what he pleases; but when his heart is fully set in him to do evil, there is no principle from which a saving change can take place. He must be renewed by the Spirit of God. He must be created anew in Christ Jesus unto good works.

5

THE NEW DIVINITY TRIED[1]

In the autumn of the year 1831 it appears that the Rev. Mr
Finney delivered a sermon on making a new heart, founded
on Ezekiel 18:13. The Rev. Mr Rand, being one of his auditors,
took notes of the discourse, which he published, attended with
a series of strictures, in a periodical work of which he was the
editor. As these notes, in the judgment of Mr Finney's friends,
presented an imperfect view of his sermon, one of their number
obtained the outline used by the preacher himself, and sent the
requisite corrections to Mr Rand, who availed himself of the
aid thus afforded. The notes and strictures were afterwards
published in a pamphlet form, under the title, 'The New
Divinity Tried'. It is the review of this pamphlet by an anonymous writer, of which we propose to give a short notice.

We are not prepared to justify the course pursued by Mr
Rand in thus bringing Mr Finney before the public without his
knowledge or consent. The considerations which evince the
general impropriety of such a step are obvious and are forcibly
stated in the Review. That there may be cases in which the

[1]By Charles Hodge. Published in 1832 in review of a pamphlet entitled 'The
New Divinity Tried; or An Examination of the Rev. Mr Rand's Strictures on
a Sermon Delivered by the Rev. C. G. Finney on Making a New Heart.'

evil produced by a popular preacher constantly presenting erroneous views in his discourses is so serious that the usual etiquette of literary proceedings should be sacrificed in order to counteract its influence we do not doubt. Nor do we question that Mr Rand felt the present to be such a case.

As the publication has not only been made but noticed by the friends and advocates of Mr Finney, there can be no impropriety in our calling the attention of our readers for a few moments to the contents of this Review. It is an elaborate production, distinguished both by acuteness and research and pervaded by a tone of moderation. These are its favourable characteristics.

On the other hand, it is lamentably deficient in open, manly discussion. Instead of a clear and bold statement of the distinguishing principles of the New Divinity and a frank avowal of dissent from the Old Divinity of New England, there is an anxious, attorney-like mincing of matters; a claiming to agree with everybody and an endeavour to cast off his opponent into the position of the solitary dissentient, and overwhelm him with the authority of great names. The evidence on which this judgment is found will appear in what follows; of its correctness the reader must judge.

We gather from the Review itself (for we have in vain endeavoured to obtain in season a copy of Mr Rand's pamphlet), that the leading objections to the New Divinity are those which have been urged from various quarters against some of the doctrines of the *Christian Spectator.* Indeed, the reviewer, to show that Mr Rand was not obliged to publish the notes of an extemporaneous discourse in order to bring the opinions which it advocated before the public, tells us the doctrines of the sermon are those which have been repeatedly presented in the *Spectator* and elsewhere. We need therefore be at no loss for the distinguishing features of the New Divinity.

It starts with the assumption that morality can only be predicated of voluntary exercises; that all holiness and sin consists in acts of choice or preference. When this principle is said to be one of the radical views of the New Divinity, neither Mr Rand nor anyone else can mean to represent the opinion itself as a novelty. It is on all hands acknowledged to be centuries old. The novelty consists in its being held by men professing to be Calvinists and in its being traced out by them to very nearly the same results as those which the uniform opponents of Calvinism have derived from it. Thus Dr John Taylor, of Norwich, presents it as the grand objection to the doctrines of original sin and original righteousness; and in defending these doctrines, President Edwards laboriously argues against this opinion.

Yet it is in behalf of this radical view of the new system that the authority of Edwards, Bellamy, Witherspoon, Dwight, Griffin, Woods, as well as Augustine and Calvin, is quoted and arrayed against Mr Rand. Almost every one of these writers not only disclaims the opinion thus ascribed to them, but endeavours to refute it.

Thus President Edwards, after stating Dr Taylor's great objection to the doctrine of original sin to be that 'moral virtue in its very nature implieth the choice and consent of the moral agent', and quoting from him the declaration, 'to say that God not only endowed Adam with a capacity of being righteous, but moreover, that righteousness and true holiness were created with him, or wrought into his nature at the same time he was made, is to affirm a contradiction, or what is inconsistent with the very nature of righteousness,' goes on to remark, 'With respect to this I would observe that it consists in a notion of virtue quite inconsistent with the nature of things and the common notions of mankind.'

That it is thus inconsistent with the nature of things he proceeds to prove. In the course of this proof we find such assertions as the following: 'The act of choosing what is good is no further virtuous than it proceeds from a good principle, or virtuous disposition of mind. Which supposes that a virtuous disposition of mind may be before a virtuous act of choice, and that therefore, it is not necessary there should first be thought, reflection, and choice before there can be any virtuous disposition.' 'There is no necessity that all virtuous dispositions or affections should be the effect of choice. And so, no such supposed necessity can be a good objection against such a disposition being natural, or from a kind of instinct, implanted in the mind in its creation.'[1]

[1] Edwards, *Works*, vol. 1 (Edinburgh: Banner of Truth, 1974), p. 177.

Again, page 178, in showing Dr Taylor's inconsistency, he says, 'If Adam must *choose* to be righteous before he was righteous', then Dr Taylor's scheme involves a contradiction, etc. A mode of expression which clearly shows the position against which he argues. Again, 'Human nature must be created with some dispositions; a disposition to relish some things as good and amiable, and to be averse to other things as odious and disagreeable.' But if it had any concreated dispositions at all, they must have been right or wrong; and he then says, if man had at first a disposition to find happiness in what was good, his disposition was morally right; but 'if he had a disposition to love most those things that were inferior and less worthy, then his dispositions were vicious.' 'This notion of Adam's being created without a principle of holiness in his heart, taken with the rest of Dr Taylor's scheme, is inconsistent with' the history in the beginning of Genesis (p. 179).

It would, however, be an endless business to quote all that might be adduced to prove that Edwards did not hold the opinion which the reviewer imputes to him. There can, it would seem, be no mistake as to his meaning. These are not mere casual expressions which he afterwards retracts or contradicts. Neither is there any room for doubt as to the sense in which he uses the words 'disposition', 'principle', 'tendency', etc., because he carefully explains them and characterizes the idea he means to express by every one of the marks which the reviewer and others give, in describing what they spurn and reject under the name of 'principle,' 'holy or sinful taste'.

They mean something distinct from and prior to volitions; so does President Edwards; it is that which, in the case of Adam, to use his own word, was 'concreated'; it was a disposition to love – not love itself – a relish for spiritual objects, or adaptation of mind to take pleasure in what is excellent; it was a kind of instinct, which, *as to this point*, (*i.e.* priority as to the order of nature to acts), he says is analogous to other instincts of our nature. He even argues long to show that unless such a principle of holiness existed in man prior to all acts of choice, he never could become holy.

Again, the 'principle' or 'disposition' which they object to is one which is represented as not only prior to voluntary exercises, but determines their character, and is the cause of their being what they are. So precisely President Edwards, 'It is a foundation laid in the nature of the soul, for a new kind of exercises of the faculty of the will.'[1] This he assumes in the case of Adam to have existed prior to his choosing God, and determined his choice; what in the case of men since the fall he assumes as the cause of their universally sinning; and in those which are renewed, as the cause of their holy exercises. If President Edwards did not hold and teach the doctrine which the reviewer rejects and denounces, then no man ever did hold it or ever can express it.

The case is no less plain with regard to Dr Dwight, who also gives the two characteristic marks of the kind of disposition now in question, viz. its priority to all voluntary exercises and its being the cause of the character of those exercises. Both these ideas are expressed with a frequency, clearness, and confidence which mark this as one of his most settled opinions. Take a single specimen: 'There is a reason,' he says, 'why one being is holy and another sinful.' This reason, or 'cause of moral action is indicated by the words *principle,* affections, nature, habits, tendency, propensity'. That he does not intend by this 'cause of moral action' an act, exercise or volition, is plain; first, because he says, 'these terms indicate a cause which to us is wholly unknown'; secondly, because he expressly and repeatedly asserts the contrary:

We speak of human nature as sinful, intending *not the actual commission of sin,* but a general characteristic of man, under the influence of which he has committed sins heretofore, and is prepared and is prone to commit others. With the same meaning in our minds, we use the phrases *sinful propensities, corrupt heart, depraved mind;* and the contrary ones, holy or virtuous dispositions, moral rectitude of character, and many others of like import. When we use these kinds of phraseology, we intend that a reason exists, although undefinable and unintelligible by ourselves, why one mind will either usually or uniformly be the subject of holy volitions, and another of sinful ones. We do not intend to assert that any one, or any number of the volitions of the man whom we characterize, has been, or will be, holy or sinful, *nor do we mean to refer to actual volitions at all.*

[1] Edwards, *The Religious Affections* (London: Banner of Truth, 1961), p. 134.

Instead of this, we mean to indicate a state of mind generally existing, out of which holy volitions may in one case be fairly expected to arise, and sinful ones in another.[1]

Again:

When God created Adam, there was a period of his existence after he began to be, antecedent to that in which he exercised the first volition. Every man who believes the mind to be something besides ideas and exercises, and who does not admit the doctrine of casualty, will acknowledge that in this period *the mind of Adam was in such a state;* that it was propense to the exercise of virtuous volitions rather than sinful ones. This state of mind has been commonly styled *disposition, temper, inclination, heart,* etc. In the Scriptures it usually bears the last of these names. I shall take the liberty to call it disposition. This disposition was the *cause* whence his virtuous volitions proceeded: the reason why they were virtuous and not sinful. Of the metaphysical nature of this cause, I am ignorant . . . This cause of necessity preceded these volitions, and therefore certainly existed in that state of mind which was previous to his first volition.[2]

This idea enters essentially into his views of several important doctrines. Thus he says Adam was created holy; *i.e.,* with holy or virtuous dispositions, propense to the exercises of holy volitions. See his *Sermon on Man,* and that on *Regeneration.* Again, he makes original sin, or depravity derived from Adam, to consist in this sinful disposition – a contaminated moral nature – and argues that infants are depraved before they are 'capable of moral action'. And again, he represents regeneration to consist in 'a relish for spiritual objects, communicated to it by the power of the Holy Ghost,' and explains his meaning by a reference to 'the state of mind of Adam, in the period antecedent to that in which he exercised his first volition'.

The soul of Adam was created with a relish for spiritual objects. The soul of every man who becomes a Christian is renewed by the communication of the same relish. In Adam this disposition produced virtuous volitions. In every child of Adam, who becomes the subject of virtue, it produces the same effects.[3]

[1] *Works of Timothy Dwight* (1752–1817), p. 410–411.
[2] *Ibid.,* p. 419.
[3] *Ibid.,* p. 214.

It is impossible, we should think, for any man to force himself to believe that Dr Dwight held the doctrine that 'moral character is to be ascribed to voluntary exercises alone'. To reconcile all the declarations which we have quoted, and a multitude of others with which his works abound, is an impossibility; unless, indeed, we admit that he did not really believe what he over and over declares to have been his faith, and really adopted an opinion against which he earnestly protests and ably argues, or that he was so little master of the English language as to be unable to communicate ideas at all.

The reviewer may possibly say that he does not deny that Dr Dwight and others held to the existence of a metaphysical something as the cause of moral actions; but they did not attribute to this something itself a moral character; that it was called holy or sinful, not from its nature, but only from its effects. To this, however, the reply is obvious; Dr Dwight not only speaks of this disposition as virtuous or vicious, calls it a sinful or holy propensity, principle, nature, habit, heart; terms which in themselves, one would suppose necessarily imply that the thing to which they apply had a moral character: but he in so many words declares it to be 'the seat of moral character in rational beings'; it is that which mainly constitutes the moral character; it is what we mean, he says, when we use the phrases *corrupt heart, depraved mind*; or the contrary ones, holy disposition, moral rectitude, holiness of character. He tells us he intends by these phrases 'a state of mind' which is not a voluntary exercise, but the cause of volitions. 'This cause is what is so often mentioned in Scripture under the name of *the heart*; as when it is said "The heart is deceitful above all things, and desperately wicked".'

Will the reviewer have us believe Dr Dwight taught there was no moral character in this cause of voluntary exercises, which he supposed the Bible meant when it speaks of a desperately wicked heart? Besides, he tells us the communication of a holy disposition, or relish for spiritual objects, constitutes regeneration – is not the moral character changed in regeneration? Has that no moral character, the reception of which constitutes a man a new creature in Christ Jesus? Yet this, Dr Dwight says, is not a volition (p. 418, vol. ii.), but 'a relish for spiritual objects', 'a disposition which produces virtuous volitions'. Again: the very same objections which the reviewer and other advocates of the New Divinity urge against the idea of moral principles prior to voluntary exercises and determining their character, Dr Dwight considers and refutes.

And finally, the reviewer tells us that he and his friends agree on this point with the advocates of 'the exercise scheme', the very persons from whom Dr Dwight most earnestly dissents as to this very point, which, he says, no one but a friend of that scheme, or of the liberty of indifference, would think of maintaining. Very much to the same purpose, President Edwards says that this opinion concerning virtue (as entirely depending on choice and agency) arises from the absurd notions in vogue concerning the freedom of the will as if it consisted in the will's self-determining power.[1]

If anything could be more wonderful than the reviewer's claiming the authority of Edwards and Dwight in favour of the opinion under consideration, it would be his claiming Dr Griffin in the same behalf; a theologian who is almost an ultra on the other side. Our limits and time utterly forbid our exhibiting the evidence in every case of the lamentable misrepresentations by the reviewer of the opinions of the authors to whom he refers. In the case of Dr Griffin it is the less necessary, as his *Park Street Lectures* are so extensively known, and as he has so recently proclaimed his dissent from the New Divinity in his *Sermon on Regeneration*. We refer the readers to these works. In the former, they will find him speaking of sin as an 'attribute of our nature' derived from our original parents, 'propagated like reason or speech (neither of which are exercised at first), propagated like many other propensities, mental as well as bodily – propagated like the noxious nature of other animals' (p. 12).

As to poor Augustine and Calvin being represented as holding the radical doctrine of Pelagius, we must think it a great oversight in the reviewer. It destroys the whole verisimilitude of his story. It forces the reader to suspect the writer of irony, or to set down his statements with regard to less notorious authors, for nothing. Calvin defines original sin: 'an hereditary depravity and corruption of our natures diffused through every

---

[1] Edwards, *Works*, vol. 1, p. 178.

part of the soul [strange definition of a voluntary exercise,] which first makes us obnoxious to the wrath of God, and then produces those works which the Scriptures denominate the works of the flesh.'

Do not the 'works of the flesh' include all sinful exercises? and is there not here asserted a cause of those exercises which has itself a moral character? Infants, he says, at their birth, are liable to condemnation, 'for though they have not at that time produced the fruits of their unrighteousness, yet they have the seed enclosed in them; nay, their whole nature is a mere seed of sin, so that it cannot but be odious and abominable to God' (*Institutes*, lib. ii., cap. 1, 8). And in another place he speaks of men being sinners, '*non pravae duntaxat consuetudinis vitio sed naturae quoque pravitate* (not depraved by corruption of practice only, but by a depravity of nature also)'. Is this the language of Mr Finney?

Could any advocate of the New Divinity say with Calvin, that the 'whole nature' of man prior to the production of the works of the flesh, 'is odious and abominable to God'? If not, why quote Calvin as agreeing with them as to this very point, that all sin consists in voluntary exercises? The reviewer himself represents Calvin as teaching that original sin consists in 'inherent corruption', a mode of expression constantly employed by such writers to indicate moral depravity as distinct from actual sins, and prior to them.

With regard to Augustine, the case is still more extraordinary. The reviewer quotes from De Moor the following passage from this father: 'Sin is so far a voluntary evil that it would not be sin if it were not voluntary', in proof that he also held that 'a moral character was to be ascribed to voluntary exercises alone'. And yet De Moor immediately adds, in answer to the appeal which he says Pelagians make to this passage, that Augustine did not wish the declaration to be understood of original sin, but restricts it to actual sin, and quotes in proof from his work against Julian an explicit statement that the principle was to be so restricted. Says Augustine: 'This is properly said in reference to the proper (or actual) sin of each one, but not of the original contagion of the first sin.' With this declaration before his eyes, how could the reviewer make such a representation?

It is this reference to such men as Edwards, Bellamy, and Dwight, besides older writers, as holding opinions which they not only did not hold, but which in every form, expressly and by implication, they rejected and condemn, that we consider unfair and uncandid. We are painfully anxious to have this course on the part of the reviewer and others explained. We wish to know on what principle such statements can be reconciled with honesty. We take it for granted they must have some esoteric sense, some private meaning, some *arrière pensée,* by which to clear their consciences in this matter; but what it is we cannot divine. This has become so common and so serious an evil that we are not surprised to find some of the leading theologians of Connecticut saying, 'It is surely time that the enemies of truth were relieved of the burden of making doctrines for us, or of informing us what we ourselves believe.'[1]

It is just as easy to make Mr Rand agree with Mr Finney as it is President Edwards or Dr Dwight. All that is necessary is to take some declaration which is intended to apply to one subject and apply it to another; and adopt the principle that language is to be interpreted not according to the writer's views of the nature of the subject, but according to those of the reviewer. If he say with Dr Griffin, 'Men are voluntary and free in all their wickedness'; or ask with Dr Witherspoon, 'Does any man *commit* sin but from his own choice? or is he hindered from any duty to which he is sincerely and heartily inclined?', then he holds that 'a moral character is to be ascribed to voluntary exercises alone'. These identical passages, referring as the very language implies, to actual sins, are quoted by the reviewer in his defence of that position and as implying that a moral character can be ascribed to nothing anterior to such voluntary exercises. It matters not, it would seem, that these declarations are perfectly consistent with the belief in moral principles, dispositions, or tastes, as existing prior to all acts, or that their authors express such to be their belief. This is gross misrepresentation of a writer's real opinions, whatever be its motive, or on whatever principle its justification may be attempted.

[1] From the prospectus of a monthly religious periodical to be entitled the *Evangelical Magazine* to be published by the Connecticut Doctrinal Tract Society.

We have already admitted that there was no novelty in this fundamental principle of the New Divinity, but that the novelty consisted in its being adopted by nominal Calvinists and traced to much the same results as it ever has been by the open opposers of Calvinism. Thus Mr Finney says with great plainness, 'A nature cannot be holy. The nature of Adam at his creation was not holy. Adam was made with a nature neither sinful nor holy. When he began to act he made it his governing purpose to serve God.' This declaration is, at least, in apparent opposition to the statements so constantly occurring in theological writers – that the nature of Adam was holy at his creation; that the *nature* of man since the fall is sinful; and others of similar import.

The method which the reviewer adopts of reconciling this apparent discrepance is, as usual, entirely unsatisfactory. He tells us there are three senses in which the word nature is used as applied to moral beings; first, it indicates something which is an original and essential part of their constitution, not resulting at all from their choice or agency and necessarily found in them of whatever character and in whatever circumstances; second, it is used to designate the period prior to conversion, as when Paul says, 'we are by nature', *i.e.,* in our unregenerate state, 'the children of wrath'; and 'a third sense is an expression of the *fact* that there is something in the thing spoken of which is the ground or occasion of a certainty that it will, in all appropriate circumstances, exhibit the result or quality predicated of it'. What the preacher meant and only meant, according to the reviewer, was that 'holiness was not an essential part of Adam's constitution at his creation, so as not to result at all from his choice and agency' (pp. 9, 10).

There is in all this statement a great want of precision and accuracy. The reviewer uses the expressions '*essential* part of the constitution' and 'not resulting from choice or agency' as synonymous, though he must be aware that Mr Rand and the great body of Christians agree in saying that holiness and sin are not and cannot be essential attributes, in the sense of the reviewer. An essential attribute is an attribute which inheres in the essence of a thing and is necessary to its being. Thus the attributes of thought and feeling are essential to mind; without them it is not mind. Whoever maintained that holiness was so essential a part of man's constitution that he ceased to be man when he lost it? Whoever maintained that either sin or holiness resided in the essence of the soul, or was a physical attribute? The reviewer knows as well as anybody that this Manichean and Flacian doctrine was spurned and rejected by the whole Christian church.

But does it follow from this that holiness and sin must depend entirely on choice and agency; that there can be nothing of a moral character prior to acts of preference? Certainly not. For this simple reason, that while the Christian church has rejected the idea of the substantial nature of sin and holiness, it has with equal unanimity held the doctrine of moral propensities, dispositions, or tendencies, prior to all acts of choice. It is in this sense that they have affirmed, and it is in this sense the New Divinity denies, that 'a nature may be sinful or holy'. And this denial, as Mr Rand correctly states, is a denial of the doctrines of original righteousness and original sin. 'The doctrine of *original righteousness,* or the creation of our first parents with holy principles and dispositions, has a close connection,' says President Edwards, 'with the doctrine of original sin. Dr Taylor was sensible of this; and accordingly he strenuously opposes this doctrine in his book on original sin.' 'Dr T.'s grand objection against this doctrine, which he abundantly insists on, is this: that it is utterly inconsistent with the nature of virtue that it should be created with any person; because, if so, it must be by an act of God's absolute power without our knowledge or concurrence, and that moral virtue, in its very nature, implieth the choice and consent of the moral agent.'

This is the notion of virtue which he pronounces quite inconsistent with the nature of things. Human nature, he afterwards says, must be created with some dispositions; these concreated dispositions must be right or wrong; if man had a disposition to delight in what was good, then his dispositions were morally right (vol. ii., pp. 406, 413). This is the view which has been well nigh universal in the Christian church; this is the idea of original righteousness which the New Divinity rejects, urging the same objection to it which Dr Taylor of Norwich, and Pelagians and Socinians long before him, had done. We are not, any more than the reviewer, discussing the truth of these doctrines, but merely endeavouring to correct his very uncandid representations, as they appear to us.

It is further objected to the New Divinity, that it rejects the doctrine of original sin. This the reviewer denies. What is this doctrine? If this point be ascertained, the question whether the objection is well founded or not can be easily answered. Let us advert, then, to the definitions of the doctrine as given in the leading Protestant Confessions. In the *Helvetic Confession*, the *Confessio et Expositio brevis,* etc., cap. viii., after stating that man was at first created in the image of God, but by the fall became subject to sin, death, and various calamities, and that all who are descended from Adam are like him exposed to all these evils, it is said: 'Sin we understand to be that native corruption of man, derived or propagated from our first parents to us, by which we are immersed in evil desires, averse from good, prone to all evil,' etc. 'We therefore acknowledge *original sin* to be in all men; we acknowledge all other sins which arise from this,' etc.

The *Basel Confession* of 1532: 'We confess that man was originally created in the image of God,' etc., 'but of his own accord fell into sin, by which fall the whole human race has become corrupt and liable to condemnation. Hence our nature is vitiated,' etc.

The *Gallican Confession*, 1561: 'We believe that the whole race of Adam is infected with this contagion which we call original sin, that is a depravity which is propagated, and is not derived by imitation merely, as the Pelagians supposed, all whose errors we detest. Neither do we think it necessary to inquire how this sin can be propagated from one to another,' etc.

The ninth of the Church of England's *Articles of Religion* states: 'Original sin standeth not in the following of Adam (as the Pelagians do vainly talk), but it is the fault and corruption of every man that naturally is engendered of the offspring of Adam, whereby man is very far gone from original righteousness, and is of his own nature inclined to evil, so that the flesh lusteth always contrary to the Spirit.'

The *Belgic Confession* says: 'We believe that by the disobedience of Adam, original sin has been diffused through the whole human race, which is a corruption of the whole nature and a hereditary depravity, by which even infants in their mother's womb are polluted, and which, as a root, produces every kind of sin in man, and is so foul and execrable before God that it suffices to the condemnation of the human race.'

The *Polish Confession*, Article iii.: 'All men, Christ only excepted, are conceived and born in sin, even the most holy Virgin Mary. Original sin consists not only in the entire want of original righteousness, but also in depravity or proneness to evil, propagated from Adam to all men.'

The *Augsburg Confession*, Article ii.: 'This disease or original depravity is truly sin, condemning and bringing even now eternal death to those who are not renewed by baptism and the Holy Spirit.'

And the *Forma Concordantiae:* 'Not only actual transgressions should be acknowledged sins, but especially this hereditary disease should be regarded as a horrible sin, and indeed as the principle and head of all sins, whence, as from a root, all other transgressions grow.'

We have referred to the leading confessions of the period of the Reformation to show that they all represent as the constituent essential idea of original sin – a corrupted nature, or hereditary taint derived from Adam, propagated by ordinary generation infecting the whole race, and the source or root of all actual sin. This is not the doctrine therefore of Calvinists merely, but of the reformed churches generally, as it was of the catholic church before the Reformation. It is the doctrine, too, of the great body of Arminians. It is unnecessary to refer to individual writers after this reference to symbols which express the united testimony of thousands as to what original sin is. That the more modern Calvinists (with the exception of the advocates of the exercise scheme) unite in this view is as plain, and as generally acknowledged, as that it was held by the Reformers.

Thus President Edwards defines original sin to be 'an innate sinful depravity of heart'. He makes this depravity to consist 'in a corrupt and evil disposition' prior to all sinful exercises. He infers from the universality and certainty of the sinful conduct of men, first, 'that the natural state of the mind of man is attended with a propensity of nature to such an issue'; and secondly, that their 'nature is corrupt and depraved with a moral depravity'. He speaks of this propensity as 'a very evil, pernicious, and depraved propensity'; 'an infinitely dreadful and pernicious tendency'. He undertakes to prove that 'wickedness belongs to the very nature of men'. He devotes a chapter to the consideration of the objection that 'to suppose men born in sin without their choice, or any previous act of their own, is to suppose what is inconsistent with the nature of sin'; and another to the objection that 'the doctrine of native corruption' makes God the author of sin. Precisely the objections of the New Divinity to the common views on this subject.

Dr Dwight is not less explicit; he makes this depravity to consist in 'the corruption of that energy of the mind whence volitions flow, and which is the seat of moral character in rational beings' (vol. i., p. 488). He proves that infants are contaminated in their moral natures from the sinful conduct of 'every infant who lives long enough to be capable of moral action.' Here then is moral pollution prior to moral action.

Dr Woods also maintains the doctrine of depravity as natural, innate, and hereditary in his letters to Dr Ware. 'Sin,' according to Dr Griffin, 'belongs to the nature of man as much as reason or speech [which we do not believe; but it serves to show to what lengths the reviewer has permitted himself to go when he quotes this writer in support of the position that all sin consists in voluntary exercises] though in a sense altogether compatible with blame, and must be derived, like other universal attributes, from the original parent; propagated like reason or speech (neither of which is exercised at first); propagated like many other propensities, mental as well as bodily, which certainly are inherited from parents; propagated like the noxious nature of animals.' He afterwards argues: 'If infants receive their whole nature from their parents pure', 'if they are infected with no depravity' when born, 'it is plain that they never derived a taint of moral pollution from Adam'. 'There can be no conveyance after they are born, and his sin was in no sense the occasion of the universal depravity of the world, otherwise than merely as the first example.[1]

---

[1] *Park Street Lectures*, pp. 12–18.

We think it must be apparent that Mr Rand was perfectly justifiable in asserting that the New Divinity rejects the doctrine of original sin. What is the meaning of this assertion? Is it not that the idea commonly expressed by that term is discarded? This idea, as we have shown, is that of natural hereditary depravity, or of a corrupt moral nature derived from our first parent. Sometimes, indeed, more is included in the term, as the idea of imputation. Sometimes the phrase is explained with more and sometimes with less precision, some resolving the idea of corruption into its constituent parts – the want of original righteousness and tendency to evil – and others not; but with a uniformity almost unparalleled in theological language and opinion, has the idea of innate corruption been represented as the essential constituent idea of original sin. The very distinction between original and actual sin, so common, shows that the former expression is intended to convey the idea of something which is regarded as sin, which is not an act or voluntary exercise. The obvious sense, therefore, of Mr Rand's assertion is correct.

The reviewer's answer is a little remarkable. He tells us there are various senses in which the phrase 'original sin' has been used in orthodox confessions and standard writings, in some one of which senses Mr Finney may and doubtless does, hold to 'original sin' (p. 13). He then undertakes to enumerate eight different senses, mainly by representing as distinct, different modes of stating the same idea: 1. The first sin of the first man. 2. The first sin of the first man and woman. (Is it not clear the reviewer was anxious to swell his list?) 3. Natural or inherent corruption. 4. Want of original righteousness and inclination to evil. (Identical with the preceding.) 5. Imputation of Adam's sin, and the innate sinful depravity of the heart. 6. Something not described, but distinct from natural corruption and that came to us by the fall of Adam. (This specification is founded on the answer given in the form of examination before the communion in the Kirk of Scotland, 1591, to the question 'What things come to us by that fall?' 'Answer: Original sin, and natural corruption.' Where it is plain that by original sin is meant the guilt of Adam's first sin.) 7. The guilt of Adam's first sin, the defect of original righteousness, and concupiscence. 8. The universal sinfulness of Adam's posterity as connected with his first sin by divine constitution – *Dr Hopkins*.

No one, we presume, could imagine that Mr Rand intended to charge Mr Finney with denying the fact that Adam sinned, when he said he denied the doctrine of original sin. The first and second, therefore, of the foregoing specifications, might safely have been omitted. As to all the others, excepting the last, they amount to the simple statement of President Edwards, that the phrase is commonly used to indicate either the guilt of Adam's first sin, or inherent corruption, sometimes the one and sometimes the other, but most frequently both conjoined. The cases in which original sin is said to include both the want of original righteousness and corruption of nature are, as we before remarked, but examples of greater precision in the description of the thing intended, and not statements of an opinion diverse from that expressed by the single phrase 'innate depravity'. The absence of light is dark-ness, the absence of heat is cold, the absence of order is confusion, and so the absence of original righteousness is depravity; and this is all that President Edwards intended to express in the passage quoted by the reviewer, in which he says there is no necessity in order to account for a sinful corruption of nature, yea, a total native depravity of the heart of man, to suppose any evil quality infused, but that the absence of positive good qualities is abundantly sufficient.

The reviewer, we presume, knows very well that this is the common view adopted by those who hold the doctrine of *physical* depravity, as it is styled by the New Divinity. He knew that according to their views it is just as supposable that man might be created with an 'instinctive' disposition to love God, as with the disposition to love himself, love society, his children, or anything else; that Adam was actually thus created, that this disposition was not constitutional in the sense in which the instinct of self-love is constitutional, but super-natural, resulting from his being in communion with the Spirit of God; that the human soul, instinct with the dispositions of self-love, natural appetite, etc., and destitute of any disposition to take delight in God or holiness, is not in its normal state, but in a state of moral degradation and ruin; that they believe there is a great difference between the state of the soul when it comes

into existence since the fall, and the state of Adam's soul;
between the soul of an ordinary man and the state of the soul
of the blessed Jesus; that this difference is prior to all choice or
agency, and not dependent upon them, and it is a moral
difference, Adam being in a holy state, instinct with holy
dispositions, and men being in a state of moral corruption at
the moment of their coming into existence.

He doubtless knew also, as his own enumeration shows, that
the phrase 'original sin' has been with great unanimity
employed to designate this state of the soul prior to moral
action, and that the fact that all men actually sin, and that
their sinfulness is *somehow* connected with the sin of Adam, is
not the fact which the term has been employed (to any extent)
to express; that, on the contrary, the one fact (the universally
sinful conduct of men) has been the standing argument to
prove the other fact, viz., innate inherent depravity; and he
should, therefore, have seen that it is preposterous to assert
that the fact of all men actually sinning, and that this is *somehow* connected with Adam's sin, is the fact expressed by the
term 'original sin'. If this be so, then all Pelagians, and all
Socinians, and all opposers of the doctrine of original sin, still
hold it. For they all believe that men universally sin, and that
this is *somehow* (by example, etc.) connected with Adam's sin.

The reviewer's saying that 'men sin, and *only* sin, until
renewed by the Holy Ghost', although it may make a difference as to the extent of the wickedness of men, makes none in
the world as to the doctrine of original sin. This doctrine, as it
has been held by ninety-hundredths of the Christian church,
he rejects just as much as the Pelagians do.[1] We presume this
will be called an *ad invidiam* argument. It little concerns us
what it is called, if it is but just and proper in itself.

What is the state of the case? Here are a set of men who hold
certain opinions which they assiduously and ably advocate.
Not content with allowing them to stand on their own merits,

[1] The appeal which the reviewer makes to writings of the disciples of
Dr Emmons, is, as he must know, entirely unsatisfactory. Though as to the
verbal statement that sin consists in voluntary acts, there is an agreement,
the whole view and relations of the doctrine as held by him and them are
different, and some of the most zealous opponents of the New Divinity are
these very Emmonites to whom he is constantly appealing for protection.

they seek to cover them with the robes of authority asserting that this, and that, and almost every man distinguished for piety and talents, has held or does hold them. When currency and favour are thus sought to be obtained for these opinions by claiming in their behalf the authority of venerable names, is it not a duty to say and show that this claim is unfounded, if such be really the case? What means this arraying against Mr Rand the authority of Augustine, Calvin, Edwards, Bellamy, Dwight, etc, etc.? What is the object of this array, if it is not to crush him and sustain Mr Finney? And yet we presume there is no fact in the history of theological opinions more notorious than that as to the points in debate, they agree with Mr Rand and differ from Mr Finney.

The earliest advocate of some of the leading doctrines of the New Divinity, the author of *Views in Theology,* instead of pursuing this objectionable and unworthy course, came out with a distinct avowal of dissent from the generally received doctrines on this subject. The same honourable course was taken by Dr Cox; by the late Mr Christmas, in his sermon on *Ability;* by Mr Duffield, in his recent work on *Regeneration;* and we venture to commend it to the reviewer as the right course, and, if such a consideration need be suggested, as the most politic. We have little doubt some of the advocates of the New Divinity have suffered more in public confidence from taking the opposite course than from their opinions themselves. And we suspect the reviewer's pamphlet will be another millstone around their neck.

Another inference from the leading idea of this new system is that regeneration is man's own act, consisting in the choice of God as the portion of the soul, or in a change in the governing purpose of the life. Mr Finney's account of its nature is as follows. He says:

I will show what is intended in the command in the text (to make a new heart). It is that a man should *change the governing purpose of his life.* A man resolves to be a lawyer; then he directs all his plans and efforts to that object, and that for the time is his governing purpose. Afterwards, he may alter his determination and resolve to be a merchant. Now he directs all his efforts to *that* object, and so has changed his heart, or governing purpose.

Again:

It is apparent that the change now described, effected by the simple volition of the sinner's mind through the influence of motives, is a sufficient change, all that the Bible requires. It is all that is necessary to make a sinner a Christian.

This account of making a new heart, the reviewer undertakes to persuade the public, is the orthodox doctrine of regeneration and conversion. This he attempts by plunging at once into the depths of metaphysics, and bringing out of these plain sentences a meaning as remote from their apparent sense as ever Cabalist extracted from Hebrew letters. He begins by exhibiting the various senses in which the words *will, heart, purpose, volition,* etc., are used.

We question the accuracy of his statements with regard to the first of these terms. He is right enough in distinguishing between the restricted and extended meaning of the word, that is, between the will considered as the power of the mind to determine on its own actions, and as the power to choose or prefer. But when he infers from this latter definition that not only the natural appetites, as hunger and thirst, but also the social affections, as love of parents and children, etc., are excluded by Edwards and others who adopt it, from the will, we demur. Edwards says that 'all liking and disliking, inclining or being averse to, being pleased or displeased with', are to be referred to the will, and consequently it includes these affections.

However, it is not to our purpose to pursue this subject. The reviewer claims, as usual, to agree with Edwards, and excludes all such affections as love of parents, love of children, etc., from the will, until they involve a preference or choice; as though every exercise of these affections did not in their own nature involve such a preference as much as love, when directed to any object.

He then makes the will and heart synonymous (thus excluding love of children, etc., from the heart), and proceeds to enumerate the various classifications of volitions into *principal, ultimative, subordinate, immanent,* and *imperative,* and winds up his elucidation and defence of Mr Finney's statement by making his 'governing purpose' to be equivalent with an '*immanent volition*', or 'the controlling habitual preference of the soul'.

We cannot understand by what rule of interpretation this sense can be got out of the preacher's expressions in their connection in the sermon. Certain it is, the common usage of language would never lead any reader to imagine that, in a plain popular discourse, not in a metaphysical essay from an avowed advocate of the exercise scheme, the phrase a 'governing purpose' meant an 'immanent volition'; or 'to alter a determination' meant to change the supreme controlling affection or choice of the soul. The reviewer himself betrays his conviction that this is not the proper acceptation of the terms, for he complains of Mr Rand for making Mr Finney's governing purpose mean no more than a mere determination of the mind; and yet the preacher substitutes one of these expressions for the other, as in his own view, synonymous. He tells us 'a man alters his determination, and *so* has changed his heart or governing purpose.'

But supposing we should admit that, taken by themselves the words 'governing purpose' might bear the sense the reviewer endeavours to place on them, how is this to be reconciled with the preacher's illustrations?

A man resolves to be a lawyer; then he directs all his plans and efforts to that object, and that for the time is his governing purpose: afterwards he may alter his determination and resolve to be a merchant; now he directs all his efforts to *that* object, and so has changed his heart or governing purpose.

What is the nature of the change involved in the alteration of a man's purpose, with regard to his profession? Is it a radical change of the affections, or is it a mere determination of the mind, founded on considerations of whose nature the determination itself can give us no certain information? As one man may make the change from one motive, and another from another: one from real love to the pursuit chosen, and another from extraneous reasons; it is evident the change of purpose does not imply nor necessarily involve a change in the affections. When therefore Mr Finney tells his hearers that the change required of them is a change analogous to that which takes place when a man alters his determination as to his

profession, and that this is all that is required, all that is
necessary to make a sinner a Christian, he is justly represented
as making religion to consist in a mere determination of the
mind. Whatever may be his esoteric sense, this is the meaning
his words convey, and his hearers, we have no doubt, in nine
cases out of ten, receive.

This impression would be further confirmed by their being
told that it is a very simple change effected by a simple volition
of their own minds; and that it is a very easy change, it being
as easy to purpose right as wrong. The reviewer's defence of
this mode of representing a change, which is said in Scripture
to be effected by the mighty power of God, strikes us as
singularly weak. He tells us:

There are two different senses in which a moral act may be said to be
easy or difficult to a man; the one referring to the nature of the act
and the capacity of the agent, that is, his possession of the requisite
powers for its performance; and the other referring to the disposition
and habit of his mind in reference to the act.

Thus we may say, it is as easy to be generous as covetous,
and that it is very difficult for a covetous man to be generous.
It is admitted, then, that it is very difficult for a man to do anything contrary to the disposition or habit of his mind, and of
course it must be exceedingly difficult to make an entire and
radical change in the affections.

But Mr Finney says it is very easy to change the heart – to
alter one's purpose. Would not this prove that he supposed the
thing to be done was not the thing which the reviewer represents to be very difficult? Does it not go to confirm the
impression that he makes the change in question to consist in
a mere determination of the mind, to the exclusion of a change
in the affections?

When the ease of the work to be done is urged as a motive for
doing it, we have a right to suppose that an easy work is
intended. But the transferring the affections from one object to
another of an opposite character; to love what we have been
accustomed to hate, and to hate what we have been in the
habit of loving, is a difficult work, and therefore not included
in the mere alteration of one's purpose which is declared to be,
and in fact is, so easy.

Not only, therefore, the mode of expression employed in describing a change of heart, but the illustrations of its nature and the mode of enforcing the duty, are adapted to make precisely the impression which Mr Rand received from the sermon, that conversion, in the judgment of the preacher, is a very trifling affair, effected as easily as a change in our plans of business; and we have reason to know that this is the impression actually produced on the minds of hearers by the preachers of this class, and on the minds of the friends and advocates of the new system themselves. Such, we think, is the natural and fair impression of the popular mode of representing the subject; and we very much question whether the metaphysical explanation of it amounts to anything more.

It is one of the most singular features of the review under consideration, that although the writer seems willing to take shelter under any great name, his principal reliance is on the advocates of Emmonism. Yet it so happens that his system and theirs are exactly the poles apart. In the one, divine agency is exalted to the real exclusion of that of man; in the other, very much the reverse is the case. According, to the one, it is agreeable to the nature of sin and virtue to be created; according to the other, necessary holiness is no holiness, there cannot be even an 'instinct' for holiness, to borrow President Edwards' expression. The same expression, therefore, in the mouth of the advocate of the one theory may have a very different meaning from what it has in that of an advocate of the other; and even if the idea be the same, its whole relations and bearings are different.

It is not, then, to the followers of Dr Emmons we are to go to learn what is meant by the immanent volitions, primary choices, or governing purposes of the New Divinity. We must go where the reviewer himself in another part of his pamphlet sends us, to the advocates of the new system itself.

We find that when they come to give their philosophical explanation of the nature of regeneration, it amounts to little more than the popular representations of Mr Finney. In the *Christian Spectator*, for example, we find regeneration described as the choice of God as the chief good, under the impulse of self-love or desire of happiness. The sinner is therefore directed to consider which is adapted to make him most happy, God or the world; to place the case fairly before his mind and, by a great effort, choose right.

This, as we understand it, is a description not of an entire and radical change in the affections, but of a simple determination of the mind, founded on the single consideration of the adaptation of the object chosen to impart happiness. If I determine to seek one thing because it will make me more happy than another (and if any other consideration be admitted as determining the choice, the whole theory is gone), this is a mere decision of the mind; it neither implies nor expresses any radical change of the affections.

On the contrary, the description seems utterly inappropriate to such a change. Does any man love by a violent effort? Does he ever, by summoning his powers for the emergency, by a volition and in a moment, transfer his heart from one object to another? Was it ever known that a man deeply in love with one person, by a desperate effort and at a stroke, destroyed that affection and originated another? He may be fully convinced his passion is hopeless, that it will render him miserable, but he would stare at the metaphysician who should tell him it was as easy to love one person as another, all he had to do was to energize a new volition and choose another object, loving it in a moment with all the ardour of his first attachment

As this description of an immanent volition does not suit the process of a change in the affections in common life; as no man, by a simple act of the will and by a strenuous effort, transfers his heart from one object to another; so neither does it suit the experience of the Christian. We have no idea that the account given in the *Spectator* of the process of regeneration was drawn from the history of the writer's own exercises, nor do we believe there is a Christian in the world who can recognize in it a delineation of his experience.

So far as we have ever known or heard, the reverse of this is the case. Instead of loving by a desperate effort or by a simple volition effecting this radical change in the affections, the Christian is constrained to acknowledge he knows not how the change occurred. 'Whereas I was blind, now I see' is the amount of his knowledge. He perceives the character of God to be infinitely lovely, sin to be loathsome, the Saviour to be all he needs; but why he never saw all this before, or why it all appears so clear and cheering to him now, he cannot tell. We cannot but think that the impression made by the mode of representation adopted by the New Divinity of this important subject is eminently injurious and derogatory to true religion; that the depravity of the heart is practically represented as a very slight matter; that the change, and the whole change, necessary to constitute a man a Christian is represented as a mere determination of his own mind, analogous to a change of purpose as to his profession; that a sense of his dependence on the Spirit of God is almost entirely destroyed, and of course the Spirit himself dishonoured.

This latter evil results not merely from the manner in which the nature of the change of heart is described and the ability of the sinner to effect it is represented, nor from the fact that this dependence is kept out of view; but also from the ideas of the nature of agency and freedom of the will, which, as we have before had occasion to remark, appear to lie at the foundation of the whole system as it has been presented in the *Christian Spectator,* and from the manner in which the Spirit's influence is described by many of the most prominent advocates of the theory. These views of human agency are such that God is virtually represented as unable to control the moral exercises of his creatures; that notwithstanding all that he can do, they may yet act counter to his wishes and sin on, in despite of all the influence which he can exert over them consistently with their free agency. If this be not to emancipate the whole intelligent universe from the control of God, and destroy all the foundations of our hopes in his promises, we know not what it is.

When sinners are thus represented as depending on themselves, God having done all he can, exhausted all his power in vain for their conversion, how they can be made to feel that they are in his hands, depending on his sovereign grace, we cannot conceive. What the nature of the sinner's dependence on the Spirit of God, according to Mr Finney, is, we may learn from the following illustration. Says the reviewer:

To illustrate the different senses in which making a new heart may be ascribed to God, to the preacher, to the truth or word of God, and to the sinner himself, Mr F. supposed the case of a man arrested when about to step over a precipice by a person crying to him, *'Stop';* and said, This illustrates the use of the four kinds of expression in the Bible in reference to the conversion of a sinner, with one exception. In the case supposed, there was only the voice of the man who gave the alarm, but in conversion there is both the voice of the preacher and the voice of the Spirit; the preacher cries *'Stop',* and the Spirit cries *'Stop'* too.

On this subject, however, the advocates of the system profess not to be united. Mr Finney and others maintain that there is no mystery about the mode of the Spirit's operation; the reviewer is inclined to think there is: The one says, 'There is no direct and immediate act'; the other, if he must adopt a theory, is disposed to admit that there is an immediate influence on the mind. The reviewer lays little stress on the difference, as both views, he says, have not only been held by many Calvinistic divines, but in connection with a firm belief of the absolute necessity and universal fact of the special agency of the Holy Spirit in producing conversion.

We are aware of the diversity of representation as to this special point among orthodox writers, but we are fully persuaded that whatever may be the private opinions of those who preach as Mr Finney is represented to have done in this sermon, the impression made on their audience of the necessity of divine influence, of the sinner's dependence, is immeasurably below the standard of the divines to whom the reviewer appeals in their justification.

For an audience to be told that all the Spirit does for them is to tell them to *stop;* that, antecedently even to this influence, they *may* and *can* do all that God requires; and, what is part of the system of the *Spectator,* that subsequently or during the utmost exertion of this influence, they *may* and *can* resist and remain unconverted; is surely a representation from which those divines would have revolted, and which has a necessary tendency to subvert what the reviewer calls the fundamental doctrine of the absolute necessity of the special agency of the Holy Ghost in producing conversion.

We believe that the characteristic tendency of this mode of preaching is to keep the Holy Spirit and his influences out of view; and we fear a still more serious objection is that Christ and his cross are practically made of none effect. The constant exhortation is to make choice of God as the portion of the soul, to change the governing purpose of the life, to submit to the moral Governor of the universe. The specific act to which the sinner is urged as immediately connected with salvation, is an act which has no reference to Christ. The soul is brought immediately in contact with God; the Mediator is left out of view. We maintain that this is another gospel. It is practically another system, and a legal system of religion. We do not intend that the doctrine of the mediation of Christ is rejected, but that it is neglected: that the sinner is led to God directly; that he is not urged, under the pressure of the sense of guilt, to go to Christ for pardon, and through him to God; but the general idea of submission (not the specific idea of submission to the plan of salvation through Jesus Christ) is urged, or the making a right choice. Men are told they have hitherto chosen the world, all they have to do is to choose God; that they have had it as their purpose to gain the things of this life, and they must now change their purpose and serve God.

Our objection is not now to the doctrines actually held by these brethren, but to their characteristic method of preaching, the effects of which we have had some opportunity of learning. Conviction of sin is made of little account, Christ and his atonement are kept out of view, so that the method of salvation is not distinctly presented to the minds of the people. The tendency of this defect, as far as it extends, is fatal to religion and the souls of men.

The happiness is that sinners are not under the influence of this kind of preaching alone; their religious character is not entirely formed by this mode of representing what God requires; but when excited by the pungency and power with which these brethren frequently address the conscience, and when aroused to the necessity of doing something to secure the favour of God, they are influenced by the truth already lodged in their minds or derived from the immediate perusal of the Scriptures; and hence, under the influence of the Spirit of God, instead of following the directions of their teachers, which would lead to God in some other way than through Christ, they feel their need of the Saviour and go to him as the gospel directs. It is in this way, we have no doubt, much of the evil of this lamentable neglect of the grand doctrines of the gospel is prevented. But just so far as this defective mode of representing the mode of salvation has any influence, it is to introduce a radically new system of religion. We again remark, we do not doubt that if these preachers were asked if they meant to leave Christ thus out of view and to direct sinners to God without his intervention, they would answer, No. But we are not speaking of what they may believe on the subject, but of the manner in which, both from the press and the pulpit, the great duty of the sinner under the gospel is presented.

It was our intention to call the attention of our readers to the panacea which the reviewer has discovered (or rather undertaken to recommend) for the cure of all doctrinal differences. But our notice of his pamphlet has already been protracted to three times the length we originally intended, and we therefore have time to say but little on the subject. His prescription is to draw a distinction between the doctrines of religion and the philosophy of the doctrines, which, he justly remarks, is an important distinction, which it is of the highest moment should be understood and properly applied.

The doctrines of religion are the simple facts of Christianity. The philosophy of the doctrines is the mode adopted of stating and illustrating those facts in their relations to each other, to the human mind, to the whole character and government of God. From this distinction results the following most important practical principle of Christian fellowship and of theological discussion. *All who teach the leading facts or doctrines of Christianity are orthodox, though they differ greatly in their philosophy of those doctrines.*

The reviewer gives these passages in *italics* to note his sense of their importance. We are constrained, however, to think that although they contain a very obvious and familiar truth, they are of little consequence for his purpose. The truth they contain is that there is a distinction between the essentials and non-essentials of a doctrine. We care little about his calling doctrines *facts*. But how is this to aid anyone in deciding on what is heresy and what is not?

The reviewer chooses to say that the fact which all the orthodox must receive respecting sin is that it exists, and that it is a dreadful evil. But how its existence is accounted for is philosophising about it. But if I assert it exists by the immediate efficient agency of God, do not I assert a fact as much as when I say it exists? Or, if I say it exists because God cannot control a moral agent, do I not assert a fact? Again, the orthodox fact about man's natural character is that in consequence of the fall of Adam, men sin, and only sin, until renewed by the Holy Spirit; the philosophy is in accounting for it. But is it not obvious that when the church declares that the universality of actual sin is to be accounted for by a sinful corruption of nature, she means to declare that the Scriptures account for one fact by another? When it is said we are condemned for the sin of Adam, is not a fact again asserted? We think, therefore, the reviewer's distinction between facts and the philosophy of them, perfectly futile.

The use he would make of it is still worse. 'All who teach the leading facts of Christianity are orthodox.' But what are these facts? Let the reviewer state them and then he is orthodox; let Edwards state them and he is a heretic. The substance of the fact regarding man's character is that *somehow,* in consequence of the fall, he sins, and only sins, etc. Is not this a bald begging of the question? That *somehow* may be the very thing which the Scriptures clearly reveal, and reveal as a *fact.*

Again: it is a fact that we are saved by the death of Christ – this we have stated as the *doctrine* of atonement. Yet, as so stated, there is not a Socinian in the world who is not orthodox on this point. This fact is not all that the Scriptures teach, nor that it is necessary to believe. The death of Christ saves us, and saves us as a sacrifice. That it operates in this mode, and not in another, is as much a matter of fact as that it operates at all.

Again; it is a fact that men are renewed and sanctified by the Holy Spirit. But here again, all Arminians, Pelagians, and even Socinians, are orthodox; for they admit the fact, as much as the reviewer does (allowing them to make the Spirit of God mean 'divine energy'). They and he might philosophise rather differently about it; but the fact they all admit. How the Spirit does the work is a matter of explanation; some say, by an immediate influence on the mind; others, by moral suasion, or presenting motives; others, by having revealed the truth in the

Scriptures; so that the result may be ascribed either to the truth as the immediate cause or to its revealer, the Spirit.

And so, finally, though illustrations might be multiplied without end, the Scriptures are a divine revelation; here is a fact in which it would seem all might acquiesce and be orthodox, without asking how God reveals truth to man. Yet this fact the neologists of Germany hold and proclaim. It is true, when they come to the *philosophy* of the fact, they tell us they mean that the Scriptures are a providential revelation from God in the same sense as the *Dialogues* of Plato.

It is too obvious to need comment that the reviewer's position is all that any man in the world who professes any form of Christianity needs to prove his orthodoxy. Let him have the stating of scriptural facts, and he will do as the reviewer in many cases has done, state them so generally that Arminians, Pelagians, and Socinians, as well as Calvinists, can adopt them, and, according to this standard, be orthodox.

We have spoken of this anonymous pamphlet with sincerity: that is, as we really felt. We view it as highly objectionable in the respect to which we have principally referred. Whoever the writer may be, we think he has more reason to lament having given occasion to the Christian public to ask how his statements can be reconciled with notorious facts, than to be offended at the strictures to which it may, and ought to, subject him.

6

ON REVIVALS
OF RELIGION[1]

We congratulate the friends of truth and order on the appearance of these publications. We have never had any doubt what would be the decision of the public mind respecting the New Divinity and New Measures system of our day, if its distinctive features could be brought out to the light and exposed to general observation. History warrants us in cherishing this our confidence. The truth is, that this system contains but little that is *new*. It is mainly, if not entirely, composed of exploded errors and condemned heresies. The church has already once and again pronounced judgment upon it; and we have no doubt therefore, that the same sentence of condemnation will be repeated by the Presbyterian church of the present day, whenever the case is fairly presented for decision.

The chief reason why the condemnation of this system has at all lingered, is, that its true character has not been generally known. Its advocates, when charged with teaching certain

---

[1]By Albert B. Dod. Published in 1835 in review of *Lectures on Revivals of Religion* and *Sermons on Various Subjects* by the Rev. C. G. Finney.

obnoxious doctrines, and, in their religious meetings, violating the sobrieties of good sense as well as of Christian order, have evaded or denied the charge, and complained piteously of misrepresentation. Much has been done to blind the minds of those who were not able to bear the things they had to say, to the undisguised character of the doctrines they have taught in the lecture room and the chapel.

We rejoice, therefore, in the publication of Mr Finney's sermons and lectures. The public can now learn what the new system is from the exposition of one of its chief promoters. He has stated his own case, and out of his own mouth may he now be justified or condemned.

The lectures on revivals were delivered by Mr Finney to his congregation in Chatham-street chapel last winter. They were first published weekly in the columns of the *New York Evangelist*, from reports furnished by the editor of that paper. They were subsequently collected, and after having been submitted to the author for correction, published in a volume. The work, we perceive, has already reached a fifth edition. Much diligence is employed in efforts to give it an extended circulation. It is recommended as a suitable book for Sabbath-school libraries; and no pains are spared to spread it abroad through the length and breadth of the land. Its friends evidently have a strong persuasion of its extraordinary merits. Their zeal for its circulation proves that they consider it a fair and able exposition of the new system.

The sermons appear to be a monthly publication. We have obtained seven of them, which are all, we presume, that have yet been published. They discuss the several topics: 'Sinners bound to change their own hearts'; 'How to change your heart'; 'Traditions of the Elders'; 'Total Depravity'; 'Why sinners hate God'; and 'God cannot please sinners'. These sermons, with the lectures on revivals, give a pretty full exhibition of Mr Finney's peculiar views. If we may judge from the tiresome degree of repetition in these productions, the perpetual recurrence of the same ideas, phrases, and illustrations, we should suppose that he can have nothing new to say; nothing, at all events, that would materially add to or modify what he has already said. We may consider ourselves fairly in possession of his system.

To the interpretation of that system we shall now proceed, having it less for our object to refute, than merely to exhibit its peculiarities. We shall endeavour to gather up the plain, obvious meaning of Mr Finney's statements, taking it for granted that there is no hidden, esoteric sense attached to them.

Of the literary merit of these productions we have but little to say. The reporter deprecates, or rather defies all criticism upon their *style,* affirming that the critic 'will undoubtedly lose his labour'. No doubt he will, so far as the amendment of the author is concerned. But the reformation of an offending author is not the sole object of criticism. The reporter himself (the Rev. Mr Leavitt) says of Mr Finney's language, that it is 'colloquial and Saxon'. Words are but relative in their meaning. What kind of 'colloquies' the Rev. Mr Leavitt may have been used to, we do not pretend to know; but for ourselves we must say, that we desire never to have a part, either as speakers or hearers, in any colloquy where such language is current, as Mr Finney often permits himself to employ.

If his other epithet, Saxon, means simply, not English, we have no objection to it. For, surely, it has not often fallen to our lot to read a book, in which the proprieties of grammar as well as the decencies of taste were so often and so needlessly violated; and in which so much that may not inappropriately be termed *slang* was introduced. But we have higher objects before us than detailed criticism upon Mr Finney's style. We should not have made any allusion to it, but that we deemed it worth a passing notice, as forming part and parcel of the coarse, radical spirit of the whole system.

We proceed to examine, in the first place, the *doctrines* of this new system. Mr Finney does not pretend to teach a slightly modified form of old doctrine. He is far from claiming substantial agreement with the wise and good among the orthodox of the past and present generation. On the contrary, there is a very peculiar self-isolation about him. Through all his writings there is found an ill-concealed claim to be considered as one called and anointed of God, to do a singular and great work. There is scarcely a recognition of any fellow-labourers in the same field with him. One might suppose indeed, that he considered himself the residuary legatee of all the prophetic and apostolical authority that has ever been in the world, so arrogantly does he assume all knowledge to himself, so loftily does he arraign and rebuke all other ministers of the gospel. He stands alone in the midst of abounding degeneracy, the only one who has not bowed the knee to Baal. The whole world is wrong, and he proposes to set them right. Ministers and professors of religion have hitherto been ignorant what truths should be taught to promote revivals of religion, and he offers to impart to them infallible information.

It is true, in his preface, he disclaims all pretensions to infallibility, but in his lectures, he more than once substantially assumes it. He tells his hearers, in relation to promoting revivals, 'If you will go on to do *as I say,* the results will be *just as certain* as they are when the farmer breaks up a fallow field, and mellows it, and sows his grain.' He speaks repeatedly of the '*endless train of fooleries*', the '*absurdities*', the '*nonsense*', which, up to his time, have been taught both in private and from the pulpit. He declares, 'there is only *here and there a minister* who knows how to probe the church,' etc. 'This is a point where *almost all ministers* fail.' 'When *I* entered the ministry so much had been said about the doctrine of election and sovereignty, that I found it was the *universal* hiding place, both of sinners and the church, that they could not do anything, or could not obey the gospel. And *wherever I went,* I found it necessary to demolish these refuges of lies.' 'There is and has been *for ages,* a striking defect in exhibiting this most important subject.' 'For *many centuries* but little of the real gospel has been preached.' 'The truth is, that very little of the gospel has come out upon the world, *for these hundreds of years,* without being clogged and obscured by false theology.'

What can be more evident than that Mr Finney considers himself a great reformer? He comes forth with the avowed purpose of clearing away the errors by which the true gospel has been so overlaid as to destroy its efficiency. He comes to declare new truths, as well as to unfold new methods of presenting them to the mind.

The first of these new doctrines to which we call the attention of our readers, has relation to the *government* of God. It will be remembered that a few years since, Dr Taylor, with some other divines, publicly announced and defended the proposition that

God could not prevent the introduction of sin in a moral system. At least he was very generally, if not universally, understood to teach this proposition. And it is strange, if not actually unprecedented, that a writer of an honest and sound mind, understanding the language he employs, and having it for his serious purpose to convey to his readers certain important information, should be misunderstood as to the main purport of his message by those best qualified, from education and otherwise, to comprehend it.

But Dr Taylor did complain that he was misunderstood. He insists that he did not intend to teach that God could not prevent the existence of moral evil, but only that it is impossible to prove that he could prevent it. His object was to unsettle belief in all existing theories upon this subject, and then to substitute this negative one in their place; in other words, to inculcate absolute scepticism upon this point.

This is the ground now occupied by the New Haven divines. We fear, therefore, that they will be alarmed by the position which Mr Finney has taken. He has evidently neglected, since his return from his foreign tour, to post up his knowledge. He has not acquainted himself with the improvements made during his absence. He teaches, without any qualification, the doctrine which the New Haven school was at first understood to teach. He complains that sinners 'take it for granted that the two governments which God exercises over the universe, moral and providential, *might* have been so administered as to have produced universal holiness throughout the universe'. This, he says, is a '*gratuitous* and *wicked* assumption'. It is *wicked,* then, to believe that God could have produced universal holiness.

Mr Finney further adds, 'There is no reason to doubt that God so administers his providential government, as to produce upon the whole, the highest and most salutary *practicable* influence in favour of holiness.' This sentiment, it is true, is susceptible of a correct interpretation through the ambiguity of the word *practicable*. But another quotation will make it evident that he means this word to include nothing more than the resisting power of the human will. 'The sanctions of his law are absolutely *infinite:* in them he has embodied and held forth the highest possible motives to obedience.' 'It is vain to talk of his omnipotence preventing sin: if *infinite* motives will not prevent it, it cannot be prevented under a moral government; and to maintain the contrary is absurd and a contradiction.' A more explicit and confident statement of this doctrine could hardly be given. It is *absurd* and *contradictory* to maintain that God could have prevented the introduction of sin into our world.

The only semblance of an argument which Mr Finney urges in support of this opinion is 'that mind must be governed by *moral* power, while matter is governed by *physical* power'.

If to govern mind were the same as to govern matter – if to sway the intellectual world were accomplished by the same power that sways the physical universe, then indeed it would be just from the physical omnipotence of God, and from the existence of sin, to infer that God prefers its existence to holiness in its stead.

Again he says, 'To maintain that the *physical* omnipotence of God can prevent sin is to talk nonsense.' We see not the least ground for this distinction between the moral and physical power of God; nor do we believe that Mr Finney himself can attach any definite meaning to his favourite phrase, 'physical omnipotence'. By the omnipotence of God we understand a power to do anything without those hindrances and restrictions by which we and all created beings are beset. It must be the same power which sways the intellectual and physical universe unless we are to make as many different species of power as there are objects upon which it may be exerted.

This distinction, however, were it well-founded, would avail Mr Finney nothing in defence of his position. The power of God, by whatever name called, can be limited in its exercise only by the laws which he has himself immutably fixed. The power of the Creator was without any limit; the power of the Governor labours under no other restrictions than the ordinances of the Creator have imposed upon it.

It is often said that God cannot achieve impossibilities, such as to make a body exist in several places at the same time. All such limitations of the divine power are found in those relations and properties of things which he has himself established. A body cannot be made to exist in several places at once, for if it could it would no longer be a body.

So in the nature of man we may trace certain properties and laws which lay a similar restriction, if so it may be called, upon the exercise of the divine power. God cannot make a sinner happy while he continues a sinner, for he has already so made man that his happiness must come to him as the consequence of the right action of his powers, and he would cease to be man if this law of his nature were altered.

Now is there any similar restriction in the nature of moral agency? Does it enter into our notion of a moral agent, and go to make up the definition of one, that he cannot be subjected to any other influence than that of motive? Suppose that God should, in some inscrutable way, so act upon his will as to dispose it to yield to the influence of motive, would such action make him cease to be a moral agent? If not, we have no right to deny the power of God to effect it.

It is impossible to conceive that his power can be restrained by anything exterior to himself. The only bounds beyond which it cannot pass must be those that have been established by his own nature, or his previous acts. Unless he has so made moral agents that it is a contradiction in terms to assert that they can be influenced in any other way than by motive, it is in the highest degree unwarrantable and presumptuous to deny that God can act upon them by other means. But a moral agent, while possessed of the necessary faculties, and not forced to act contrary to his will, or to will contrary to his prevailing inclinations and desires, remains a moral agent still. Would, then, the operation of any other influence than that of motive upon him, destroy his liberty of action or his freedom of will? Certainly not. And as certainly, no man can deny that God can influence men as he pleases without thereby denying his omnipotence. A more groundless, gratuitous assumption could not well be found than Mr Finney has made in asserting that it is impossible for God to affect his moral subjects in any other way than by motive.

Let it be observed that we use the word *motive,* as Mr Finney himself has evidently used it, to denote simply the objective considerations presented to the mind as they are in themselves, without taking into account the state of the mind in relation to those considerations. This is the only sense of the word in which it can be at all maintained that '*infinite* motives' have been urged upon man for the prevention of sin and the promotion of holy obedience.

If the state of the mind, which always determines the apparent qualities of the object, be included, as it generally is, in the term motive, then it is not true that the mind could resist 'infinite motives'. In this sense of the word, it is self-evident that the will must always be determined by the strongest motive. An 'infinite motive', by which can be meant only a motive infinitely strong, or stronger than any other we can conceive of, would of course prevail and carry the will with it. Then it would be just to infer, from infinite motives having been presented to bear man onward in the paths of holy obedience, that God had done all that he could to prevent sin. And then too it would be impossible that any sin could exist, or that sin could ever have entered our world.

But granting what we have shown to be the gratuitous assumption that God cannot influence men in any other way than by the objective presentation of truth to the mind, Mr Finney has given us no reasons for adopting the opinion that 'he has done all that the nature of the case admitted to prevent the existence of sin', while we can see many reasons which forbid us to receive it.

The state of the question, as we are now about to put it, in conformity with Mr Finney's representations, does indeed involve the *three* gratuitous assumptions: 1. That God could not have made man a moral agent and yet give him a greater degree of susceptibility of impression from the truth than he now possesses; 2. That, man being as he is, God could not have devised any external considerations to affect him, in addition to those which are actually placed before his mind; and 3. That, man and the truth both being as they are, God cannot reach and move the mind of man in any other way than by the truth.

These are by no means axioms, and Mr Finney would be sadly perplexed in the attempt to prove any one of them. But, for the sake of showing that even with these bold and barefaced assumptions he cannot maintain his position, we will admit them all. Man could not have been a moral agent had he been more yielding to the truth than he now is. 'Infinite motives' to obedience have been provided; by which, as we have already shown, can be meant only that *all the truth* which could possibly affect the human mind has been revealed to it. And thirdly, man cannot be moved but by the truth.

The 'nature of the case' being supposed to demand all these admissions, does it still follow that God has done all that he could to prevent the existence of sin? Mr Finney himself shall answer this question. His theory of the nature of divine influence is, that the Spirit 'gets and keeps the attention of the mind' – 'he pours the expostulation (of the preacher) home' – he keeps the truth, which would else have been suffered to slip away, 'in warm contact with the mind'. Here is of course the admission, and we are glad he is willing to concede so much power to his Maker, that God can gain the attention of the mind, and keep before it and in contact with it, any or all of the 'infinite motives' which he has provided to deter it from sin. Connect this admission with another class of passages, in which Mr Finney teaches that 'When an object is before the mind, the corresponding emotion will rise', and who does not see in the resorting consequence a glaring inconsistency with the doctrine that God has done all that he can to prevent the existence of sin?

To make this more plain, we will take the case of Adam's transgression, of which Mr Finney has, out of its connection with the subject we are now discussing, given us the rationale. He says:

Adam was perfectly holy, but not infinitely so. As his preference for God was not infinitely strong, it was possible that it might be changed, and we have the melancholy fact written in characters that cannot be misunderstood, on every side of us, that an occasion occurred on which he actually changed it. Satan, in the person of the serpent, presented a temptation of a very peculiar character. It was addressed to the constitutional appetites of both soul and body; to the appetite for food in the body, and for knowledge in the mind. These appetites were constitutional; they were not in themselves sinful, but their unlawful indulgence was sin.

The temptation in this case was the motive addressed to Adam's constitutional appetites. The reason why this motive prevailed was that it was kept before the mind to the exclusion of adverse considerations. The emotions of desire towards the

forbidden fruit were not unlawful until they had become
sufficiently strong to lead Adam to violate the command of his
Maker. If, then, just at the point of unlawfulness, the attention
of Adam's mind had been diverted from the forbidden fruit to
the consideration of God's excellency and his command, 'the
corresponding emotion' would have arisen, and he would not
have sinned. But the Spirit has power to 'get and keep the
attention of the mind'. Certainly then he could have directed
the attention of Adam's mind to those known truths, though at
the moment unthought of, which would have excited the
'corresponding emotions' of reverence for God, and preserved
him thus in holy obedience.

But though Mr Finney holds forth the views here given of
the Spirit's agency in presenting truth to the mind, it would
evidently be a great relief to his theological scheme if he were
fairly rid of the doctrine of divine influence. The influence of
the Holy Spirit comes in only by the way, if we may so speak,
in his account of the sinner's regeneration and conversion. We
will cast away this doctrine, therefore – we will grant him even
more than he *dares* to ask – and still his position is untenable,
that God has done all that he can to prevent the existence of
sin.

Before he can demand our assent to this proposition, he must
prove, in the case already presented, that God could not have
prevented the entrance of Satan into the garden. Admitting
that the volitions of Satan were beyond the control of his
Maker, he must investigate the relation of spirit to space, and
prove that it was impossible for God to have erected physical
barriers over which this mighty fiend could not have passed.
He must show that it was impossible for God so to have
arranged merely providential circumstances, that our first
parents should have been kept out of the way of the tempter, or
that the force of the temptation should have been at all diminished. Until he has proved all this, and then proved that his
three assumptions which we have pointed out are true, we
must prefer the 'absurdity' and 'nonsense' of rejecting his
doctrine, to the wisdom of receiving it.

The argument thus far has been a direct one, and we should
not fear to leave it as it now stands. But we cannot refrain from
adverting to some of the consequences of the doctrine we have

been examining. If God has done all that he can to prevent the existence of sin, and has not succeeded in his efforts, then must he have been disappointed. If he cannot control at pleasure the subjects of his moral kingdom, then must he be continually and unavoidably subject to grief from the failure of his plans. Instead of working all things according to his good pleasure, he can do only what the nature of the case will permit – that is, what his creatures will allow him to do. He in whose hands are the hearts of all men, and who turns them as the rivers of waters are turned, is thus made a petitioner at the hands of his subjects for permission to execute his plans and purposes.

Accordingly, we find Mr Finney using such language as this: 'God has found it *necessary to take advantage* of the excitability there is in mankind, to produce powerful excitements among them before he *can* lead them to obey.' He speaks of a 'state of things, in which it is *impossible for God* or man to promote religion but by powerful excitements'. And of course there may be states of things in which neither by excitements nor by any other means will God be able to effect the results he desires. Then may we rightly teach, as some at least of our modern reformers have taught, that God, thwarted in his wishes and plans by the obstinacy of the human will, is literally grieved by the perverse conduct of men; and sinners may properly be exhorted as they have been to forsake their sins from compassion for their suffering Maker!

It is a sufficient condemnation of any doctrine that it leads by an immediate and direct inference to so appalling a result as this. We know of nothing which ought more deeply to pain and shock the pious mind. If the perverseness of man has been able in one instance to prevent God from accomplishing what he preferred, then may it in any instance obstruct the working of his preferences.

Where, then, is the infinite and immutable blessedness of the Deity? We cannot contemplate this doctrine, thus carried out into its lawful consequences, without unspeakable horror and dismay. The blessedness of the Deity! What pious mind has not been accustomed to find in it the chief source of its own joy? Who does not habitually turn from the disquieting troubles and scenes of misery that distress him here, to 'drink of the river of God's pleasures'? Who can bear the thought that the

infinitely holy and benevolent God should be less than
infinitely happy? We see not how any heart that loves God can
feel happy itself, unless it believes him to be, as he deserves to
be, infinitely blessed. Nor can we find any security for the
felicity of the creature but in the perfect and unchangeable
felicity of the Creator. If God, therefore, be as this doctrine
represents him, unable to produce states of things which he
prefers, and if his benevolent feelings are thus continually
exposed to grief from obstructions to their operation, the voice
of wailing and despair should break forth from all his moral
subjects. We can see, indeed, but little to decide our choice
between such a God as this and no God.

Another consequence of this doctrine is that God cannot
confirm angels and saints in holiness. If he could not prevent
the introduction of sin into our world, we see not upon what
principles we are entitled to affirm that he can prevent its
re-introduction into heaven. We see not how he can at any time
hinder the standard of rebellion from being yet once more
uplifted among the bright and joyous throng that now cast
their crowns at his feet.

We are perfectly aware of the answer which Mr Finney will
make to this objection. He will contend that the additional
motives furnished by the introduction of sin, such as the visible
and dreadful punishment of the sinner, and the display of the
divine character thereby afforded, are sufficient to enable God
by the use of them, together with the means and appliances
previously existing, to confirm holy beings in holiness.

Now, independently of other insuperable objections to this as
a sufficient reply, how does it consist with that other part of the
scheme, that 'infinite motives' had been already arrayed
against the introduction of sin? If these motives were infinite,
then no addition could possibly be made to them. We leave Mr
Finney to reconcile this contradiction, or to admit that we have
no reason to expect that the gates of heaven will be barred
against sin.

This doctrine also takes away from the sinner all just ground
for the dread of everlasting punishment. Its advocates, we
know, have contended that it is the only position from which
Universalism can be effectively assailed. But if, when man was
tempted to sin by so insignificant a motive as the forbidden

fruit while 'infinite motives' were drawing him back, God could not prevent him from yielding, it must surely be impossible for him to prevent the sinner in the other world from obeying the impulse of the infinite motives which, more strongly there than here, will urge him to holiness.

The sinner, then, may dismiss his apprehensions of the everlasting experience of the miseries of a wicked heart. If God could not prevent Adam from sinning, under the influence of a small motive, there is no reason to fear that he can prevent any inhabitant of hell from becoming holy, under the influence of infinite motives.

We have dwelt upon this subject at greater length than was at first intended. Our excuse is that the question at issue is a very serious and important one; and the views of it presented by Mr Finney seem to be so dishonouring to the character of God, as well as subversive of some of the most important truths of religion, that they should be carefully examined. Had our object been simply to criticise, Mr Finney might have been more briefly despatched. There is in his pages a surpassingly rich treasure of contradictions, which might at every turn have furnished us with an *argumentum ad hominem,* had we been disposed to avail ourselves of it. But we have felt that the matter in hand was of too grave and weighty an import to be thus managed.

We invite the attention of our readers, in the next place, to Mr Finney's views of the *nature of sin, depravity* and *regeneration.* He contends that all sin consists in acts, and assures us that those who teach otherwise are guilty of 'tempting the Holy Ghost', and of a 'stupid, not to say wilful perversion of the Word of God'. He deems it absurd beyond expression to suppose that there can be a sinful disposition prior to sinful acts; nay, he solemnly affirms that 'millions upon millions have gone down to hell' in consequence of the doctrine of what he is pleased to call 'physical depravity' having been so extensively taught.

He seldom approaches this subject without breaking out in some such paroxysm as the following: 'O the darkness and confusion, and utter nonsense of that view of depravity which exhibits it as something lying back, and the cause of all actual transgression!' Our readers will soon be able to judge for themselves whether Mr Finney has cleared away any of the darkness which rests upon this subject.

In the prosecution of our inquiries into the nature of sin, two questions very naturally present themselves for decision; first, whether there can exist anything like what has been called *disposition,* distinct from mental acts; and secondly, whether, if such an attribute of mind can and does exist, it may be said to possess any moral character. Mr Finney, with much convulsive violence of language, continually denies that there can be any such thing as a mental disposition, in the sense in which we have used the word. He employs the term, it is true, but he says he means by it a mental act; and that it is nonsensical to attach to it any other meaning.

His arguments against the possibility of the existence of mental dispositions, apart from mental acts, may be briefly despatched; for we do not reckon among the arguments his violent outcries of darkness, confusion, absurdity, nonsense, doctrine of devils, etc., nor his assertions that God himself cannot lead the sinner to repentance without first dispossessing him of the erroneous notion that his nature as well as his conduct needs to be changed.

All the arguments on the point now before us, that lie scattered through his many pages, may be reduced to two. It is impossible, he contends, to *conceive* of the existence of a disposition of mind; and again, if there be a disposition distinct from the faculties and acts of the mind, it must form a part of the substance of the mind, and hence follow physical depravity and physical regeneration with all their horrid train of evils.

When he asserts the impossibility of *conceiving* of a disposition of mind, we suppose he means that it is impossible to frame an image of it, or form a picture in which this disposition shall stand visible to the mind's eye. It is only in this sense that his assertion is true. It is true that we cannot form such a *conception* of a mental disposition, but we will not insult the common sense of our readers by attempting to prove that this is no argument against its existence.

The other argument on which Mr Finney relies to prove the non-existence of any disposition of mind, is that if there be any such thing it must form a part of the substance of the mind, it must be incorporated with the very substance of our being, with many other phrases of like import. Hence he charges those who teach that there are such dispositions, and that they possess a moral character, with teaching physical depravity, and representing 'God as an infinite tyrant'. He avers, in a great variety of forms, that their preaching has a direct and legitimate tendency to lull the sinner in his security, to make men of sense turn away in disgust from such absurd exhibitions of the gospel, and to people hell with inhabitants.

These are grave charges; and as, if substantiated, they would affect the fair fame and destroy the usefulness of nine-tenths of the ministers of the church to which Mr Finney belongs, so, if groundless, Mr Finney must be regarded as a slanderer of his brethren, guilty and odious in proportion to the enormity of the unsustained charges against them.

In one respect at least Mr Finney is guilty of bringing false accusations against his brethren. He continually represents them as holding and teaching all his own inferences from their doctrines. This is more than uncharitable; it is calumnious. He has a perfect right to develop the absurdities of what he calls physical depravity and present them as so many reasons for rejecting any doctrine which can be proved to result in such consequences; but he has no right to endeavour to cast the reproach of teaching these inferred absurdities upon men who have uniformly, and if more decently, yet not less strongly than himself, disclaimed them.

But we contend that these absurdities do not lawfully flow from the doctrine that the mind has tastes and dispositions distinct from its faculties and acts. It is easy to show, in contradiction to Mr Finney, that it may possess such attributes, which nevertheless will not form any part of the substance of the mind. Nay, we can make Mr Finney himself prove it. In one of his sermons, where he has lost sight for a brief space of physical depravity, he speaks on this wise:

Love, when existing in the form of *volition,* is a simple preference of the mind for God and the things of religion to everything else. This preference may and often does exist in the mind, so entirely separate from what is termed emotion or feeling, that we may be *entirely insensible to its existence.* But although its existence may not be a matter of *consciousness* by being felt, yet its influence over our conduct will be such, as that the fact of its existence will in this way be made manifest.

Here is a state of mind recognised which Mr Finney, with an utter confusion of the proprieties of language, chooses to call 'love existing in the form of volition', but which we call a 'disposition'. But by whatever name or phrase it may be designated, it is not a faculty of the mind; it is not the object of consciousness, has no sensible existence, and cannot therefore in any proper sense be called an act of the mind, nor yet does it form any part of the substance of the mind.

It is not without an object (what it is will be presently seen) that Mr Finney makes so queer a use of the term *volition* in the above quotation; but the insertion of this word does not alter the bearing of the passage upon the point now in question. His subsequent qualifications show that he is describing something different from an act of the mind: and the single question now before us is, whether there can be in the mind any disposition distinct from its acts, and comprising within it tendencies and influences towards a certain course of action, which yet does not form a part of the substance of the mind. The passage quoted is clear and explicit, as far as this question is concerned.

Let us hope, then, that we shall hear no more from Mr Finney on the subject of *physical* depravity; or at least that when he next chooses to harangue his people on this favourite topic, he will have the candour, the plain, homespun honesty, to tell them that there is not a single minister in the Presbyterian church who teaches the odious doctrine, or anything that legitimately leads to it, but that he has brought this man of straw before them to show them how quickly he can demolish it. We have a great aversion to this Nero-like way of tying up Christians in the skins of wild beasts that the dogs may devour them.

But it will be said that the dispositions which have been shown to exist in the mind are formed by the mind itself, in the voluntary exercise of its powers; such would not be the case with a disposition existing prior to all action. This is true, but it is not of the least moment in settling the question of the *physical* character of the disposition. If a disposition may be produced by the mind itself, which so far from being itself an act makes its existence known only by its *influence,* and which yet is not incorporated with the substance of our being nor entitled to the epithet *physical,* then such a disposition might inhere in the mind prior to all mental action, without possessing a physical character. There is not the least relevancy or force, therefore, in the argument commonly and chiefly relied upon, that if there be such an antecedent disposition, it must be physical. The only argument that can be urged here is that experience shows us what is the formative law of our dispositions, that these are always generated by the mind's own action; and it is absurd therefore to suppose that any disposition can exist in the mind anterior to all action.

The conclusion to which this argument arrives is wider than the premises. Its fallacy, and it is an obvious one, lies in extending a law, generalised from observation upon the mind's action, to a case in which by hypothesis the mind has never yet acted, and to which, of course, the law can have no application.

There is here a fallacy of the same nature as would be involved in a process of reasoning like this: All our observation proves to us that no tree can be produced but by calling into action the germinative power of its seed. The seed must be planted in a fitting soil, and be subjected to a certain class of influences; it must decay and then send forth the tender shrub, which, in its turn, must be sustained by appropriate nourishment; and years must elapse before the tree will lift its tall head to the skies. No man has ever seen a tree produced by any other means, and the nature of things is such that a tree cannot be produced in any other way. *Therefore,* no tree could have originally come into being but through the same process. The error in reasoning is here apparent, nor is it less so in the case which this was intended to illustrate.

Here again it will be urged, and at first sight the objection may seem to gather force from the illustration we have just employed, that if there be any such antecedent disposition as we are contending for, formed previous to any action of the mind, it must be the direct effect of creative power; and if it possess any moral character, as we shall offer some reasons for believing it does, then God is the immediate author of sin.

This is the form in which this objection is always put by Mr Finney and others, and we have therefore adopted it, although it assumes what has been shown to be untrue, that a disposition of mind, in the sense in which we use the term, implies the idea either of a physical entity or a spiritual substance. It does not and cannot include any such idea, and can in no case be considered, therefore, as the effect of *creative* power.

But does it follow that a primitive disposition such as we speak of, must be the direct product of the agency of the Deity? Is it not evident, on the contrary, that this is only one out of an infinite number of modes in which it may possibly have been produced? The first tree might have been called into being by the power of God and sprung up in an instant, complete in all its proportions; but it might also have been produced in an endless number of ways, through the operation of some law, different of course, from the existing law of vegetable production, but requiring as much time for the completion of its process, and removing its final result to any assignable distance from the direct interference of divine agency.

So is it possible, too, that a primitive disposition of mind may be produced in an infinite number of ways; and the mode of its formation may be such that it cannot be considered the effect of the divine power in any other sense than that in which all the movements and actions, both of matter and mind throughout the universe, are said to be of God.

We think we have now shown that there are such states of mind as have been designated by the term disposition; that a disposition of mind may exist anterior to all mental action; that this disposition does not form any part of the substance of the mind; and that it is not necessary to suppose that God is the author of it, in any other sense than that in which he is the author of all we feel and do.

We come now to discuss the question of the moral character of mental dispositions. Mr Finney, with his accustomed violence and lavish abuse of those who teach a different doctrine, denies that a disposition of mind, granting its existence, could possess any moral character. Most of his arguments on this point have been already despatched by our preliminary discussion. If it be true that a disposition is sinful, then sin is a substance, instead of a quality of action: then, too, God is the author of sin, and he is an infinite tyrant, since he damns man for being what he made him. This sentence comprises within it the substance of most that wears the semblance of argument in what Mr Finney has said on this subject; and how perfectly futile this is has been made sufficiently apparent.

He argues from the text, 'Sin is a transgression of the law', that sin attaches only to acts, and cannot be predicated of a disposition. As well might he argue from the assertion, man is a creature of sensation, that he possessed no powers of reflection. Until he can show what indeed he has asserted very dogmatically, but of which he has offered no proof, that this text was meant to be a strict definition of sin, it will not serve his purpose.

The only other arguments worthy of notice, which Mr Finney adduces in support of his position, that all sin consists in acts, are drawn from the considerations that '*voluntariness* is indispensable to moral character.'

There is undoubtedly a sense in which it is true that nothing can be sinful which is not *voluntary*. And in this sense of the word all our dispositions *are* voluntary. There are two meanings attached to the word 'will'. It sometimes denotes the single faculty of mind called will; and sometimes all the active powers of the mind, all its desires, inclinations and affections. This double meaning has proved a great snare to Mr Finney. He either never made the distinction, or perpetually loses sight of it, and hence is often inconsistent with himself.

In seeking to exhibit the meaning which he prevalently attaches to the words 'will', 'voluntary', etc., we shall have occasion to present to our readers a very singular theory of morals. 'Nothing,' he says, 'can be sinful or holy which is not directly or indirectly under the control of the will.' But over our emotions

the will has no direct influence, and can only bring them into existence through the medium of the attention. Feelings or emotions are dependent upon *thought,* and arise spontaneously in the mind when the thoughts are intensely occupied with their corresponding objects. Thought is under the direct control of the will. We can direct our *attention* and meditations to any subject, and the corresponding emotions will spontaneously arise in the mind. Thus our feelings are only *indirectly* under the control of the will. They are sinful or holy only as they are thus indirectly bidden into existence by the will. Men often complain that they cannot control their feelings; they form overwhelming attachments which they say they cannot control. They receive injuries, their anger rises, they profess they cannot help it. Now while the attention is occupied with dwelling upon the beloved object in the one case, the emotions of which they complain will exist of course; and if the emotion be disapproved by the judgment and conscience, the subject must be dismissed from the thoughts and the attention directed to some other subject, as the only possible way of ridding themselves of the emotion. So in the other case, the subject of the injury must be dismissed and their thoughts occupied with other considerations, or emotions of hatred will continue to fester and rankle in their minds.

Again, in another place, he says:

If a man voluntarily place himself under such circumstances as to call wicked emotions into exercise, he is entirely responsible for them. If he place himself under circumstances where virtuous emotions are called forth, he is praiseworthy in the exercise of them, precisely in proportion to his voluntariness in bringing his mind into circumstances to cause their existence.

Again, he says, 'If he (a real Christian) has voluntarily placed himself under these circumstances of temptation, he is responsible for these emotions of opposition to God rankling in his heart.' We might quote pages of similar remarks.

These passages would afford ground for comment on Mr Finney's philosophy. He shows himself here, as on all occasions when he ventures upon the field of mental science, a perfect novice. But we are chiefly concerned with the theological bearings of the passages quoted.

It is evident that Mr Finney here uses the words 'will', 'voluntarily', etc., in their restricted sense; and hence we have the dangerous theory of morals that nothing can possess a moral character which is not under the control of the volitions of the mind. But our emotions cannot be thus controlled. They rise *spontaneously* in the mind, they *must* exist when the thoughts are occupied with the objects appropriate to their production. Hence all our emotions, affections and passions, according to Mr Finney, possess a moral character only in consequence of the power which the mind has, by an act of will, to change the object of thought and thus introduce a different class of feelings.

Now, we might object to this view of the matter that the will does not possess the power here attributed to it. Our trains of thought are in some degree subject to our volitions; but the will has by no means an absolute control over the *attention* of the mind. Attention is generally indeed but another name for the interesting character of the idea to which the mind is attending, and is no more directly subject therefore to the bidding of the will than is the state of mind which imparts its interest to the present object of thought. The grounds and the force of this objection will be evident to anyone who will reflect upon states of mind which he has been in, when his whole soul was so absorbed in the contemplation of some subject, that all his efforts to break away from the scenes which riveted his attention only served to break for a moment their fascinating power. But we will wave this objection, not because it is not sufficiently strong to be fatal to Mr Finney's theory, but because it lies aside from our present course.

A still more serious objection is that upon this theory it is impossible that our emotions should possess any moral character. If they are moral 'only as they are indirectly bidden into existence by the will', then they cannot be moral at all. If it is necessary to go back to the act of will which introduced the object in view of which these emotions necessarily arise to find their moral character, then upon no just grounds can morality be predicated of them. If a man has put out his eyes, he cannot justly be accounted guilty for not being able to read, nor for any of the consequences which result from his blindness. These consequences, if he could have foreseen them, do indeed accumulate the greater guilt upon the act of putting out his eyes; but that act is all for which he is fairly responsible.

So in the other case, it is upon the act of the will which brought the mind into contact with the objects, which of necessity awakened its emotions, that we must charge all the responsibility. All the virtue and vice, the holiness and sin of which we are capable, must lie solely in the manner of managing the power of attention. He is a perfect man whose mind is so trained that it takes up whatever subject of meditation the will enjoins; and he is a sinful man, whose mind, without a direct volition to that effect, reverts as if by instinct to holy themes and heavenly meditations and adheres to them even though the will should endeavour to force it away.

All the foundations of morality and religion are virtually swept away by this theory. If its assumptions be true, we should discard all the motives and means now employed to promote virtue. As it makes all moral excellence reside in the readiness and skill with which the power of attention is managed, the most efficient means for the promotion of virtue, beyond all comparison, would be the study of the mathematics. Such are the ridiculous extremes to which Mr Finney is driven in carrying out his doctrine that all sin consists in acts.

It can hardly be maintained that we have caricatured his doctrine or run it out beyond its intrinsic tendency. For if, as he says, a man is praiseworthy or blamable in the exercise of his emotions only because *he has placed himself* under circumstances where these emotions are called forth, then it is plainly unjust to charge responsibility upon anything else than the act of placing himself under the circumstances.

But without charging upon his theory anything beyond what he has developed as its admitted consequences, who does not see upon the face of his own statements absurdity enough to condemn any doctrine which necessarily involves it? A man is responsible for his emotions, he says, only when he has voluntarily brought himself under such circumstances as to call them into existence.

Let us suppose then, two men, brought without any direct agency of their own under the same set of circumstances. We will imagine them taken by force and placed in a grog shop, filled with tipplers quaffing the maddening drink and uttering blasphemies that might make 'the cheek of darkness pale'. Emotions are at once awakened in both the spectators. The desires of the one go forth over the scene; he takes pleasure in those who do such things; he longs to drink and curse with them; he knows that this is wrong, and endeavours to change the subject of meditation, but his sympathy with the scene before him is so strong that his thoughts will not be torn away from it, and his mind continues filled with emotions partaking of its hideous character. The heart of the other instantly revolts at the scene. Every time he hears the name of God blasphemed, he thinks of the goodness and glory of the Being thus dishonoured, and while wondering that others can be blind to his excellency, the liveliest feelings of adoration and gratitude are awakened in his heart.

Now, according to Mr Finney, there is no moral difference between these men; they are not responsible for emotions thus awakened. The one has not sinned, nor is the other praiseworthy. This is no consequence deduced from something else that he has said. It is a case put in strict accordance with his explicit statements. Such is the monstrous absurdity to which he is driven by denying that the state of mind which would, under the circumstances above supposed, have disposed one of the spectators to descend and mingle in the filth and wickedness of the scene, and the other to rise from it to heaven in his holy desires and emotions, does of itself possess a moral character.

Another illustration of the absurdities in which he has involved himself is furnished by his declaration that man is praiseworthy in the exercise of his emotions, 'precisely *in proportion* to his voluntariness in bringing his mind into circumstances to cause their existence'. Mr Finney's common method of expressing the incomprehensibility of anything is by saying, 'It is all algebra'; and we must really doubt whether he knows the meaning of the term *proportion*. For upon his principles, the ratio between the merit or the demerit of any two actions whatever must be a ratio of equality. Voluntariness, in his sense of the word, does not admit of degrees. The will either acts or it does not to bring the man under the peculiar circumstances. There are no degrees in its consent or refusal; and of course there can be no degrees in moral worth, or in guilt.

If two men have each received the same injury, and each by an act of will directed the attention of the mind to the injury and him who committed it, then they are equally guilty for their feelings of hatred, however much those feelings may differ in strength. There can be no difference of degree in the moral demerit of their emotions, although the one should hate his adversary enough to work him some slight injury in return, and the other hate him so much that nothing less than the murder of his victim will satisfy his thirst for vengeance. The two men were *equally* voluntary in bringing their minds under the circumstances which awaken their emotions, and must of necessity, according to Mr Finney's canon of morality, be equally guilty.

There is indeed another class of passages in Mr Finney's writings, in which he brings forward a further criterion of morality. He says, 'When the will is decided by the voice of conscience, or a regard to *right,* its decisions are virtuous.' The change of preference, or the decision of the will, which takes place in regeneration must be made 'because to act thus is *right*'. The will must decide 'to obey God, to serve him, to honour him, and promote his glory, because it is reasonable, and right, and just'. 'It is the *rightness* of the duty that must influence the mind if it would act virtuously.' And again, 'When a man is fully determined to obey God because it is *right* that he should obey God, I call that principle.'

In these passages, and there are many more like them, he seems to resolve all virtue into rectitude. It is evident why he does so, for he is thus enabled to require a mental decision, an act of the mind, in relation to the rectitude of any emotion or action, in order to constitute it virtuous; and thus defend his position that morality can attach only to acts.

He has here fallen into the mistake, however, of making the invariable quality of an action the motive to its performance. It is true that all virtuous actions are right, but it does not follow from this that their rectitude must be the motive to the performance of them. If this be so, then the child who in all things honours his parent does not act virtuously unless each act of obedience is preceded by a mental decision that it is right for him to obey. Mr Finney desired to take ground which would enable him to deny that there is anything of the nature of holiness in the Christian's emotions of love to God when prompted by his *disposition* to love him; but he has evidently assumed an untenable position.

We could easily bring forward more errors into which he has been betrayed in carrying out his false doctrine that morality can be predicated only of acts. But we have surely presented enough. And this exposure renders it unnecessary that we should repeat what have been so often produced and never refuted, the positive arguments for believing that our dispositions, or states of heart, including the original disposition by

which we are biased to evil, possess a moral character and are
the proximate sources of all the good and evil in our conduct.
Some of Mr Finney's pretended arguments against this
opinion we have not answered simply because they are so
puerile that, though we made the effort, we could not condescend to notice them. All of them that had the least
plausibility we have shown to be without any real force. And
if any man can reject this opinion on account of the difficulties
with which it is still encumbered, and adopt the monstrosities
connected with Mr Finney's rival doctrine, we must think that
he strains at a gnat and swallows a camel.

As might have been expected from what has already been
said, Mr Finney denies that there is any such thing as *natural
depravity*. His views on this subject are easily exhibited. We
might describe them all, indeed, in a single phrase by saying
that they are neither more nor less than the old Pelagian
notions. 'This state of mind,' he says, describing the commencement of sin in a child, 'is entirely the result of temptation
to selfishness, arising out of the *circumstances* under which the
child comes into being.'

If it be asked *how* it happens that children universally adopt the
principle of selfishness, unless their nature is sinful, I answer that
they adopt this principle of self-gratification, or selfishness, because
they possess *human* nature, and come into being under the peculiar
circumstances in which all the children of Adam are born since the
fall . . . The cause of outbreaking sin is not to be found in a sinful
constitution or nature, but in a wrong original choice . . . The *only*
sense in which sin is *natural* to man is, that it is natural for the mind
to be influenced in its individual exercises by a supreme preference or
choice of any object.

On reading this last extraordinary declaration, the text of an
inspired apostle came to mind, in which he assures us that we
are 'by *nature* children of wrath'. If both those declarations be
true, we have the curious result that we are children of wrath
not because we are sinners, but because we are so made as to
be influenced by a supreme choice! But texts of Scripture are as
nothing in Mr Finney's way. He makes them mean more or
less, stretches or curtails them, just as occasion requires. His

system is a perfect Procrustean bed, to which the Bible, no less than all things else, must be fitted. An illustration of this is found in his manner of dealing with the passage, 'I was shapen in iniquity, and in sin did my mother conceive me.' This text would seem, at first sight, to present a very serious obstacle to his views. And what does he do with it? He first gravely proves that it does not mean 'the substance of a conceived foetus is sin'! He then jumps to the conclusion, 'All that can be possibly meant by this and similar passages is that we were always sinners from the commencement of our *moral* existence, from the earliest moment of the exercise of moral agency.' That is, when David and the other sacred writers make these strong assertions, they only mean to inform us that the moment we adopt the principle of supreme selfishness as our rule of action, we do wrong; or, in other words, that just as soon as we begin to sin, we sin! May we not well say that he has a marvellous faculty for making a text mean anything, or nothing, as suits his purpose?

Another illustration of this is furnished by his interpretation of the text, 'The carnal mind is enmity against God, for it is not subject to the law of God, neither indeed can be.' The carnal mind, he says, means a *minding of the flesh,* a voluntary action of the mind, a choice that is supremely selfish. While men act upon the principle of supreme selfishness, obedience is impossible.

This, he says, is the reason why the carnal mind, or the minding of the flesh, is not subject to the law of God, neither indeed can be. Wonderful discovery! So the apostle, in this passage, meant nothing more than the stale truism, that a man cannot be sinful and holy at the same time – that he cannot, *in the same act,* transgress the law and render obedience to it.

Pelagians have always found a difficulty in reconciling their theory with the salvation of infants by the *grace* of Jesus Christ. Pelagius himself was sorely pressed on this point. Infants are in no way answerable for the sin of Adam, or otherwise evilly affected by it than that it brings them into circumstances of temptation, and they have no sin of nature; how then can they be subjects of pardon? What interest can they have in the atonement of the Saviour? Let us see how Mr Finney disposes of this difficulty.

Had it not been for the contemplated atonement, Adam and Eve would have been sent to hell at once, and never have had any posterity. The *race* could never have existed . . . Now every infant *owes its very existence* to the grace of God in Jesus Christ; and if it dies previous to actual transgression, it is just as absolutely indebted to Christ for eternal life as if it had been the greatest sinner on earth.

We have no words to express our aversion to this egregious trifling with sacred subjects. The Bible teaches us that all of our race who are saved are redeemed from sin; that they are *saved,* not born, by virtue of the atonement of Jesus Christ. And when we ask Mr Finney how this can be reconciled with his theory that there is nothing connected with infants that *can* be atoned for, he very gravely tells us that they owe their BIRTH to the grace of God!

He does not tell us why he baptizes infants. We do not know, indeed, whether he ever administers this ordinance to children previous to the supposed commencement of moral action. Certainly, upon his principles, it could have no meaning. He rejects, with utter scorn and ridicule, the idea that in regeneration and sanctification there takes place anything that can be properly symbolised by 'the washing off of some defilement'. The *water* of baptism then, to whomsoever this rite be applied, cannot have any emblematical meaning; and the apostle committed a rhetorical error, to say the least of it, when he wrote, 'But ye are *washed,* but ye are *sanctified.*' But with what propriety this ordinance can be administered to children, who, having never actually transgressed, are not sinners, who are just what they ought to be, we cannot conceive. Surely consistency requires Mr Finney to assign to infant baptism a place among those hated abominations, upon which he so much dwells, that the 'traditions of the elders' have introduced into the church.

We shall not undertake to show in detail the inadequacy of Mr Finney's theory to account for the sin there is in the world. This has often been done. And it still remains perfectly inexplicable why, if men come into the world with just such a nature as they ought to have, prone no more to evil than to good, and are surrounded at the same time with 'infinite motives' to holiness, and 'circumstances' that tempt them to sin, that they should all, with one accord, obey the force of the finite circumstances rather than the infinite motives. If this be the state of the case, we might naturally expect all mankind to become holy, excepting here and there some luckless one, who, not having sufficient skill so to manage the attention of his mind as to keep before it the infinite motives to holiness, would fall into sin.

Here too we might ask, what has become of the doctrine that God has done all that he could to prevent the present degree of sin? If he can so influence some men, after their hearts are set in them to do evil, that they shall become holy, could he not have induced them at the first to choose holiness instead of sin?

We cannot pass from this part of our subject without developing one of the many singular results afforded by the comparison of different parts of Mr Finney's writings. The one we are now about to present is so very peculiar that we solicit for it special attention. He rejects the common doctrine of depravity, because it makes man a sinner by necessity – it makes God the author of sin – it is a constitutional or physical depravity, and leads to physical regeneration, etc. He frequently blows off the superfluous excitement produced in his mind by this view of depravity, in sentences like the following: 'That God has made men sinners, incapable of serving him – suspended their salvation upon impossible conditions – made it indispensable that they should have a physical regeneration, and then damns them for being sinners, and for not complying with these impossible conditions – monstrous! blasphemous! Believe this who can!'

Now let us see how he gets rid of this *physical necessity,* which he falsely but uniformly charges upon the common opinions respecting depravity. According to his theory, the cause of men becoming sinners is to be found in their possessing human nature and coming into being under circumstances of temptation – in the adaptation between certain motives which tempt to undue self-gratification, and the innocent constitutional propensities of human nature. But in one of his lectures, where he is endeavouring to persuade his hearers to use the appropriate means for promoting a revival, and presenting on that account such truths and in such forms as seem to him most *stirring,* he says:

Probably the law connecting cause and effect is more *undeviating* in spiritual than in natural things, and so there are fewer exceptions, as I have before said. The paramount importance of spiritual things makes it reasonable that it should be so.

In the use of means for promoting revivals, he says again: 'The effect is *more certain* to follow' than in the use of means to raise a crop of grain.

Now, upon his system, the efficiency of all means for promoting revivals may be traced up ultimately to the tendency of eternal *motives* to influence the mind. We have here, then, the position, distinctly involved, that *motives,* when properly presented, when so presented as to produce their appropriate effect, operate by a surer law than any of the physical laws of matter. The effect of the proper presentation of a motive to the mind is more *certain,* and of course more *inevitable,* than that the blade of wheat should spring from the planted seed or a heavy body fall to the ground. Now he will not deny that the motives to sin, which meet man soon after his entrance into the world, are thus adequately presented; for the sad proof of it is found in the uniform production of their effect. That effect must of course be *inevitable,* beyond any idea of necessity that we can form from the operation of physical laws.

From the parts of his scheme already presented, our readers will be able to anticipate Mr Finney's theory of *regeneration.* The change which takes place in regeneration he, of course, represents as a change in the mind's method of acting. As it originally chose sin instead of holiness, so a new habit consists in choosing holiness instead of sin. The idea that there is imparted to the heart a new relish for spiritual objects, or that any new principle is implanted, he rejects; to teach this, he says, is to teach a physical religion, which has been the great source of infidelity in the church. 'It is true,' he says,

the constitution of the mind must be suited to the nature of the outward influence or motive; and there must be such an adaptation of the mind to the motive, and of the motive to the mind, as is calculated to produce any desired action of the mind. But it is absurd to say that this constitutional adaptation must be a holy principle, or taste, or craving after obedience to God. All holiness in God, angels, or men, must be *voluntary,* or it is not holiness. To call anything that is a part of the mind or body, holy – to speak of a holy substance, unless in a figurative sense, is to talk nonsense.

We remark here, in passing, that this is the uniform style in which Mr Finney caricatures the opinions from which he dissents. From one form of statement he habitually passes to another as completely synonymous, which has not the remotest resemblance to it. He assumes here that a principle, or taste, cannot be *voluntary,* whereas it cannot but be voluntary, in the only sense in which voluntariness is essential to moral character; and also that it must be a substance, or form a part of the mind or body – an assumption than which nothing can be more groundless and absurd.

He adds, 'The necessary adaptation of the outward motive to the mind, and the mind to the motive, lies in the *powers of moral agency,* which every human being possesses.' Understanding, conscience, and the power of choice, he supposes, are all that is needful to enable man to receive the truth of God and act under its influence.

There is nothing new in all this. It is at least as old as the fifth century. It has been broached repeatedly since the days of Pelagius, and as often shown by arguments that have not yet been refuted to be utterly inadequate to account for the facts of the case. We have indeed its radical unsoundness fully exposed to us by the apostle Paul, where he declares, 'The natural man receiveth not the things of the Spirit of God; neither can he know them, for they are spiritually discerned.'

This passage of Scripture will bear no interpretation which does not place it in irreconcilable contradiction with Mr Finney's theory. He generally asserts that the sinner knows all the truth that is necessary to induce him to make to himself a new heart, and that the only reason why it fails to produce this effect is because he will not *consider* the truth.

We say *generally,* because here, as in everything else, Mr Finney is inconsistent with himself. At one time he talks thus: 'It is indeed the pressing of truth upon the sinner's consideration that induces him to turn. But it is not true that he is ignorant of these truths before he thus considers them. He *knows* that he must die – that he is a sinner – that God is right, and he is wrong', etc. But again, when he is seeking to make an impression upon the sinner, he assures us that 'the idea that the careless sinner is an intellectual believer is absurd – the man that does not feel, nor act at all, on the subject of religion, is an *infidel,* let his professions be what they may'. But we will leave him to explain how an *infidel* can be said to *know* that to be true, which he does not *believe* to be true. The uniform tenor of his representations, when treating of the subject of regeneration, is that the sinner wilfully refuses to *consider* known truths, and on that account alone, has not a new heart.

The apostle, on the contrary, declares the natural man receiveth not the things of the Spirit of God, neither *can* he know them. We presume that no one but Mr Finney himself can doubt to which of these authorities we should bow.

If the testimony of the apostle needed any confirmation, we might find it abundantly in human experience. Every man knows that his perception of moral truths depends upon the state of his heart. It is a matter of familiar experience that truths which sometimes affect us scarcely at all, will, at another time, act so powerfully as to break up all the fountains of feeling within us. And this difference is not owing to the greater or less degree of consideration bestowed upon the truth; we may think of it as profoundly in the one case as in the other.

Who has not felt that a familiar truth occurring to the mind in the same terms with which it has often before been clothed, will suddenly display a hitherto unseen richness of meaning which at once wakes up all the feelings of the heart? What is it that can thus modify our powers of moral perception but the state of the mind?

And how can we expect, then, that the spiritual truths of God's holy Word should produce their appropriate effect upon the mind of the sinner, who is destitute not only of any fellowship with those truths, but of the disposition of heart by which their meaning is discerned? We cannot understand how the unrenewed heart, if as Mr Finney says, 'it hates God with mortal hatred', can even understand the real meaning of the truth 'God is love'; or feel that this truth is a motive for subduing its hatred. Nor are we able to see how any of those considerations most frequently presented in the sacred Scriptures can prevail with the sinner and produce upon him their appropriate effect, unless his mind be illuminated, his heart renewed, by the influences of the Holy Spirit.

Mr Finney's own pages will furnish us with evidence that he himself considers the mind as needing some further adaptation to the motives of the Bible than the powers of moral agency. This evidence is found in the fact that the motives which he most frequently and importunately urges are not those which are commonly employed in the sacred Scriptures. He seems to have a kind of instinct of the insufficiency of the considerations presented by the inspired writers to answer his purpose.

The most common form in which he sets forth the change that takes place in regeneration is that of a change in the choice of a *Supreme Ruler.* He divides the world into two great political parties, the one with God, the other with Satan, at its head. When a man makes for himself a new heart, he changes sides in politics – he gives up the service of Satan and submits to the government of God. The great duty which he urges upon the sinner is unconditional submission to God. This duty, as presented by him, is very rarely intended to include submission to the terms of salvation revealed in the gospel – it is a submission to God as the great creator and ruler of the world – the God of providence rather than of grace.

Now it will at once occur to every reader of the Bible that this is not the duty which the sacred writers most frequently urge upon the sinner. They call upon men to repent and believe in the Lord Jesus Christ. But Mr Finney says, 'It is *generally* in point, and a safe and suitable direction, to tell a sinner to *repent.*' Marvellous! that he should consider it generally, but not always *safe* to tell a sinner to do that which the apostles, with great uniformity, tell him to do.

The other part of the apostolic exhortation to sinners, 'Believe in the Lord Jesus Christ,' he seems to think, should no longer be given in any case save where an individual is unwilling to admit that Christ is the Messiah of God. This exhortation he considers as exclusively suitable to the days of the apostles, 'when the minds of the people were agitated mainly on the question whether Jesus was the true Messiah'. 'They bore down,' he says, 'on this point, because here was where the Spirit of God was striving with them, and consequently this would probably be the first thing a person would do on *submitting* to God.' He does indeed number among the directions to be given to sinners that 'they should be told to *believe* the gospel'; but he explains this to mean nothing more than 'that trust or confidence in the Scriptures that leads the individual to act as if they were true'. Of that specific act of faith in which the soul apprehends the Lord Jesus as its Saviour and receives pardon and justification, he seems not to have the least idea. The sole value of repentance or faith he finds in the manifestation which they afford of the heart's willingness to *submit to the authority* of God. 'Whatever point,' he says, 'is taken hold of between God and the sinner, when he *yields* that, he is converted. When he yields one point to *God's authority,* he yields all.'

This is evidently another gospel. The apostles urge all men to believe in the Saviour because faith is in itself a proper and a most important duty – but Mr Finney deems it of no importance, save as it manifests submission to the authority of the Great Ruler, and thinks it unsuitable to urge it upon any sinner therefore, unless it be one whose heart has assumed a hostile attitude towards the claims of Jesus Christ to be the true Messiah. How widely, indeed, does this differ from the gospel revealed to us from heaven, which places faith at the head of human duties, teaching us that it is the instrumental cause of our forgiveness, that it unites us to the Lord Jesus Christ and is the mediate source of all our spiritual strength!

As the duty presented by Mr Finney to the sinner's mind is different from that commonly urged in the Bible, so does he employ different motives to induce compliance. The chief motive upon which he relies is that it is *right* to acknowledge God and submit to him as our Great Ruler.

We can now see another reason why he assumed the strange position upon which we have already commented, that 'it is the *rightness* of a duty that must influence the mind if it would act virtuously'. Man in his natural state can be made to see that it is *right* for him to submit to God, but he cannot be made to perceive his moral glory or to feel that his character is lovely.

As he cannot receive the things of the Spirit of God, Mr Finney is therefore driven to the necessity of seeking other things which he can receive. He endeavours by developing the useful tendency of the principles of the divine government in

contrast with the injurious influence of selfishness, to produce
a conviction in the sinner's mind that it is right for God to
reign; and upon this conviction he relies to induce the sinner to
change his voluntary preference and submit to the righteous
rule of his Creator.

In one of his sermons, after describing to the sinner how he
must change his heart, he goes through a kind of rehearsal of
the performance. He begs the sinner to give him his attention
while he places before him 'such considerations as are best
calculated to induce the state of mind which constitutes a
change of heart'. In presenting these best considerations, he
dwells upon 'the unreasonableness and hatefulness of selfishness', 'the reasonableness and utility of benevolence', 'the
reasons why God should govern the universe', etc. His
remarks upon these topics are protracted through ten or twelve
octavo pages, in the whole of which, about as many lines are
devoted to a frigid allusion to the justice and mercy displayed
in the atonement of Jesus Christ. In a previous passage of the
same sermon he says, 'The offer of reconciliation annihilates
the influence of despair and gives to conscience its utmost
power.' He seems here to limit the efficacy of the gospel, to its
opening the way for the operation of existing motives upon the
heart of man.

And his practice is certainly consistent with this low view of
the gospel. The considerations which he brings forward as best
adapted to induce the sinner to change his heart are almost
exclusively such as are furnished by natural religion. We hear
next to nothing of the grace and glory of God as they shine in
the face of Jesus Christ, of the wondrous love of a dying
Saviour, of the demerit of sin as illustrated by his death, or of
the guilt of the sinner in remaining insensible to the motives
which address him from Calvary. Our Saviour intimates that
all other sin is comparatively lost in the sin of rejecting him;
and the apostles refer to the neglect of the 'great salvation'
provided for man as presenting the most odious form of human
guilt. To the life and death of Jesus Christ, indeed, do they
continually recur for the illustration and enforcement of all
human duties. They make known nothing save Jesus Christ,
and him crucified. This is the great central source of light and
heat. Whatever may be the point of departure, how uniformly

do they carry us to the cross and bid us thence look at the character of God and the duty of man.

But when Mr Finney professedly addresses himself to the task of presenting the considerations best adapted to move the heart of the sinner, he thinks he can find a better point of view. He takes his stand amidst the wonders of creation; he finds in the character there developed and the relations there established between man and his Maker, the right and the duty of God to govern and man's obligations to obey – 'the reasonableness and utility of virtue – the unreasonableness, guilt, and evil of sin': – hence he charges the sinner with having 'set his unsanctified feet upon the principles of eternal righteousness, lifted up his hands against the throne of the Almighty, set at naught the authority of God and the rights of man'!

We do not deny the validity of these considerations, upon which he chiefly dwells; but we do deny that the truths involved in them are the peculiar truths of the gospel, or that they are those which the apostles deemed best adapted to become 'the wisdom of God and the power of God unto salvation'. Throughout his whole system indeed, it is painful to see how small a space is allotted to the cross of Christ. Often where it might be expected to stand forth conspicuous, it seems to be, of set design, excluded. In this same sermon, when defending the reasonableness of the 'conditions of the gospel', he tells the sinner that *faith* is reasonable because 'nothing but faith in what God tells him can influence him to take the path that leads to heaven'. The faith of which he here speaks is a 'condition of the gospel', and yet he represents it in no other light than as a general belief in the truth of God's word; and justifies its requirement solely on the ground of its tendency to make man holy. There is no hint of that faith in the Lord Jesus Christ so often mentioned in the Scriptures, by which the soul commits itself to him as its Saviour and becomes a partaker of the benefits of his redemption – no allusion to the reasonableness of this condition on the ground of its rendering to God all the glory of our salvation. We see not how any pious mind accustomed to look to Jesus Christ for all its strength and joy and glory can pass through this new system without being constrained at every step to cry out, 'Ye have taken away my Lord, and I know not where ye have laid Him.'

Another illustration, trifling it is true when compared with the one we have just presented, but yet worthy of notice, of the difficulty under which Mr Finney labours in carrying out his views of regeneration, is found in the necessity which is laid upon him of violating the established meaning of words. A new heart is a new act. In regeneration no principle is implanted in the mind, but the beginning and end of the process is in a new act; and consequently the process of the divine life in the soul of man is a series of acts – there is no growth of anything which lays the foundation of those acts and disposes to the performance of them.

He not only believes this to be true, but thinks it vastly important that others should be convinced of its truth. The world has hitherto been ignorant of the true nature of religion and the method of its progress in the heart. He expresses his doubt whether one professor of religion out of ten in the city of New York, if asked what sanctification is, could give a right answer. They would speak of it 'as if it were a sort of washing off of some defilement' – or they would represent it as the growth of some principle, or germ, or seed, or sprout, implanted in the soul. 'But sanctification,' he says, 'is *obedience.*' Of course, to sanctify must mean to obey; and to be sanctified is to be obeyed. Now we charitably hope that Mr Finney has underrated the number of those who could give a right answer to this question; for we presume that more than nine out of ten of the professors of religion in New York have been at school and can read a dictionary, if not the Bible and the catechisms of their church, and surely not one, thus qualified, could ever think of giving his definition of sanctification.

We have already exposed the insufficiency of Mr Finney's theory; and in testimony thereof have adduced his own departure, in carrying out his theory, from the instructions and motives developed in the gospel. He thus evidently betrays his own conviction that the duties which the apostles commonly urge upon the impenitent are not consistent with his scheme; and that the motives they present are of such a nature as to require a corresponding disposition of heart.

The force of the objections we have brought forward is not at all diminished by the different form in which he sometimes states his doctrine of the new heart. He has a class of passages in which he represents the spiritual heart, as 'that deep-seated, but voluntary preference of the mind which lies back of all its other voluntary affections and emotions, and from which they take their character'. If by 'preference' be meant such an inclination as he has elsewhere described under that name, which is not an object of consciousness and makes itself known only by its influence over our acts; and by its being 'deep-seated' that is, seated in the will itself, using the term in its larger sense, and for that reason entitled to the epithet 'voluntary', we should have no objection to this account of the matter. This is precisely our idea of a disposition.

But this is not his meaning. The preference which he here intends is a conscious act of the mind. It still remains then for him to show how the mind can be induced to prefer the glory of God as the supreme end of pursuit, when it is blind to that glory, and if we may credit the apostle, in such a state that, until renewed, it cannot know it.

Another difficulty, too, is started by the passage we have just quoted from him. It seems that we are to look back from every other voluntary affection and emotion of mind to this 'deep-seated preference' to find their moral character. But as this preference is itself but a voluntary exercise of mind, and differs from its other voluntary exercises only by being more deep-seated, it would seem that we ought to look back to something else for its moral character. It is impossible for us to imagine how one voluntary exercise of mind can possess a moral character independent of the subjective motives which prompted it, while all other affections and emotions are good or evil only through their connection with this one. Is it not wonderful that with such beams in his own eye, he should be endeavouring to pluck out motes from the eyes of others!

Mr Finney asserts the perfect, unqualified *ability* of man to regenerate himself. It is easier, indeed, he says, for him to comply with the commands of God than to reject them. He tells his congregation that they 'might with much more propriety ask, when the meeting is dismissed, how they should go home, than to ask how they should change their hearts'. He declares that they who teach the sinner that he is unable to repent and believe without the aid of the Holy Spirit insult his understanding and mock his hopes – they utter a libel upon

Almighty God – they make God an infinite tyrant – they lead the sinner very consistently to justify himself – if what they say is true, the sinner ought to hate God, and so should all other beings hate him – as some have humorously and truly said, they preach, 'You can and you can't, you shall and you shan't, you will and you won't, you'll be damn'd if you do, you'll be damn'd if you don't.' It has been reserved, we imagine, for the refined and delicate taste of Mr Finney to discover the *humour* of this miserable doggerel. He is obviously much delighted with it and, like all his other good things, has worked it up more than once. We hope the next compiler of the beauties of American poetry will pay a due deference to his commendation and assign a conspicuous place to this precious morsel.

Most professors of religion, he says, pray for sinners that God would *enable* them to repent. Such prayers he declares to be an insult to God. He thinks it a great error to tell the sinner to pray for a new heart or to pray for the Holy Ghost to show him his sins. 'Some persons,' he says,

seem to suppose that the Spirit is employed to give the sinner power – that he is unable to obey God without the Spirit's agency. I confess I am alarmed when I hear such declarations as these; and were it not that I suppose there is a sense in which a man's heart may be better than his head, I should feel bound to maintain that persons holding this sentiment were not Christians at all.

We have certainly never met with a more singularly extravagant and unfortunate declaration than the one last quoted. Who are the persons who have held and taught this sentiment, so inconsistent with Christianity? Why, at the head of the list stand our Saviour and his apostles. 'No man,' said Christ, *'can* come to me except the Father which hath sent me draw him.' And the apostles refer continually to the absolute dependence of man upon God for the necessary strength to perform his duties aright.

Not one of those holy men felt that he was of himself 'sufficient for these things'. Their uniform feeling seems to have been, 'I *can* do all things through Christ, who strengtheneth me.' Mr Finney not only believes that we *can* do all things without any strength from Christ, but he makes this one of the fundamental doctrines of Christianity.

The apostles exhorted men to be strong in the grace that is in Christ Jesus, and they prayed for those to whom they wrote that the Lord would *strengthen* them with might by his Spirit – that he would make them perfect, establish, strengthen, settle them. But Mr Finney says that to pray that God would help the sinner to repent is an insult to God; as if God had commanded the sinner to do what he cannot do. Now the Christian has at least as much ability to be perfectly holy as the sinner has to repent. God commands Christians to be perfect, and of course, when the apostles prayed that the Lord would *strengthen* them and make them perfect, they prayed 'as if God had commanded the Christian to do what he cannot do'. These prayers, then, uttered under the inspiration of the Holy Ghost, must have been 'an insult to God'! Mr Finney cannot relieve the character of his reckless, irreverent assertions by saying that the sacred writers meant to represent nothing more than the unwillingness of the sinner to do his duty. Beyond all dispute they represent this unwillingness under the form of an inability, and it is against those who describe it by precisely equivalent terms that Mr Finney raves with such infuriate bitterness.

There is a question here, not between him and us, but between him and the apostles, whether they employed proper and safe language in describing the moral condition of man and the nature of his dependence on divine aid. He may perhaps say that the language employed by the apostles was perfectly proper at that time, but as their statements have been perverted and become the source of ruinous errors, it is now necessary to employ more explicit and guarded language. We suppose this will be the nature of his defence, as he distinctly takes the ground that it will not answer to preach the same class of truths, or to exhibit them in the same manner, in any two ages of the Church, or in any two places. At each time and place the sinner is entrenched behind his own peculiar errors, and the preacher must be careful not to present any truth which he can so pervert as to fortify himself in his refuges of lies.

But is it true that any such change can take place from age to age in the natural character or the accidental circumstances of man, as to call for any important change in the matter or manner of religious instruction? What error has ever existed that does not find its refutation in some revealed truth? It is a very dangerous principle to admit that we are at liberty to omit such truths of the Bible as we deem unsuitable to existing emergencies, and to exhibit others in a very different light from that in which they are left by inspired writers. It virtually suspends the whole of the divine revelation upon the discretion and wisdom of man. But if true, it has no application to the case now before us.

There is no evidence that the perversion of the truth which Mr F. thinks can only be met by varying the manner in which the apostles represent man's dependence, is a modern error. On the contrary, it is undeniable that this very error prevailed in the days of the apostles. Paul met with the same objections that are now current, drawn from the divine sovereignty and human dependence; and how does he refute them? By a flat denial that man is unable of himself to do his duty? Or by a modification, a softening down of his previous statements? No – he re-asserts the perverted doctrines in the face of the objections raised against them. He does not, nor does any one of the sacred writers, affirm in a single instance that the sinner is able to obey the divine commands. Not a text of Scripture can be found in which this is declared, while a multitude can be produced which explicitly and in so many words deny it.

Will Mr F. say that the apostles urged upon men obedience to the divine commands and thus *virtually* declared their ability to obey? Then why does he not declare it in the same virtual manner? The same reasons existed then as now for a direct assertion of the sinner's ability, and yet it was in no case made. Why, then, should he make it now, and dwell upon it, and magnify it into an important, nay, an essential part of the gospel, so that he who disbelieves it cannot be a Christian at all?

But it is not true that in urging the commands of God, the sacred writers teach the entire and independent ability of man to obey. Mr Finney does not pretend to bring forward a single passage of Scripture in which his doctrine is directly taught; he finds it proved in no other way than by his own inferences from such commands as 'Make to yourself a new heart' and 'My son, give me thy heart'. His brief argument for human ability is, God commends man to obey, therefore he can obey. He does not even allude to the distinction often taken between natural and moral ability. He teaches broadly without any qualification whatever that a divine command implies the possession of all the ability necessary to obedience. Obligation and ability, he says, must be commensurate. And how does he prove the truth of this last proposition? In no other way than by repeating, times without number, that to teach otherwise makes God an infinite tyrant.

But the Bible does not inform us that there is any tyranny in God's commanding men to do what they cannot do. It teaches us directly the contrary, by making known the duty of man to receive the things of the Spirit of God, while it at the same time declares that without divine assistance he *cannot* receive or know them. He must refer, then, for the truth of this maxim, to our natural sense of justice. We might object to this reference of a case already so clearly decided by a higher authority; but we have no fear that there will be found here any discrepance between the teachings of revelation and the testimony of man's conscience, if the latter be rightly interpreted. Our natural sense of justice does indeed teach us that no obligation can rest upon man to perform any duty for which he has not the necessary faculties; and that he is not responsible for failure in anything which he was willing to do, but was hindered in the execution by causes beyond his control.

When applied to such cases as these, there is a self-evidence belonging to the maxim in question which places its truth beyond all dispute. Mr Finney's mistake lies in extending it to cases which lie altogether beyond the limits within which it was generalised. We deny that the common sense of mankind has ever required that we should possess the ability to change our *inclinations* as the condition of our responsibility for their exercise.

To illustrate this, let us suppose the case of a man under the influence of any dominant passion. Before he has long indulged this passion, it would be comparatively easy for him to relinquish it. As he gives way to its impulses, however, its power over him increases, until at length it binds in complete subjection to itself all the other affections of his nature. At each step of its progress the *difficulty* of subduing it is increased;

and yet who will deny that the sin of cherishing is accurately proportioned to this difficulty? The law of continuity, which has place in moral reasoning, as well as in that 'algebra' which is to Mr F. the symbol of incomprehensibility, would teach us hence to infer that the guilt is greatest when the difficulty is greatest, and that the former has its highest form of aggravation in the insurmountable character of the latter. The language of the whole world is framed in recognition of this truth. We speak familiarly of the difficulty which men find in changing their inclinations, without ever conceiving that we thereby lessen their obligation; nay, we consider the cup of their guilt full to the brim, when they have so destroyed their ability to become virtuous that we may properly say of them, 'They *cannot* cease to do evil, and learn to do well.'

When a paramount inclination, like a strong man armed, has taken possession of the heart and, with a despotism peculiar to itself, banished all but its own ideas and emotions, how can it be dispossessed? Will it yield to a volition of the mind? We all know it will not, and Mr Finney himself admits it. He says that our affections will not obey the bidding of the will – we cannot summon or dismiss them by a volition.

This admission is fatal to him. The mind, he says, can operate upon its inclinations and affections only by changing the object of thought; and this change it certainly cannot effect in a moment. When any strong inclination is in exercise, the mind has an attraction for those ideas and considerations which tend to sustain and increase its present emotions, while it repels all others to an unseen distance, and some little time at least is necessary before it can succeed in calling up and keeping before it those objects of thought which may introduce a different class of feelings. Upon his own account of the matter, no man *can,* in an instant, change a strong inclination. And yet if that inclination be an evil one, the obligation to an *immediate* change is evident. What, then, has become of the maxim that obligation and ability are commensurate?

The sinner who perceives the opposition of the divine government to his selfish plans, and whose heart is on that account filled with emotions of hatred towards God, cannot *instantly,* if at all, turn his mind to such views of the divine character as will inspire him with love. And yet the duty of immediate, instant submission is very evident. We see, then, that power is not the exact measure of obligation. One instance of the failure of the truth of this maxim is as good as a thousand, since one is enough to destroy its generality and leave the arguments for the inability of the sinner standing in all their force, unless they can be overthrown by considerations drawn from other sources.

We do utterly deny that the sinner is able, in the sense which Mr Finney contends for, to obey the divine commands. In proof of this we say that he is dead in trespasses and in sins, and as the dead man is insensible to all things, so is he to those objects which, if rightly perceived, would be adapted to kindle within him holy desires and affections. Until renewed, he cannot know the things which he must know before he can discharge his duty. And the arguments which we urge from reason and Scripture in defence of these views are not touched by the assertion that obligation and ability must be commensurate with each other.

We have already produced one instance in which, upon Mr Finney's own admission, this maxim fails to be true: and we are now about to bring forward another, in which he virtually confesses that it is never true when the affections and inclinations of the heart are in question. In explaining why there can be no repentance in hell, he says, when a man's 'reputation is so completely gone that he has no hope of retrieving it, in this state of despair there is no *possibility* of reclaiming him; no motive *can* reach him and call forth an effort to redeem his character'.

Now, in view of this admission, let it be true that obligation and ability are commensurate, and what is the consequence? Why, that when a man has become so vicious as to ruin his reputation – when he has reached such a confirmed state of iniquity that he himself and all others despair of his ever becoming virtuous – when he has severed the last link that bound him to humanity and is floating loose from his species, a demon or a brute – then is he released from all accountability! Mr Finney adds, that in hell 'the sinner will be in despair, and while in despair it is a moral *impossibility* to turn his heart to God'. But will he deny that the sinner in hell is under any less obligation to love God on account of this admitted impossibility of loving Him? Betraying, as he here does, his knowledge of the limitations to which his favourite standard of obligation is subject, we should suspect him of a set design to deceive, when he uses it so often in its broad, unqualified sense, and takes his stand upon it to thunder out his furious anathemas against others, had he not furnished us, through all his writings, with such abundant evidence of his incapacity to take into view more than a very small part of one subject at the same time.

With the exposure of the error involved in his position, that God cannot consistently command man to do that which he cannot perform, we shall take our leave of this part of the subject, for he has not brought forward the semblance of an argument in favour of the sinner's ability to regenerate himself, which does not directly involve the universal truth of this erroneous maxim.

We have already occupied so much space that we cannot exhibit as fully as we would wish Mr Finney's views of the doctrine of *divine influence*. His theory on this subject is expressed in the following extract:

The work of the Holy Spirit does not consist merely in giving instruction, but in compelling him to *consider* truths which he already knows – to *think* upon his ways and turn to the Lord. He urges upon his *attention* and *consideration* those motives which he hates to consider and feel the weight of.

Again he says: 'It is indeed the pressing of truth upon the sinner's *consideration* that induces him to turn.'

It will be at once perceived that he limits the agency of the Holy Spirit in the regeneration of the sinner to the simple presentation of truth to the mind. Said we not truly, that the influence of the Holy Spirit comes in here only by the way? It is strictly parenthetical, and has about as much fitness and meaning, in connection with the rest of his scheme, as 'the grace of God' has in the REX, DEI GRATIA on the disk of a Spanish dollar.

He maintains that the truth of God, if adequately considered, would convert the sinner; and that he has a perfect and independent power to keep that truth before his mind. Surely, then, the agency of the Spirit is superfluous. It is a new cause introduced to account for the production of an effect for which we already have an adequate cause.

But though he has, inconsistently we think, retained the doctrine of divine influence, he has so modified it that it has but few, if any, points of resemblance with the scriptural representations of this subject. His common method of illustrating the nature of the Spirit's agency is by a reference to the manner in which a lawyer *persuades* a jury, or an orator *sways* his audience. The Spirit merely presents the truth, and the moral suasion of the truth regenerates the sinner, or rather induces him to regenerate himself.

It is not thus that the Scriptures represent it. What mind can read his frequent illustration of an advocate persuading his hearers, and then pass to the scriptural one, of a power that raises from death unto life, without feeling that the agencies which can be properly set forth under such dissimilar symbols must be specifically and widely different from each other? If he has given us the correct account of the divine agency exerted in the salvation of man, then it cannot be denied that the language of the sacred writers, on this subject, is most delusively extravagant.

He does sometimes describe the Spirit as forcing the truth home with tremendous power – pouring the expostulation home – keeping the truth in warm contact with the mind – gathering up a world of motive and pouring it in upon the soul in a focal blaze. Of these and similar expressions, the 'warm contact' and the 'focal blaze' seem to be his favourites, as he has most frequently repeated them. They are but the rays with which he seeks to conceal from his own view and that of others his meagre skeleton of a Scriptural truth. He seems to resort to these expressions because he feels the inaptness and poverty of his plain statements. But it is as bad to lose one's self in a fog of metaphor, as in that 'fog of metaphysics' which he so much dreads. His 'close contact' and 'warm contact' and 'focal blaze' and 'pouring home' mean nothing more than that the Spirit presents the truth to the mind.

However the form of expression may be varied, this exhausts the subject of his interference. He does nothing to awaken the attention any further than the truth which he offers awakens it; nothing to arouse the feelings – nothing to make the scales fall from the eye of the mind that it may perceive the truth – nothing to change the disposition of the heart so that it may love the truth and feel its constraining influence.

Mr Finney expressly and warmly excludes any direct operation of the Spirit upon the mind or heart. To suppose any such agency, he says with an irreverence of which we hope but few could be guilty, is to suppose a 'physical scuffling' between the Holy Spirit and the sinner! As the Spirit awakens no inclination of the heart to go forth and embrace the truth, the warm contact with the mind into which he brings it can refer only to its continuous presentation. When the truth is placed before the mind and the attention is fixed, the contact is complete and cannot be rendered any closer or warmer but by the instrumentality of the affections, upon which Mr F. asserts the Spirit exerts no agency. We have already shown the utter inadequacy of this account of the mode of regeneration. Whether the truth remains for a short or a long time, in cold or in warm contact with the unrenewed heart, it will feel in the considerations before it no sufficient motive for loving God.

It will be seen from Mr F.'s account of the Spirit's influence, that the agency which he exerts in the regeneration of the sinner is the same in kind as that exerted by the preacher. Both call his attention to the truth, and neither of them does anything beyond this. If you go to a drunkard and urge upon him the motives which should induce him to abandon his cups, you have done for him precisely what the Holy Spirit does for the sinner in his regeneration. The preacher, upon this scheme, has the same right that God has to assume to himself the glory of the sinner's salvation.

Indeed Mr F. fully admits this in answering the objection that his view of the subject 'takes the work out of God's hands and robs him of his glory'. His defence is that the glory belongs to God inasmuch as he caused the sinner to act. And mark the meaning and force of his illustration: 'If a man,' he says, 'had made up his mind to take his own life, and you should, by taking the greatest pains and at great expense, prevail upon him to desist, would you deserve no credit for the influences you exerted in the case?'

Is it not amazing that any man with the Bible in his hands and professing to love its sacred truths, could divide, as this passage fully does, the glory of the sinner's salvation between God and man, ascribing the work in the same sense to the Holy Spirit and the preacher, and distributing to each a similar meed of praise!

Mr Finney seems to have a great objection to the preaching of the doctrine of divine influence in any manner. There was a tract published in New York entitled *Regeneration is the Effect of Divine Power*. He twice declares that, 'The very title to this tract is a stumbling block.' He says that, 'While the sinner's attention is directed to the subject of the Spirit's influences, his submission is impossible'; and that if the apostles on the day of Pentecost had gone off to drag in such subjects as dependence upon the Holy Spirit, it is manifest that not one of their hearers would have been converted. 'The doctrine of election and divine sovereignty', he asserts, 'has nothing to do with the sinner's duty – it belongs to the government of God.' And in another place he says, 'To preach doctrines in an abstract way, and not in reference to practice, is absurd.'

As the doctrine of divine sovereignty then has nothing to do with the sinner's duty, we suppose that he intends that it should not be preached at all. Thus does he distort, thus would he conceal from view, a doctrine which runs through the whole Bible, is incorporated with all its revelations, and is the basement principle of so many emotions and actions!

It is obvious why he is thus hostile to divine sovereignty. This doctrine he thinks is calculated to keep men easy in their sins. If they are dependent upon God, they will be led to wait for his action upon them before they begin to act. No doubt the truth may be thus perverted. But is not his doctrine greatly more liable to perversion? He teaches the sinner that he has all the requisite power to convert himself. What more natural than for the sinner to say, I love my sins and therefore as I can at any moment forsake them and make myself holy, I will continue to indulge myself?

It is worthy of remark that when Mr Finney is exposing, in one of his most moving paragraphs, the unfitness of a deathbed as a place for repentance, he alludes only to the difficulty of thinking and keeping the mind in warm and distressing contact with the truth during the agonies of dissolution. He does not refer in the most distant manner to the danger that the sinner, justly abandoned of God, may be unable on that account to change his heart.

Is there no danger, too, that the sinner, so repeatedly assured that God would be an infinite tyrant if he had commanded him to do what he cannot do, should find in his own experience that he cannot of himself make a new heart, and thus be led to condemn the justice of the divine requirements? May he not also very consistently say to his instructor, It is at least as easy for you to be perfectly holy as it is for me to repent – I retort upon you your charges that I am a wicked rebel, and that my heart has been case-hardened in the fires of hell – Physician, heal thyself. If it is easier for me to love God than to hate him, it is easier for you to be perfect than to remain imperfect. It is easier indeed for you to he holy, even as your Father in heaven is holy, than it is for you to walk home; to do the latter requires that you should both be willing and exert the proper muscular action, but to do the former only requires you to be willing. You must be the wickedest being in the universe, then, to refuse to perform a duty so obvious and so easy.

We here dismiss this subject for the present. As we have occupied ourselves with Mr Finney's doctrines, we have been led to seek them chiefly in his sermons, from which most of our extracts have been taken. We propose in our next number to examine his lectures more particularly and develop the *measures* and the *spirit* of this new system. As we have shown that its doctrines are not those of the Bible, so will it be seen that its *spirit* is anything rather than the spirit of Christianity.

We have not shown the discrepances between Mr Finney's doctrines, and the standards of the church to which he belongs. This would be holding a light to the sun. It is too evident to need elucidation that on all the subjects which we have gone over, his opinions are diametrically opposed to the standards of the Presbyterian church, which he has solemnly adopted. Many of the very expressions and forms of stating these doctrines upon which he pours out his profane ridicule are found in the Confession of Faith.

Why then does he remain in the church? He will hold up to the detestation of his people a man who refuses to pay his subscription to the Oneida Institute because he conscientiously

believes that institution is doing more harm than good, asserting that he is not honest, and more than insinuating that he
cannot go to heaven. And can he see no moral dishonesty in
remaining in a church whose standards of faith he has
adopted, only to deny and ridicule them?

It is a remarkable fact that this man, thus incorrect in his
doctrinal views, thus dishonest in his continuance in a church
whose standards he disbelieves and contemns, should have
been appointed a professor of theology to assist in training up
ministers for our churches.

The trustees of Oberlin Institute had, to be sure, a perfect
right to appoint him; but it seems to us very remarkable that
they should have selected him, and rather more so that he
should have felt willing to undertake the office of an instructor
in theology. We suppose, however, that his object was to show
the church the way in which her ministers should be trained.

We give him credit for his good intentions. He declares it to
be a solemn fact that there is a great defect in the present mode
of educating ministers, and that the training they receive in our
colleges and seminaries does not fit them for their work. He
assures his readers that all the professors in our theological
seminaries are unfit for their office; some of them are getting
back towards second childhood and ought to resign; and none
of them are such men as are needed in these days.

Now is it not very kind in Mr Finney, when the church
is thus destitute of men who can adequately instruct her
ministers, to step forward and take the office upon himself? No
doubt the whole Presbyterian church ought to break forth in
rejoicings.

But we confess we would rather he should make the
experiment of his ability in this line out of our church. He will,
doubtless, think this very unkind and ungrateful, but we
cannot help it. We tender him our thanks for the substantial
service he has done the church by exposing the naked deform-
ities of the New Divinity. He can render her still another, and
in rendering it perform only his plain duty, by leaving her
communion and finding one within which he can preach and
publish his opinions without making war upon the standards
in which he has solemnly professed his faith.

SECOND ARTICLE

We proceed to exhibit to our readers the *measures* recommended and the *spirit* displayed in Mr Finney's *Lectures on Revivals*. We do this at the known hazard of being denounced as enemies to revivals and friends of Satan. But it is a very small thing with us that we should be judged of Mr Finney's judgment. We, in common with all the friends of pure and undefiled religion, have a sacred duty to discharge in relation to this subject, from which no considerations of fear or favour should deter us. Mr Finney and his followers have shown a resolute determination to persevere in their course. It is surely then the duty of those who believe that course to be detrimental to the best interests of religion to proclaim their dissent. We believe, therefore will we speak.

Our first remark is upon the disingenuousness of which Mr Finney is guilty, in stating the question of New Measures. These measures, he says, are opposed 'on the ground that *they are innovations*'. Now he knows perfectly well, and all the world knows, that this is not the ground on which they are opposed. Of the many testimonies against them which have been published, we defy him to point to a single one in which their novelty is made the cause of their condemnation. And yet he seeks continually to make upon his reader the impression that naught has been or can be said against them, save that they are *new*.

Who but himself ever supposed that they were *new?* Who does not know that he has picked up his measures, as well as his theology, among the castaway rubbish of past times? The only novelty in the matter is that these measures should be employed in the Presbyterian church, in combination with a false theology and a fanatical spirit. Why then, when Mr Finney is professedly defending his course from the objections which have been urged against it, does he confine himself so exclusively to the single ground of opposition, that his measures are new? Why, if he felt himself equal to the task, did he not fairly and honestly meet the real objections which have been urged against him? Such disingenuous evasions always injure the cause in defence of which they are employed.

A similar artifice may be detected in his enumeration of New Measures. 'They are Anxious Meetings, Protracted Meetings, and the Anxious Seat.' He must have known while uttering this sentence that the public estimation has never ranked these three things together; and we very much doubt whether he has ever heard the term New Measures applied to the Inquiry Meeting or the Protracted Meeting. Meetings[1] of the kind thus designated have been held in all parts of our church, and, when wisely instituted and controlled, have never within our knowledge met with any opposition.

Why then should he place the 'anxious seat' in the same category with these institutions, unless it were furtively to borrow for it a portion of their admitted respectability? Doubtless he intended that his triumphant vindication of things which no one has opposed should leave a general impression on the reader's mind, of which the Anxious Seat might receive the benefit. But does he not know that while there are some who will be imposed upon by such chicanery, there are others who will penetrate the flimsy deception and turn with disgust from a cause thus advocated? Or does he take it for granted that among his 'fit audience', would that we could add 'though few', there will be no discrimination of mind?

In his formal defence of his peculiar measures, Mr Finney undertakes to establish the position 'that our present forms of public worship, and everything, so far as measures are

[1] We are aware that the Editor of the *New York Evangelist* has said that 'before Mr Finney arose, Mr Nettleton was much blamed for his irregularities and imprudence'. This piece of information it seems came to Mr Leavitt, all the way round by St Louis. Such statements are intended to cast over Mr Finney the broad mantle of Mr Nettleton's reputation; or possibly the design may be to make Mr N. jointly responsible for the evils which are now seen to be pouring in upon the church through the flood-gates which the modern reformers have hoisted. Whatever may be the object, it is exceedingly unfair and dishonourable to attempt to associate the name of Mr Nettleton with a class of men of whom we know, and they too, he has ever said, 'Oh, my soul, come not *thou* into their secret!' Would it not be well for the Rev. Editor, before putting forth statements which reach him by such a circuitous route, to make some inquiry as to their truth nearer home? Mr Nettleton's life has been spent chiefly in New England, and we challenge Mr Leavitt to produce as authority for his statement the opinion of any settled minister in New England of the denomination to which Mr N. belongs, who was not an avowed enemy to all revivals.

concerned, have been arrived at by degrees and by a succession of New Measures'. His remarks under this head are so curious that we are sure they would amaze our readers. We wish we could quote them all. He descants with most admirable perspicacity and force upon cocked-hats, fur caps, bands, silk gowns, stocks, cravats, wigs, and small-clothes. He then passes on to the discussion of Psalm Books, lining the hymns, choirs, pitch-pipes, whistles, and fiddles.

In the course of his profound and edifying remarks upon these topics, he relates several stories, of which the following may be taken as a specimen:

I have been told that some years ago in New England, a certain elderly clergyman was so opposed to the new measure of a minister's wearing pantaloons that he would on no account allow them in his pulpit. A young man was going to preach for him who had no small-clothes, and the old minister would not let him officiate in pantaloons. 'Why,' said he, 'my people would think I had brought a fop into the pulpit, to see a man there with pantaloons on, and it would produce an excitement among them.' And so, finally, the young man was obliged to borrow a pair of the old gentleman's small-clothes, and they were too short for him and made a ridiculous figure enough. But anything was better than such a terrible innovation as preaching in pantaloons.

Again, he says:

I remember one minister who, though quite a young man, used to wear an enormous white wig. And the people talked as if there was a divine right about it, and it was as hard to give it up, almost, as to give up the Bible itself.

We dare not reproach him for these instructive little stories in which he abounds, since he is a strenuous advocate for the propriety, nay, the necessity, of telling such stories from the pulpit. 'Truths not thus illustrated,' he says, 'are generally just as well calculated to convert sinners as a mathematical demonstration.' But as, besides himself, 'there are very few ministers who dare to use these stories', he calls upon them to 'do it, and let *fools* reproach them as story-telling ministers.' Speaking, too, of such as contend for the dignity of the pulpit, he cries out, 'Dignity, indeed! Just the language of the *devil*.'

We do not pretend to be as well acquainted as Mr Finney seems to be with the language of the devil; but knowing who it is that has said, 'Whosoever shall say, Thou *fool,* shall be in danger of hell-fire', we would rather abide the consequences of the malediction against those who censure 'storytelling ministers' than stand in the predicament of him who uttered it. 'Fool' and 'devil' are in truth very hard names, but we will not be angry with Mr Finney for employing them; we can bear them from him, and it would be cruel to deny him the use of his most effective weapons. We trust that we may be excused, however, from attempting to reply to such arguments.

Nor can it be reasonably expected that we should answer his stories about cocked-hats, wigs, whistles, etc.; or controvert the important truths they were intended to illustrate. Indeed, so far are we from wishing to controvert them that we will furnish him with an additional truth of like kind, and one of such vital moment that we can only wonder how it escaped his penetrating survey.

It is unquestionably true that the ministers in New England within the last half century were very generally in the habit of wearing long *queues* and riding on switch-tailed horses; and if he will apply to us, we can furnish him with some instructive stories to illustrate this truth. We shall leave to him, however, the duty of explaining how the 'new measure' of cutting off the *queues,* carried through like that of wearing pantaloons, black stocks, and round hats, in the face of persecution and danger, was made instrumental in promoting the purity and power of revivals of religion. We should be glad if he would inform us too, whether the men who in the spirit of martyrs introduced these innovations regarded conformity to them as the only credible evidence of true piety. Did any of these worthies ever say of 'wearing pantaloons instead of small clothes', as he has said of the 'anxious seat', that it occupied the precise place that *baptism* did with the apostles? Or has the signal honour been reserved for him of discovering and introducing a measure co-equal in importance with a divine institution?

The object of Mr Finney, in this miserable farrago, is to produce the impression that the objections which have been brought against his measures are as trivial and ridiculous as those which were urged against the innovations of which he here speaks. Whether he has succeeded, however, in making any other impression than that of pity for the man who can thus ineptly trifle with a serious subject we leave our readers to judge.

It has often been objected against the modern reformers that granting the beneficial tendency of their measures, they unduly magnify their importance. This charge they have denied and have maintained that they considered them important, but yet unessential, circumstances attending and favouring the exhibition of truth. We rejoice that evasion of this kind is no longer possible. Mr Finney throughout his *Lectures* insinuates and often directly asserts the paramount importance, nay, the indispensable necessity of the new measures. 'The object of the ministry,' he says, using that 'Saxon colloquialism' which his reporter so much admires,

is to get all the people to feel that the devil has no right to rule this world, but that they ought all to give themselves to God and vote in the Lord Jesus Christ as the governor of the universe. Now what shall be done? What measures shall we take? Says one, 'Be sure and have nothing that is new.' Strange! The object of our measures is to gain attention, and you *must have something new.* As sure as the effect of a measure becomes stereotyped, it ceases to gain attention, and you *must try something new.*

In the exercise of a wise economy 'of our new things', he thinks public attention

may be kept awake to the great subject of religion for a long series of years, until our *present* measures will by and by have sufficient novelty in them again to attract and fix the public attention. And so we shall never want for something *new.*

All this would be abundantly unintelligible if interpreted by the light of Mr F.'s own definitions. On the page preceding that from which it is taken, he says, 'building houses for worship, and visiting from house to house, etc., are all *measures,* the object of which is to get the attention of the people to the gospel.' And in another *Lecture* from which we have made some extracts, he dignifies with the name of 'measures' the several articles of the clergyman's dress, the chorister's pitch-pipe, and various other like things. As 'building houses for worship' is a 'measure', it must, according to his theory, soon cease to produce its effect; and the gospel cannot gain attention then unless we 'try something new', such for instance as preaching in tents instead of our present church edifices. In the revolving cycle of these 'measures', too, the time will come when the cocked hat, small clothes, and wig, must be restored to their former honours, or the truth cannot make any impression upon the minds of men. Will Mr Finney calculate the length of this cycle, that the public may know when they will be favoured with the opportunity for observing the impulse which will be given to the spread of the truth by the return of these ancient observances?

Admitting the truth of Mr Finney's favourite maxim that 'obligation and ability are commensurate', he cannot perhaps be considered bound to write with anything like logical precision or consistency. But we have a right to expect honesty. We are entitled to demand that he shall not use terms in one sense, when seeking to relieve his system from odium, and then artfully change the meaning to subserve his purpose. This he has evidently done in the passage above quoted.

Let us assign, however, to the term 'measures' in this extract the signification which it was intended here to bear, and yet how revolting is the doctrine taught! According to this theory, the gospel, which its divine author left complete in all its parts and proportions and most admirably adapted to secure its destined ends, must utterly fail of its effect unless there be added to it a set of machinery of man's invention.

A great, if not the chief part of ministerial wisdom is made to consist 'in devising and carrying forward measures' for exciting public attention. The very perfection of Christian wisdom, the height of religious prosperity, are to be sought in that state of things in which 'we shall never want for something that is *new*'.

How is the temple of God dishonoured by this alleged necessity for a continual shifting of its services, like the scenes of some raree-show, to attract the vulgar gaze! How is the gospel degraded by being thus made dependent for its effect upon a kind of jugglery which shall be studiously adapted to surprise and startle beholders and thus 'attract their attention'! It is the very nature of truth to be severely simple;

and in this simplicity she delights to go forth to win her victories. She leaves to error the use of stratagem and guile.

The quotation we have made is not a solitary passage in which the writer in an unguarded moment has claimed for his new measures a degree of importance, which in his more sober moods he would rather disavow. Deliberately and often does he assert the unqualified *necessity* of these new measures to the success of the gospel. 'Without new measures,' he says, 'it is impossible that the church should succeed in gaining the attention of the world to the subject of religion.' And again, 'But new measures, we *must have.*'

It will be seen in the sequel that this is only one illustration of Mr Finney's disposition to claim infallibility and supreme importance for all his own opinions, even when the smallest matters are in question. His argument, in the paragraph from which the sentences last quoted are taken, may certainly claim the merit of originality.

There are so many exciting subjects constantly brought before the public mind, such a running to and fro, so many that cry 'Lo here' and 'Lo there', that the church cannot maintain her ground, cannot command attention, without very exciting preaching and sufficient novelty in measures to get the public ear.

He then proceeds to explain what these 'exciting subjects' are which call upon the church to institute specific measures for producing a counteracting excitement. They are such as 'the measures of politicians, of infidels and heretics, the scrambling after wealth, the increase of luxury', etc.

It should seem, then, that the church must vary the method of celebrating divine worship and modify all the arrangements for presenting religious truth to the minds of men according to the dainties of their tables and the elegance of their furniture and equipage, the degree of commercial enterprise among them, or the extent of infidel machinations, the number of railroads and canals in progress, and of Presidential candidates in the field. The measures we must use are some determinate function of all these variable quantities; and its form should be, in each case, most carefully calculated. Every change in the state of speculation, trade, or politics must call for such a change of measures as will be 'calculated to get the attention of men to the gospel of Christ' under these new circumstances. Religion must descend from her vantage ground, and on the level with all this world's concerns and by kindred arts must she bustle, contrive, and intrigue 'to get the public ear'. To make use of one of Mr Finney's own illustrations, because

the politicians get up meetings, circulate handbills and pamphlets, blaze away in the newspapers, send their ships about the streets on wheels with flags and sailors, send coaches all over town with hand-bills to bring people up to the polls, all to gain attention to their cause and elect their candidate

the church is bound to imitate their wisdom and institute a similar system of manoeuvres.

Where then is the contrast which Paul so often draws between the weapons of our warfare and those with which the world contends? How widely do these *ad captandum* measures differ from the direct, single-hearted course of the apostles! They evidently relied upon the truth as the only instrument they could lawfully employ in the accomplishment of their errand.

Their miracles were not intended like the glaring show-bill of some exhibition, to attract the attention of the public; their object was to convince, not to amaze the people. They felt that they were the heralds of God, commissioned to bear a weighty message to the children of men; and while to their miracles they appealed for the proof of their commission, upon the intrinsic overwhelming importance of their message they founded their claim to the public attention. If we may credit their own statements, they 'renounced the hidden things of dishonesty, not walking in craftiness, nor handling the word of God deceitfully, but by *manifestation of the truth,* commending themselves to every man's conscience in the sight of God.' They seem to have had no idea that they must set in operation some preliminary mechanism to awaken the attention of conscience to the truth.

If this complicated and ever-shifting system of 'exciting measures' is necessary to the success of the gospel, why do we find no trace of it in their practice, and not a syllable of it in their writings? If, as Mr F. says, 'new measures are *necessary* from time to time to awaken attention and bring the gospel to bear upon the public mind', why has it been left for him to reveal to us these necessary means for the propagation of the gospel?

Mr Finney refers distinctly to the character of the present age as furnishing a special argument for the use of new measures in religion and as determining the kind of measures to be employed. The substance of his argument is that this is an age of great excitement, and therefore the same kind of preaching and of measures which did very well in the days of our fathers will not answer now; we must have something more exciting, or religion cannot obtain a hearing. From the same premises, we should arrive at a very different conclusion.

This is, indeed, an age of extraordinary excitement. The great improvements in the mechanic arts and the wide diffusion of knowledge have given a strong impulse to the popular mind; and everywhere the social mass is seen to be in such a state of agitation that the lightest breath may make it heave and foam. This being the case, should religion fall in with this excitement and institute measures for fostering it up to a certain point, that she may gain a favourable moment for presenting her claims? We had thought that one great object of religion was to allay this undue excitement of the human mind; to check its feverish outgoings towards earthly objects and to teach it without hurry or distraction, in self-collectedness, to put forth its energies in a proper direction and to their best advantage. This self-possession being included in the final result at which religion aims, can it be wise to commence the attempt to produce it by exasperating the contrary state of mind?

Paul was once placed among a people who were proverbial for their excitability. Their feelings would kindle and flame with the lightest spark, and like all persons of this mercurial temperament, they delighted in excitement and were continually seeking its procuring causes. 'For all the Athenians and strangers which were there spent their time in nothing else, but either to tell or to hear some *new* thing.' Here, then, according to Mr Finney's theory, was the very people upon whom it would be necessary to play off some preparatory measures to excite them and gain their attention to the Word.

But the apostle appears to have felt that nothing was necessary beyond the simple declaration of the Word. He looked upon the truth declared by his lips and prospered in its course by the energy of the Holy Spirit, as amply sufficient to secure the needful attention and accomplish the purpose whereunto it was sent. Nay, so desirous was he to prevent the surprise of *novelty,* that he represents himself as aiming, by the truth which he exhibits, merely to supply a chasm in their knowledge which they had themselves discovered. He presents Jehovah to them as the God of an altar already existing, and declared to them him, whom they had ignorantly worshipped.

Nor did this apostle ever vary his course to suit the latitude of the place he was in or the temperament of the people around him. Among the pains-taking and thrifty Jews; the learned and witty Athenians; the dissolute Corinthians; the more phlegmatic and martial Romans, he employed but one measure, the declaration of the truth.

Will it be said that in his day the gospel was so novel, its truths so surprising, that the necessity for other measures was superseded, but that now, when men have become familiar with the revelations of the gospel, something else than the 'thrice-told tale' must be employed to awaken public attention? And is it conceivable, then, that the Great Head of the Church, foreseeing that the time would come when the preaching of the gospel would lose its effect and other means become necessary for its propagation, should leave human reason to grope in the dark for these additional measures? Such imperfection does, indeed, often mark the ways and proceedings of man, but may not be attributed unto him 'whose thoughts are not as our thoughts, nor his ways as our ways'.

We have assumed thus far that the new measures cannot be defended under the pretext that they are only a particular mode of preaching the gospel or of exhibiting the truth, and are therefore virtually comprised in the appointed means for the promotion of religion. The measures for which Mr Finney pleads are something distinct from the truth, aside from it, and intended to exert a separate influence. He plainly presents them as the precursors of the gospel, to prepare the way for its coming. It is surely incumbent on him, therefore, to explain why the Scriptures make no allusion to these indispensable appendages, or rather prefixes, of the gospel.

Pressed with this difficulty, and unable to work a miracle in confirmation of his right to supply the deficiencies of the revelation already made, will he yield the position that these new measures are necessary.and content himself with maintaining that, as they tend to favour the impression of the truth, and it is our duty to preach the truth in its most efficient form, it is both expedient and right to make use of them? Upon this ground some of Mr Finney's fellow labourers have rested their cause and have constructed for it a much better defence than he has made.

The principle is here assumed that it is the right and the duty of every man to make use of any measures for promoting religion that seem to him well adapted to co-operate with the truth and aid in its work; and this principle is, within certain limits, both just and safe; but when pressed beyond them it is false and dangerous. If there be no restraint upon the application of this principle, then are the means for the diffusion of Christianity left, as before, at the mercy of human discretion.

Each minister should, in this case, be keen as a Metternich in foreseeing the final effect of the machinery he puts in operation; and the most eagle-eyed would often find themselves mistaken. Hence experiment after experiment must be made to try the efficacy of different measures; and the house of God becomes transformed into a kind of religious laboratory. Upon this same principle the Roman Catholic church has introduced the worship of images and pictures and overlaid the simplicity of the gospel with the tinsel and glare of her pompous ritual. She has cast upon religion such a profusion of ornaments wherewith to deck herself that she has expired beneath the burden. The measures of the Catholic church, though adopted with the honest design of favouring the operation of the truth, are readily condemned by all Protestants.

We might imagine, too, many other measures which would temporarily assist the impression of the truth and which would yet meet with universal condemnation. It was Domitian, we believe, who invited some of his senators on a certain occasion to sup with him, and when they arrived at his palace they were ushered into a room hung with black and against the walls of which were placed coffins, each one, by the dim, blue light of a sulphur lamp placed within it, showing the name of one of the horror-stricken guests. At a signal from the emperor, execution-ers rushed into the room, each with a drawn sword in his hand. There can be no doubt that a homily on death delivered just then would have produced a wonderful effect upon the audience. But would any one recommend such measures for giving effect to the truth of man's mortality? Or would any one, save the preacher and the trumpeter who are said to have actually tried the trick, approve of stationing a man in the belfry of the church to give emphasis by a blast from his horn to the preacher's account of the blowing of the archangel's trump? Phosphoric paintings might be drawn upon the walls of the church, which being rendered suddenly visible by the extinguishment of the lights at the proper point in the preach-er's discourse, would most powerfully aid the impression of the truth he was delivering. A thousand devices equally effective, and equally objectionable, might be invented by the exercise of a little ingenuity.

Where then shall we draw the line between what is right and what is wrong? If compelled to run this boundary line, we should make it divide between those measures which might be considered vehicles of the truth or intended simply to provide for the exhibition the truth, and those which are designed of themselves to produce an effect.

There are various methods in which the truth may be presented, such as from the pulpit, in Bible classes, or Sunday-schools, and in private conversation. Of all such measures, if measures they must be called, those are best which are best adapted to make the truth effective. Means must also be provided for the proper exhibition of truth, such as building convenient houses for public worship, collecting children in Sunday-schools, visiting from house to house, forming Bible and other benevolent societies. To this class may be referred also protracted meetings and inquiry meetings.

The design of these meetings is simply to collect the people together that they may hear such truths as are deemed suitable to their state of mind. It was never intended that the mere institution of such a meeting, or the act of going to attend upon it, should produce any religious effect. Such arrangements as these may undoubtedly be made if they are fitted to favour the operation of the truth. And this limitation will be found to include the condition that the measures themselves, the bare mechanism of the arrangements for the presentation of the truth, instead of being constructed with the design and the tendency to surprise and captivate the attention, should be so ordered as to attract no notice. The perfection of pulpit eloquence is when the manner of the preacher attracts no attention, and the truth is left to work its unimpeded effect upon the hearer; and so those are the best measures which themselves pass unregarded and suffer the mind to be entirely occupied with the truth.

The measures which are peculiar to Mr Finney and his followers are of a very different class. The *anxious seat*, for instance, is intended to produce an effect of its own. Its object is not simply to collect in one place those who are in a particular state of mind, that they may be suitably instructed and advised. No, there is supposed to be some wonder-working power in the person's rising before the congregation and taking the assigned place. This measure then, and all that resemble it in its tendency to occupy and excite the mind, we should condemn on scriptural grounds as inexpedient and unauthorised.

The distinction we have here made we think is just and important: and we could urge many reasons why it should be taken as the dividing line between right and wrong measures for promoting religion. But this position might be contested by some, and we are anxious here to reason from premises universally conceded. There are many cases where right and wrong run into each other, and the bounding line between them, like that between neighbouring states, is involved in dispute and doubt.

We will grant therefore, to save all cavil, the universal truth of the principle that it is right to make use of any measures in our efforts to promote religion that are adapted to aid the truth in its operation upon the minds of men. Here then we are called upon to examine the tendency of the particular measures proposed and insisted upon by Mr Finney; and when he shall have worn out these and, in accordance with his Athenian notion that we must continually find something new, introduced others, we shall be under the necessity of testing them in like manner.

For reasons already given we shall throw out of consideration inquiry meetings and protracted meetings. We shall first consider what Mr F. calls the *anxious seat*. His formal definition of this measure is 'the appointment of some particular seat in the place of meeting, where the anxious may come and be addressed particularly and be made subjects of prayer and sometimes conversed with individually'. Let this definition be well marked. It points out with sufficient distinctness the nature and design of this measure.

What then will be the surprise of the reader to learn that on the same page he implicitly admits that the real *design* is totally different from the avowed one! In defending this measure from objection, he says, 'the *design* of the anxious seat is undoubtedly philosophical and according to the laws of mind: – it has two bearings.' These two bearings are that 'it gets the individual (who is seriously troubled in mind) willing to have the fact known to others'; and secondly, 'it uncovers the delusion of the human heart and prevents a great many spurious conversions by showing those who might otherwise imagine themselves willing to do anything for Christ that in fact they are willing to do nothing.'

In defending this measure, who would not have supposed that his arguments would have been drawn from the importance of having those who were troubled in mind collected together that they might 'be addressed particularly', etc.? But there is not one word of his defence that has the remotest connection with the avowed object of this measure. He was evidently thrown off his guard; and the plainness with which he thus incautiously reveals the true, in distinction from the professed, design is only a new instance to illustrate the difficulty of maintaining a consistent system of deception. We have understood from the beginning the guileful character of this measure, and it has constituted in our minds a strong objection against it; but we had not expected to find so distinct an acknowledgment of it in Mr Finney's defence.

Can any measures thus marked by insidiousness, be lawfully employed in the promotion of religion? How careful is the Apostle Paul to inform us that he did 'not walk in *craftiness*'; and when some of his enemies at Corinth charged him with having 'caught them with *guile*', how promptly did he repel the odious accusation! We are told too that in the Saviour's lips, 'there was found no guile'; but that his enemies used *crafty* measures to ensnare him. Christian wisdom becomes worldly cunning the moment that it ceases to be united with the artlessness and simplicity of the dove. But we need not multiply arguments to prove that deception can never be lawfully employed in the support and furtherance of the truth. The only difficulty heretofore has been to substantiate the charge of guile against the new measures, and Mr Finney has saved us all further trouble on this score.

Deception may seem for a time to aid the progress of truth, but its ultimate effects must always be injurious. In the case now under examination, it is easy to foresee the evil. Many will doubtless go to the anxious seat, and finding that no counsels of prayers are offered on their behalf which might not have been delivered with as much propriety and effect while they occupied their former seats, will perceive that the apparent and professed design of this measure was intended merely as a lure to draw them within the sphere of its real operation. They will feel that they have been deceived, and there is nothing which the mind more instinctively and quickly resents than the least approach to fraud or imposition upon itself – nothing which more surely awakens its unfriendly and hostile feelings. A still larger class will see at once the deception of this measure and will turn away in disgust from a cause which calls in the aid of such fantastic trickery – a disgust which we should not hesitate to pronounce reasonable, if the conduct which excites it were lawful and right.

The best cause imaginable on trial before a jury would be prejudiced and probably lost by any appearance of fraud in the matter or management of it. What impression then must be made respecting religion, when her friends employ such measures and represent them as essential to the success of the gospel! What multitudes will conclude and conclude justly, if the sayings and doings of these reformers are true and right, that the cause itself thus supported must be a bad one! The character of religion is known to the world chiefly from the conduct of its professed friends; and they cannot be too careful, therefore, to pursue such an open and honest course as will plainly show that in the strong consciousness of the merits of their cause, they reject with disdain the tortuous policy and intriguing arts of worldly men.

The substance of Mr Finney's first argument in defence of the anxious seat is comprised in the following extract.

When a person is seriously troubled in mind, everybody knows that there is a powerful tendency to try to keep it private that he is so, and it is a great thing to get the individual willing to have the fact known to others. And as soon as you can get him willing to make known his feelings you have accomplished a great deal.

The anxious seat he supposes will produce this willingness, will 'get him to break away from the chains of pride', and thus 'gain an important point towards his conversion'.

It is true that there is often found the tendency, here spoken of, to conceal the state of the feelings from public observation. But this is not always the effect of pride. However strange and inconceivable it may be to Mr Finney, there can be no doubt that there is such a thing as a diffidence which has its origin in modesty rather than pride. There are those, and they form perhaps a much larger class than he supposes, whose minds shrink from everything like a parade or public display of feeling. Every refined mind possesses more or less of this retiring delicacy. Its tenderest, most cherished feelings are those which are least exposed save to the objects of them; it feels indeed, that its affections would be profaned by being laid open to the stare of vulgar curiosity.

It is easy to see how such a mind will be affected by the anxious seat. In proportion ordinarily to the intenseness of the feelings awakened within a man of this mood will be his aversion to make the public exhibition of them which is demanded. He knows that there is in every community a circle of religious gossips who are always found among the earliest and warmest patrons of the anxious seat, and who attend continually upon it to satisfy their prurient curiosity and gather materials for conversation from the disclosures there made of the feelings of their neighbours. And he cannot bear the thought that his most private and sacred emotions should be thus idly bruited about. After a severe struggle of mind, he will decide not to go to the anxious seat and, as he has been taught to consider this step necessary to his conversion, there is much reason to fear that his decision not to take it will put an end to his seriousness. The spark which properly fostered might have been kindled into a bright and ever-during flame is thus quenched by a kind of rude and harsh dealing for which the Word of God affords no warrant.

There are others in whom the unwillingness to make known their religious concern proceeds from the dread of ridicule. This dread has a place in most minds, and with some men it constitutes one of the strongest feelings of their nature. There are many young men who could better brave almost any danger than endure the laugh or face the sneer of their thoughtless companions. The religious anxiety of such must become deep and strong before it will drive them to break through the restraints which this fear imposes upon them. Can it be deemed wise or safe then to expose them unnecessarily to so severe a trial as the anxious seat? This trial may in some cases effect, so far as this is concerned, the desired result, but there is a dreadful risk incurred of repelling some, upon whom the truth had taken hold, to their former state of thoughtless unconcern.

And what is the counterbalancing advantage to warrant this risk? Why, the anxious seat, argues Mr Finney, 'gets the individual, who is seriously troubled in mind, willing to have the fact known to others; and as soon as you can get him willing to make known his feelings, you have accomplished a great deal.'

The true state of the question is here very artfully concealed from view. The real operation of the anxious seat is not to make the individual upon whom it takes effect willing to have his feelings known to *others*; it is to make him willing to display them before the *whole congregation*. And this is so far from being 'an important point gained towards his conversion' that it should be deprecated as fraught with almost certain evil. It is important that some one or more should be made acquainted with his state of mind, that he may receive the instructions adapted to his case; but it is highly undesirable that the whole community should know it, lest the thought that he is the object of general observation and remark should turn away his mind from the contemplation of the truth and call up an antagonist influence which shall prevail over that which had begun to work within him. The risk, then, which is involved in the use of this measure, is incurred for the attainment of an end which is of itself a positive and serious disadvantage.

In this connection, too, we would remark that the tendency of the anxious seat, and of the whole system of public pledging, voting, etc., or as Mr Finney calls it in his Saxon English, 'of speaking right out in the meeting', is *to obstruct the operation of the truth.* They distract the mind and divert it from the truth by producing a distinct and separate excitement. Suppose an individual listening to the message of God feels the truth manifested to his conscience. As the preacher proceeds, the truth takes deeper hold upon him, the penitential tear starts from his eye, and he resolves that he will begin to seek the Lord. When the sermon is closed his heart still meditates upon the truth he has heard, and his feeling of anxious concern becomes each moment more intense.

But now comes the call to the anxious seat. He hears himself exhorted in the most impassioned manner to exchange the seat he now occupies for another designated one; and the vehemence with which this measure is urged upon him, and the motives and illustrations employed to enforce it, seem to imply that the salvation of his soul depends upon his taking this step. Here is a new subject presented to his mind, and one of a very agitating nature. The divine truth which was but now occupying his mind is forced away while he revolves the questions, Shall I go or not? Who else will go? What will they say of me? The excitement thus produced obliterates the impressions which the truth had made and, but for the consideration we are now about to present, it would then be a matter of small moment whether he went to the anxious seat or not.

The consideration just alluded to is the tendency of the anxious seat *to form and cherish delusive hopes.* Mr Finney has indeed assigned as his second argument, and the only additional one to that already examined in favour of this measure, that its bearing is 'to detect deception and delusion, and thus prevent false hopes'.

This argument would have astonished us beyond measure had we not ceased to be startled by anything which Mr Finney can say or do. He has worn out all our susceptibilities of this kind, and no measures from him in argument or action, however new, could now surprise us. This case is but one out of several similar ones, in which Mr F. resorts to the forlorn hope of reversing what he knows and feels to be the most formidable objections against him, and changing them into arguments in his favour.

As might have been anticipated in every attempt of this kind, he has utterly failed. He supposes that the anxious seat operates as a test of character. He says:

Preach to him (the awakened sinner), and at the moment he thinks he is willing to do anything – but bring him to the test, call on him to do one thing, to take one step that shall identify him with the people of God, or cross his pride – his pride comes up, and he refuses; his delusion is brought out and he finds himself a lost sinner still; whereas, if you had not done it he might have gone away flattering himself that he was a Christian.

This argument involves the capital error that no sinner who is truly awakened can refrain from obeying the call to the anxious seat. It assumes that to go to the anxious seat is 'to do something for Christ' and that it is impossible for him who refuses to go to be a Christian. It supposes that these things are true, and that every awakened sinner is ignorant or undiscerning enough to believe them true.

Some test of this kind, he says, the church has always found it necessary to have. 'In the days of the apostles, *baptism* answered this purpose. It held the precise place that the *anxious seat* does now, as a public manifestation of their (the people's) determination to be Christians.'

So it appears that baptism, like all other measures, wears itself out and must be replaced by something new. Will Mr Finney inform the church how long we must wait before this measure will be again fitted to accomplish the purpose for which the Saviour intended it? Though he supposes that the anxious seat occupies 'the precise place' that baptism did, we can by no means consent to receive it as an equivalent. Baptism was indeed a test of character, since obedience or disobedience was exercised in view of a divine command; but the anxious seat cannot operate thus, except by arrogating to itself a similar authority. We trust that this may be deemed a sufficient answer to Mr F.'s argument for the anxious seat as a test of character.

The tendency of this measure to foster delusion and create false hopes is very evident. There are some persons who are fond of notoriety and ever ready to thrust themselves forward on any occasion or in any manner which will attract to them the notice of others. To such the anxious seat holds out a powerful temptation. This measure, if used at all, must be used without discrimination. It applies the same treatment to all, and does not permit us, according to the apostolic direction, to make a difference, 'having compassion on some' 'and pulling others out of the fire'. While it unduly discourages and in many cases overwhelms with despair the timid and diffident, it invites forward the noisy and bustling who need to be repressed. Others again will go to the anxious seat who are not properly awakened, upon whom indeed the truth has produced no effect; but they go because they have been persuaded that to do so is 'to do something for Christ' and that it will be 'an important point gained towards their conversion'.

Mr Finney agrees with us in supposing that such public manifestations will often be made by persons who have not the feelings indicated; for however irrational a man's theories may be, he cannot refrain sometimes, out of connection with them, from talking common sense. On one occasion, when he is out of his controversial attitude, he says to his congregation, 'perhaps if I should put it to you now, you would all rise up and *vote* that you were agreed in desiring a revival, and agreed to have it now'; and he then goes on to prove to them that nevertheless they are not agreed.

Doubtless it would be so, and in like manner will many go to the anxious seat who are not 'anxious'. And the great majority of all who go will go under the influence of erroneous impressions and wrong excitement. Whatever may be the theory of the anxious seat, in practice it is not used for the purpose of making visible and thus rendering permanent the impressions made by the truth, nor is such its effect. This is most fully disclosed by Mr Finney.

Those who have been affected by the truth and who obey the summons to the anxious seat will not go with the view of making known their state of mind to their spiritual advisor.

They will ordinarily make this 'pilgrimage to Mecca' because they have been deceived into the belief that it is a necessary step towards their salvation; and that they are rendering to Christ an acceptable service by thus attending upon an institution which is as good as baptism, or perhaps a little better.

The excitement which draws persons of these different classes to the anxious seats, not being produced by the truth and yet partaking of a religious character, must tend to conduct the mind to error and delusion. Some, no doubt who in the heat of the moment, have taken this step before so many witnesses, will feel that they are committed, and rather than be talked of as apostates through the whole congregation, they will be induced to counterfeit a change which they have not experienced. We have not been surprised, therefore, to learn what is an unquestionable fact, that where this measured has been most used, many hypocrites have been introduced into the church – men professing godliness, but living in the practice of secret wickedness.

And a still greater number, through the operation of the same influence, have been led to cherish false hopes. In the mind of an individual who has gone to the anxious seat, an important place will be filled by the desire to come out well in the estimation of the multitude who have looked upon this declaration of his seriousness; and, already too much disposed to judge favourably of himself, he will be thus still more inclined to rest satisfied with insufficient evidences of a gracious change. Every extraneous influence of this kind which is brought to bear upon a mind engaged in the delicate business of forming an estimate of itself, must tend to mislead and delude it.

The anxious seat, no matter how judiciously managed, is liable to the objection here advanced. It excites the mind and thus urges it forward at the same time that it thrusts aside the truth, the attractive power of which is alone sufficient to draw it into its proper orbit. But the intrinsic tendency of this measure to lead the mind astray is very greatly enhanced by the manner in which it is conducted by Mr Finney and his imitators.

The ordinary course of proceeding with those who come forward to occupy the anxious seat is on this wise. They are exhorted to submit to God during the course of the prayer which the preacher is about to offer. They are told that this is a work which they can perform of themselves. They have only to summon up all their energies and put forth one herculean determination of will, and the work is done. A strong pull, as in the case of a dislocated limb, will jerk the heart straight, and all will be well.

At the conclusion of the prayer, they are called upon to testify whether they have submitted. All who make this profession, without any further examination, are at once numbered and announced as converts. Sometimes a room or some separate place is provided to which they are directed to repair. Those who remain are upbraided for their rebellion and again urged to energize the submitting volition during another prayer. And this process is continued as long as there is a prospect of its yielding any fruit.

Does it need any argument or illustration to show that the anxious seat, thus managed, must be a very hot-bed of delusion? The duty here urged upon the sinner is not, as we have shown in our former article, the duty which the Bible urges.

We are at no loss to understand why Mr Finney presents the sinner's duty in this form. Submission seems to be more comprised than some other duties within a single mental act, and more capable of instant performance. Were the sinner directed to repent, it might seem to imply that he should take some little time to think of his sins and of the Being whom he has offended; or if told to believe on the Lord Jesus Christ, he might be led to suppose that he could not exercise this faith until he had called up before his mind the considerations proper to show him his lost condition and the suitableness of the offered Saviour. Repentance and faith, therefore, will not so well answer his purpose. But with submission, he can move the sinner to the instant performance of the duty involved, or, as he says in his Saxon way, can 'break him down', 'break him down on the spot', 'melt him right down clear to the ground, so that he can neither stand nor go'. In the mental darkness consequent upon this unscriptural exhibition of his duty, and while flurried and bewildered by the excitement of the scene, the sinner is to perform the double duty of submitting and of deciding that he has submitted.

Who can doubt that under these circumstances multitudes have been led to put forth a mental act and say to themselves, 'There, it is done,' and then hold up the hand to tell the preacher they have submitted, while their hearts remain as before, except, indeed, that now the mists of religious delusion are gathering over them? Had this system been designed to lead the sinner in some plausible way to self-deception, in what important respect could it have been better adapted than it now is to this purpose?

The test-question propounded to the occupant of the anxious seat is not always made as definite as we have represented. Sometimes it is proposed in as loose and vague a form as this: 'Would you not be willing to vote that God should be the Supreme Ruler?' and an affirmative answer to this question has been deemed and proclaimed adequate evidence of submission, and the assenting individual filed off among the 'new converts'.

So unbecoming and foreign from the true nature of religion have been the attempts often made by these preachers to produce an excitement; so indecent the anxiety manifested to force upon the anxious sinner some expression or sign which might authorize them to make use of his name to swell their list of converts, that we can liken it only to the manner in which the recruiting sergeant, by the display of drum and fife and banner, and if this will not answer, by the intoxication of his dupe, persuades him to accept a piece of the king's money and thus binds him to the service and increases his own reward. The chief difference is that the enlisted soldier soon perceives that he has been caught with guile and bitterly deplores the consequences of his delusion, but the deceived sinner will in many instances remain deceived until he learns his mistake at the bar of his Judge.

Lest the proclamation, upon the most slight and insufficient grounds, that the anxious sinner is a convert should not act with sufficient power upon his sense of character to make him counterfeit a Christian deportment or deceive himself into the belief that he is a true disciple of Christ, there is provided an additional new measure, *the immediate admission to the Lord's Supper of all who profess themselves converts.* It will be at once seen how this measure plays into the rest of the system and assists the operation of the whole. Mr Finney, to perfect his system, has but to take one step, and maintain that no church has the right to discipline any of its members who have been thrown in by the operation of the new measures. This is evidently wanting to complete his plan, which ought to provide some method for retaining his converts in the church as well as for their easy introduction into it. And why should he hesitate to make this small addition? It is surely more defensible than many other parts of his system. We should not be surprised to find a denial that the 'set of old, stiff, dry, cold elders' that have crept into our churches have any authority to discipline his converts, figuring at large in the neat pattern-card which he issues of the newest fashion in measures.

Mr Finney endeavours to show that it is the duty of the young convert to apply immediately for admission to the church, and the duty of the church to yield to this application. In Chatham-street Chapel, it seems, their practice is to propound applicants for a whole month, but the reason of this long delay is that in a city many strangers will apply, and it is necessary for the session to have opportunity to inquire respecting them. In the country, however, the church will 'sin and grieve the Holy Spirit' by debarring from the communion any who apply 'if they are sufficiently instructed on the subject of religion to know what they are doing, and if their general character is such that they can be trusted as to their sincerity and honesty in making a profession'.

'Great evil,' he says, 'has been done by this practice of keeping persons out of the church a long time to see if they were Christians.' No doubt great evil has been done to the credit of his system wherever the converts made by it have been thus tried, but this is the only evil that we have ever known to result from the practice. Under the ordinary ministrations of the gospel there is much that springs up having the semblance of piety but without root, so that it soon withers away. And it cannot be doubted that much more than the usual number of these fair-looking but rootless plants will start up in Mr Finney's forcing-bed.

Surely, then, the voice of wisdom and of duty calls upon the church to wait until the blossom, if not the fruit, shall have appeared. When the seeming but deceived convert has been once admitted within the pale of the church, the motives and means of continued self-deception are so greatly multiplied as to leave but little ground for hope that he will ever be awakened from his false security until the dawning light of another world breaks in upon him.

The church also owes a duty to herself in this matter. The addition of unworthy members to her communion, by rendering frequent acts of discipline necessary, will expose her to distraction within and to scandal without. But these weighty considerations, plainly involving the eternal welfare of individuals and the true prosperity of the church, must all give way to provide for the effectual working of Mr Finney's system. Better that the church should be filled with the hypocritical and the deluded than that the new measures should lose their credit.

Many of Mr F.'s opinions tend to this same point, to provide for smuggling his converts into the church before they themselves or the session to whom they apply can have had full opportunity to judge whether they have undergone a change of heart. Says Mr F.:

There is no need of young converts *having* or *expressing* doubts as to their conversion. There is no more need of a person's doubting whether he is now in favour of God's government than there is for a man to doubt whether he is in favour of one government or another. It is, in fact, on the face of it, *absurd* for a person to talk of doubting on such a point, if he is intelligent and understands what he is talking about.

Though it might perplex a man of plain understanding to conceive how such instruction as this could be reconciled with the scriptural account of the deceitfulness of man's heart, yet its meaning and drift are perfectly intelligible. Its tendency, and it would hardly be uncharitable to say, its design, is to form a bold, swaggering, Peter-like confidence which may preserve the fresh convert from misgivings of mind during the brief interval of a few hours, or at most days, which must elapse between his professed submission and his reception into the church.

The next thing is to impress him with the belief that it is his duty to apply at once for admission to the Lord's Supper, and this is most fully done. He is told that if he waits 'he will probably go halting and stumbling along through life'. No, there must be no waiting – drive on, or the tempestuous gust will die away.

Then the church must be taught to throw open her doors, and this she is told to do under the pains and penalties of 'grieving the Holy Spirit' if she refuse. Some examination, however, must be held, and the result of this might be to show that many of the applicants had been insufficiently or erroneously instructed in the plan of salvation. And see how beautifully Mr Finney provides for this difficulty. 'In examining young converts for admission to the church, their consciences should not be ensnared by examining them too extensively or minutely *on doctrinal points.*' The meaning of the phrase 'too extensively or minutely' may be readily understood from the exposition we have given of Mr Finney's theological system.

The church session who should ask of one of these converts, What is the ground of your hope of salvation? might receive for an answer, 'My submission to God: the world is divided into two great political parties, the one with Satan, the other with God at its head; and I have energised a mighty volition and resolved to join the latter and vote in the Lord Jesus Christ as governor of the universe.'

Suppose the examination to proceed a little further – Have you been led to see the depravity of your heart? 'I know nothing of a depraved heart. All I know on this subject is that ever since Adam sinned, every person begins to sin when he becomes a moral agent.' – But does not David say, I was shapen in sin? 'Yes, but the substance of a conceived foetus cannot be sin, and David only meant that he sinned, when he sinned.'

Have you any reason to believe that your soul has been washed in the fountain set open for the remission of sin? 'I know nothing of any such operation. I have been taught that it is a great error introduced into the church by the accursed traditions of the elders to speak as though in religion there occurred anything like the washing off of some defilement.'

Upon whom do you rely for strength in the conflict which is before you? 'Upon the might of my own arm.' – Do you not pray to God to strengthen you and enable you to discharge your duties? 'No, it would be an insult to God to pray thus, as though he had commanded me to do what I am not able to perform.'

Do you believe that God is all-powerful? 'Yes; that is, I believe he can do some things, and others too, if his creatures will not oppose him.' – Can he preserve and promote the prosperity of the church? 'Yes, by taking advantage of excitements.

The session, somewhat dissatisfied, we may suppose, with this examination, resolve to question the candidate more closely on some of these points. But – 'Hold, hold,' cries Mr Finney, 'take care how you ensnare the conscience of this young convert by examining him too extensively or minutely on doctrinal points.'

The way is thus laid perfectly open for the entrance of his converts into the church. But how shall they be kept there? There are two new measures proposed by him that might seem to aim at this end, but both of them inadequate. The first is that they shall be kept in ignorance of the standards of the church they have entered. Young converts, he says, ought to be indoctrinated, but he avowedly excludes from the means of indoctrination 'teaching the catechism'. This would answer if he could only keep in the first ones until he had introduced a majority into every church who should know nothing of the catechism or confession of faith.

The other measure proposed is that his converts should not be made to 'file in behind the old, stiff, dry, cold members and elders'. No doubt, if they could be permitted to take the lead and manage all things in their own way there would be no difficulty. But there is reason to apprehend that age, combined with Christian experience and clothed with official pre-eminence, will still insist upon its right to direct the young and inexperienced.

Nothing can be more evident than that these new measures are remarkably adapted to form and propagate a false religion. Indeed, we have little doubt that the whole system has originated in a total misconception of the true nature of religion. This charge was, in substance, alleged against Mr Finney several years since, and substantiated from the only production

which he had then given to the public.[1] It was fully made out
to the conviction, we imagine, of every candid mind that
examined the evidences, but its only effect upon Mr Finney, so
far as we can perceive, has been to induce him to throw in an
unintelligible paragraph upon the difference between emotion
and principle:

One of the first things young converts should be taught is to
distinguish between emotion and principle in religion ... By emotion
I mean that state of mind of which we are conscious and which we
call *feeling,* an involuntary state of mind that arises of course when
we are in certain circumstances or under certain influences. But these
emotions should be carefully distinguished from religious principle.
By principle, I do not mean any substance or root or seed or sprout
implanted in the soul. But I mean the voluntary decision of the mind,
the firm determination to act our duty and to obey the will of God, by
which a Christian should always be governed.

Does he intend here, by maintaining that our emotions are
involuntary, to deny them any moral character? Does he mean
to tell us that the emotion of complacency towards holiness is
not an adequate or proper motive for the cultivation of
holiness in ourselves? Are all those actions which are prompted
by our emotions divested of morality, or, if moral, are
they sinful? And then, what a definition of a *principle,* as
distinguished from an emotion? A voluntary decision of mind?
A man decides to do some act because he thinks it right. His
decision is a principle. He has stumbled into this arrant
nonsense, over his dislike to mental dispositions.

[1] See a pamphlet, published in 1828, entitled *Letters of the Rev. Dr Beecher
and the Rev. Mr Nettleton on the New Measures in Promoting Revivals of
Religion*. This pamphlet contains a masterly discussion of the subject.
Though it was written before the new measures had as fully disclosed themselves as now, its allegations have been more than sustained, and all its
prophecies of evil, time has already converted into history. We fear that the
continued press of new publications has crowded this pamphlet out of sight.
It deserves more than an ephemeral existence, and we shall be glad if this
notice has in any degree the effect of calling attention to it. It has never been
answered. Mr Finney, we are told, makes it his rule never to reply to any
attacks upon him – it should have been added, save by bitter vituperations
from the pulpit. A very convenient principle this.

But we will not puzzle ourselves or our readers in the attempt further to analyse this mysterious paragraph. Whatever may be its meaning or design, it will not turn aside the charge that the general tendency of Mr Finney's representations is to give an undue predominance to the imaginative emotions in religion.

We are susceptible of two very different classes of emotion – the one connected with the imagination, the other with the moral sense; the one awakened by objects that are grand, terrible, etc., the other called into exercise by the perception of moral qualities. These two kinds of emotion produce widely different effects upon the animal frame. Let a predominant emotion of terror fill the mind and it will fever the blood, quicken the pulse, blanch the cheek, and agitate the whole frame. Each moment that the emotion becomes more intense, the bodily excitement increases, and it may be heightened until life is destroyed by it. But let the mind be occupied with disapprobation of moral evil, and in the intensest degree of this emotion, how feeble in comparison is its effect upon the powers and functions of animal life? This close sympathy of the imaginative emotions with the bodily frame gives them a dangerous pre-eminence.

The same object often calls into simultaneous action emotions belonging to both these classes. The contemplation of his sinful life may call up at once in the mind of a man abhorrence of sin and dread of its evil consequences, and there is reason to fear that, without great care, the latter feeling will absorb the former.

Now, it is just here that we think Mr Finney has erred and gone over into the regions of enthusiastic excitement. He is evidently possessed of an ardent temperament, and the calm and gentle excitement attending the exercise of the moral emotions disconnected with the imaginative has not sufficient relish for him. It is comparatively tame and tasteless. For the same reason, he discards as 'animal excitement' all the gentler feelings; such as, like the 'soft and plaintive note of an Eolian harp', spread themselves through the soul and dissolve it in tender sadness or pity. He turns from these to the stronger and more boisterous emotions which, stirring both soul and body like the sound of the trumpet, can yield the luxurious play and revel of intense sensation. When a feeling of this character is awakened by religious objects, though it should swallow up the accompanying emotion inspired by conscience, yet the imaginative mind entertains no doubt of the religious character of the passion which fills and moves it.

It is in this region, where prevails the awakening din of the storm and tempest of pious passion, that Mr Finney, as it appears to us, has constructed the chief dwelling-place of religion. For the proof of this, we appeal to the general tone of swelling extravagance which marks all his sentiments and to the habitual tenor of his illustrations and instructions.

He teaches in various places and ways that the progress of religion in the heart cannot properly be set forth under the symbol of the growth of 'any root or sprout or seed, implanted in the mind'. Now it so happens that one of these figures, the growth of a seed, was employed for this very purpose on more than one occasion by our Lord himself and by his apostles. And it must be acknowledged that this is a very fit and instructive emblem, if the progress of religion be dependent on the growth of *principle* – that is, of that which is the *beginning*, or which lays the ground for a series of actions and determines them to be what they are; but inappropriate and deceptive, as he represents it to be, if religion has its origin in a 'deep-seated' act of the mind, and for its increase depends on the fitful gusts of passionate fervour.

To the same effect are the many representations which he puts forth of the repugnance which the Christian will feel when brought into contact with a fellow Christian who is more spiritual than himself. This electric repulsion will take place only when their minds are under the dominion of the imaginative emotions. The Christian whose religion is the offspring of principle, and has its range among the emotions of the moral sense, will love Christian excellence and be attracted by it in proportion to its purity and brightness. The effect of greater holiness than his own, whether seen in men, in angels, or in God, will be to increase his admiration and draw him onward in the divine life.

This repellent effect of the exhibition of greater piety, Mr Finney supposes, will take place only in those who are considerably below it. If those around are anywhere 'near the mark', it will 'kindle and burn' among them until it has warmed them all up to its own temperature. Hence, in a prayer meeting, if a spiritual man leads who is 'far ahead' of the rest, 'his prayer will repel them'; but it 'will awaken them if they are not *so far* behind as to revolt at it and resist it'. And again he says, 'in the midst of the warm expressions that are flowing forth, let an individual come in who is cold and pour his cold breath out, like the damp of death, and it will make every Christian that has any feeling want to get out of the meeting.' A precise account this of the operation of a kind of religion which has cut loose from principle and conscience, and surrendered itself to the emotions of the imagination.

And in accommodation to this species of religion must all the arrangements of the prayer meeting be ordered. 'There should be,' he says, 'but one definite object before the meeting.' Forgetful – perhaps we ought to say, reckless – of the model our Saviour has given us, in which there are as many objects brought before the mind as it contains sentences, he censures and ridicules every prayer which is not confined to a single point.

Unless some short passage of Scripture can be found which bears upon this specific point, he says, no portion of the Bible should be read at the meeting. 'Do not drag in the Word of God to make up a part of the meeting as a mere matter of form – this is an insult to God.'

There must be no 'joyful singing'. 'When singing is introduced in a prayer meeting, the hymns should be short and so selected as to bring out something solemn, some *striking* words.'

There must be no adoration of the Deity. Yes, incredible as it may appear, Mr Finney proscribes and burlesques that sublimest, holiest exercise of the human mind, in which it rises to the contemplation of Infinite Excellence and prostrates itself before it, rehearsing the perfections which it feels it cannot worthily celebrate. 'Some men,' he says, 'will spin out a long prayer in telling God who and what he is!!'

The tendency of all this is easily perceived. We have mentioned the correspondence which always takes place between the movements of imaginative emotions and of the animal frame. Mr Finney contends that the spirit of prayer is in its very nature and essence a spirit of agony; and he mentions with commendation a state of mind in which 'there is but one way to keep from *groaning,* and that is by resisting the Holy Ghost'. Nay, he brings forward with very special praise the case of a man 'who prayed *until he bled at the nose!!*' Another pattern is afforded by a woman who got into such a state of mind that she could not live without prayer. She could not rest day nor night unless there was somebody praying. Then she would be at ease; but if they ceased, *she would shriek with agony.* Of himself he says,

Brethren, in my present *state of health,* I find it impossible to pray as much as I have been in the habit of doing, and continue to preach . . . Now will not you, who are *in health,* throw yourselves into this work, and bear this *burden,* and lay *yourselves out* in prayer?

Again, it is well known that persons who are under the dominion of imagination soon become a prey to delusion. All their inward impressions are projected into the form of external realities. Their forebodings of mind are to them the shadows of coming events, and they assume the character and authority of prophets. This peculiarity is fully endorsed by Mr Finney under the name of 'spiritual discernment'.

There was a woman in a certain place – almost all his stories of this kind are about women – who

became anxious about sinners and went to praying for them – and she finally came to her minister and talked with him and asked him to appoint an anxious meeting, for she *felt* that one was needed. The minister put her off, for he *felt* nothing of it. The next week she came again and besought him to appoint an anxious meeting; she *knew* there would be somebody to come, for she *felt* as if God was going to pour out his Spirit. He put her off again. And finally she said to him, 'If you don't appoint an anxious meeting *I shall die,* for there is *certainly* going to be a revival.' The next Sabbath he appointed a meeting.

The result of course was, as in all other *published* predictions of this kind, that the oracle was fulfilled.

He had several other stories to the same effect; and the expectation of these women, founded on no evidence save that of individual feeling, he calls 'spiritual discernment'; and gives warrant to those who possess it to arraign their ministers and elders and fellow members of the church as 'blind' and 'sleepy'. 'Devoted, praying Christians,' he says, 'often see these things so clearly and look so far ahead, as greatly to stumble others. They sometimes almost seem to prophesy.' They do indeed not only almost, but altogether, seem to prophesy, and so has many an enthusiast before them. This disposition to put faith in spectral illusions is indeed a very common mark of enthusiasm, and the reason of it is well understood by all who are acquainted with the philosophy of the human feelings.

In like contradiction to the true nature of religion, but in perfect keeping with the false notion of it which we suppose Mr Finney to have adopted, are his opinions respecting the absolute necessity of excitement to the general prosperity of religion in the world and to its growth in the Christian's heart. 'The state of the world is still such, and probably will be till the millennium is fully come, that religion must be mainly promoted by these excitements.' His professed theory on this subject is that there must be an alternation of excitement and decline – that after a great religious stir among the people, they will decline and keep on declining 'till God can have time, so to speak, to shape the course of events so as to produce another excitement' – then comes another decline, and so on.

He represents this same spasmodic action as taking place in each Christian's experience. It is impossible, he thinks, to keep a Christian in such a state as not to do injury to a revival, unless he pass through the process of 'breaking down' every few days. 'I have never laboured,' he says, 'in revivals in company with any one who could keep in the work and be fit to manage revival continually who did not pass through this process of *breaking down* as often as once in two or three weeks.' He adds, 'I was surprised to find a few years since that the phrase *breaking down* was a stumbling block to certain ministers and professors of religion – they laid themselves open to the rebuke administered to Nicodemus, "Art thou a master in Israel, and knowest not these things?"'

We are surprised that anyone should have been ignorant of the meaning of this 'breaking down'. It is very intelligible. In consequence of the law to which we have several times referred, when the imaginative emotions are strongly excited the bodily frame sympathizes powerfully with the excitement, and all the chords of the system are so tensely strung that they cannot long bear it. Hence follows reaction, exhaustion, 'breaking down'. If religion be founded in principle, if its peculiar and cherished emotions be those of the conscience, then can there be no call for this breaking down and jumping up – this cicadic movement.

But we have dwelt at sufficient length upon this point. We were anxious to present as complete evidence of the truth of our position as our limits would permit; for we do believe that Mr Finney's mistaken views of the nature of religion lie at the bottom of his measures and have given to them their character and form; and that these measures, therefore, wherever used, will tend to propagate a false form of religion.

These measures might have had their origin in the 'New Divinity', for they are in harmony with the theology as well as the religion of the system. Historical facts, however, have guided us in assigning their origin to erroneous views of religion. The New Measures, we believe were in full action before the theology of New Haven shed its light upon the world. We recollect that it was matter of surprise to many when the conjunction took place between the coarse, bustling fanaticism of the New Measures, and the refined intellectual abstractions of the New Divinity. It was a union between Mars and Minerva – unnatural, and boding no good to the church. But our readers will have observed that there is a close and logical connection between Mr Finney's theology and his measures. The demand created for the one by the other and the mutual assistance which they render are so evident that we will spend no time in the explanation of them.

There is one argument of Mr Finney in favour of the new measures which we have not noticed, and to which we should not now allude, but for a purpose which will soon disclose itself. This argument is, in true importance, on a perfect level with that drawn from the small-clothes, wigs, and fur caps. It consists in producing the names of a great number of wise and eminent men who have been prominent in introducing innovations. All this has nothing to do with the question – it is perfectly puerile indeed to introduce it – unless these men introduced such innovations as he contends for. Among these new-measure men he introduces the name of President Edwards. And on several occasions he makes such a use of the name of this great man as is calculated to leave upon the reader's mind the impression that Edwards had sanctioned his proceedings. He has no right thus to slander the dead or impose upon the living.

It is well known that Davenport, against whose extravagant fanaticism Edwards wrote at length is *redivivus* in Mr Finney, and that the same scenes over which he grieved and wept have been re-enacted in our day under Mr Finney's auspices. For one of his measures, lay exhortation, he does distinctly claim the authority of Edwards. 'So much opposition,' he says, 'was made to this practice nearly a hundred years ago that President Edwards actually had to take up the subject and write a laboured defence of the rights and duties of laymen.'

We were not surprised by Mr Finney's ignorance in confounding Mary, Queen of Scots, with 'bloody Queen Mary' of England; we do not demand from him historical accuracy; we do not look indeed for anything like a thorough knowledge of any one subject, for, should he obtain it, it would surely pine away and die for want of company. But we were not quite prepared for such ignorance of Edwards's opinions and writings. Can it be ignorance? Charity would dispose us to think so, but we cannot. In the same work from which Mr Finney has taken long extracts and to which he often refers as if familiar with its contents, Edwards makes known with all plainness his opposition to lay exhortation. He expressly condemns all lay teaching which is not 'in the way of conversation'. He censures the layman

when in a set speech, of design, he directs himself to a multitude, as looking that they should compose themselves to attend to what he has to say . . . and more still, when meetings are appointed on purpose to hear lay persons exhort, and they take it as their business to be speakers.

In a published letter of his to a friend who had erred in this matter, he tells him:

You have lately gone out of the way of your duty and done that which did not belong to you, in exhorting a public congregation . . .

you ought to do what good you can by private, brotherly, humble admonitions and counsels; but 'tis too much for you to exhort public congregations or solemnly to set yourself by a set speech, to counsel a room full of people, unless it be children or those that are much your inferiors.

These are the sentiments of Edwards, and it is hardly possible that Mr Finney should have been unacquainted with them. Whence then this bold misrepresentation? This is one illustration of that unscrupulousness in the use of means for the attainment of his ends which he too often manifests. With perfect nonchalance he will make figures, facts, Scripture, everything, bend to the purpose he has in hand. We have often been reminded while reading his pages of the calculator who, being applied to, to make some computations, asked his employer with perfect gravity, 'On which side, Sir, do you wish the balance to come out?'

Another illustration of Mr F.'s peculiar facility in this way is at hand, and we will give it. In one of his *Lectures*, when endeavouring to persuade the people not to contradict the truth preached by their lives, and as usual inflating every sentiment to the utmost degree for the accomplishment of his purpose, he says, 'If Jesus Christ were to come and preach, and the church contradict it, it would *fail – it has been tried once.*' But in another *Lecture*, where he is labouring might and main to prove that every minister will be successful in exact proportion to the amount of wisdom he employs in his ministration, he is met with the objection that Jesus Christ was not successful in his ministry.

But, reader, you do not know the man if you imagine that this difficulty staggers him at all. Not in the least. In disposing of it he begins by showing that 'his ministry was *vastly more successful* than is generally supposed', and ends by proving that 'in fact, he was *eminently successful*'. And no doubt, if his argument required it, he could prove that Christ was neither successful nor unsuccessful.

This unscrupulous use of any means that seem to offer present help, whether for the attainment of their objects within the camp or without, was early noted as a peculiar mark of the new-measure men. Dr Beecher says, in a letter written eight years since, 'I do know, as incident to these new measures, there is a spirit of the most marvellous duplicity and double-dealing and lying surpassing anything which has come up in my day.'[1] And the heaviness of this accusation will not be much lightened by any one who has been an attentive observer of their movements since.

These were Dr Beecher's sentiments in 1827. Since that time he is understood to have patronised the Corporal when he visited Boston; and but lately he delivered a high eulogy upon him at the West, in the course of which he says, 'I have felt the beating of his great warm heart before God', and professes to have heard more *truth* from him than from any other man in the same space of time. Dr B.'s opinions, expressed in the letter from which we have quoted, profess to have been formed from the most full and accurate acquaintance with facts. Dr Beecher has an undoubted right to change any of his opinions, but he cannot expect the public to give him their confidence if he makes such changes as this, without rendering a more satisfactory account of them than he has yet given of this one.

There only remains to be noticed the argument for the new measures which Mr Finney draws from their *success*. We shall not stop to dispute with him the position which he assumes, that the success of any measure demonstrates its wisdom and excellence. No man can maintain the ground which he takes upon this subject, denying that it forms any part of the plan of

---

[1] This letter was addressed to the Editor of the *Christian Spectator*. It seems that there had been some symptoms of a disposition on the part of this Editor to compromise with the new measures, from a desire to promote the circulation of his work in those regions where these measures were then burning in all their fury. Dr B. immediately writes this letter of strong remonstrance, in which in the most rousing strain he exhorts to firm, open and decided resistance. 'The more thoroughly we do the work', he says, 'of entire demolition of these new measures, the sooner and safer we can conciliate.' His opinion of Mr Finney at that time may be gathered from the following extract: 'Now, that such a man as he (Mr Nettleton) should be traduced and exposed to all manner of evil falsely in order to save from *deserved reprehension* such a man as Finney (who, whatever talents or piety he may possess, is as far removed from the talent, wisdom, and judgment, and experience of Nettleton, as any corporal in the French army was removed from the talent and generalship of Bonaparte), is what neither my reason, nor my conscience, nor my heart will endure.'

God in the government of the world, to bring good out of evil. But there is no need of discussing this matter now. We will grant him the benefit of the criterion.

It is too late in the day for the effect of this appeal to success. The time was when an argument of this nature might have been plausibly maintained. Appearances were somewhat in favour of the new measures. At least wherever they were carried converts were multiplied, and though the churches were distracted, ministers unsettled, and various evils wrought, yet it might have been contended that on the whole, the balance was in their favour. But it is too late now for Mr Finney to appeal, in defence of his measures, to the number of converts made by them, to the flourishing state of religion in the western part of New York, where they have been most used, and to the few trivial evils which have been incident to them. Indeed, he seems to have a suspicion that the public possess more information on this subject than they did a few years since, and he pours out his wrathful effusions on the informers. He is animated with a most special dislike to letter-writing. 'Some men,' he says, 'in high standing in the church have circulated letters which never were printed. Others have had their letters printed and circulated. There seems to have been a system of letter-writing about the country.' 'If Christians in the United States expect revivals to spread, they must give up *writing letters,*' etc. 'If the Church will do all her duty, the millennium may come in this country in three years; but if this *writing of letters* is to be kept up, etc. . . . the curse of God will be on this nation, and that before long.' 'Go forward. Who would leave such a work and go to writing letters?' 'If others choose to publish their *slang and stuff,* let the Lord's servants keep to their work.' Who will not feel thankful that Jack Cade's day is gone, and a man cannot now be hung 'with pen and ink-horn around his neck' for being able to write his name?

But thanks to these much abused letter-writers, we have received their testimony, and neither Mr Finney's assertions nor his ravings will shake the public confidence in it. It is now generally understood that the numerous converts of the new measures have been, in most cases, like the morning cloud and the early dew. In some places, not a half, a fifth, or even a tenth part of them remain. They have early 'broken down' and have never got up again. And of those that yet remain, how many are found revelling in the excesses of enthusiastic excitement, ready to start after every new vagary that offers, and mistaking the looming appearances, the *fata Morgana*, of the falsely refracting atmosphere in which they dwell, for splendid realities! How many more, the chief part of whose religion consists in censuring the established order of things around them, in seeking to innovate upon the decent and orderly solemnities of divine worship, and in condemning as unconverted, or cold and dead, the ministers, elders, and church members, who refuse to join them!

From the very nature of these measures they must encounter the conscientious and decided opposition of many devout Christians, and hence wherever they have been introduced, the churches have been distracted by internal dissensions and in many cases rent asunder. Ministers who have opposed them have been forced to abandon their charges; and those who have yielded to them have been unsettled by their inability to stimulate sufficiently the seared surface of the public mind; so that it is now a difficult matter among the western churches of New York to find a pastor who has been with his present flock more than two or three years.

Change and confusion are the order of the day. New ministers and new measures must be tried, to heighten an excitement already too great to admit of increase, or to produce one where the sensibility has been previously worn out by overaction. Rash and reckless men have everywhere rushed in and pushed matters to extremes, which the originators of these measures did not at first contemplate. Trickery of the most disgusting and revolting character has been employed in the conduct of religious assemblies; and the blasphemous boasts of the revival preachers have been rife throughout the land. Mothers have whipped their children with rods to make them submit to God; and in this have done right, if there be truth in the theology and fitness in the measures of Mr Finney. Men of taste and refinement have been driven into scepticism by these frantic absurdities of what claims to be the purest form of religion, or they have sought refuge in other denominations from these disorderly scenes in ours.

Doctrinal errors and fanatical delusions of the wildest kind have started into rank existence. The imposture of Matthias and the Perfectionism of New Haven, are monster-growths, in different directions, of this same monster-trunk.[1] And no one can tell what new and yet more monstrous growths it will cast out. No form of enthusiasm develops at once or soon all its latent tendencies. Though its present course may be comparatively regular and near the truth, no mind can predict in what erratic wanderings it may be subsequently involved. The path of the comet within the limits of the solar system can scarcely be distinguished by the nicest observations, from the regular orbit of the planet; but it ultimately rushes off into unknown fields of space: and the course of enthusiasm while in sight, like that of the comet, will not suffice to furnish us with the elements of its orbit. To what blackness of darkness it may finally rush, we know not. We might fill a volume with describing evils already wrought by the new divinity and new measure system, and then fill many more by collating this system with history and showing what evils are yet within the limits of its capabilities.

We would not be understood to mean that no good has been produced under the preaching of the new divinity and the operation of the new measures. They have doubtless in some cases been overruled for good and been made instrumental in producing true conversions. But we do maintain, for we fully believe it to be true, that the tendency of this system, of all that is peculiar to it as a system of doctrine and of action, is unredeemedly bad. We have brought forward every argument which we could find in Mr Finney's pages in favour of his reforms, and in canvassing them have presented our own objections. And our readers must now judge between us.

[1] See the history of *Matthias and His Impostures* by Col. William L. Stone. Col. Stone has rendered an important service to the public by the publication of this work. It furnishes a train of facts which will astonish those who have looked upon this noted imposture as a sudden and isolated freak of the human mind. It was our purpose to make copious extracts from this work to illustrate the opinion of its author, that the delusion of Matthias and of his victims 'originated in the same spirit of fanaticism which has transformed so many Christian communities in the northern and western parts of New York, and states contiguous, into places of moral waste and spiritual desolation.' But we must content ourselves with this reference. We hope the work will circulate widely. It furnishes a salutary lesson of warning to all who can learn from the past.

We have one more objection still to present, and it would alone be sufficient to outweigh all the considerations which Mr Finney has presented in favour of his measures. We mean the *spirit* which accompanies them. We shall be under the necessity of giving a much briefer development and fewer illustrations of this spirit than we had intended, but we shall succeed, we think, in showing that it is the essential spirit of fanaticism.

The first feature of it to which we invite attention, is its *coarseness* and *severity*. Mr Finney's language is habitually low and vulgar. He revels in such Saxonisms as these: 'Let hell boil over if it will, and spew out as many devils as there are stones in the pavement.' 'Look at that sensitive young lady; is she an impenitent sinner? Then she only needs to die to be as very a devil as there is in hell.' 'Devil' and 'hell' are, indeed, familiar to him 'as household words'. The young men in some of our theological seminaries, he says, 'are taught to look upon new measures as if they were the very inventions of the devil. So when they come out, they look about and watch and start as if the devil was there.' We imagine that all the young men in our seminaries know that there are *men* who are equal to these things without any help from the devil.

In condemning those who pray, 'Lord, these sinners are seeking thee, sorrowing,' he says, 'It is a LIE.'

The men who had promised to pay, each, a yearly sum to the Oneida Institute, but who afterwards refused on the ground, as one of them assured us, that the pledge under which they subscribed, that a thorough course of instruction should be established in the institution, had been violated, are rated after this manner:

Is this honest? Will such honesty as this get them admitted into heaven? What! break your promise, and go up and carry a *lie* in your right hand before God? If you refuse or neglect to fulfil your promise, you are a *liar,* and if you persist in this you shall have your part in the lake that burns with fire and brimstone.

He subsequently adds, 'You cannot pray until you pay that money.'

In dealing with impenitent sinners, he will allow no symptoms of compassion or pity. The church, in all her conduct, must show that she 'blames them'. We must at all times make it plain by our deportment that we 'take God's part against the sinner.' He thinks it a dreadful error even for us to make use of our Saviour's language in praying for sinners, 'Father, forgive them, they know not what they do.' Every sentence and every term must be charged with fierce accusation against them.

To this harsh severity all the tender amenities of social intercourse and the still more tender charities of the domestic affections must be sacrificed. He maintains that parents can never pray for their children 'in such a way as to have their prayers answered, until they feel that their children are *rebels*'. And he narrates a story to show that no mother can expect her son to be converted 'until she is made to take *strong ground against him as a rebel*'.

Had we space for comment here, we might easily show that no spirit can claim fellowship with the gospel of Jesus Christ which thus runs rough-shod over all the tender sympathies and affections of the human heart. But it is thoroughly consistent with the fierceness of fanatical zeal, which has its play among the stronger passions of our nature and looks with contempt upon whatever is kind, tender, gentle, or compassionate.

The next feature of Mr Finney's spirit to which we turn, is its *extravagance*. It is a peculiar mark of the fanatic that every dogma, every little peculiarity to which he is attached, is made to be infallibly certain and infinitely important. Should he admit anything less than this he would feel the ground sliding from under him. To hold natural sentiments and express them plainly and with proper limitations would be to sink all his advantage and bring himself down to a level with others.

His own mind, too, is often in an uneasy and self-doubting state which needs confirmation. Hence, for the double purpose of making a strong impression on others and of strengthening himself, every opinion and sentiment are inflated entirely beyond their natural limits. To quote all the illustrations of this disposition to extravagance which Mr Finney's lectures afford would be to cite no inconsiderable portion of the whole volume which contains them. The minutest things are made matters of indispensable necessity. Every rag which he touches is henceforth endowed with the power of working miracles. He is himself addicted to telling stories and parables from the pulpit to illustrate the truth, and we have no objection to this provided it is done – as Mr F. says the devil wishes it done – so as to comport with the proper dignity of the pulpit. We have known many preachers who excelled in this style of preaching. But Mr F. is not content with maintaining that this is a good and, for some men, the best way of presenting and enforcing the truth. No, nothing less will satisfy him than that 'truths not thus illustrated are generally just as well calculated to convert sinners as a mathematical demonstration'. Many excellent men who have no taste or turn for this illustrative method of preaching will be astonished and grieved to learn that to deliver a plain, unvarnished statement of scriptural truth to their congregations is as hopeless a means of doing good as to prove to them that two sides of a triangle are greater than the third side.

Again, Mr Finney is given to extemporaneous preaching, and of course this is not merely the best, it is the *only way,* of preaching. He can find no resting place for the sole of his foot but on the broad ground that 'we never can have the *full meaning* of the gospel till we throw away our notes'.

We do not like forms of prayer, not thinking them adapted to promote the spirit of prayer; and we shall always oppose them, unless they should be found necessary to protect us from such prayers as Mr Finney is in the habit of offering. But we can by no means agree with him in saying that 'forms of prayer are not only absurd in themselves, but they are the very device of the devil'.

We have seen many a pious old lady, when she had finished reading a portion of her Bible, placing a piece of paper or a string, or perchance her spectacles, between the leaves, that she might readily open to the place again, and it certainly never occurred to us that this custom was any evidence of want of piety. But Mr Finney says to all such, 'The fact that you fold a leaf or put in a string demonstrates that you read rather as a *task* than from love or reverence for the word of God.'

Of the prayers of pious females who have assembled by themselves without inviting impenitent sinners to be present, he says, 'such prayers will do no good – *they insult God*'. To those who are in the habit of praying with submission to the divine will, he says, 'You have no right to put in an *if,* and say,

Lord, *if it be thy will,* give us thy Holy Spirit; *this is to insult God'*.

Mr Finney, like all other fanatics, makes additions of his own to the scriptural code of morals. Matthias forbade his disciples the use of pork. Mr Finney condemns tea, coffee, and tobacco, evening parties, ribbons, and many other things. He is just as confident in supporting his false standard, as extravagant too in denouncing those who transgress it, and in launching against them the thunderbolts of divine vengeance, as if it had been communicated to him by express revelation. He says, 'If you are not doing these things' – among which he has enumerated *the disuse of tea, coffee and tobacco –* 'and if your soul is not agonized for the poor, benighted heathen, why are you such a *hypocrite* as to pretend to be a Christian? Why, your profession is an *insult* to Jesus Christ.'

Again, he says, 'Perhaps he is looking upon it (the use of tobacco) as a small sin', and he then proceeds to prove that the sin is as gross as a merchant's clerk would commit in robbing the money drawer. He lifts up his hands in astonishment at an agent who is in the city soliciting funds for some charitable purpose and actually uses all three of these abominations; and he enters his protest against the Home Missionary Society for aiding churches in which the members use tea, coffee, or tobacco. Again, speaking of the *ministry* as refusing to give up the use of coffee, he cries out, 'Is this *Christianity*? What business have you to use Christ's money for such a purpose?' Matthias surely could not have raved in better style over a delinquent caught in the horrible act of eating a piece of pork.

Of evening parties, even when none but 'Christian friends are invited so as to have it a religious party', he says, 'this is the *grand device* of the devil.' These social assemblies are often concluded with prayer: – 'Now this,' he says, 'I regard as one of the worst features about them.' When there is to be a circle of such parties in a congregation he advises them

to dismiss their minister and let him go and preach where the people would be ready to receive the word and profit by it, and not have him stay and be distressed, and grieved, and *killed,* by attempting to promote religion among them while they are engaged *heart and hand in the service of the devil.*

To the young lady who wears 'a gaudy ribbon and ornaments upon her dress', he cries, 'Take care. You might just as
well write on your clothes, *No truth in religion.*' And over this
fondness for dress, tight-lacing, etc., he says, 'Heaven puts on
the robes of mourning, and hell may hold a jubilee.'

The man who stands aloof from the temperance cause has
'his hands all over *red with blood*', – he who drinks cider, beer,
or anything else, until 'you can smell his breath' is a *drunkard*
– and no slave holder 'can be a fit subject for Christian
communion and fellowship'.

We had marked some twenty other passages, many of them
worse than any we have given, but we suppose enough has
been furnished to satisfy our readers of Mr Finney's extravagance.

We turn, then, to his *spiritual pride* and *arrogance*. We have
not been able to find one sentence in his book which wears the
semblance of humility. But there is arrogance and assumption
beyond anything which it has ever been our fortune previously
to encounter. Such a swelling, strutting consciousness of self-
importance looks forth from almost every page, that we have
been compelled again and again to turn from it, not in anger
but in pity.

Any one who should read his book and believe it would be
led to suppose that until he came forth in the plenitude of his
wisdom and goodness to instruct mankind, all had been darkness. The Bible had been misunderstood and its doctrines
perverted; ministers had been preaching 'an endless train of
fooleries'; the pulpit had never 'grappled with mind'; 'very
little common sense had been exercised about prayer meetings'; everything had been managed in the most ignorant and
bungling way. But he comes and all things are set right, or at
least would be if his measures were not opposed. All the wise
and good, however, fully agree with him.

We encounter this arrogant and exclusive spirit at the very
outset. In his preface he says, 'But whatever may be the result
of saying the truth as it respects some, I have reason to believe
that the great body of *praying* people will receive and be
benefited by what I have said.' Speaking, in one of his lectures
of 'ministers, who by their lives and preaching give evidence to
the church that their object is to do good and win souls to

Christ', he says, '*This class of* ministers will recognise the truth of *all* that I have said or wish to say.'

In the full magnitude of a self-constituted bishop of all the churches, fully entitled by his superior wisdom to rebuke with authority all other ministers, he exclaims in another place, 'I will never spare ministers from the naked truth.' 'If the whole church,' he says, 'as a body had gone to work ten years ago and continued it as *a few individuals whom I could name* have done, there would not now be an impenitent sinner in the land.' The greatest appearance of modest humility which we have seen in him is his refusing on this occasion to name himself at the head of the 'few individuals'.

He claims, in no guarded terms, the exclusive approbation of God for his doctrines and measures. 'They' (the church) 'see that the *blessing of God* is with those that are thus accused of new measures and innovation.' Desirous as he is to monopolize the favour of heaven, we do not wonder at finding him in another place declaring with great *naïveté*, 'I have been pained to see that some men, in giving accounts of revivals, have evidently felt themselves obliged to be particular in detailing the measures used, to avoid the inference that *new measures* were introduced.' And if the accounts of all the revivals that have occurred without any help from the new measures were as much noised abroad as those aided by them have been, he would be still more 'pained' by the more abundant evidence that the symbol of the Divine presence does not shine exclusively upon his camp.

In presenting to his hearers 'the consequences of *not being filled with the Spirit*', he says to them:

You will be much troubled with fears about fanaticism – you will be much disturbed by the *measures* that are used in revivals; if any measures are adopted that are *decided* and *direct,* you will think they are all new, and will be *stumbled* at them just in proportion to your *want of spirituality: you* will stand and cavil at them because you are *so blind* as not to see their adaptedness, while *all heaven is* rejoicing in them.

Again, of those that are opposed to 'new measures', to 'this new-light preaching', and to 'these evangelists who go about the country preaching', he says, '*Such* men will sleep on till they are awakened by the judgment trumpet without any revival, unless they are willing that God should come *in his own way.'*

This fanatical claim to the exclusive favour of God, this arrogant identification of all his opinions and measures with the divine will, is very frequently put forth. After having proved that his system has been greatly prospered, that it has been successful beyond anything the world had yet seen, he says, 'If a measure is *continually and usually blessed,* let the man who thinks he is wiser than God call it in question – take care how you *find fault with God.'*

Of the Cedar-street church in New York, which had taken a decided stand against the new divinity and new measures, or as Mr Finney states it, had pursued a course 'calculated to excite an unreasonable and groundless suspicion against many ministers who are labouring successfully to promote revivals', he says, 'They may pretend to be mighty pious and jealous for the honour of God, but *God will not believe* they are sincere.' Of this same church he afterwards says, in allusion to their requiring an assent to the Confession of Faith from all applicants for admission to the Lord's Supper, a step which would exclude his converts, unless their consciences should be as elastic as their teacher's, 'No doubt *Jesus Christ is angry* with such a church, and he will show his displeasure in a way that admits of no mistake if they do not repent.'

In the prospect of a rupture with France, he tells his people, 'No doubt' – it will be observed that he never has any *doubt* about the divine feelings when his measures are in question – 'No doubt God is holding the rod of war over this nation; the nation is under *his displeasure* because the church has conducted in such a manner with respect to revivals.'

The 'dear fathers' who have the training of our young men for the ministry, he thinks unfit for their office, and in this opinion he is perfectly confident that he has 'the mind of the Lord'. 'Those dear fathers,' he says, 'will not, I suppose, see this; and will perhaps think hard of me for saying it; *but it is the cause of Christ.'*

But we have given specimens enough of this offensive self-glorification.

In close connection with this trait stands his *censoriousness*. The passages we have already adduced for other purposes so far illustrate this disposition that it will not be necessary to produce many in addition. Of those who have circulated what he calls 'slanderous reports of revival men and measures', he says, 'It is impossible, from the very laws of their mind, that they should engage in this work of death, this mischief of hell, if they truly loved the cause of Christ.'

'Hell' is with him nothing more nor less than the state prison of his system, to which all are condemned who dissent or doubt. Again he says, 'No doubt the devil laughs, if they can laugh in hell, to hear a man pretend to be very much engaged in religion and a great lover of revivals, and yet all the while on the look-out for fear some *new measures* should be introduced.' And of prayers which ask 'that sinners may have more conviction', or 'that sinners may go home, solemn and tender, and take the subject into consideration', he says, 'All such prayers are just such prayers as *the devil wants.*'

This is but a common and very vulgar method of cursing. It contains no argument. It would be very easy for his opponents to reply that the devil is thus exclusively busy among the adversaries to the new opinions and measures, because he is aware that among their friends his work is well enough done without him. And the argument would be as good in the one case as in the other.

Mr Finney has some mystical notions respecting the 'prayer of faith' – notions in which none, we believe, out of his own *coterie* agree with him.[1] Here as elsewhere, he condemns without mercy all dissentients. Having spoken of a public examination at a theological seminary, in the course of which his peculiar opinions on this subject were controverted, he says, 'Now, to teach such sentiments as these is to trifle with

---

[1]It was our purpose, had our limits permitted, to notice at length his wild opinions on this subject. We the less regret the necessary exclusion of our intended remarks on this topic, as we are able to refer the reader to a very excellent discussion of it, in two Lectures, lately published, from the pen of Dr Richards, of the Auburn Seminary. Since the publication of these Lectures, Mr Finney no doubt has another argument for proving that this venerable servant of Christ is not 'such a man as is needed for training our young ministers in these days of excitement and action'.

the word of God.' And he declares that all persons who have not known by experience the truth of his enthusiastic views of this matter 'have great reason to doubt their piety' and adds, 'This is by no means uncharitable.'

Everything which has, at any time or in any quarter of the land, been said or done that seems adapted to operate to the prejudice of his measures, is dragged into the pulpit and made the occasion of denunciation against the transgressors. 'Some young men in Princeton came out a few years ago with an essay on the evils of revivals.' We cannot see what necessity there was for Mr Finney to tell the people of Chatham-street Chapel that the young men in Princeton some years before had published their opposition to the new measures. But he does tell them, and adds, 'I should like to know how *many* of those young men have enjoyed revivals among their people since they have been in the ministry; and if *any* have, I should like to know whether they have not *repented* of that piece about the evils of revivals?' We can inform Mr Finney, that that 'piece' affords 'no place for repentance' though it should be sought 'carefully with tears'.

He tells his people again, that 'one of the professors in a Presbyterian theological seminary felt it his duty to write a series of letters to Presbyterians, which were extensively circulated'; and in these letters the new measures were condemned. This incident is made the occasion of a tirade, in the course of which he breaks out with the exclamation, it is a

shame and a *sin* that theological professors, who preach but seldom, who are withdrawn from the active duties of the ministry, should sit in their studies and write their letters, advisory or dictatorial, to ministers and churches who are in the field and who are in circumstances to judge what needs to be done.

And he says it is *'dangerous* and *ridiculous* for our theological professors, who are withdrawn from the field of combat, to be allowed to dictate in regard to the measures and movements of the church.' We shall see whether his theological professorship will put a bridle on his tongue. It will be seen that no venerableness of years or wisdom or Christian excellence can turn aside the fulminations of his displeasure. To disapprove of his measures, no matter with what otherwise excellent qualities this disapproval may be associated, is to give decisive evidence of wickedness, and not only to offend him, but to insult God.

Nor is he ever startled by the number of his victims. All, whether a few individuals or a whole church, who will not fall down and worship the golden image which he has set up, are doomed to the fiery furnace. The General Assembly, a few years since, issued a Pastoral Letter in which the new measures were condemned. But neither Mr Finney's modesty nor his tenderness is at all troubled by the array of the whole church against him. When he saw their pastoral letter he says, 'My soul was sick, an unutterable feeling of distress came over my mind, and *I felt that God would visit* the Presbyterian church for conduct like this.' How to the very life is the fanaticism of this sentence – this turning from general opposition to solace and strengthen himself in the singular prerogative which he enjoys of a back-door entrance into the court of heaven, and of unquestioned access to its magazines of wrath.

In a like spirit he says of the 'Act and Testimony warfare' that 'the blood of millions who will go to hell before the church will get over the shock, will be found *in the skirts of the men* who have got up and carried on this dreadful contention'. And of the General Assembly, that 'No doubt there is a jubilee in hell every year about the time of meeting of the General Assembly.' Of all ministers, be they few or many, 'who will not turn out of their tracks to do *anything* new', he says, 'they will grieve the Holy Spirit away, and God will visit them with his curse.'

At the close of these extracts, for we must put a period to them from other causes than lack of materials to furnish more like them, we would ask, was there ever a fanatic who was more intelligible in his claim to a close relationship of his own with the Most High, or more indiscriminate and wholesale in his condemnation of those who refused submission to his peculiar dogmas? Was there ever a Dominic who was more exclusive or more fierce?

There remains one more feature of Mr Finney's spirit to be noticed, his *irreverence* and *profaneness*. This is a topic which we would gladly have avoided. It is painful to us to contemplate this trait of character, and we would not willingly shock the minds of others, as we have been shocked by some of the passages which we must quote under this head. But it is necessary to a correct understanding of the spirit of the new measures that this feature should be exhibited. It has been seen all along that Mr Finney's theology is not a barren vine, and we trust it has at the same time been seen that its fruit is the grapes of Sodom and the clusters of Gomorrah.

We will now show what are the practical results of his theory of the divine government; though for reasons just hinted, we shall give no more illustrations under this allegation than are necessary distinctly to sustain it.

In urging the necessity of new measures to the production of revivals, he says, 'Perhaps it is not too much to say, that it is *impossible for God himself* to bring about reformations but by new measures.' Here we might pause, for the man who is capable of uttering such a sentence as this is capable of almost any degree of profaneness.

But lest it might be urged that this may be a solitary instance of unpremeditated rashness, we must furnish a few more. He says of a certain class of people that 'they seem determined to leave it to God alone to convert the world, and say, If he wants the world converted let him do it. They ought to know,' he continues, 'that *this is impossible:* so far as we know, *neither God* nor man *can* convert the world without the co-operation of the church.' Again, when speaking of the duties of church members 'in regard to politics' he says, '*God cannot sustain* this free and blessed country which we love and pray for, unless the church will take right ground.' In rebuking those who do not 'exhibit their light' he tells them, '*God will not take the trouble* to keep a light burning that is hid.' To cast ridicule upon a certain kind of prayers, he says that they who offer them pray in such a manner that 'everybody wishes them to stop, and *God wishes so too,* undoubtedly'. And in reference to the subscribers to the *New York Evangelist* who have neglected to pay in their dues, he says, 'Why, it would *be disgraceful to God* to dwell and have communion with such persons.'

We will close these extracts with two passages of a still more extraordinary character. Speaking of the Saviour, he says, '*He was afraid* he should die in the garden before he came to the cross.' And yet again, and more astounding still, he says:

Jesus Christ when he was praying in the garden was in such an agony that he sweat as it were great drops of blood, falling down to the ground; – I have never known a person sweat blood, but *I have known a person pray till the blood started from the nose!*

Who that has ever dwelt in holy contemplation over the sacred mysteries of his Saviour's sufferings does not feel indignant at this unhallowed, vulgar profanation of them? And what extremes can appal the mind that could perpetrate this without shrinking?

Let it be noted that the spirit which we have here pictured is not the spirit of Mr Finney alone. Had it belonged to the man, we should not have troubled ourselves to exhibit it. But it is the spirit of the system, and therefore deserves our careful notice. And it is seen to be, as Dr Beecher called it eight years ago, 'a spirit of fanaticism, of spiritual pride, censoriousness, and insubordination to the order of the gospel'.[1] It is prurient, bustling and revolutionary – harsh, intolerant and vindictive.

Can the tree which produces such fruit be good? The system from which it springs is bad in all its parts, root, trunk, branches, and fruit. The speculative error of its theology and religion is concrete in its measures and spirit. Let it prevail through the church, and the very name *revival* will be a by-word and a hissing. Already has it produced, we fear, to some extent this deplorable result. Such have already been its effects that there can be no doubt, if it should affect still larger masses and be relieved from the opposing influences which have somewhat restrained its outbreakings, it will spread desolation and ruin, and ages yet to come will deplore the waste of God's heritage. To the firm opposition of the friends of truth, in reliance upon the Great Head of the Church, and prayer for his blessing, we look for protection from such disaster.

We have spoken our minds plainly on this subject. We intended from the beginning not to be misunderstood. It is high time that all the friends of pure doctrine and of decent order in the house of God should speak plainly.

[1] See Dr Beecher's *Letter* in the pamphlet on New Measures, before referred to.

Mr Finney was kindly and tenderly expostulated with at the commencement of his career. Mr Nettleton, than whom no one living was better qualified or entitled to give counsel on this subject, discharged fully his duty towards him. Others did the same. But their advice was spurned, their counsels were disregarded. To envy or blindness did he impute their doubts of the propriety of his course. He had a light of his own, and by it 'he saw a hand they could not see'. All the known means of kindness and expostulation have been tried to induce him to abandon his peculiarities, but without success.

It is the clear duty of the Church now to meet him and his co-reformers with open and firm opposition. Let us not be deluded with the idea that opposition will exasperate and do harm. Under cover of the silence and inaction which this fear has already produced, this fanaticism has spread, until now twelve thousand copies of such a work as these *Lectures on Revivals* are called for by its cravings. And there is danger that this spirit will spread still more extensively. The elements of fanaticism exist in the breast of every community and may be easily called into action by causes which we might be disposed to overlook as contemptible.

We conclude this article, as we did our former, by pointing out to Mr Finney his duty to leave our church. It is an instructive illustration of the fact that fanaticism debilitates the conscience, that this man can doubt the piety of any one who uses coffee, and call him *a cheat* who sends a letter to another on his own business without paying the postage; while he remains, apparently without remorse, with the sin of broken vows upon him.

In this position we leave him before the public. Nor will we withdraw our charges against him until he goes out from among us, for he is not of us.

7

SANCTIFICATION[1]

This judicious and excellent treatise presents, in a small compass, the substance of the modern controversy on the doctrine of entire sanctification in the present life. The author's statements are calm and clear, his method logical, his arguments conclusive, and his style simple and dignified. Though it is not long since we called the attention of our readers to this subject, especially in the form in which it is presented by the Oberlin professors, we think they will not regard the following pages as misapplied when they consider how ceaseless are the efforts of the advocates of error to propagate a doctrine which the history of the church teaches us seldom fails to become, in one form or other, an apology for sin.

The notion of the actual attainment, in some instances, of perfect virtue in this life is so gratifying to human pride that we need not wonder at its adoption by some in nearly every age of the world. Contrary as it is to Scripture and experience, it is too deeply radicated in man's selfishness not to find apologists and advocates among the conceited, the enthusiastic, and

[1]By John Woodbridge. Published in 1842 in review of *The Scriptural Doctrine of Sanctification Stated and Defended against the Error of Perfectionism*, by W. D. Snodgrass, D.D., Philadelphia.

such as are unaccustomed to an impartial scrutiny of their own hearts. It flatters exceedingly all those pretensions to superior sanctity which are disjoined from humility, penitence, and ardent aspirations after entire assimilation to the perfection of the divine moral character. In most of the false religions of the earth, the doctrine of human perfection, manifested in at least some peculiarly favoured instances, has, if we mistake not, formed an essential article of belief; and in all countries, perhaps, individuals have been found possessing an exemption from the common frailties of their race. A kind of perfection has been claimed for Greek and Roman sages, for Hindoo devotees, for Mahommedan saints; and even for the savage warrior, smiling in death at the impotent efforts of his enemies to extract from his agonising nature the shriek or the groan of suffering.

That Pantheism which is the philosophical basis of most of the popular systems of idolatry, assumes as a fundamental position such a union of man to the Deity as constitutes the leading principle of modern perfectionism in its purest and most sublimated form. Hence originates the deification of men as well as the divine worship paid to stocks, stones, rivers, mountains, wind, and all the inferior parts of the creation; Pantheism (elevating a creature of yesterday to the rank of a divinity), which is supposed by many to have been of more ancient date than the universal deluge, was maintained in all the following ages till the time of Christ, and was not entirely relinquished even by some of his professed disciples. Holding such a principle, they were prepared to adopt other opinions equally preposterous and unchristian.

To this perhaps should be attributed, in part at least, the antinomianism and perfectionism of some of the heretics in the apostolic age – so the Nicolaitans and Simonians – who maintained that they were released from all obligation to the law and that none of their actions, however contrary to the letter of the precept, were really opposed to the divine will and worthy of punishment: and how could they, who were parts of God, or rather identical with him, commit sin?

The Gnostics of the first and second centuries, and the Manichaeans of the third, believed human souls to be particles of the celestial light, of the same essential nature with God himself, and no otherwise corrupt or corruptible, than by being combined with sinful matter. The new Platonists of Egypt held substantially the same opinions. Hieronymus, in the preface to his dialogues against Pelagius, says that Manichaeus, Precillian, Evagrinus, Hyperborius, Flavinian, Origen, and the Menalians of Syria, were perfectionists.[1]

The brethren and sisters of the Free Spirit, in the thirteenth, fourteenth and fifteenth centuries, held that all things flowed by emanation from God; that rational souls were portions of the divine essence; that the universe was God; and that by the power of contemplations they were united to the Deity and acquired hereby a glorious and sublime liberty both from sinful lusts and the common instinct of nature.[2] In the latter part of the seventeenth century, the disciples of Michael de Molinos in Spain, France, and Italy were perfectionists.[3]

It is worthy of remark that in none of all these, during so many successive centuries, do we trace any evidence of the belief of the direct agency of the Holy Spirit on the heart, turning its affections to God and securing the perfection of its obedience. For the most part, they asserted that regeneration and complete deliverance from sin could be effected by contemplations and the soul thus be so identified with God as to constitute them not two things united, but one being; and in this way they explained the indwelling and controlling agency of the Most High in man. Of the reality and presence of native and moral corruptions as maintained by consistent Calvinists they seem to have had no conception.[4] Pelagius and Coelestius, in the fourth century, who denied the innate sinfulness of the human heart and the consequent necessity of efficacious grace in its renewals, maintained with entire systematic consistency that men might live without sin during the whole period of their life; that some had actually so lived for so many years, and that others, restored by repentance after transgressions, had subsequently continued perfect in holiness to the close of their days.[5]

[1] *Literary and Theological Review*, vol. iii, p. 28.
[2] Buck's *Theological Dict. and Mosheim.*
[3] *Literary and Theological Review*, as above.
[4] *Ibid.*
[5] *Ibid.*, vol. iii., p. 29, where we have in a note a curious specimen of the arguments of Coelestius on this subject. Also Wigger's *Hist. of Augustinism and Pelagianism.*

The primitive Quakers, the French Prophets, the Shakers, Jemima Wilkinson, Joanna Southcott, and the great body of Mystics in every communion held to perfection in this life as the attainment of the privileged few; and the advocates of this doctrine have usually represented the denial of it as involving great licentiousness and a state of utter spiritual bondage.

The views of the famous John Wesley, the father of Arminian Methodism, are well known to the reading part of the religious community. He affirmed, as Whitefield asserts 'that no Baptist or Presbyterian writer whom he had ever read knew anything of the liberties of Christ'; to which statement Whitefield replied, in his own pointed and emphatical manner:

What! neither Bunyan, Henry, Flavel, Halyburton, nor any of the New England and Scotch Divines? See, dear sir, what narrow-spiritedness and want of charity arise from your principles; and then do not say aught against election any more on account of its being destructive of meekness and love. I know you think meanly of Abraham, though he was eminently called the friend of God, and I believe also of David, the man after God's own heart.[1]

Wesley gives us an account of the steps by which he was led, during a course of many years, to embrace what he calls the doctrine of 'Christian perfection', which, as he explains it, though it includes the idea of freedom from sin, implies neither perfection in knowledge nor infallibility nor security against temptations and infirmities.[2] According to the system of the Romish church, good men may not only attain to perfections but perform, moreover, works of supererogation, serving as a fund of merits for the advantage of believers of inferior spiritual attainments.

It is not till lately that Perfectionism has been professed within the pale of Congregational and Presbyterian churches. By our fathers it was accounted heresy, inconsistent with the express testimony of the Scriptures, contradictory to Christian experiences, and subversive of the entire scheme of the gospel. But in consequence of certain Pelagian speculations

[1] Gillies' *Life of Whitefield,* New Haven edition, 1812, p. 256.
[2] Wesley's *Plain Account of Christian Perfection,* New York edition, 1837, p. 3, 18, *et passim.*

concerning moral agency, human ability, and the divine influence in sanctification – errors that have become extensively popular – individuals once reputed most zealous for revivals of religion have been led to join Pelagius and other kindred spirits in their views of the attainableness of perfection in the present life. Such, as we believe, is the philosophical origin of Perfectionism as held by the professors at Oberlin and their theological friends.

That we may not misrepresent the meaning of those to whom we refer, we will state their doctrine of perfection in their own language.

'What is perfection in holiness? In answer to this inquiry I would remark,' says Mr Mahan, 'that perfection in holiness implies a full and perfect discharge of our entire duty, of all existing obligations in respect to God and all other beings. It is perfect obedience to the moral law.'[1] With respect to the attainableness of perfection in this life, the same writer says, 'We have evidence just as conclusive, that perfect and perpetual holiness is promised to Christians, as we have that it is required of them.' 'We have the same evidence from Scripture, that all Christians may, and that some of them will, attain to a state of entire sanctification in this life, that they will attain to that state in heaven.' 'There is positive evidence that some of them did attain to this state.'

Mr Finney affirms, and in this we suppose he expresses the opinion of his associates at Oberlin, that sinless perfection for the time being is implied in the lowest degree of true piety. 'It seems to be a very general opinion,' says he,

that there is such a thing as imperfect obedience to God, *i.e.*, as it respects one and the same act; but I cannot see how an imperfect obedience, relating to one and the same act, can be possible. Imperfect obedience! What can be meant by this, but disobedient obedience! a sinful holiness! Now, to decide the character of any act, we are to bring it into the light of the law of God; if agreeable to this law, it is obedience – it is right – wholly right. If it is in any respect different from what the law of God requires, it is wrong – wholly wrong.[2]

[1] *Christian Perfection*, pp. 4, 27, 38.
[2] *Oberlin Evangelist*, vol. i.

Here we have the doctrine that all Christians are sometimes perfect or are perfect so far as they have any true holiness; and it is a very natural inference from such premises that believers may attain to a confirmed state of perfection in the present life. This conclusion is adopted by Mr Finney, as well as Mr Mahan.

To disprove the perfectionism taught in the above extracts, or to show that none of the saints are entirely free from sin in the present life, will be our object in this essay.

We shall begin with noticing the principal arguments which are commonly adduced by perfectionists of different descriptions in support of their views of this subject. We shall next exhibit direct evidence of the sinful imperfection of the heart of the saints in this life; and lastly, we shall show the great practical importance of the doctrine for which we contend, in opposition to the error which it controverts.

The arguments of the perfectionists are first to be considered. *The command of God requires perfection,* is one of their arguments. Answer. It is doubtless true, that the Most High does command us to be perfect; and to enjoin anything less than perfection would be inconsistent with his own purity and those eternal principles of rectitude according to which he governs the universe. The law expresses his feelings towards moral objects; but it leaves wholly undetermined the question whether his rational creatures will acknowledge or reject his authority. His command, in any instance, neither supposes that it will be obeyed, nor implies any insincerity in him, provided he foresees that it will not be obeyed. The contrary supposition would be incompatible with some of the most undeniable facts of revealed religion.

Does the divine command to be perfect prove that some may or will obey this righteous precept? Then, for the same reason, the divine prohibition of all sin in mankind equally proves that some of them may pass through a long life without a single act of transgression. It is by no means certain, therefore, that all the human race are or have been sinners: and, of course, the doctrine of universal depravity, unequivocally and frequently as it is taught in the Scriptures, may be false. It is as easy to imagine that some never sin, as that they become perfectly holy after they have acquired a sinful character. The opinion of

Pelagius with regard to this subject was therefore more specious and more logical than is the notion of those who make God's requirement of perfect sanctification an argument that some are perfectly sanctified in this life; while with strange inconsistency, they assert the universal moral depravity anterior to conversion of such of mankind as have sufficient knowledge to be moral agents.

Besides, entire holiness is plainly obligatory on all rational creatures; and no strength of depraved affection or hopelessness of condition can release any from the demands of the law of God. On this principle, the devils, in their place of torments are bound to love their Maker and yield themselves implicitly to his authority. To say they are not thus bound is to take their part against their Maker and pronounce them entirely excusable and innocent in their present rebellion, rage, and blasphemy. But does it follow, because they are under law, that they will therefore ever return to their duty? The Bible, on the other hand, assures us that their misery, and consequently their enmity to God, will be without end.

The command of God, it is alleged, implies our ability to obey, and it is reasonable to suppose that where ability exists, it will sometimes at least manifest itself by obedience. This argument has been strongly urged, both to account for the existence of sin (for where there is ability to obey, there is also supposed to be ability to disobey, or 'the power of contrary choice'), and to show the practicability of obedience, in the highest degree, to all the divine requisitions. 'Were it not,' says Mr Finney,[1] 'that there is a sense in which a man's heart may be better than his head, I should feel bound to maintain that persons holding this sentiment, that man is unable to obey God without the Spirit's agency, were no Christians at all – obligation is only commensurate with ability.'

Again he says,[2] 'Certain it is that men are able to resist the utmost influence that the truth can exert upon them, and therefore have ability to defeat the wisest, most benevolent, and most powerful exertions which the Holy Spirit can make to effect their sanctification.' Mr Mahan says,[3] 'I infer that a state

[1] *Lectures on Revivals of Religion*, p. 17.
[2] *Oberlin Evangelist*, Lect. 21, p. 193.
[3] *Christian Perfection*, p. 28.

of perfect holiness is attainable in this life from the commands
of Scripture addressed to Christians under the new covenant.'

The philosophy from which perfection is thus inferred had
been previously asserted by certain divines of celebrity in
Connecticut. In proof of this, the reader is referred to two or
three citations from the *Christian Spectator,* formerly published at New Haven. 'Free moral agents can do wrong under
all possible preventing influence.'[1] 'We know that a moral
system necessarily implies the existence of free agents with the
power to act in despite of all opposing power. This fact sets
human reason at defiance, in every attempt to prove that some
of these agents will not use that power and actually sin.'[2]
Again: 'God not only prefers on the whole that his creatures
should for ever perform their duties rather than neglect them,
but purposes on his part to do all in his power to promote this
very object of his kingdom.'[3] In all these statements, the
implication is clear, that men are, of course, able to do whatever God requires of them; and that the mind is in reality
self-moved in all its moral exercises.

We readily admit that men have the requisite faculties to
obey God; in other words, that they are moral agents. And this
is often what is meant by natural ability. We admit also that
the inability of sinners is a moral inability inasmuch as it
relates to moral objects, arises from moral causes, and is
removed by a moral change. The possession, however, of
natural ability in the sense just stated does not establish the
conclusion contended for in the preceding argument. Because
men or devils have the requisite intellectual or physical
faculties to serve their Creator, does it certainly follow that
they will serve him?

As it regards moral ability, it is absurd to imagine that the
rule of duty is to be measured by this. On this supposition there
is really no rule of light except the inclinations of creatures; or,
guilt is diminished in proportion to the stubbornness and
virulence of the principle of evil to be overcome; which is
but saying, in other language, that the more sinful, the more
bent on rebellion any one is, the less is he to blame for his

[1] *Christian Spectator,* 1830, p. 563.
[2] *Ibid.,* 1831, p. 617.
[3] *Ibid.,* 1832, p. 660.

disobedience. Mankind by nature, then, are perfectly innocent in hating God and in rejecting the manifold overtures of the gospel; for it is clear from this inspired volume that they are 'dead in trespasses and sins'. Their disinclination to obedience is affirmed to be so great that it can be overcome by nothing less than the direct exertion of Almighty power. 'No man,' says Christ, 'can come unto me, except the Father who hath sent me draw him.'

Accordingly, the commencement of holiness in the sinner's heart is again and again described by such phrases as indicate the highest manifestation of the immediate and creative agency of God. It is the donation of a new heart – a second birth – a new creation – a resurrection from the dead. These figures, strong as they are, are doubtless used with the utmost propriety as most happily expressive of the inveteracy of the evil disposition to be vanquished, of the sinner's moral help-lessness, and of his absolute dependence on sovereign grace. The continuance of believers in obedience is also constantly ascribed to the same power by which they were originally renewed after the image of God. 'Without me,' says Jesus Christ, 'you can do nothing.' 'Ye have not chosen me, but I have chosen you and ordained you, that ye should go and bring forth fruit and that your fruit should remain.'

Here we learn that the growth of the fruit in the first instance and its permanency afterwards are both owing to the choice, purpose, and effectual agency of the Redeemer. 'We are not sufficient of ourselves,' says Paul, 'to think anything as of ourselves; but our sufficiency is of God.' 'Being confident of this very thing, that he which hath begun a good work in you will perform (finish) it until the day of Jesus Christ.' The good work here intended is doubtless, as appears from the connection, the implantation of holiness in the heart by the efficacious grace of God. 'Who are kept,' says Peter, 'by the power of God, through faith, unto salvation.'

From these passages, and indeed from the whole tenor of the Bible, it is evident that whatever may be men's natural power or freedom as moral agents, their depraved propensities present as effectual an obstacle to obedience as the want of liberty itself would do. At the same time, they are constantly blamed for that disinclination or moral inability which, but for the interposition of Omnipotent grace, insures their destruction. They have ruined themselves; and their only hope is in the mercy and unconquerable might of their injured Creator, who may justly leave them to perish in their perverseness.

There is no reason then, for the conclusion that because men have the natural ability, they will therefore obey the law of God, any more than there is ground for arguing with Pelagius that a portion of the human race will live without sin from the commencement of their existence till death; and, consequently, that for them no repentance, no pardon, no Saviour, will be necessary; or, than there is ground for inferring with Universalists the future probable, if not certain, return of devils and the spirits of lost men in hell to their duty and to happiness. The argument from ability therefore, in this instance is of too wide a sweep in its general application to be admitted as of any force; for it manifestly goes to undermine the whole gospel and overthrow all the revealed principles of the moral government of God.

Another argument connected with the foregoing in favour of Perfectionism is founded in an erroneous philosophy concerning the nature of sin. This affirms that those propensities which we cannot overcome by the force of our own sovereign determination are merely constitutional susceptibilities, or physical attributes, having no moral character, the extirpation, or extinguishment of which is consequently not necessary to sinless perfection. Thus it has been argued that the most selfish innate desires and passions are in themselves innocent, being nothing more than incentives or occasions to sin, which must be expected to continue after the heart has become completely sanctified.

This summary method of disposing of the subject must doubtless be very gratifying to those who choose rather to find an apology for their sins than to confess and mourn over them before God. Where there is no sin there is surely no occasion for godly sorrow on account of sin. Let the standard of duty be low enough, and it will be easy to show that perfection belongs to many men, or to all men, or even to the inhabitants of hell themselves. Suppose, for example, that malice, hatred of God, enmity to creatures, and furious blasphemy, under circumstances of hopeless suffering are not criminal, and it will follow incontrovertibly that these feelings and acts are perfectly innocent in Satan and his hosts in their present state of misery. God cannot therefore, with propriety, punish them for their present irreconcileable malignity and that conduct which flows spontaneously from their hearts. In this view of the subject, the devils are as truly perfect now as they were when they existed enthroned seraphs in the heavenly paradise. Their condition has, indeed, been changed; but then the divine law has been altered to suit their new condition.

To bring this reasoning to bear on the case before us – if the natural passions of anger, revenge, covetousness, pride, and ambitions be not in themselves wrong, and if nothing but strong resolutions against sin, a resistance of our evil propensities, a devout and moral life, and reliance on the grace of Christ be needful to constitute a sinless character, then we admit that many of the human race have attained to perfection in this life. Yea, verily, according to this philosophy, sinless perfection is consistent with an eternal war in the breast between principle and passion; and as there is reason to suppose that the physical attributes of the soul will continue after death, it is next to certain that the saints in glory will be obliged to maintain an unceasing conflict with such innocent things as their love of self-indulgence, their fondness for distinction and power, and their constitutional susceptibility to resentment and revenge. Deny the principle of concupiscence to be sinful, and what hinders its existence, its disquieting irruptions, its violent onsets, even within the walls of New Jerusalem ?

This philosophy requires an exposition of the law entirely contrary to the Scriptures. The sacred volume condemns the first risings of inordinate desire and, of course all vicious tendencies to transgression in the soul. 'Whoso hateth his brother is a murderer.' 'Whosoever looketh upon a woman to lust after her, hath committed adultery with her already in his heart.' It requires us not merely to choose and strive after, but to possess and exercise right affections and passions; to love God and our neighbour, to feel kindly even to our enemies. 'Thou shalt not covet', is one of its express prohibitions. Yet coveting may exist, when from the restraints of conscience and fear there is no effort, no purpose to obtain the desired object. The affection is wrong and is forbidden, though it lead to no correspondent external acts or conscious determinative volition of the mind.

It was an apprehension of the spirituality of the law which convinced the Pharisee, Saul of Tarsus, of the exceeding corruption of his heart and destroyed all his self-righteous hopes. 'I had not known sin but by the law; for I had not known lust' (concupiscence), that is, I had not known that it was sin, 'except the law had said, thou shalt not covet.' 'For I was alive without' (a just apprehension and sense of) 'the law once; but when the commandment came' (with a clear view of its spiritual requirements and immutable obligation), 'sin revived and I died.' Thus plain it is, that whether we call the principle of concupiscence constitutional or not, it is still sinful in the eye of the law. Words may create confusion in the mind, but they do not change the nature of things. So long as the Christian is agitated in any degree by excessive or ill-directed desires, he is deficient in his obedience and therefore continues to be a transgressor.

Changing his ground, the advocate of the doctrine of perfection in this life sometimes asserts that though Christians cannot accomplish their own sanctification and ought not to attempt it, yet if they cast themselves upon Christ for this boon it will be bestowed upon them. Instead of working themselves, they must come to Christ to work in them, both to will and to do, and he will make them perfect. This notion too is affirmed by the very men who contend, when it suits their purpose, that sinners have perfect ability to change their own hearts, and believers perfect ability to do all that is required of them. 'I am willing to proclaim it to the world,' says Mr Mahan, 'that I now look to the very God of peace to sanctify me wholly.'

I have for ever given up all idea of resisting temptations subduing any lust, appetite, or propensity, or of acceptably performing any service for Christ, by the mere force of my own resolutions. If any propensities which lead to sin are sacrificed, I know it must be done by an indwelling Christ . . . If you will cease from all efforts of your own, and bring your sins, and sorrows, and cares, and propensities, which lead to sin, to Christ, and cast them all upon him – if with implicit faith you will hang your whole being upon him and make it the great object of life to know him, for the purpose of receiving and reflecting his image – you will find that all the exceeding great and precious promises of his word are, in your own blissful experience, a living I reality . . . You shall have a perpetual and joyful victory . . . Everywhere and under all circumstances, your peace in Christ shall be as a river.[1]

From these and other similar passages in the writings of the new Perfectionists, it would seem that Christians have nothing to do but to lie passively in the hands of Christ and 'roll the responsibility' of their sanctification upon him. What mean, then, the numerous scriptural inculcations upon believers to strive, to run, to wrestle, to fight, to put on the whole armour of God? It is manifest from the inspired volume that we are to come to Christ not for the purpose of saving ourselves the trouble of a personal warfare, but that we may engage in such a warfare with good motives, with becoming zeal, with persevering energy, and with success. The effect of faith is not drowsiness, but vigilance: not self-satisfied repose, but self-distrust; not slothfulness, but untiring activity. When Christ works in us, both to will and to do, of his own good pleasure, it is that sustained, quickened by his power, we may work out our own salvation with fear and trembling.

The present is not the first time in which Pelagian self-sufficiency and Antinomian indolence have been found co-inhabitants of the same dwelling, interchangeably occupying one another's places, and adopting one another's phraseology. But how are these apparent contradictions to be reconciled? They cannot be; yet, after all, it is not intended by the writers to whom we refer to ascribe all holiness to divine agency.

Their meaning appears to be that Christ will sanctify us wholly if we look to him for such a blessing; yet there is no provision in their system to secure the act of looking itself. Man begins to turn, and God completes the sanctification of man. Hence it is affirmed that, notwithstanding the promises of the new covenant insuring perfection in this life, comparatively few of the saints do ever become perfect on this side of the grave.

[1] *Christian Perfection*, pp. 189, 190, 191.

The fact that the saints are in Scripture sometimes said to be perfect has been alleged as another argument in favour of Perfectionism.

We answer that the word *perfection* is used in different senses. It is sometimes employed to express advancement and maturity in the Christian character and in knowledge, as distinguished from the comparatively low conceptions, weakness, and inconsistencies of mere infants in the divine life. 'We speak wisdom among them that are perfect', that is, the thoroughly instructed. 'Let us therefore, as many as be perfect, be thus minded.'

It is sometimes used to denote evangelical uprightness or sincere piety, in distinction from an empty profession of godliness. In this sense of the word, perfection belongs to all real saints. Thus the Psalmist says, 'Mark the perfect man, and behold the upright, for the end of that man is peace.' Here *perfect* and *upright*, agreeably to a well known rule of Hebrew construction, are evidently synonymous terms. A perfect man in this place, then, is a man who is sincere in his religious profession, a real friend of God and an heir of heaven. The wicked are said to 'shoot in secret at the perfect', that is, at the regenerated children of God. 'For the upright', says Solomon, 'shall dwell in the land, and the perfect shall remain in it.' In this passage, too, the terms uprightness and perfection have the same meaning.

Noah is said to have been a perfect man, yet the phrase is immediately explained as signifying the reality of his piety or his humble walk with God. That he was not without the remains of moral corruption is manifest from a subsequent instance of intoxication with which he is charged in the Scriptures. Job is also affirmed to be a perfect man. But that it was not intended to assert his freedom from sin is apparent from his conduct which is recorded, for he afterwards cursed the day of his birth. He also himself confessed his want of sinless perfection. 'If I justify myself, mine own mouth shall condemn me: if I say I am perfect, it shall also prove me perverse.' 'If I wash myself with snow-water, and make my hands never so clean, yet shalt thou plunge me in the ditch, and mine own clothes shall abhor me.' 'Behold I am vile; what shall I answer thee? I will lay mine hand upon my mouth.'

In the same sense we are to understand the phrase as used by Hezekiah, when he says, 'Remember now, how I have walked before thee in truth, and with a perfect [that is, with a sincere] heart.' That sinless perfection was not intended seems evident from what the Scriptures tell us concerning his conduct soon after the prayer in which these words are contained. 'But Hezekiah rendered not again according to the benefit done unto him, for his heart was lifted up; therefore wrath was upon him, and upon Judah and Jerusalem. Notwithstanding, Hezekiah humbled himself for the pride of his heart.' Most clearly, therefore, though he was perfect in the sense of sincere, or truly pious, he was yet far from being sinless. Of several of the kings of Judah it is said that their heart was perfect with the Lord, yet actions are attributed to them utterly inconsistent with the supposition that they were exempt from all sinful defects. The obvious meaning of the phrase as applied to those good men is that they were sincere believers, and maintained by their example and public acts the doctrines, institutions, and laws of true religion in their dominions.

It is affirmed of Zacharias and Elizabeth, that 'they were both righteous before God, walking in all the commandments and ordinances of the Lord blameless'. In this passage it is plainly the design of the inspired writer to teach us that Zacharias and Elizabeth were eminent saints, maintaining an example of impartial and universal obedience. That he did not mean to attribute to them sinless obedience is manifest, because in the context Zacharias is charged with criminal unbelief, for which he was punished with the temporary loss of the power of speech. What! a perfectly holy man subject himself to the divine displeasure and struck dumb for his distrust of God's Word!

Paul calls upon those whom he had addressed as perfect to be followers of him (*Phil.* 3:15, 17); yet, in the same connection he says, 'Not as though I had already attained, either were already perfect.' It is certain, therefore, that, in the one instance, the word has a different meaning from what it has in the other; for it is absurd to suppose that a wise and humble man who confessed himself to be still imperfect would exhort those whom he regarded as sinless, to look to him as an example. Some have understood by the *perfect,* whom Paul

addressed, full grown men in Christian knowledge, in distinction from children. Accordingly, Beza translates the passage,
'*quotquot itaque adulti sumus, hoc sentiamus* (as many as are
mature or *adult*)'.

One of the arguments of Mr Mahan on which he strongly
insists is expressed in the following terms: '*The Bible
positively affirms that provision is made in the gospel for the
attainment of a state of perfection, and that to make such
provision is one of the great objects of Christ's redemption.*'[1]

This language is ambiguous in several respects. It may mean
that God has revealed it as his determination that his people,
or some of them, shall become perfect in the present world;
and, in this sense it is but an assumption of the doctrine to be
proved. It may mean that God's plan includes the complete
sanctification of his children at some future period of their
existence; a fact which no one questions and which proves
nothing with respect to the subject in dispute. God has also
made provision for the deliverance of his people from sickness,
pain, and all afflictions, and for the enjoyment of the Redeemer's presence in glory; but this purpose concerning the elect is
not accomplished till they are released from the present world
by death.

Does Mr Mahan mean that nothing hinders the perfect
obedience of Christians but their own culpable abuse, or dis-
regard of their privileges? Very well; and it may with equal
truth be said that nothing different from this hinders the
perfect obedience of impenitent sinners. Does he mean merely
that believers might be perfect but for their own fault? It is also
true, as the apostle assures us, that the very heathen are without excuse; and the damned themselves are doubtless
inexcusably criminal for their present rebellion.

Does he mean that the atonement secures the perfect holiness
of Christians in the present life? This is simply a begging of the
question; and it is moreover contradicted by fact; since the
great body of believers are, by the acknowledgment of
Mr Mahan himself, far from perfect holiness.

Does he mean that the Spirit of God is able and gracious
enough to make them perfect? So the Spirit of God is able and
gracious enough to make the whole world perfect and even to

[1] *Christian Perfection*, p. 20.

exclude all sin from the universe. But his power and mercy are ever regulated in their exercises by his wisdom and his supreme regard to the interests of universal being.

The only question in reference to this subject is, what is God's revealed purpose? Has he anywhere told us that his people, or a part of them, will become perfectly holy during their abode in this world? If not, the removal of external obstacles to their perfection no more proves that they will be perfect than God's readiness to receive every true penitent justifies the conclusion that all mankind will repent and cordially embrace the overtures of the gospel.

The loose manner in which Mr Mahan expresses himself makes it difficult to say what he does mean, except that he intends to assert that God has done or will do something that renders it certain a part of his people will grow to a state of perfection before they exchange earth for heaven. Excellent, therefore, as Dr Woods' discussion of this subject mainly is, we cannot agree with him in saying that 'devout Christians and orthodox divines have in all ages maintained the same doctrines' with Mr Mahan, concerning 'the provisions of the gospel'. We must know what Mr Mahan means by 'the provisions of the gospel' before we can say anything like this. In all 'the practical writings of Calvin, Flavel, Owen, Bunyan, Watts, Doddridge, President Davis, and Good', not a sentence can be found which implies that God has, in such a sense, made provision for the complete sanctification of his children while they 'abide in the flesh', that his plan includes this result of his administration towards them; and if Mr Mahan does not mean so much as this, he means nothing to his purpose.

Mr Mahan also affirms that 'perfection in holiness is promised to the Christian in the new covenant under which he is placed'.[1]

If it be true that God has promised that his people shall become perfect in this life, the question is settled. But what are the proofs adduced of this fact? Why, he cites a number of passages which, if they are at all relevant to his designs, prove that all Christians become completely holy at the moment of their regeneration. The promises he mentions belong to all under the new covenant. These are contained in such passages

[1] *Ibid.*, p. 22.

as Jeremiah 31:31–34 and Hebrews 8:8–11; Deuteronomy 30:10; Jeremiah 1:20; Ezekiel 36:25–27; Isaiah 59: 21, and Luke 1:74, 75, etc. God circumcises the hearts of all his people; he puts his law in their inward parts; he takes away the stony heart out of their flesh; and he causes them to walk in his statutes. But does Mr Mahan believe (as he should, in order to be consistent with himself) that all the elect are completely sanctified at the very instant of their conversion? So far from it, he says, 'the great men of the church are slumbering in Antinomian death or struggling in legal bondage with barely enough of the evangelical spirit to keep the pulse of spiritual life faintly beating.'[1]

But does Mr Mahan believe that the promises of the new covenant have failed with respect to 'the great mass of the church'? How then can he argue from these promises that any part of the church will be completely sanctified in this life? Again, he says, 'from the evangelical simplicity of their first love, they (*i.e.*, the great mass of Christians) fall into a state of legal bondage, and after a fruitless struggle of vain resolutions with the world, the flesh, and the devil, they appear to descend into a kind of Antinomian death.' 'The spirit of Antinomian slumber prevails, and death, not a present Christ, is looked for as the great deliverer from bondage.'

What does this mean? Has God forgotten his covenant? Or is it simply conditional? But a conditional covenant, from its very nature, does not insure the compliance of a single individual with its proposals. The truth, however, is that the promises enumerated by Mr Mahan have their incipient fulfilment here, and will be accomplished, in the broadest extent of their meanings, hereafter. God, therefore, is faithful, though it remain true that none are entirely free from sin on this side of heaven

Some have insisted on those texts in which God promises to cleanse his people from all sin, as an evidence that they may attain to perfection in this life.

In some instances, to be *cleansed from sin* is equivalent to pardon, or gratuitous justification. Thus, in Psalm 51: 'Wash me thoroughly from mine iniquity, and cleanse me from my sin'; that is, save me from the deserved consequences of my

[1] *Christian Perfection*, pp. 100–1.

disobedience. Again, in allusion to ceremonial purification, which represented atoning blood, David says in the same Psalm, 'purge me with hyssop, and I shall be clean, wash me and I shall be whiter than snow.' Thus, in Jeremiah 33: 8: 'And I will cleanse them from all their iniquity whereby they have sinned against me.' That this refers to justifying grace rather than sanctification seems evident from what immediately follows: 'and I will pardon all their iniquities whereby they have sinned, and whereby they have transgressed against me.' Thus, also, in 1 John 1:7–8: 'The blood of Jesus Christ, his Son, cleanseth us from all sin,' that is, obtaineth our pardon, for it is not the atonement but a direct divine influence which removes the power and pollution of sin. Again: 'If we confess our sins he is faithful and just to forgive us our sins, and to cleanse us from all unrighteousness.' Here, to *forgive sins*, and to *cleanse from all unrighteousness* appear to be equivalent phrases. In the sense of pardon or free justification, all believers are cleansed from sin, since they are all acquitted and viewed and treated as perfectly righteous for the Redeemer's sake.

Where deliverance from the dominion of sin is promised, reference is in part had to what takes place in this world, but, more especially, to the future perfection of the heavenly state. The purifying process begins in the new birth and is gradually carried forward in sanctification, till the work is completed in glory. But how does the promise of future entire emancipation from the thraldom of sin prove that this blessing will be obtained immediately, or during the brief term of our earthly existence? It is also promised to believers that they shall be delivered from all sorrow, that they shall vanquish completely death and hell, and shall live and reign with Christ; and it might as well be argued, that these promises will have their full accomplishment here, as those which relate to the entire purgation of the saints from their moral defilement.

The truth is, God's faithfulness peculiarly appears in sustaining his people amidst the temptations and difficulties connected with a state of sinful imperfection till death is swallowed up in victory. Every good thing which the Lord has spoken will be shortly accomplished; and is his veracity to be distrusted because he does not give to his children in this world the perfect rest and triumph of heaven? Was God unfaithful to his ancient saints because he did not send them the promised Messiah in the time of Moses?

I may remark in general that if we regard not the scope of a passage, nor the peculiar import of scriptural phrases, nor the analogy of the faith, we may from insulated texts, deduce doctrines as preposterous as any that were ever advanced by the greatest heretics. Thus from the passages 'Behold the Lamb of God, who taketh away the sin of the world', we might argue, in opposition to the repeated declarations and general tenor of the Scriptures, that Christ sanctifies or pardons and saves the whole human race. Whereas the truth intended to be taught in these words is the reality and universal extent of the atonement of Christ.

'I argue,' says Mr Mahan,[1] 'that perfection in holiness is attainable in this life, and that the sacred writers intended to teach the doctrines from the fact that inspired men made the attainment of this particular state the subject of definite, fervent, and constant prayer.'

So we have examples of inspired men praying for the purity and blessedness of the heavenly state. But do believers, while sojourning on earth, ever literally become companions of the glorified? Paul was continually pressing toward the mark, for the prize of the high calling of God in Christ Jesus; the acquisition of this prize was the object of his most earnest labours, of his most fervent prayers; and Mr Mahan supposes[2] that the 'mark' at which the apostle so strenuously aimed was the 'resurrection of the dead'. But was Paul actually raised from the dead during the period of his abode in this world? Or does it follow, because he continued to sigh and groan, being burdened, that he did not pray in faith for a glorious resurrection? Christ taught his disciples to pray, 'Thy kingdom come, thy will be done on earth as it is in heaven.' This prayer was offered by the apostles and has been offered by the most devoted Christians in all later ages; yet to this day, much the greater part of mankind continue the slaves of sin and ignorant of the way of salvation by the Mediator. Are we to conclude therefore that this prayer has been so long and by such multitudes of the excellent of the earth, offered in vain?

[1] *Christian Perfection*, p. 34.
[2] *Ibid.*, p. 60

Perfectionists have urged the prayer of Christ recorded in John 17:21–23 as a proof of their doctrine: 'That they all may be one, as thou, Father, art in me, and I in thee, that they also may be one in us: that the world may believe that thou hast sent me.' 'I in them, and thou in me, that they may be perfect in one.' 'The union here prayed for,' says Mr Mahan, 'is a union of perfect love.' 'We must admit that this love and consequent unions will exist among believers, or maintain, first, that Christ prayed for that which he requires us to believe that it is not for the glory of God to bestow on his children. Second, that the world are never to believe in Christ.'[1]

That this prayer was offered in behalf of all God's children cannot admit of a doubt. But if it was offered for all, it has been answered in part at least, with respect to all, since the supplications of the Son are ever prevalent with the Father. However imperfect Christians may be, they are all united to their Head by a living faith, they all have essentially the same views of the gospel; they approve of one another's character, and rejoice in the prosperity of the kingdom of which they are all subjects; they all hate sin and love the same divine objects; they have all been washed in the same blood, have been renewed by the same Spirit, have become partakers of the same hope, and have been made heirs of the same salvation. The union among believers, as it is far more pure and sacred than that which subsists among worldly men, is destined to grow in strength, while all earthly friendships decay, and to endure for ever. Nor, apparently defective as it is, has it been wholly ineffectual in carrying a conviction to the ungodly of the divine reality and power of the gospel. In consequence of the example of Christians, notwithstanding the many inconsistencies with which it has been marred, the 'world' have been constrained to admit the divine mission and character of the Redeemer.

But Mr Mahan seems to suppose that this prayer is not answered at all, except with regard to those who become perfectly sanctified in the present life. What must be the inference? Plainly this – that with respect to the great body of Christians hitherto, during their mortal pilgrimage, the prayer of the Saviour has been followed by no correspondent effect.

[1] *Christian Perfection*, p. 33.

According to Mr Mahan's interpretation, therefore, Christ has failed to secure the object which he sought; for this writer supposes that comparatively few of the saints have attained to that perfection which their Master prayed they should possess. But if the prayer has failed of an answer till now with respect to millions of Christians, what evidence is there that it will not equally fail in all future ages of time?

It is reasonable therefore to conclude, not that the great Intercessor has prayed in vain, but that the perfectionists have misapprehended and misinterpreted his prayer. Our Lord said, 'I pray not thou shouldst take them out of the world, but that thou shouldst keep them from the evil.' The word evil may be understood to include both sin and suffering as well as the temptations and buffetings of Satan. If therefore we forget facts and the general testimony of the Scriptures in our exposition of particular texts, we may infer from this last cited passage that all real believers have done with conflicts and enjoy perfect freedom from afflictions and sorrows.

Mr Mahan thinks that Paul's proposing himself as an example to other Christians 'shows that he had arrived to a state of entire sanctification'.[1]

Paul does not propose himself as a perfect example. He was worthy of imitation in many respects; and so are many other good men, who would be the last persons on earth to claim the character of entire obedience. That Paul was imperfect, and that after all his attainments he felt himself to be so, will fully appear in the sequel. As for the passages which Mr Mahan cites to prove the perfection of Paul's obedience, they assert nothing more than the sincerity of his faith, the eminency of his self-denial, and his fidelity as an apostle and minister of Christ. When he declared that he was pure of the blood of all men, he referred merely to the clearness and fulness with which he had preached the gospel. But can none, save one who is perfectly holy, declare to his hearers all the counsel of God?

Some have considered 1 John 3:9 as proving that saints may be entirely free from sin in this life. 'Whosoever is born of God doth not commit sin; for his seed remaineth in him, and he cannot sin, because he is born of God.'

---

[1] *Christian Perfection*, p. 39.

It is the opinion of some writers that the apostle here refers to the sin of total and final apostasy, against which all true Christians are secured by the power and presence of God. The connection, however, seems to warrant the conclusion that John's object is to exhibit one of the distinguishing evidences of true religion, which is obedience. Some in the primitive church were Antinomians, supposing, with many modern perfectionists, that Christians were freed from the rule of duty and were at liberty to live according to their inclinations. To meet this impious dogma, as well as excite believers to the diligent pursuit of holiness, the sacred writer affirms that regeneration implies the implantation of a virtuous 'seed', or 'principle', which by its own proper tendency prompts to all the works of faith and labours of love. The real Christian, therefore, cannot be the committer or doer of sin, in such a sense as implies an habitually and totally depraved character. He longs for perfect holiness and assiduously strives to keep all the commandments of God. In other words, he is habitually a new man, both in his heart and in the overt actions of his life.

The connection, both preceding and following the text, accords with this interpretation. The tenth verse is, 'In this the children of God are manifested, and the children of the devil: whosoever doeth not righteousness is not of God, neither he that loveth not his brother.' Such are the scope and design of the passage. The other interpretation is moreover attended with difficulties not easy to be removed:

1. It overthrows a leading doctrine of the greater part of the perfectionists (who are Arminians), concerning the defectibility of the saints. Here we learn that regeneration includes the idea of permanency or certain perseverance in obedience, 'his seed remaineth in him'. Most surely, then, Wesleyans and other Arminian perfectionists ought not to cite this passage as an evidence of their doctrine; since if it proves anything in their favour, it proves too much for their cause.

2. Admit the interpretation of the perfectionists, and it will follow that none but the perfectly holy had been born of God or are real Christians. The language of the apostle is very explicit: 'Whosoever is born of God doth not commit sin.' If by not committing sin here be intended absolute perfection, then the smallest sin, either external or internal, is enough to

demonstrate a professor of religion to be a hypocrite. On this ground, therefore, the difference between saints and sinners must be, not in the nature of some or all of their exercises, but the perfection of the former and the imperfection of the latter. The last part of the text is, if possible, stronger than the first: 'He cannot sin, because he is born of God.' If the meaning be he cannot sin at all, then of course no one who does sin at all, has within him the smallest spark of true religion.

3. The interpretation adopted by the perfectionists makes John contradict himself in this very epistle; for he does expressly affirm that none of the children of men in this world are entirely free from sin. In chapter 1 verse 8, he tells us, 'If we say that we have no sin' (as some pretended that all their actions as believers were pure), 'we deceive ourselves, and the truth is not in us.' In the language of the New Testament, the affirmation that the truth is not in one, seems to be the same as saying that he is not a real Christian. Paul speaks of men of 'corrupt minds, and destitute of the truth', that is, devoid of the Christian spirit or of evangelical piety. John, in the second chapter of this epistle, uses the same phrase. 'He that saith I know him, and keepeth not his commandments, is a liar, and the truth is not in him.' Elsewhere the same apostle speaks of the truth as being in Christians, as dwelling in them; and them he represents as walkers in the truth.

Thus he teaches us that the boast of perfection indicates not superior sanctity, but gross self-ignorance or intentional falsehood, and a destitution of the genuine traits of the Christian character. In chapter 3 verse 3 he says, 'and every one that hath this hope in him purifieth himself even as he is pure.' Macknight has the following note on this passage:

The apostle, as Beza observes, doth not say, 'hath purified himself', but 'purifies himself'; to show that it is a good man's constant study to purify himself, because no man in this life can attain to perfect purity. By this text, therefore, as well as by 1 John 1:8, those fanatics are condemned who imagine they are able to live without sin.

From the foregoing passages, it is apparent that John taught a very different doctrine from that of sinless perfection in this life. And is it credible that he has been guilty of gross self-contradiction in the course of a single brief letter?

It may be said in favour of the doctrine of perfection of the saints in this life that *it is honourable to Christ, and implied in his all-sufficiency as the Saviour of his people.* Will he not, it may be asked, be all to his people that they need or desire?

We answer that he will be all to them that he has promised, but that he will do nothing for them contrary to his own express declarations and the wisdom of his general counsels. We are ill-qualified to judge what, except so far as he has revealed his purpose in his Word, it is wisest and best for him to do. There are some things which he will not do for his people. He will not, for example, make them all of gigantic stature and herculean strength; nor render them immortal upon the earth, nor cause them to live to the age of Methuselah, nor raise them at once in intellect and knowledge to an equality with the angels, nor free them, while they continue here, from the universally experienced pains and ills of this mortal existence. To expect from him such achievements betrays either infidelity or the utmost extravagance of enthusiasm. That he will ultimately accomplish the entire sanctification of his people is certain: this they are bound to believe; but to look to him without any warrant from his word for such a manifestation of his grace in this world betokens rather weakness and presumption than suitable confidence in his faithfulness and power.

When he assures us that he will do for us whatever we ask, it is with the express or implied condition that our petitions are in accordance with his purposes as made known in the Scriptures. Has he ever told us in the Bible that he will, if we ask him, purify us from all sin in the present world? If not, it seems opinionated pride and ignorance, rather than eminent faith and holiness, to expect him, out of a regard to our wishes, thus to turn aside from the course of his ordinary gracious operations. Besides, so long as we continue here, we must come to him as needy, as empty, as sinners. But these are not the characteristics of such as are completely sanctified. They have as truly entered into their rest as any of the saints with Christ in Paradise.

'*But some have professed to be perfectly holy.*'

Such were not the saints of whom we have an account in the Scriptures. These all confessed their continual proneness to sin;

and depended all their life long on the resources of rich, free, superabounding grace. Some, indeed, have claimed perfection, but they resembled the Pharisee who thanked the Lord for his moral superiority over other men, much more nearly than the contrite Publican who smote upon his breasts saying, 'God be merciful to me a sinner.'

The church of Rome, too, has claimed infallibility. A man's favourable opinion of himself is but a poor argument to show that he is either good or great. 'He that trusteth in his own heart is a fool.' 'There is,' says Solomon, 'a generation that are pure in their own eyes, and yet are not washed from their filthiness.' It is the self-righteous hypocrite who cries, 'stand by thyself, come not near to me, for I am holier than thou.' 'These,' says God, 'are a smoke in my nose, a fire that burneth all the day.'

Many poor enthusiasts have believed themselves inspired and capable of working miracles; and some have affirmed their possession of attributes strictly superhuman and divine. Are the Behmenites, the French Prophets, the disciples of Ann Lee, and the Mormons, then, to be acknowledged as the divinely illuminated messengers of God? 'Not he that commendeth himself is approved, but whom the Lord commendeth.'

When a man professes an eminence in holiness surpassing that ascribed to any of the Scripture saints, he is for that reason to be distrusted; and if he boasts of a perfection which the Bible denies to pertain to any of the human race in this world, he is to be at once regarded, without the trouble of further examination, either as a deceiver or the subject of a morbid fanaticism.

It is not for a moment to be deemed possible – whatever may be his professed experimental knowledge of religion, or his zeal, or the apparent blamelessness of his life – that he is in the right, in opposition to the explicit declaration of the Scriptures. 'Let God be true, but every man a liar.' 'To the law and to the testimony; if they speak not according to this word, it is because there is no light in them.' At all events, if one come to us with a professedly new revelation, he is not worthy of attention from us until we find him performing works which are plainly and incontestably miraculous.

It is, moreover, said by perfectionists that *the common orthodox doctrine on this subject is discouraging and leads to licentiousness.*

The same objection has been made to the doctrines of entire depravity, regeneration by effectual grace, election, justification by faith alone, the atonement of Christ, and indeed the whole scheme of evangelical truth contained in the Bible. Infidels, too, have professed to reject the sacred volume on the ground of the alleged evil tendency of many of its narratives, precepts, and exhibitions of divine character. Does it follow, then, that the influence of the doctrines of grace is bad, or that the Bible does not give us the most just and consistent view of God? Certainly not.

He who needs the expectation of perfect holiness in this life to stimulate his efforts in religion is yet a stranger to the ingenuous nature of that faith which is the fruit of divine grace. The true Christian loves holiness, and will therefore strive to make advances in the divine life. Did Baxter, Brainerd, Martyn, and Payson labour any the less diligently for Christ because they did not expect perfect rest on this side of heaven? Has any advocate of perfectionism ever surpassed those holy men in watchfulness, in fervent prayers, in the most self-denying sacrifices, and in unwearied attention to all the demands of duty?

The common doctrine concerning the imperfection of the heart of the saints in this world is adapted to produce and strengthen some very important branches of the Christian character – particularly humility, a great fear of sin, watchfulness against temptation, and habitual active dependence on the teaching and power of the Holy Spirit. 'Oh,' says the believer convinced of this truth, 'how potent must be my corruptions; and how hopeless, but for Almighty grace, my state!' It teaches in the most impressive manner the unwearied faithfulness of the Redeemer, who, inconstant and unworthy as they all are, will never leave one of his ransomed people to perish. How sweet, how tender the gratitude which such a view of his unceasing care cannot fail to inspire!

The doctrine at the same time serves to wean the believer from the world, where he is ever to bear the burden of sin, and dispose him to seek with the most intense desires for the freedom, rest, and blessedness of heaven. It helps to make welcome the grave and eternity. To one who knows the evils of his heart, it is fitted, when clearly understood, to impart a hope which would be otherwise impossible; since it assures him that the struggles he feels within him have been common to others, who now love and adore in the unclouded vision of the Lamb. He is therefore animated to press forward in his holy warfare till he shall drop all the sorrows of his mortal state and lay down his arms at the side of the grave.

We now proceed to state the more direct evidence of the sinful imperfection of all the saints in this life.

1. *The first argument is derived from the direct testimony of the Bible.*

Not a single text can be adduced which, properly understood, attributes perfection to good men in this life. On the contrary, the criminal imperfection of them all is most plainly asserted. Witness Ecclesiastes 7:20: 'For there is not a just man upon earth that doeth good and sinneth not.' It is as evident from this passage that no one on earth is perfectly holy, as that any are imperfect. Proverbs 20:9: 'Who can say, I have made my heart clean, I am pure from my sin?'

Mr Mahan suggests that reference is here had to a man's past life. The language, however, supposes present imperfection. Should one say, 'I have made my heart clean', the words would imply not that his heart had always been clean (for that which has never been impure needs no cleansing), but that he had accomplished his perfect sanctification. To say 'I am pure from any sin' is equivalent to saying 'I am free from that depravity which was once my character'. The passage, then, strongly denies the sinless perfection of any of the human race in this world.

1 Kings 8:46: 'There is no man that sinneth not.' Mr Mahan contends that this means simply that every man is peccable, or liable to sin. If so, the passage supposes that all men here are in a very different state from that of the angels and saints in heaven, who are in no danger of apostatizing from God. Is it not natural, then, to conclude that there is in the hearts of the saints here something which peculiarly exposes them to sin? And what can this be but a sinful propensity? Mr Wesley

disposes of the passage in a different manner. 'Doubtless,' says he, 'thus it was in the days of Solomon: yea, and from Solomon to Christ, there was no man that sinned not.' But he supposes that the declaration is not applicable to the times of the gospel.

With such as have a suitable reverence for the Scriptures, this method of explaining away the text requires no comment. 'What,' says Eliphaz, the Temanite, 'is man that he should be clean, and he which is born of a woman that he should be righteous?' 'If I say I am perfect' (or sinless), remarks Job, 'it shall also prove me perverse.'

'How does this declaration,' asks Mr Mahan, 'which Job applies to himself and to no other person, prove that all other saints, and Christians even, are imperfect?' It is sufficient to reply that Job was one of the best men of his own or any other age; that he is celebrated as such in the book of Ezekiel, and that he is proposed to Christians in the New Testament as a model of distinguished patience. 'And the Lord said unto Satan, hast thou considered my servant Job, that there is none like him in the earth, a perfect and an upright man?' And is it not evidence of perverseness in men of far inferior moral attainments to boast of their perfection?

'Who', says the Psalmist, 'can understand his errors? Cleanse thou me from secret faults.' Here it is intimated that all have errors or faults from which they need to be purified by the grace of God. The New Testament is no less explicit on this subject than the Old. We need not here adduce the passages already quoted from the first epistle of John, as they must be fresh in the reader's remembrance.

James 3:2: 'For in many things we offend all', or are all offended. We can see nothing in the connection or in the nature of the thing which limits this declaration to any particular description of men. The apostle evidently includes himself and his fellow Christians.

2. *Many of the exhortations addressed to Christians, and the prayers offered in their behalf, imply that they are not at present completely sanctified.* They are required to make advancement in piety. 'To grow in grace.' But where one is perfect in holiness, he can 'grow in grace' only by an increase of his natural capacity. His whole duty is done; and can he do more than his duty? 'Giving all diligence, add to your faith

virtue, and to virtue knowledge, and to knowledge temperance, and to temperance patience, and to patience godliness, and to godliness brotherly kindness, and to brotherly kindness charity.' Could such an exhortation with any propriety be addressed to one whose obedience, according to his capacity, was as perfect as that of Gabriel?

A large portion of the precepts written to Christians in the New Testament import the necessity of improvement, of progress, in the divine life. 'Now our Lord Jesus Christ himself, and God, even our Father, comfort your hearts, and stablish you in every good word and work.' Would this be a suitable prayer in behalf of those already stablished in perfect goodness? 'We pray exceedingly that we might see your face, and might perfect that which is lacking in your faith.' 'The Lord make you to increase and abound in love.' 'The God of peace sanctify you wholly.' 'Now the God of peace make you perfect in every good work to do his will, working in you that which is well pleasing in his sight.'

The prayer for perfect sanctification supposes that the blessing has not already been obtained, as the prayer that sinners may be regenerated assumes that they are yet in an unrenewed state. The foregoing passages may serve as a specimen of the prayers of inspired men in behalf of their brethren; and while they prove the moral imperfection of those for whom they were presented, they give us no reason to conclude that a full answer to them was obtained on this side of the tomb. To infer the contrary would be as unreasonable as to infer that a sincere prayer for the deliverance of believers from all evil must secure its object perfectly in the present world.

3. *It is the duty of all men daily to ask of God the forgiveness of their sins.* This is evident from the form of prayer which our Lord taught his disciples, which is given as a general guide to our daily devotions, and which contains in substance the petitions needful for Christians during their whole life. That the prayer, as it respects the subjects which it brings into view, whether the precise form be adopted or not, is designed for daily use, is manifest from one of its petitions. 'Give us this day our daily bread.' It is then added, 'and forgive us our trespasses, as we forgive those who trespass against us.' We shall all therefore need daily to pray for pardoning mercy.

But the daily need of forgiveness supposes the daily commission of sins to be forgiven. The daily prayer implies daily confession of sin. And does Christ require us to confess offences of which we are not guilty? The insertion of this petition among the rest was doubtless intended to remind us of the sinful imperfection of all our services in the present world. Mr Mahan's evasion of this argument, that it involves the supposition that 'the kingdom of God will never come', and that 'the Christian will never be in a state in this life in which he will not be subject to injuries from others' is rather confirmatory than subversive of the inference I have maintained. Mr Mahan virtually allows, then, that so long as Christians are 'subject to injuries from others', this prayer is suitable for all believers. And are they not still 'subject to injuries'? The prayer, therefore, is with propriety used by Christians at this day; and it remains to be proved that it will cease to be appropriate to their circumstances so long as the sun and the moon endure.

4. *The same doctrine is evident from the history which the Holy Ghost has given us in the Scriptures of the most eminent saints in ancient times.* Noah was once intoxicated; Abraham practised dissimulation concerning his wife; Isaac indulged sinful partiality towards Esau; Jacob sometimes indulged criminal distrust; Lot was shamefully overcome by temptation; Moses spoke unadvisedly with his lips; Aaron was too accommodating to the sinful wishes of his countrymen, and formed an image for idolatrous worship; David committed crimes for which his holy soul was afterwards humbled in the dust; Solomon's old age was disgraced by his idolatries; Job and Jeremiah impatiently cursed the day of their birth. Shall I speak of the faults of Eli, and Samuel, and Jehoshaphat, and Asa, and Hezekiah, and Josiah? Unpleasant as the recollection of their failings is, it may be profitable to impress upon us the necessity of continual vigilance and prayer. It is important to observe that to those holy men, the remembrance of their sins was grievous and the burden of them was intolerable.

Let us look now at the saints of whom we have an account in the New Testament. Not one of them is presented to us with a faultless character. In the little family of Christ we observe the spirit of worldly ambition. We hear the disciples inquiring

among themselves, who shall be greatest? They were warm in
dispute; and carry their mutual complaints to their meek and
compassionate Lord.

Who can think of the confidence of Peter and his subsequent
lapse, though so soon followed by his repentance, without
exclaiming, 'What are the holiest men, unaided and
unsustained by the grace of God!' Much as Peter's character
afterwards was improved, his sanctification was still imperfect. 'But when Peter', who was in that instance too much
actuated by motives of carnal policy, 'was come to Antioch, I',
says Paul, 'withstood him to the face, because he was to be
blamed.' Thus, weak in himself and liable to trangress was
that great apostle, whose very name denotes firmness and
constancy.

James and the gentle, affectionate John, actuated by a spirit
of revenge, would fain have commanded fire to come down
from heaven and consume the Samaritans, who refused to
receive their Master. Yet Mr Mahan thinks that John became
perfectly holy in this life. Because John was conscious of the
sincerity of his obedience it is inferred that he was free from
sin.

Paul and Barnabas contended and divided with a spirit of
acrimony, ill-befitting their eminent meekness, self-denial, and
devotion to the cause of the Redeemer. Yet in Mr Mahan's
view it is at least 'doubtful' whether Paul, in that instance,
deviated in the smallest degree from perfect holiness.

The same writer makes the apostle attest his own perfection
in a number of passages which simply assert the reality of his
faith and piety, though he expressly says, 'Not as though I
had already attained, either were already perfect; brethren,
I count not myself to have apprehended: but this one thing I
do; forgetting those things which are behind, and reaching
forth unto those things which are before, I press toward the
mark for the prize of the high calling of God in Jesus Christ.'

In the apostolical epistles to the churches, faults are specified and reproved, which render it certain that the religion
of the primitive Christians was by no means such as
dreaming perfectionists claim for themselves. Thus do
Bible facts on this subject explain and establish the Bible
doctrine.

5. *The most holy men mentioned in Scripture have confessed, and that in their best frames, their remaining sinfulness.* 'Against thee, thee only,' says David, 'have I sinned.' 'Mine iniquities have gone over my head; as an heavy burden, they are too heavy for me.' 'Behold I am vile,' says Job, 'what shall I answer thee?' Nehemiah and Daniel include themselves in their confessions of the sins of their people. Paul again and again renounces all dependence on his own righteousness, and casts himself without reserve on the atonement and perfect obedience of the Saviour. These were among the best men that ever lived; and if they felt themselves to be still imperfect, is it not evident that others who regard themselves as purified from all sin are miserably deceived?

6. *The warfare which the Scriptures teach us exists through life in the bosoms of good men, implies the imperfection of their obedience, or the continuance of evil principles, however mortified and weakened, in their hearts.* It is nowhere intimated that any of the saints have arrived at such a state that they have nothing more to do in opposing sin in their hearts. On the contrary, they are all exhorted to continual watchfulness and diligence, lest they be overcome by temptation. 'Be sober, be vigilant.' It is clearly implied in many exhortations that Christians will be obliged to fight the good fight of faith till they die. Is it not plain from this that there will always be sin in them to resist? Would it not be absurd to direct men to fight an enemy already completely vanquished and destroyed?

To evade this argument, shall we be told of innocent susceptibilities to sin which render perpetual resistance necessary? On this principle, as we have already observed, there must be an inward warfare in heaven, since men carry with them their innocent mental susceptibilities into the regions of endless purity. But is there any warfare in that world? Were the saints here perfectly holy, we see no reason why they should be any more troubled with internal conflicts than are the glorified spirits in heaven.

According to the more common interpretation of orthodox divines, the apostle, in Romans 7, is describing his own experience and that of every believer in this world. In that chapter he speaks of sin dwelling in him; of willing what he could not perform; of finding a law that when he would do good, evil was present with him; of delighting in the law of God after the inward man, and yet seeing another law in his members warring against the law of his mind, and bringing him into captivity to the law of sin in his members; and he adds the pathetic exclamation, 'O wretched man that I am, who shall deliver me from the body of this death?' He speaks as if two distinct persons within him were contending for the mastery; and he rests all his hope of the final victory of the good principle over its opposite on the mere grace of the Redeemer. 'I thank God, through Jesus Christ our Lord. So then with the mind, I myself serve the law of God, but with the flesh the law of sin.'

No real difficulty exists from the connection in supposing this passage to be descriptive of the Christian experience of Paul himself, and of other true saints. It has been appropriated by the best of men as most happily expressive of their own views of themselves; while most of the opponents in modern times of its application to true Christians have also had Arminian or Pelagian notions of the great doctrines of grace. The orthodox interpretation is the most natural, and such as the plain unlettered Christian who had no system to support would be most likely to adopt.

Some of the phrases employed express a state of feeling which is never found in a totally depraved sinner. Can such an one truly say that he allows not the evil which he commits, that he hates what he does, and that he delights in the law of God after the inward man? The Psalmist represents it as one of the characteristics of a good man, that 'his delight is in the law of the Lord.' 'O Lord, how love I thy law!' 'Delight thyself also in the Lord, and he shall give thee the desires of thy heart.' As for the confession 'I am carnal, sold under sin', it merely expressed the strong sense which Paul had of the power of indwelling sin as it was manifested in the effects which he noticed in the following connection.

In Galatians 5:17, the apostle speaks of an inward spiritual conflict as common to Christians. 'The flesh lusteth against the spirit, and the spirit against the flesh: and these are contrary the one to the other, so that ye cannot do the things that ye would.' By the flesh here, as is evident from what follows, is intended the corrupt nature, or sinful disposition of mankind. This flesh is affirmed to exist in Christians and to counteract the impulses of their new or spiritual nature. The combatants being thus in the field, the contest can never be intermitted till the foe is finally routed and destroyed.

7. *The temper, represented in the Scriptures as necessary to acceptable prayer, implies on the part of the offerers the consciousness of remaining sin.* None are permitted to mention their own goodness as the meritorious ground of acceptance. Humility and penitence are indispensable to a right approach to the throne of grace. We read of one who, without any confession of sin, boasted before God of his good deeds; but we are assured by the supreme Judge that this man found no favour with his Maker. Observe Daniel's prayer. After confessing his own sin as well as the sin of his people, he said, 'We do not present our supplications before thee for our righteousness, but for thy great mercies. O Lord, hear; O Lord, forgive; O Lord, hearken and do: defer not, for thine own sake, O my God; for thy city and thy people are called by thy name.' Observe the prayer of the Psalmist: 'Enter not into judgment with thy servant; for in thy sight shall no man living be justified.' Observe the prayer of Isaiah:

Behold thou art wroth, for we have sinned; in thy ways is continuance, and we shall be saved. For we are all as an unclean thing, and all our righteousnesses are as filthy rags; and we all do fade as a leaf: and our iniquities, like the wind, have taken us away. And there is none that calleth upon thy name, that stirreth up himself to take hold of thee; for thou hast hid thy face from us, and hast consumed us, because of our iniquities. But now, O Lord, thou art our Father: we are the clay, and thou our potter; and we all are the work of thy hand. Be not wroth very sore, O Lord, neither remember iniquity for ever; behold, see, we beseech thee, we are all thy people.

Here we see the church relinquishing all confidence in herself, in her strength, in her goodness, taking to herself everlasting shame and reposing all her hope in the sovereign mercy and gracious covenant of her God. In the spirit of this passage Jeremiah prays, 'Though our iniquities testify against us, do thou it for thy name's sake.' Of that penitent submission which prostrates the pride of the heart and all the powers of the soul before the divine Majesty, we are most impressively taught the necessity in the parable of the Publican and Pharisee. He whose prayer was graciously accepted had no good actions to enumerate, no apology to offer for his transgressions. His only plea was mercy, through the great propitiation provided for the guilty and the lost. The Pharisee, on the other hand, seemed to regard himself as perfect.

See the repenting prodigal. He tells of no good that he has done. He speaks not even of his compunction, his sorrow, his long and painful journey, to regain the parental mansion and sue for an abused parent's love. No, with shame and weeping he cries 'Father, I have sinned against heaven and before thee, and am not worthy to be called thy son.' The current language of the Bible accords with these examples. The Lord fills the poor with good things, but he sends the rich empty away. 'He will regard the prayer of the destitute; he will not despise their prayer.'

But what have such promises to do with those who believe that they have already attained to perfection? Are they poor, destitute in their own eyes? What, they who have only to be thankful for the forgiveness of what is past, and to be satisfied with their present purity and worthiness? This is pharisaism, this is arrogance indeed, if anything can deserve the name. 'Thou sayest I am rich, and increased with goods, and have need of nothing, and knowest not that thou art wretched, and miserable, and poor, and blind, and naked.'

8. *The same doctrine is confirmed by the testimony of those in later times who have given the best evidence of eminent meekness, humility and a disinterested consecration of themselves to the service and cause of God.* In the confessions and writings of the great Augustine, the power of indwelling sin is acknowledged with a strength and pungency of expression which proves the depth of his convictions and the intenseness of his penitential sorrow. The ardent and intrepid Luther is full of this most humiliating subject, that he may drive the church from every other refuge to the atoning sacrifice and the immaculate righteousness of her Redeemer. Baxter, Owen, Flavel, Charnock, Bates, Howe, Bunyan, and a host of their godly contemporaries, unite in their acknowledgements of the exceeding potency of remaining sin in the hearts of the best of

God's people. Who has not observed the strong language of Edwards, Brainerd, and Payson as they confessed and mourned over the sins that were mixed with, and defiled, their holiest services? John Newton, Winter, Scott, Martyn, and indeed most of those who have seemed eminently spiritual, have been full and constant in expressing their conviction of the criminal imperfection of their best works, the strength of their innate corruptions, and their entire dependence on the power and sovereign grace of God to direct and uphold them.

And if these were not real saints, who in modern times are entitled to the appellation? Are they, who profess to depend on their good life for acceptance with God, while they oppose, calumniate, and hold up to ridicule the peculiar doctrines of the gospel? Are those zealots, proud, censorious, and dogmatical, who boast of their perfect deliverance from sin? 'By their fruits ye shall know them; do men gather grapes of thorns, or figs of thistles?

On this subject the great and good Wilberforce says:

To put the question concerning the natural depravity of man to the severest test; take the best of the human species, the watchful, diligent, self-denying Christian, and let him decide the controversy, and that not by inferences drawn from the practices of a thoughtless and dissolute world, but by an appeal to his personal experience; go with him to his closet, ask him his opinion of the corruption of the heart, and he will tell you that he is deeply sensible of its power, for that he has learned it from much self-examination and long acquaintance with the workings of his own mind. He will tell you that every day strengthens this conviction; yea, that hourly he sees fresh reason to deplore his want of simplicity in intentions, his infirmity of purpose, his low views, his selfish unworthy desires, his backwardness to set about his duty, his languor and coldness in performing it; that he finds himself obliged continually to confess that he feels within him two opposite principles, and that he cannot do the things that he would. He cries out in the language of the excellent Hooker, 'The little fruit which we have in holiness, it is, God knoweth, corrupt and unsound; we put no confidence at all in it, we challenge nothing in the world for it, we dare not call God to reckoning, as if we had him in our debt books; our continual suit to him is, and must be, to bear with our infirmities, and pardon our offences.'

9. *The Bible teaches us to look for the accomplishment of our perfect conformity to God as a part of that peculiar and glorious reward which is reserved for a future life.* 'I shall be satisfied, when I awake with thy likeness.' 'It doth not yet appear what we shall be; but we know that, when he shall appear we shall be like him; for we shall see him as he is.'

Is not the implication clear and unanswerable that our moral assimilation to Christ will not be completed till we awake in eternity and behold him in his unveiled glory? But according to the scheme of the perfectionists, that which makes heaven most attractive to the pious heart may be fully enjoyed upon earth; we may be as sinless and, according to our capacity, as much conformed to the Redeemer here as are any of the saints in his immediate presence before the throne.

Why then should Christians so eagerly, as the Bible represents them as doing, fix the eyes of their faith and desire on the celestial paradise? Why do they so joyfully anticipate the second coming of their victorious Prince and deliverer? We are assured that 'the spirits of just men made perfect' are collected together in 'the city of the living God, the heavenly Jerusalem.' Why are we not told that their dwelling-place is upon earth, as well as in the distant country beyond the tomb?

10. *God deals with the best of his people here as in a state of imperfection.* They are subject to the discipline of affliction. The voice of divine Providence, as well as of the Word to them, is, 'Arise ye, for this is not your rest; for it is polluted.' It is plainly a doctrine of Scripture that mankind suffer only because they are sinners. Sickness, pain, disappointments, and the other calamities of life are, in innumerable passages, represented as divine judgments or expressions of God's righteous displeasure against the wickedness of the world. 'When thou with rebukes dost correct man for iniquity, thou makest his beauty to consume away like a moth.' 'There is no soundness in my flesh, because of thine anger; neither is there any rest in my bones, because of my sin.' 'For we are consumed by thine anger, and by thy wrath are we troubled.' 'Wherefore doth a living man complain, a man for the punishment of his sins?'

Our blessed Lord was exposed to suffering in the capacity of our substitute. Had he not acted in this character, his life would have been as happy as it was innocent and holy. 'The Lord laid upon him the iniquity of us all', and therefore he was bruised, tortured, and put to death upon the accursed tree. His was a peculiar case, unparalleled in the history of our world; the result of an expedient of the divine government to save the guilty, in consistency with the demands of righteousness and the maintenance of the honour of God. The sufferings of no other person are strictly vicarious or avail to the removal of the divine anger against transgressors.

With respect to Christians, however distinguished by their attainments in piety, afflictions are affirmed to be fatherly chastisements and proofs of the paternal faithfulness of their covenant God.

If his children forsake my law, and walk not in my judgments; if they break my statutes, and keep not my commandments; then will I visit their transgression with the rod, and their iniquity with stripes. Nevertheless, my loving-kindness I will not utterly take from him, nor suffer my faithfulness to fail.

From this passage it is plain that believers are never visited with the 'rod' and with 'stripes', except on account of their 'transgression' and their 'iniquity'.

Whom the Lord loveth he chasteneth, and scourgeth every son whom he receiveth. If ye endure chastening, God dealeth with you as with sons; for what son is he whom the father chasteneth not? But if ye be without chastisement, whereof all are partakers, then are ye bastards and not sons.

None of God's children, then, in this world, can wholly escape chastisement; and the reason is they all need correction. 'As many as I love,' said Christ, 'I rebuke and chasten.' He told his disciples that 'in the world' they should have 'tribulation'. 'We must,' said Paul, 'through much tribulation enter into the kingdom of God.' 'For we that are in this tabernacle do groan, being burdened.' 'For they verily for a few days chastened us, after their own pleasure: but he for our profit, that we might be partakers of his holiness.'

The plain doctrine of the apostle here is that after believers have become fully partakers of the divine holiness, the end designed to be answered by God's chastisement will have been accomplished. The undeniable inference, therefore, is that then their sufferings will cease. And this is what we should have reason to expect.

Is it credible that a wise and merciful parent will inflict needless pain on his own children? Mr Mahan himself virtually admits the force of this reasoning:

The rod, properly applied, brings the child into a state in which the rod is no more needed. So of the rod in the hand of our own heavenly Father. Its object is to render us partakers of his holiness. Till this end is accomplished, the rod will be used. When this end is accomplished, it will no longer be needed.[1]

But we have already seen that all God's people here are, to a greater or less degree, the subjects of affliction. Will Mr Mahan pretend that they who claim to be perfect are less liable than other professors of religion to the common natural evils of this life? If not, their claim, according to the principle allowed by himself, can have no good foundation.

Will it be said that believers suffer according to general laws? Be it so; but by whom, I ask, were those general laws established, and were they not formed by their author in view of all the wants which would ever take place under their operation? Besides, who does not know that the Scriptures in numerous instances ascribe all the calamities which befall creatures to the sovereign appointment and direct agency of that Being on whom are dependent all the laws of nature and all the results to which they gave birth? A few passages to this effect have already been quoted. It is apparent from these, and many other texts, that the hand of God is as much to be acknowledged in the evils we suffer as in those events that are strictly miraculous and which occur without the intervention of means or second causes.

Since, then, affliction is ordained on account of sin, the perfectly obedient ought to be as exempt from affliction as are any of the saints in heaven. Every bereavement, therefore, that the perfectionist sustains, every pain he feels, demonstrates the falseness of his creed. Were he what he professes to be, this poor dying world would be a most unsuitable residence for him; and he would without doubt ascend at once to join his

[1]*Christian Perfection*, p. 66.

kindred in the skies and swell the shouts of their praise. The entire system of divine Providence here proceeds upon the assumption that the whole human race are so depraved as to need perpetual restraints and the intermingling of painful inflictions with the attractive influences of mercy.

We have now to show the *great practical importance of correct views of this subject.*

Some have said that if the doctrine we have maintained be true, it is not worthy of being contended for, especially at the risk of peace; and it has been sometimes intimated that the contrary scheme, though erroneous, may excite Christians more powerfully than the truth would do, to the indefatigable pursuit of holiness. This notion directly contradicts the Bible. There we learn that believers are sanctified through the truth; and we are urged to 'buy the truth and sell it not'. No portion of revealed truth can be of little consequence; since we are told on the best authority that 'all Scripture is given by inspiration of God, and is profitable'.

The common doctrine here defended, therefore, provided that it be scriptural, cannot be of small importance in its relation to truth and duty. Nor has it been received as of small importance by either its enlightened friends or its enemies. Great stress was laid upon it by Augustine and the Reformers; and it has been deemed of vital moments by the most distinguished later theologians in our own country and in Europe. While it has been held by the orthodox, it has been strongly opposed by the wildest and most erratic of the opposers of evangelical doctrines. This fact indicates clearly the tendency of the different schemes on this subject. In every well-instructed and well-balanced mind, the scriptural doctrine of the imperfection of good men in this life stands not as an isolated truth but as an inseparable part of a system of religious belief, experience and practice.

The perfectionist, if consistent with himself, must have different apprehensions of God from those which are possessed by the advocates of orthodoxy. Where is the perfectionist who has clear and correct views of the universality, definiteness, and immutability of the divine purposes? Can an instance be found of such an one who does not confound the decrees of God with his commands; thus virtually undermining the stability of the divine governments, and taking away the foundation of our confidence in the ultimate prevalence of truth and holiness over error and wickedness? Besides, as holiness is the same in all beings, he who regards himself as perfectly sanctified must believe that he is, in proportion to his capacity, as pure and as good as his Creator. How far below the representations of the Bible must be such a man's views of the righteousness and moral glory of the adorable Supreme!

Perfectionism explains away or virtually repeals God's holy and unchangeable law. In some instances its advocates directly affirm that the obligations of the law have been abrogated with respect to all believers; and that Christ has so fulfilled its demands that his people are not in any sense answerable for their delinquencies. They are said to cease from their works, and to 'roll the responsibility of their future and eternal obedience on the everlasting arm'.[1]

In order to maintain the dogma of personal perfection, it is necessary to make it consist in something far short of the consummate virtue required in the Word of God. Hence real sins are called weaknesses, frailties or innocent constitutional temptations. Concupiscence is reduced to the blameless, though, when they become excessive, somewhat dangerous cravings of physical appetite. Supreme self-love is declared to be an essential characteristic of intelligent moral agency, against which there is no law; which is the spring of all virtue as well as of vice, and to which no more blame can be attached than to the pulsations of the heart or the vibrations of a pendulum. Affections, as such, have no character; they are but the innocent susceptibilities of our nature, and their most violent workings are innocent, except so far as they are produced or modified by a previous deliberate act of the will. In all other cases they are passive emotions like the involuntary impressions made upon the brain by the bodily senses.

It follows on this principle that love to God and hatred of him, are equally indifferent things; and that they become praiseworthy or criminal solely in consequence of their connection with some previous purpose of the mind. It must hence be inferred that when God commands us to love him, he does not mean what he says; but that he is to be understood as

---

[1] *Literary and Theological Review*, vol. i., p. 558.

simply requiring us to do what we can to approve of his character and yield obedience to his commands. Thus his law, in his high and spiritual import, is frittered down to an accommodation to the taste, or moral inability of mankind. Observe the language of Mr Finney:

It is objected that this doctrine lowers the standard of holiness to a level with our own experience. It is not denied that in some instances this may have been true. Nor can it be denied that the standard of Christian perfection has been elevated much above the demands of the law in its application to human beings in our present state of existence. It seems to have been forgotten that the inquiry is, What does the law demand; not of angels, and what would be entire satisfaction in them; nor of Adam previously to the fall, when his powers of body and mind were all in a state of perfect health; not what will the law demand of us in a future state of existence; not what the law may demand of the church in some future period of its history on earth, when the human constitution, by the universal prevalence of correct and thorough temperance principles, may have acquired its pristine health and powers; but the question is, What does the law of God require of Christians of the present generation; of Christians in all respects in our circumstances, with all the ignorance and debility of body and mind which have resulted from intemperance and the abuse of the human constitution through so many generations? The law levels its claims to us as we are, and a just exposition of it, as I have already said, under all the present circumstances of our being, is indispensable to a right apprehension of what constitutes entire sanctification.[1]

Perfectionism often and directly leads to the most gross, palpable, and blasphemous forms of Antinomianism. It has been conjoined with the horrible notion that to the Christian all actions are alike; that sin in his case ceases to be sin; that his doings, however perverse, are not his own but are the works of Jesus Christ himself, whose will impels his perfect ones in all they think, say, and do. Hence some of the perfectionists have talked of themselves as divine; as incarnations of the Deity, possessing at once the righteousness, strength, and infallibility of the Redeemer. By many, the utility and necessity of all divine ordinances are denied as fit only for the uninstructed

[1] *Oberlin Evangelist*, vol. ii, p. 50.

and carnal, who have not yet entered into their rest. In the writings of even the more sober perfectionists of this day, expressions are found which seem to contain the germ of these extravagant and impious pretensions.

It is scarcely needful to remark that the belief in perfectionism cannot stand in connection with clear scriptural apprehensions of the total moral corruption of unregenerate men. Hence, whatever words the defenders of this scheme have used, they have universally, so far as we know, denied the essential difference, as it respects the spring and nature of their exercises, between saints and impenitent sinners. The governing motive, namely, self-love, or the desire of happiness, however it may vary in its results, is represented to be the same in both classes, or at the most, any change effected in this respect is to be attributed simply to the operation of principles which, though stimulated perhaps by a divine influence, are yet common to both. With such philosophy, to speak of any as totally depraved is to use words without meaning; or to adopt a phraseology fitted to bewilder and mislead those who are incapable of reducing doctrines to their legitimate and primary elements. The history of perfectionism shows, indeed, that most of its advocates have renounced the use of evangelical language on this subject; and have maintained, either that men are naturally no more inclined to evil than good, or that a portion of the divine moral image has been imparted to the whole human race.

Perfectionism has been commonly, as it is naturally, connected with a want of reverence for the Bible. Mr Wesley reproves those who infer from the conduct of the apostles that some are entirely free from sin in this life, in the following terms: 'Will you argue thus, if two of the apostles once committed sin, then all other Christians, in all ages, do and must commit sin as long as they live? Nay, God forbid that we should thus speak.' Again: 'What if the holiest of the ancient Jews did sometimes commit sin? We cannot infer from hence that all Christians do and must commit sin as long as they live.'[1] Thus Scripture examples are made to prove nothing against the doctrine of perfection. Mr Mahan contends that the passages in the Old Testament which assert the imperfection of good men ought not to be adduced as evidence that

[1] Wesley's *Plain Account of Christian Perfection*, pp. 19, 20.

none under the gospel are perfectly holy. His words are, 'Whatever is said of the character of saints under the old dispensation cannot be applied to Christians under the new, unless such application was manifestly intended by the sacred writer.' Speaking of the declaration in Ecclesiastes 8:20, he says, 'It was made with reference to men in the state then present, and not with reference to their condition under an entirely new dispensation.'[1] Thus easily does he dispose of passages which contradict his view. Many have supposed the prophets and primitive Christians to have been unenlightened and carnal compared with themselves.

Many perfectionists have substituted impulses, or the inward light, for the teaching of the word; and have spoken in disparaging terms of the latter as compared with the internal illumination of which they boast. In exemplification of this remark, we might refer the reader to the votaries of ancient Quakerism, Shakerism, and Mystics and Quietists of every description. And no wonder that they who are perfect undervalue that volume which condemns their creed and which was written by men who confessed themselves to be sinners. What! the perfect condescend to be taught by those who are imperfect! It is absurd in the extreme. Besides, it is natural to suppose that they who are perfectly holy should read the word of God rather on the tablet of their own minds than on the perishing pages of a book printed by human hands.

It has accordingly been no uncommon occurrence for those who imagined themselves to have attained to the highest degree of sanctification to abandon the reading of the Scriptures and trust to the supposed illapses and movings of the Spirit within them. And what is this but a species of infidelity under the guise of a superior sanctity and devotion? 'Search the Scriptures,' says Jesus Christ, 'for in them ye think ye have eternal life; and they are they which testify of me.'

We see, then, why it is that perfectionism has so generally led to the wildest enthusiasm. Notwithstanding the warnings of some of its more intelligent and sober champions,[2] it has been

---

[1] Mahan on *Christian Perfection*, p. 67.

[2] Wesley's *Plain Account*, pp. 119–20, where are some sound and important remarks on this subject. The Oberlin professors have written against some of these extravagances, yet they maintain opinions which lead to the most pernicious enthusiasm, and their paper, it is said, is read and admired by some of the most fanatical of the perfectionists in the western country.

very extensively connected with confidence in impressions, visions, and unaccountable voices, to the practical rejection of that word of truth, light, and power, which speaks from heaven. Many of its disciples have professed to be literally inspired; and with the pretext of obeying divine instruction have committed the most disgraceful excesses.

It is also the parent and the offspring of monkish austerities, inasmuch as it readily and almost necessarily attributes the source of sin to the body or the animal appetites which, though not wrong in themselves, will yet become the certain occasion of transgression, unless they be kept in subjection by the strictest regimen and a kind of unceasing penance. Most of the Romish recluses who inflicted the severest castigation upon themselves and endeavoured to drive out sin by voluntary hunger, cold, and nakedness, professed by these means to be seeking, or actually enjoying the blessing of unstained purity, and unalloyed communion with God.

Some of the Protestant preachers and believers of the doctrine in our own country seem to be verging towards the same superstition; and to imagine that such abstinence and dietetics as they inculcate, connected with a general reception of their creed, would in the course of a few generations almost entirely extirpate sin and its consequences from our world. What less can Mr Finney mean when he says, 'Is it not true, my brethren, that the mind is, in this state of existence, dependent upon the physical organization for all its developments – and that every transgression of physical law tends strongly to a violation of moral law?' Again:

I am now fully convinced that the flesh has more to do with the backsliding of the church than either the world or the devil. Every man has a body, and every man's body, in this age of the world, is more or less impaired by intemperance of one kind or another. Almost every person, whether he is aware of it or not, is in a greater or less degree, a dyspeptic and suffering under some form of disease arising out of intemperance. And I would humbly ask, is it understood and proclaimed by ministers that a person can no more expect healthy manifestations of mind in a fit of dyspepsia than in a fit of intoxication? Is it understood and preached to the church that every violation of the physical laws of the body, as certainly and as necessarily prevents healthy and holy developments in proportion to the extent of the infraction of physical law, as does the use of alcohol? I am convinced that the temperance reformation has just begun, and that the total abstinence principle, in regard to a great many other subjects beside alcohol, must prevail before the church can prosper to any considerable extent.[1]

To such an absurd extreme does this leader of perfectionism carry his notions respecting the connection between the body and the soul; and so clearly does he lay down principles of temperance, which are rather Pythagorean, Gnostical, or Papal, than conformable to the precepts and maxims of pure Christianity.

Correct views of this subject are important on account of their necessary connection with the great system of truth and duty revealed in the Scriptures. A number of errors springing from perfectionism, as the waters from a fountain, have already been noticed. As a general fact, the perfectionist is a Pelagian in his views of native depravity, decrees, election, the divine agency in regeneration, and gratuitous justification; and he denounces the doctrines of Paul, according to their plain import, as they are taught in his epistles to the Romans and the Ephesians, as injurious to the interests of holiness and in the highest degree dishonourable to God. Experience has proved that perfectionism peculiarly prepares the ground, where it is cultivated and flourishes, for an abundant crop of infidelity and the most odious forms of delusion and imposture.

As to the practical fruits of this error, may we not be permitted to ask, without subjecting ourselves to the imputation of uncharitableness, do we not see enough of them at Oberlin itself, represented by its admirers as the very focus of all moral light and of holiness, to justify the severest crimination?

What mean the constant denunciations against the church, against orthodox and faithful ministers, and against all who dare to resist the dangerous innovations which go forth like swarms of locusts from that seat of superficial learning and of bold, reckless speculation?

What mean the complaints which we hear from the West of the disorganizing spirit and conduct of the students and

---

[1] *Oberlin Evangelist*, as quoted in the April number of the *Princeton Review*, pp. 243–4.

preachers from that seminary; the divisions they have created and sought to create in once powerful churches; and the resolutions condemnatory of their proceedings adopted by ecclesiastical bodies formerly believed to be sufficiently favourable to the extraordinary opinions and measures which have characterized the theological revolution of the last fifteen or twenty years?

What mean the violent acts of some of the professedly perfect ones, blindfolding, menacing, and unmercifully beating a youthful offender accused of attempting to corrupt one of the female members of the school; and that after they had themselves deceived him and seduced his mind by a feigned correspondence and other acts of dissimulations not unworthy of the disciples of Loyola? What mean the published apologies for those disgraceful acts, under the eye, and with the sanction of the fathers of the heresy?

What mean the apparent conceit, arrogance, dogmatism, and radicalism of not a few of the ill-instructed young men who are sent out from Oberlin to preach down dead professors of religion and dead ministers, and orthodox creeds and catechisms, and to proselyte the world to the kind of sanctity taught by the faculty of that institution?

But we forbear. It is, we are persuaded, but to know Oberlin thoroughly, to be convinced of the utter falseness of all its pretensions to uncommon spiritual mortification and holiness. Perfectionism, indeed, can never bear a rigid and impartial scrutiny as to its visible effects any more than as to the radical principles which produce them. Its grapes, however beautiful in the eye of the distant or cursory spectator, are still the grapes of Sodom; and its clusters are the clusters of Gomorrah.

In proportion to the developments which are made, new evidence is afforded that this heresy however diversified or modified by circumstances, is everywhere the same in its essential features and in its tendency; arrayed alike against evangelical doctrine and order; fostering fanaticism and spiritual pride; and whether it nominally acknowledge or reject the ordinances of the gospel, taking away the grounds which support them and robbing them of the salutary influence which, in their legitimate use, they are adapted and designed to exert.

It is time to draw these extended remarks to a close.

Reader! the progress of this doctrine, the indifference of many professedly evangelical men with regard to its diffusion, and the disposition manifested by not a few to apologise for its propagation are indications most unpropitious to the cause of humble, meek, spiritual Christianity. Perfectionism, with whatever professions 'of love, tenderness, and devotion' it may be accompanied, is not the progeny of light but of darkness; and, as truly as Universalism or Socinianism, it should be viewed and treated by ministers and churches as a fundamental error. Tending as it does to sap the foundations of all true religion and genuine morality, apostasy to it should be regarded as an evidence either of a peculiar species of monomania, a profound ignorance of the meaning of the terms employed, or of the want of that humility without which all pretensions to piety are vain.

Be jealous of any system of mental philosophy, the principles of which naturally lead to the adoption of this great error so contrary to the Word of God and the conscious experience of the most eminent believers. It is worthy of very serious inquiry (if indeed there be any room to doubt on the subject), whether some modern speculations concerning moral agency and the divine influence in the production of holiness, have not contributed largely to the existence and progress of the peculiar form of this error, which has within the last few years swept like a simoon[1] over some of the fairest portions of our Zion. Guard with constant vigilance the citadel of truth at its very vestibule.

Christian reader! 'Be not carried about with divers and strange doctrines; for it is a good thing that the heart be established with grace, not with meats which have not profited them that have been occupied therein.'

This subject urges upon you most impressively the duty of an humble walk with God. Is it true that sin mixes with and pollutes all your doings – your most disinterested charities, your holiest prayers, your most grateful praises? Is it true that you will daily, hourly, every moment, need a fresh pardon and the aid of all-conquering grace, till your feet shall stand on the

---

[1] A hot, suffocating desert wind in Arabia and North Africa.

shores of the celestial Canaan, with the harp of God in your hand and the wreath of immortality encircling your brow? The dust then surely becomes you. There lie and confess your sins, and acknowledge the justice of your condemnation, and weep with ingenuous sorrow, and beg for mercy.

Unite with fervent prayer, untiring watchfulness, and diligence. To this your innumerable inward foes, ever ready for the assault, seem continually, vehemently, irresistibly, to urge you. In such a situation, can you sleep? Awake, for the powers of hell are near and are eagerly pressing on to circumvent and destroy you. 'Wherefore, take unto you the whole armour of God, that you may be able to withstand in the evil day, and having done all, to stand.'

Let not the reality of your continual imperfection be your excuse; but rather let it excite you to more ardent exertions to reach the crown of life.

Be satisfied with nothing less than perpetual progress in holiness. You have but commenced the war; there remaineth yet much land to be possessed; go on from victory to victory till not an inch of the promised territory shall continue in possession of the enemies of your Lord.

Persevere for a few days, and you will gain the perfect purity and bliss after which your glowing heart aspires. No sound of clashing arms, no opposing hosts are in heaven. Its quietude is never invaded by anxiety or fear. Its holiness is untarnished as its pure light, and enduring as its years. Triumphant termination of conflicts and of wars! Hasten, then, blessed day, so long desired by the holy creation.

Adore the grace and faithfulness of your redeeming God. He has not only forgiven the sins of your unregenerate days, but he has borne with your renewed provocations since your conversion – your ingratitude, your coldness, your worldliness, your self-seeking, your manifold abuses of his love. Nor will he leave unfinished the work which he has begun. He will guide you by his counsel and afterwards receive you to glory. Thus will he keep, bless, save, all the armies of the ransomed, to the praise of his glorious grace for ever. What patience, what condescension, what unfainting, boundless love! 'Oh that men would praise the LORD for his goodness, and for his wonderful works to the children of men!'

8

BODILY EFFECTS OF RELIGIOUS EXCITEMENT[1]

During the years 1800, 1801, 1802, and 1803, a revival of religion occurred in the southern and western sections of Kentucky, or what is generally known as the Green River country. The principal instruments were the Rev. Messrs M'Gready, Hodge, Rankin, and M'Gee. The first named individual was in the van. He was a devout, evangelical, powerful preacher; a pupil of Dr McMillan, lately deceased. These men, let it be recollected, were the original leaders and abettors of the subsequent irregularities and disorders of the Cumberland Presbytery, which will be noticed hereafter.

Previous to this revival of religion, Kentucky and all this western region was in a state of great coldness and declension. The country was new, and a heterogeneous mass from all quarters had pressed into it. Presbyterians, both clergy and people, were very formal. Sacramental services were very long, and often irksome, and apparently unedifying, or rather uninteresting, to the large mass of attendants. Communicants were heads of families generally; rarely was there to be seen a young

[1]By Thomas Cleland. The article here reprinted was originally in the form of a letter from one who was well acquainted with the facts detailed. These are highly instructive and ought to be recorded and remembered for the benefit of the coming generation [Originally published 1834; the above comment is from the 1846 reprint.]

person at the Lord's table. The services were conducted on the plan suggested in our *Directory for Worship*, chapter viii, section 6. The Sabbath was occupied in preaching, fencing, and serving the tables, as it was called, from five to eight hours. The communion was held twice in the year in those churches which had stated pastors or supplies, and in many churches only once in the year. Such was the state of things when the revival commenced, which was some time in the year 1799, in the region before mentioned.

The population there was sparse at that time and widely scattered. The work at first was no doubt a glorious work of the Spirit of God. The calls for ministerial labour were so great and extensive that it was impossible for the few clergymen recently settled there to supply the demand. This circumstance suggested the idea of protracted meetings, that the ministers might have the opportunity of meeting people at one time and one place. There were then no missionaries to go from place to place and preach to the scattered population. And inasmuch as no neighbourhood had a population sufficient to support so many people as assembled on those occasions, this gave rise to the plan of camp-meetings. A grove was selected, 'a pulpit of wood', or as we generally term it, a stand, for the clergy was erected. The multitude who intended to be stationary located themselves with their waggons, carriages, or tents, in such places around the stand as their fancy or convenience dictated. The assembly was often so great that secondary stands were erected: the congregation divided, so that three or four preachers were discoursing at the same time in different parts of the grove.

Here was the commencement of disorder and confusion. The sermon had scarcely commenced when some one or more would become the subject of bodily exercise. This was commonly called the falling exercise; or, as it was often said, such and such an one was 'struck down'. We cannot better describe this exercise than Dr McMillan has done, in his letter to President Carnahan:

It was no unusual thing to see a person so entirely deprived of bodily strength that they would fall from their feet, or off their feet, and be as unable to help themselves as a newborn child. We have seen some lie in this condition for hours, who yet said that they could hear everything that was spoken, and felt their minds more composed and more capable of attending to divine things than when their bodies were not thus affected. As far as we could observe, the bodily exercise never preceded, but always followed, upon the mind's being deeply impressed with a sense of some divine truth.

Another *fac simile,* if we may so call it, you may find in Mr Gulick's letter written on the Island of Kauai. See *Missionary Herald,* volume xxix. p. 404:

Some were seized with a kind of convulsive trembling; and in a few cases, overcome by their feelings, they fell prostrate on their faces and lay for a length of time weeping in a most affecting manner. And what, in our estimation at least, renders this work the more remarkable is that many of these very persons who now felt so deeply have for years been in the habit of hearing the most solemn and alarming truths in the Bible without the least apparent emotion. But now, without any special cause of excitement or alarm from us, they are thus deeply affected.

But now, as we conceive commenced the principal mischievous measure. When anyone would become the subject of this bodily exercise, immediately a group would collect around and commence singing, and then praying, and then exhorting. Many instances of this kind obtained in different parts of the congretation all at the same time. Hence it happened that throughout the assembly, as far as the eye could reach from the stand, there was a continual commotion and confused noise of preaching, exhorting, singing, praying, and shouting going on at the same instant. Many, from curiosity or anxiety, were seen continually running from one group to another, so that the multitude was in a perpetual state of commotion and agitation.

This scene of things continued day and night with little or no abatement. The ministry rather yielded up the reins to the multitude, who, being carried away with such a state of things, considered the pulpit of little account, if any at all. Indeed, preaching, especially of the didactic character, was considered a great hindrance to the progress of the revival.

This sentiment was not confined exclusively to the populace, for some of the leading and most popular preachers gave way to the opinion that such kind of preaching was rather an interruption to the great work that was then going on. Hence, the most zealous, arrogant, and enthusiastic of the laity, finding the ministry ready to surrender their posts, very naturally took the whole management of the service out of their hands and controlled it at pleasure.

Moreover, if a minister, however evangelical in faith and practice, did not come 'fully up to the mark', *i.e.*, if he expressed any disapprobation, ministered any caution, attempted to correct any extravagances, he was not only set down immediately as being hostile to the revival, but even interrupted and prevented from proceeding in his discourse by some of the multitude, who commenced singing, or praying, or exhorting, or shouting – whichever was at the time found most convenient by the leaders of such disorder.

It was ultimately out of this hot-bed of wild enthusiasm and disorder that there sprung up that fruitful crop of heresy and schism that afterwards assumed the shape, as well as the name, of New Lights, Schismatics, Marshallites, Unitarians, and Shakers. By these heresies the Synod of Kentucky was deprived of eight members, *viz.*, Marshall and Thomson (who afterwards recanted their errors and returned), Stone, Dunlavy, McNamer, Huston, Rankin, and Bowman. All these, except Stone and Bowman, became Shakers.

For a particular account and description of bodily exercises as they were perpetuated and fostered among the New Lights after they became a separate and distinct body, being excluded from our church, we refer to the *Evangelical Record,* p. 217, written by McNamer while one of that party, or perhaps after he turned Shaker. The description is indeed ludicrous, but so far as our knowledge and observation extended at the time, we cannot detect anything incorrect in the statement. We do not consider it exaggerated or too highly coloured.

As to these extravagances, the Presbyterian church by this time began to pause and look on these scenes as they were fully acted out by the New Lights, with a degree of wonder and disgust. Still there was enough, and more than enough, among ourselves to make us blush, on a review, and excite in us a desire to hide our mother's nakedness if we could. The work was conducted by Bishop and McChord. We return to the revival scenes.

We have seen the origin of *camp-meetings,* which have so much importance now attached to them. They originated in the Presbyterian church from *necessity*; and this necessity perhaps at the time, justified the measure. And so long as they were confined to the circumstances which seemed to call for them, were extensively accommodating and thought to be highly beneficial. The meetings at first were awfully solemn, and no doubt much good was done. But when they were extended and adopted in the more populous parts of the country, where they were attended by thousands and tens of thousands, induced by every motive good or bad, together with the lax and irregular management of them, they exhibited too much the appearance of disorder and confusion which baffled and defied all description.

It is proper to remark, however, that the form and arrangements of camp-meetings now differ very much from those in former days. Then, the people came together without any shelter but their waggons and their tents, erected where convenience or fancy might dictate. They brought provisions for themselves and horses, and whatever else was thought necessary to their continuance on the ground for many days. Now, the plan of temporary buildings of small log huts in regular order around the stand, and the space where the congregation is to assemble, is adopted. Order and solemnity generally prevail and are carefully inculcated and constantly maintained. Formerly, as we have seen, it was entirely the reverse. As for the comparative good or evil attending camp-meetings, we have nothing to say, as my acquaintance with such meetings is very limited. They appear to be lauded or condemned according to the opinions and prejudices of their advocates or opponents.

We confess ourselves at a loss to know the proper shape and size of the subject now before us; how far the plan of this history should extend; what to set down, and what to omit. To descend to particulars and minute circumstances would not be agreeable to the feelings of some yet living, nor do we know that it would be edifying.

We will state a few facts and anecdotes connected with the subject before us. The writer was licensed to preach in April 1803, both before and after which he witnessed many things, the detail of which would make a little volume. The largest meeting he attended was in June 1801, at Caneridge, Bourbon county, where B.W. Stone was then pastor. The exercises as well as the encampment were such as are described above. Many appeared to be deeply affected, and many had fallen down. There was much singing, praying, exhorting, etc., at tents, at the meeting-house, and every place where small groups were assembled around one or more of the persons who were 'struck down'.

Subsequently, during the years 1802–3, we witnessed many cases of bodily exercise, the most of which, we have reason to believe, were entirely involuntary, while some others, we thought, were the reverse, *i.e.*, either the persons conceited or fancied themselves under exercise, or desired to be, and there-fore sought for it and yielded to the first impulse, which might, however, have been successfully resisted. Many persons within my knowledge became hopefully pious, the most of whom continue unto the present, and many have fallen asleep in Jesus. The number of apostasies was much fewer than might be supposed. Indeed, when we look back on those times, we greatly wonder that there were not ten for one. The Presbyter-ian church suffered greatly, lost many members, more ministers proportionably than others; but she continued unconsumed, and was much better prepared by practical knowledge and dear-bought experience for the next revival than she was before. But to our narrative.

A contemporary brother minister, by our request, has given us, in substance, the following facts. The first personal know-ledge he had of any of the subjects of the revival was in the winter of 1800–01, near the borders of the State of Tennessee. Shortly after the people began to assemble, two or three persons appeared to swoon away, and after lying fifteen or twenty minutes, appeared to be wholly convulsed, some more than others. His attention was particularly called to a young female who, after some time lying apparently motion-less, began to move her lips. On a near approach, he found himself the subject of her prayer, from which it appeared that she was under the impression that he had come a considerable distance and from a cold region to see the great work that was going on in that place. And she prayed fervently that he might not be disappointed. When she recovered and resumed her usual posture and state of mind, there was great solicitude manifested by her minister and others to know the result of her exercise, what she had seen, etc. She informed them that she had seen that they were to have a glorious meeting that day, and the minister (Mr Rankin) said he had no doubt of it. In that same place, there were others who saw during their exercises, as they expressed themselves, certain persons (who were yet unconverted) in the act of preaching and a very great work going on under their ministry, and they appeared to expect it with as much certainty as if it had been revealed to them from heaven.

At that time and place there was a considerable mixture of wheat and chaff. On the one hand, there was manifestly an anxious disposition to converse on religious subjects, particularly about the experience and exercises of the heart, a close attention to the preaching of the word with apparent desire to profit thereby. There appeared among many a docile temper, a spirit of inquiry, with fervent prayer and cautious zeal. On the other hand, there was a prevailing sentiment that the subjects of the revival had more than common attainments in evangelical knowledge and piety; that the millennium was just at hand, even at the door, of which fact these extraordinary exercises were certain precursors and evidences. These and such like extravagant notions were, of course, attended by an arrogant boldness and self-importance which did not savour of the religion and spirit of Christ. Social meetings, catechetical instructions, etc., were almost, if not altogether, neglected.

As before intimated, the intervals between sermons were occupied by the multitude in various exercises. The ministers took, comparatively, but little interest in conducting the worship except in the time of preaching, which occupied but a small portion of the twenty-four hours. The rest of the time was spent as before described, singing with great fervour and animation, shaking hands all through the crowd, praying by fifties and hundreds all at the same moment. Such scenes we have often witnessed. Young converts were often seen passing through the assembly and on the outskirts thereof, exhorting sinners in a very lofty tone and peremptory manner to fly from the wrath to come. Others would pray for hours together until they were exhausted, and when they could stand up no longer they would sit down or recline on some other person, and then pray or exhort until completely exhausted, so that nature could exert itself no further.

These exercises were greatly applauded and highly approved as being not only certain evidences of the gracious state of the individuals themselves, but likewise as eminently useful and instrumental in furthering the revival. When some of the elder brethren were inquired of about the expediency and propriety of correcting some extravagances which appeared wild and visionary, their reply was, in substance, that they knew these things were not right, but should they interfere by attempting to rectify them at that time, it might interrupt, if not stop, the revival altogether. Here the ministry, however good the intention, was much at fault. The surrendering up the control and management of the religious exercises into the hands of mere novices, or such as were unskilful and inexperienced, was the very inlet or gateway to those errors and extravagances that soon followed.

There was, if we mistake not, one general prevailing prominent feature attending this revival everywhere: it was the strange, mistaken disposition, in a very large portion of the people, to undervalue the public means of religion and, in the place thereof, to promote a kind of tumultuous exercise in which themselves could take an active part, if not become the principal leaders. Hence, some of these would-be leaders have been known to lie down and sleep in the time of preaching and during some of the most serious and solemn addresses, and as soon as the sermon was over, suddenly rise to their feet and sing, and shake hands, and pray, and exhort, with all the apparent energy of a saint or messenger from heaven. The wild fanatical notions of some were manifested by their believing themselves under obligation to go, according to certain impressions which they considered to be from heaven: namely, that they must go to certain places, and say and do certain things, and that it must be done and said at a certain time, etc. Many such things as these, which would be tedious and unnecessary to detail here, obtained and prevailed in this revival.

We proceed to relate a case or two respecting the exercise called the 'jerks'. This succeeded some time after the falling exercise and, I believe, had its origin in East Tennessee; at least it was, to use a commercial phrase, first imported into Kentucky from that quarter. It affected the good and the bad, the aged and the young. It was entirely involuntary, dreaded and hated, and even cursed by some; while it was desired and courted and highly prized by others. It came on something like the hiccough, without any premonitory symptom, and left the subject equally without any sensible effect.

During its prevalence we made several experiments; being inexperienced in the ministry, we knew not what to do with it. While preaching we have, after a smooth and gentle course of expression, suddenly changed our voice and language, expressing something awful and alarming, and instantly some dozen or twenty persons or more would simultaneously be jerked forward, where they were sitting, with a suppressed noise, once or twice, somewhat like the barking of a dog. And so it would either continue or abate according to the tenor or strain of my discourse.

The strong sympathy and intimate correspondence between the mind and the body was fully manifested by this experiment, producing the exhibition which immediately followed. The first subject of this exercise that attracted our attention was the pious wife of one of our elders. She was affected by this operation very gently, she felt no pain whatever, but rather the reverse – a pleasing sensation – could give no satisfactory account of its operation. She went to the country village on a public day to do a little shopping; we accompanied her on our way home. She was entirely free from any operation of the jerks. We therefore determined to try an experiment, conversed freely and somewhat jocularly with her on secular matters to divert her mind as far off in that direction as we thought necessary, and then immediately changed the subject to that of a very serious and solemn character. We are certain, not two minutes had elapsed before she was considerably affected with this exercise. Her body from the saddle and upwards appeared to pitch forward half way to the horse's neck, six or eight times in a minute. We were fully satisfied she could not prevent it.

Our mind became, some time after, greatly perplexed about this exercise. We could not encourage it, and yet, being a young minister, we were afraid to say anything against it publicly, as it had many friends and advocates. At length it was found to be detrimental in various ways. Besides interrupting public worship, it deterred many from attending altogether, being impressed with the belief that it was 'catching'. But it was not confined to the public assembly; it invaded the private and domestic circle, while engaged in domestic business or travelling on the road. The same individual was frequently the subject of it, young and old, male and female, refined and unrefined, the pious and the wicked, were alike under its operation.

Take another singular case, stated to us by Mr M'Gready. A young man, son of an elder, to avoid attending a camp-meeting in the neighbourhood with the family, feigned himself sick. On the morning of the Sabbath he continued in bed until the family had all started for the meeting, he being left alone, except a few small blacks. When thus alone, he congratulated himself on his success by the deception he had practised on his parents. He raised up his head and, looking all around his room, smiled at the adventure; but lest it might not be complete, lest someone might have occasion to linger or return and so he be detected, he resumed his clinical position covering over his head, and in a short time directed his thoughts towards the camp ground. He fancied the multitude assembling, the services commenced, the bodily exercises, as he had seen them, now in operation. He fancied a certain female now in full exercise; 'Now she's at it, now she's at it.'

In a moment he was taken with the same exercise (the jerks), was hurled out of his bed and jerked hither and thither, all around the room, up against the wall, and in every fashion. He had never been affected by bodily exercise before, but now found himself perfectly unmanageable. He had heard it said, and indeed witnessed the fact, that praying would cause the jerks to cease. He tried it; the desired effect followed immediately. He felt no more the effects of the exercise than a person does after the hiccough. He supposed it all a dream, a mere conceit, illusion, or something of the kind, resumed his bed, commenced his pranks again; and again was the scene acted over, only a little worse. The same remedy was resorted to, and he again became *in statu quo*.

He arose, dressed himself, sauntered about awhile, wanted some employment to pass the time away, bethought himself of a dog-skin in the vat that needed unhairing, drew it out, laid it on the beam, rolled up his sleeves, grasped the graining knife, lifted it up to make the first scrape, when lo, it was instantaneously flirted out of his grasp and he was jerked back, over logs, against the fence, up and down, until he resorted to his old remedy and again obtained relief. Feeling as before, perfectly free from any sensible or evil effects, as strong and resolute and determined and reckless as ever, he ventured again. He assumed his instrument and resumed his posture over the subject of his intended operation when immediately, before he could make one stroke, the whole scene, only if possible, tenfold worse, was acted over again; it was much more severe, and greatly protracted.

The usual remedy at first failed. He became alarmed, thought the Lord was now about to kill him, became deeply convicted of his great folly and wickedness; became composed again in body but now greatly agitated and concerned in mind; called a little black, pointed him to the dog-skin, which he was afraid now to approach, directed where to lay it away, returned to his room weeping and crying to God for mercy, and in this condition was found on the return of the family. He shortly afterward obtained a good hope through grace, applied for the privileges of the church, gave this relation of facts to the session, was received and, in the judgment of Christian charity, gave satisfactory evidence by a scriptural experience and godly living that he was a renewed man and redeemed sinner saved by grace.

We shall add only one case more. One evening we rode six miles up Green river and preached at a Mr McWhorter's, in a Baptist settlement. The house was crowded. The people were attentive until we had finished the discourse and had prayed and were about to sing the last hymn, but were forestalled by an enthusiastic kind of man, who started a song with a lively tune. Several young women began to jerk backwards and forwards. The seats were immediately removed to afford room and prevent them from being hurt. One young woman had what we would call the whirling exercise. She went round like a top, we think at least fifty times in a minute, and continued without intermissions for at least an hour. It exceeded by far anything of the kind we had ever witnessed. We were told she had had the jerks nearly three years. She did not appear exhausted; complained of pain or distress if the bystanders did not continue singing. We became perfectly tired, our preaching seemed to be all gone and to have been rather in the way, from what took place afterwards. We remonstrated with some of them and cautioned them.

Thus you see this exercise continued, more or less, in one or another place, for a long time. It, however, in the general gradually disappeared, especially from the Presbyterian Church, and thus afforded us a very happy relief. We were heartily glad when it was entirely gone. After all these novelties left us, the church, like one enfeebled and exhausted, sank down into formality and apathy. After she had passed through the fire she came forth more refined as to doctrine and soundness in the faith. For nearly twenty years afterwards was she without a revival. But blessed be God, she has recovered and her borders have been greatly enlarged and her stakes strengthened; and we trust in God she will never see and feel such another shock. In her wisdom and experience we believe such things will never find favour and encouragement again.

The Cumberland business was the last difficulty we had to struggle with. The original Cumberland Presbytery was one of our own, formed by the Synod from the Transylvania Presbytery and shortly afterwards dissolved, being incapable of transacting business. M'Gready and Hodge acknowledged and renounced their ecclesiastical aberrations; Rankin turned Shaker; M'Gee and McAdam were under citation, but never appeared.

The whole business was finished by the Assembly in 1809, and in February 1810 the present Cumberland formed themselves into a separate body. By a subsequent assembly they have been recognised as other denominations, such as Methodists, Baptists, etc. Some of their ministers are more violent against us than the Methodists. Their preachers are generally illiterate and a little more than semi-Arminian. They have carried off by their zeal and name many members of our church, where we had no ministry. A friend in whom we can confide lately informed us that they are very friendly in

Missouri; co-operate with us heartily in the Christian enter-
prises of the day; boldly and successfully combat heresy; and
appear to manifest great anxiety and desire to becomes in some
way united with us. But this cannot be, from their present
aspect as a body. Their literary character, as well as orthodox
standard, is too low and uncertain.

Should it become expedient to branch out, in extending the
history of the revival (as we wrote of this before), it will be
necessary to trace, first, the New Lights, the sphere of whose
operations was in the eastern section of Kentucky, by Marshall,
Stone, etc. The Rev W. L. M'Calla collected materials for their
history before he left Kentucky, but I know not what he did
with them. Out of these heretics soon sprung the Shakers,
whose history is familiar.

The Cumberland is a distinct branch altogether, gradually
rising and growing out of the disorders which obtained in the
Green River country, or further down in Kentucky and in West
Tennessee, called Cumberland, we suppose, from the river of
that name running by Nashville This accounts for the name
'Cumberland Presbytery', at first given to that section of our
synod and subsequently adopted by the present Cumberlands,
as they are generally called. In their worship, they are considered more noisy and disorderly than the Methodists. In short,
to use a homely phrase, they have Presbyterian warp, but
Methodist filling.

THE JERKS

As the facts in relation to these bodily agitations are somewhat remarkable, we deem it expedient to make some addition
to what is stated above by our worthy correspondent.

The phenomenon of swooning, or suddenly falling or sinking
down under religious exercises, has not been uncommon in
times of great excitement and under very impassioned preaching. Such occurrences were very frequent under the ministry of
Whitefield and Wesley; and in this country, during the great
revivals which took place under the preaching of Whitefield,
the Tennents, Blairs, etc., such appearances were of frequent
occurrence. The same was remarkably the fact at Cambuslang
and Kilsyth in Scotland during the extraordinary religious
excitement which took place in those towns early in the last

century. We have also witnessed such effects on the body as
occurring very commonly in the meetings of the Methodists
and Baptists in the south and west. In the cases which have
fallen under our observation, the effect on the body was
entirely involuntary. Sometimes it was preceded by a universal
trembling of the whole frame; but, at other times, the falling
was as sudden as if the person had been struck with lightning.
In some cases there followed a convulsive motion of the limbs;
but most frequently the patient lay motionless, as if in a swoon.
And the only remarkable difference between these paroxysms
and those of common syncope is that in the former the person
is not unconscious of what is said and done in his presence.

But the bodily agitation called the jerks is a very different
affection; and the only appearance known to us which bears a
resemblance to it is the jumping exercise in Wales, of which Dr
Haygarth has given an account in his treatise *On the Effect of
the Imagination in the Cure of Bodily Diseases.* The same
facts are referred to in Sidney's *Life of Rowland Hill.*

This extraordinary nervous agitation commenced, as stated
by our correspondent, in East Tennessee, at a sacramental
meeting; and we have been informed that on that day several
hundreds of persons of all ages and sexes were seized with this
involuntary motion. It was at first almost uniformly confined
to the arms, and the motion proceeded downwards from the
elbow, causing the arm to move with a sudden jerk or quick
convulsive motion, and these jerks succeeded each other after
short intervals. For some time no religious meeting was held in
which this novel involuntary exercise was not exhibited by
more or less of the audience in that part of the country where
they originated. And, generally, all those who had once been
the subjects of it continued to be frequently effected, and not
only at meeting but at home, and sometimes when entirely
alone.

After the commencement of the jerks, they spread rapidly in
all directions. Persons drawn by curiosity to visit the congregations where they existed were often seized, and when they
returned home they would communicate them to the people
there. But in some instances they occurred in remote valleys of
the mountains, where the people had no opportunity of
communication with the infected. In East Tennessee and the

south-western part of Virginia their prevalence was the greatest; and in this region persons of all descriptions were seized,
from the aged grey-headed preacher down to children of eight
or ten years of age.

Soon, however, the 'exercise' began to assume a variety of
appearances. While the jerks in the arms continued to be the
most common form, in many cases the joint of the neck was
the seat of the convulsive motion and was thrown back and
forward to an extent and with a celerity which no one could
imitate, and which to the spectator was most alarming.

Another common exercise was dancing, which was
performed by a gentle and not ungraceful motion, but with
little variety in the steps. During the administration of the
Lord's Supper, in the presence of the Synod of Virginia, we
witnessed a young woman performing this exercise for the
space of twenty minutes or half an hour. The pew in which she
was sitting was cleared, and she danced from one end to the
other; her eyes were shut and her countenance calm. When the
dancing terminated she fell and seemed to be agitated with
more violent motions. We saw another who had what was
termed the 'jumping exercise', which resembled that of the
jumpers in Wales. It was truly wonderful to observe the
violence of the impetus with which she was borne upwards
from the ground; it required the united strength of three or four
of her companions to confine her down.

None of these varieties, however, were half so terrible to the
spectator as that which affected the joint of the neck. In this,
it appeared as if the neck must be broken; and while the bosom
heaved in an extraordinary manner, the countenance was
distorted in a disgusting way.

Besides the 'exercises' already mentioned, there were some
of the most curious and ludicrous kind. In one, the affected
barked like a dog; in another, they boxed with fists clenched,
striking at every body or thing near to them. The running
exercise was also one of the varieties, in which the person was
impelled to run with amazing swiftness. There were many
other singular motions in imitation of persons playing on the
violin, or sewing with a needle, etc., etc. The remarkable
circumstance in relation to these various exercises was that a
person affected with a peculiar species of the jerks, coming into

a congregation where that had not been experienced, would commonly communicate it to those who had been affected with exercises of a different kind. Thus, a lady from Tennessee, who brought into a certain part of Virginia the barking exercise, immediately was imitated by certain of those affected with the jerks, who had never seen anything of this sort before.

These nervous agitations were at first received as something supernatural, intended to arrest the attention of the careless multitude, and were therefore encouraged and sustained by many of the pious; but after a while they became troublesome. The noise made by these convulsive motions in the pews was such that the preacher could not be composedly heard; and in several of the exercises the affected person needed the attention of more than one assistant. Besides, nervous agitation or falling was so easily brought on by the least mental excitement, even at home, that many who were the subjects of the jerks became weary of it, and in some cases avoided serious and exciting thoughts, lest they should produce this effect. It is remarkable, however, that they all united in their testimony that in the most violent and convulsive agitations, as when the head would rapidly strike the breast and back alternately, no pain was experienced; and some asserted that when one arm only was affected with the jerks, it felt more comfortable than the other through the whole day. Perhaps this was imagination.

In some places the persons affected were not permitted to come to the church on account of the noise and disturbance produced. The subjects were generally pious, or seriously affected with religion, but not universally. There were cases in which careless persons, and those who continued to be such, were seized. The dread of the jerks was great in many, both religious and careless, and upon the whole, the effect produced by them was very unfavourable to the advancement of religion. All, however, were not of this opinion. Some who had much experience of them continued to speak favourably of their effects.

We have the pleasure of annexing to our account the statement of an intelligent and respectable physician who appears to have paid much attention to subjects of this kind. The opinion of such men is valuable, as they are better acquainted with the physiology of man than other persons.

The Jerks – This affection I have repeatedly witnessed in the State of Illinois in the years 1822–4. The persons subject to it were principally females in the humbler walks of life, natives of North Carolina and Tennessee. Young females (say from thirteen to thirty years old), of sanguine and nervous temperament, were more addicted to it than others. It is equally prevalent among Methodists and Cumberland Presbyterians. Their discourses are generally passionate addresses, first to the fears, and secondly to the sympathies of their hearers. At the conclusion of these addresses, hymns are sung with great animation, the leaders passing through the congregation shaking their hands. The jerks or falling generally commence at the conclusion of the sermon and increase during the singing.

Different persons are variously affected: some rise to their feet and spin round like a top, while others dance till they fall down exhausted. Some throw back their heads with convulsive laughter, while others, drowned in tears, break forth in sighs and lamentations. Some fall from their seats in a state of insensibility and lie for hours without consciousness, while others are affected with violent convulsions resembling epilepsy. Those habituated to the affection are generally attacked under the circumstances above detailed, but I have seen some persons who had become so irritable that the least mental excitement would produce the paroxysm. Others appeared to be affected from sympathy. l have seen several young women of the same neighbourhood, who were always attacked at seeing one of their number with the paroxysm. I have seen others who would be instantly attacked on seeing any person with the affection without having any previous mental excitement. During the convulsive paroxysm, recollection and sensation are but little impaired; after continuing a certain period, the person generally falls into a state of stupor very much resembling that subsequent to epilepsy. Yet the animal functions are not much impaired. The pulse is natural. The temperature that of health throughout the paroxysm. After it has subsided there is soreness of the muscles and a slight dull pain of the head, which soon pass away.

From the sex of those most subject to the affection, the time of life when they are most susceptible of it, the condition they occupy in society, the causes which excite it into action, and the effect produced by the paroxysm, I was led to the conclusion that it was a nervous disease brought on by continual mental excitement and protracted by habit, that after it has once become habitual from long continued mental excitement, sympathy will be sufficient to call it into action without mental excitement. Many of the subjects of this affection were addicted to hysterics; and all, persons easily affected by anything exciting the natural sympathies.

I have omitted to mention one fact I have often witnessed, viz., that restraint often prevents the paroxysm. For example, persons always attacked by this affection in churches where it is encouraged will be perfectly calm in other churches where it is discouraged, however affecting may be the service, and however great the mental excitement. Some of them have told me that such was the fact, and as these were the more intelligent of those addicted to such affections, I doubt not the truth of what they said.

REFLECTIONS

1. The first reflection which is suggested by the preceding accounts is that the physiology of the human system is very imperfectly understood.

2. The second is that an irregular action of the nervous system produces often very astonishing appearances.

3. Religious excitement carried to excess is a dangerous thing. Enthusiasm is the counterfeit of true religion and is a species of insanity.

4. In revivals of religion badly regulated, there may be much extravagance, and yet the work in the main may be genuine. The wise will discriminate and not approve or condemn in the lump.

5. Pious men and women are imperfect in knowledge and often form erroneous opinions which lead them astray. Bodily affections, however, are no evidence of error or enthusiasm.

6. Such bodily affections as are described in the foregoing narratives are no doubt real nervous diseases which do not destroy the general health.

7. All such things tend to the discredit of religion and should be prevented or discouraged.

Index